D1521177

Staging Governance

Staging Governance

THEATRICAL IMPERIALISM

IN LONDON, 1770–1800

Daniel O'Quinn

THE JOHNS HOPKINS UNIVERSITY PRESS
Baltimore

This book was brought to publication with the generous assistance of the Karl and Edith
Pribram Endowment.

The Johns Hopkins University Press
2715 North Charles Street
Baltimore, Maryland 21218-4363
www.press.jhu.edu

Library of Congress Cataloging-in-Publication Data

O'Quinn, Daniel, 1962–
    Staging governance : theatrical imperialism in London, 1770–1800 / Daniel O'Quinn.
        p. cm.
    Includes bibliographical references and index.
    ISBN 0-8018-7961-2 (hardcover : acid-free paper)
    1. English drama—18th century—History and criticism. 2. Imperialism in literature.
3. Politics and literature—Great Britain—History—18th century. 4. Theater—England—
London—History—18th century. 5. Political plays, English—History and criticism.
6. Theater—Political aspects—England—London. 7. Colonies in literature. I. Title.
    PR719.I45O59 2005
    822'.609358—dc22
                                                            2004026032
A catalog record for this book is available from the British Library.

For Gabriel

CONTENTS

ACKNOWLEDGMENTS

THIS PROJECT WAS SUPPORTED by a generous three-year research fellow-
ship from the Social Sciences and Humanities Research Council of
Canada. Like many other Canadian scholars, I am grateful to the various
scholars willing to commit their time to SSHRC's many initiatives and
whose intensive peer review gave me the confidence to write this book.
Funding from SSHRC allowed me to employ a small cadre of superb research assistants. Mark Stephen, Michelle Lobkowicz, Nasrin Gilbert, and
Rory McClellan immersed themselves in the relevant archives, and I owe
a great deal to their intellectual curiosity and their enthusiasm for late
eighteenth-century newspapers. At crucial stages of the research, I received
valuable assistance from staff members at the University of Guelph, at the
Thomas Fisher Rare Book Library at the University of Toronto, at the
Huntington Library in Pasadena, at the Victoria and Albert Museum in
London, at the National Library of Australia, and, perhaps most importantly, at the British Library, especially those librarians working in the
India Office and Records Collection. Eva Soos at the J. Morgan Pierpont
Library in New York, Martin Durant at the Victoria and Albert Museum,
David Rhodes in the Prints and Drawings Collection at the British Museum, and Sylvia Carr at the National Library of Australia were extraordinarily helpful when it came time to collect the illustrations. I am also indebted to the College of Arts at the University of Guelph for financial
assistance in procuring images and for facilitating my research in general.
    In its early stages, this project was developed on three separate occa-
sions as a graduate course in the School of English and Theatre Studies
at the University of Guelph. The students' enthusiasm for, and frustration
with, the issues surrounding imperial performance at this historical

juncture played no small part in shaping this project. For their patience, their candor, and their curiosity, I am grateful.

Deidre Lynch, Donna Andrew, and an anonymous reader for the Johns Hopkins University Press read the entire manuscript with extraordinary care. Their advice, their commitment, their encouragement, and, most of all, their intellectual generosity has been invaluable. I owe special thanks to Deidre and Donna, for they have been receptive listeners and astute critics of the project from its inception to its completion. Several colleagues with a special interest in Romantic theatre and/or British imperial culture–Betsy Bolton, Julie Carlson, Jeffrey Cox, Michelle Elleray, Mary Favret, Theresa Kelley, and Gillian Russell–agreed to read and comment on sections of the manuscript at different stages of its composition. I couldn't have asked for a more thoughtful and rigorous group of interlocutors. To a person, they raised crucial questions and provided me with vital information and suggestions without which certain chapters would be much less successful. All these contributions were timely and helpful, but I bear the responsibility for any residual errors. To Julie, Jeff, Gillian, Michael Gamer, and Jane Moody, I owe special thanks for helping me understand by their example how to conduct research in Romantic theatre. Natasha Eaton offered important assistance with some of the images and deserves my thanks. To Orrin Wang, Teresa Kelley, Sonia Hofkosh, Ian Balfour, Sarah Zimmerman, Reeve Parker, Mary Jacobus, David Clark, Laura Brown, Patrick Holland, Jennifer Schacker, Susan Brown, Alan Shepard, and Donna Pennee, my debts are more various and general, but no less important. Their relentless encouragement, careful critique, and timely advice had a significant impact not only on my scholarly activities but also on the composition and revision of this book.

Sections of this work were presented at a meeting of the Washington Area Romantics Group, at the University of Wisconsin–Madison, at the Romantic Orientalism conference at the University of Aberistwyth, at the American Society for Eighteenth Century Studies, and at various meetings of the North American Society for the Study of Romanticism. I would like to thank all of the audiences and organizers for their interest, questions, and suggestions. Early versions of some of the materials in chapters 6 and 7 first appeared on two highly innovative electronic resources: my discussion of Starke's *The Sword of Peace* was solicited by Michael Eberle-Sinatra and Tom Crochunis for the *British Women Playwrights around 1800* website and my analysis of *Ramah Droog* was published by *Romantic Praxis*.

During the past two years, I have been grateful to Michael Lonegro at the Johns Hopkins University Press for treating both my manuscript and my concerns with care and respect. Thanks to Juliana McCarthy, Kimberly Johnson, Alexa Selph, and Brian MacDonald for bringing the book through its final stages.

Finally, I want to thank Anne Lyden, Michelle Elleray, Arthur Irwin, Liz Noble, Jennifer Henderson, Jim Ellis, Glenn Mielke, Roger Seamon, and Barbara Seamon for their unwavering support and affection over the years. To my parents, Leo and Celeste O'Quinn, and my sister, Jennifer, I owe more than I can say. Jo-Ann Seamon's sense of fun, her political commitment, and her love infuse everything I am and everything I do. Our son Gabriel is roughly the same age as this project and this book is dedicated to him.

Staging Governance

The Supplementation of Imperial Sovereignty

BETWEEN 1770 AND 1800, transformations in the relationship between metropolitan British society and its colonial holdings, as well as changes in the concept of the nation itself, precipitated crises in governance that left Britons with a new sense of themselves. By the middle of the eighteenth century the successes of British mercantilism had effectively expanded sovereignty well beyond the shores of the British Isles. Although economically the nation and the empire were mutually constitutive, that was not the case politically.[1] In fact, this very expansion posed significant problems for the theory and practice of sovereignty and contributed to its supplementation by new governmental tactics that eventually dispersed power over a wide range of institutions. These tactics both added to and substituted for juridical sovereignty in such a way that the state form eventually made the empire the target of its operations. This book is vitally concerned with this double process, for it argues that one can track important shifts in governmentality in the theatricalization of imperial affairs in late eighteenth-century London. It is my claim that nightly plays and the discourse surrounding them not only commented on but also orchestrated national reactions to the recalibration of imperial sovereignty in the late eighteenth century.

Michel Foucault's notion of governmentality describes a complex series of events in which the juridical principle of sovereignty, which defined governmental practices through the sixteenth and seventeenth centuries, was permeated and activated in a new way by practices aimed at managing the imbrication of men and things in the emergent capitalist economy of the nineteenth century. Governmentality is "the ensemble formed by the institutions, procedures, analyses, and reflections, the calculations and tactics that allow the exercise of this very specific albeit complex form of power, which has as its target population, as its principal form of knowledge political economy, and as its essential technical means apparatuses of security."[2] Like much of the argument of this book, Foucault's horizon of analysis involves the relationship between bodies, economies, and the state-sponsored actions of the military. As a general analysis, Foucault's essay, like much of his work, marks the late eighteenth century as the moment when this ensemble emerged, and his arguments regarding the construction of docile bodies through disciplinary tactics and the correlative mobilization of biopower through the deployment of sexuality and the racialization of class identity are widely known. But, despite the efforts of some scholars, the relationship between these governmental tactics and the recalibration of the politics and economics of empire in the late eighteenth century remains obscure.[3]

Much of this obscurity derives from the term *empire* itself. Reaching back to the transitional moment between feudal and modern governance, J. G. A. Pocock reminds us that

> the primary meaning in English of "empire" or *imperium* had been "national sovereignty": the "empire" of England over itself, of the crown over England in the church as well as state, the independence of the English church-state from all other modes of sovereignty. The exercise of this sovereignty had involved England in a series of tensions and contradictions, between the crown and crown-in-parliament, between the crown-in-parliament and the government of the national church, which had given rise to a series of civil wars, dissolutions of government, conspiracies, revolutions, foreign wars and a period of dynastic and therefore ecclesiastical uncertainty which as late as 1760 was only recently terminated.[4]

Pocock's sense of the instability generated by this term is important because his analysis of imperial crisis during the reign of George III emphasizes that, as the empire extended around the world, competing definitions of the term empire had threatened the sovereignty of the British realm over itself. In this account, the American Revolution and the complex struggles over the East India Company, each in its own way, forced an almost continuous reassessment of the relationship between nation, colony, and constitution, whose implications threatened to reengage the long and violent history that had consolidated the notion of King-in-Parliament as the fundamental bulwark against perpetual civil war.

[T]he legal status of the colonies had never been determined, and . . . the identification of "empire" and "realm"—of "empire" meaning "sovereign monarchy" with "empire" meaning "extensive or enormous monarchy"—meant that the British empire altogether lacked the *jus publicum,* regulating the relations between its components under sovereignty, which would have constituted it an "empire" in the sense understood by civilian jurists.[5]

The American war underlined the problem posed by this shifting meaning, and Pocock's analysis of the dissolution of the Atlantic empire thoroughly demonstrates how the lack of a language of "confederation" meant that control of America would have to be ceded to the colonists to prevent a collapse in the governance of the metropolitan realm. To put it in the language of eighteenth-century politics, the resolution of the American conflict preserved the "sovereign monarchy" at the expense of the "extensive or enormous monarchy" in the Atlantic world.

Pocock's analysis of the imperial crisis, however, is confined to the Atlantic empire and is thus an illuminating yet partial account of British imperial politics at the time.[6] Alongside of the American conflict, one can trace an equally significant and no less violent engagement with the definition of sovereignty in the long struggle over the governmental practices of the East India Company in the 1770s and 1780s. The American problematic is suited to Pocock's combination of political theory and social history because that revolution, staged as an assault on Parliament and the Constitution, provides an entry point for discussion regarding the limits of constitutionality in the empire in the 1770s. As he has persuasively demonstrated, the American Constitution is in many ways the culmination of key elements of British political theory and history and is thus readable through the conventional language of Whig political discourse.[7] After the loss of the American colonies, British imperial interests in the Asian subcontinent were preserved such that the "extensive or enormous monarchy" either superseded or incorporated the claims of the "sovereign monarchy." This period of extreme uncertainty in the 1780s is the primary focus of this book because both the anxieties and the compensatory fantasies generated by that decade's recalibration of the empire had long-lasting effects. One of my contentions, which I take up more explicitly at the end of the book, is that our relative lack of knowledge regarding this period of social turbulence is a symptom of the resilience of the strategies used to suppress the anxieties of empire. The 1780s demand our attention because the social processes and phantasmatic compensations detailed in the ensuing chapters haunt post-imperial and neo-imperial life.

Although the largely Whig assault on the practices of the East India Company in the 1770s and 1780s cannot be characterized as a revolution, it precipitated a series of constitutional problems that were resolved in ways that explicitly exceeded the language of constitutions. The governmental actions of the East India Company sometimes followed the imperatives of a chartered company and sometimes behaved very much like a state. This hybridity emerged as a disturbing counterexample to the notion of King-in-Parliament and threatened to reveal precisely what the political practice of the state was at great pains to conceal—namely, that the pressure of imperial expansion was redefining the British polity in a fashion that was progressively undercutting the political conjunction of liberty and landed property, while reconfiguring the state relation as one between a potentially tyrannical court of directors and its shareholders.[8] For observers such as Edmund Burke, that opened the door to a level of corruption against which no amount of virtue could sustain itself:

> What, then, will become of us, if Bengal, if the Ganges pour in a new tide of corruption? Should the evil genius of British liberty so ordain it, I fear this House will be so far from removing the corruption of the East, that it will be corrupted by them. I dread more from the infection of that place, than I hope from your virtue. Was it not the sudden plunder of the East that gave the final blow to the freedom of Rome? What reason have we to expect a better fate?[9]

Critiques of Indian affairs were exceptionally volatile because the East India Company operated as a spectral example of how the imperial nation might be defined. The mismanagement of the East India Company revealed the dangers not only of fantasies of corporate rule but also of the collusion of landed and commercial interests in current practices of governance. What is challenging about this debate over the specific form of governmentality exhibited by the East India Company, whose activities would begin to play a compensatory role following the American secession, is that it effectively reengaged with the question of "empire" in a fashion that supplemented strictly juridical constructions of the state.

That history of reengagement, although no less ensconced in the archive of parliamentary debate and political pamphleteering, cannot be understood without stretching beyond constitutionality itself into the micrological practices of social regulation that Pocock identified under the rubric of manners or virtue.

> From 1688 to 1776 (and after), the central question in Anglophone political theory was not whether a ruler might be resisted for misconduct, but whether a regime founded on patronage, public debt, and professionalization of the armed forces did not corrupt both governors and governed; and corruption was a problem in virtue, not in right, which could never be solved by asserting a right of resistance. Political thought therefore moves decisively, though never irrevocably, out of the law-centered paradigm and into the paradigm of virtue and corruption.[10]

The practice of virtue and the regulation of manners were the province of a wide variety of social agents and play a crucial role not only in the resolution of the problem of revolution in British political theory but also in the day-to-day amelioration of economic and social disparity that was crucial for maintaining the tenuous stability of King-in-Parliament during a time of turbulent change. The language of virtue and manners explored by Pocock, Phillipson, and others is more narrowly defined than the micrological processes that Foucault analyzed under the rubric of disciplinary and regulatory power, but there is enough common ground to recognize that the analysis of virtuous sociability is never very far from the often arcane struggles over corruption, legitimacy, and constitutionality that pervaded the reign of George III.[11] That these analyses require one another is one of the basic assumptions of this book and, for better or worse, demands that we consider governmental tactics in both the conventional, often legal, language of political theory and the more diffuse discourse of manners, desires, and proprieties.

The clearest evidence that these apparently dissociated tactics were entwined with key transformations in the governance of the nation and the empire can be found in any of the daily papers circulating in London in the late eighteenth century. On any given day, the papers provided their readers with information regarding events in Parliament, shipping news, advertisements for any number of new and used commodities, reports on specific colonial transactions, scandalous accounts of the sex lives of fashionable society, reports on the royal household, satirical poems and bon mots, announcements for sales, reports of births and deaths, and any number of brief essays on science, social life, or public affairs presented as letters to the editor. The range of information resembles that of contemporary papers, but what is different is the complete lack of hierarchy in the presentation of this information. Events relating to the cataclysmic loss of the American colonies or the economic collapse of the East India Company sit adjacent to accounts of balls and sporting events. Reports of military triumph over native resistance in India are framed by ads for the very materials whose availability these successes ensured. Over the course of its four pages, a conventional eighteenth-century paper simply prints these stories, ads, and announcements where they fit best, and although it is possible to discern precedence in the stories themselves, their haphazard contiguity indicates something about the lives of eighteenth-century Londoners. These levels of social interaction and knowledge, swirled into a colloidal solution, capture the extraordinary flux of everyday life in London and its connection to lives lived in distant locales.

While giving us a sense of the interconnectedness of social and economic practices, the papers are also highly insusceptible to analysis. To understand the social transitions played out in the papers, we need an operator that focuses and organizes the relations between people and things so that salient developments may be discerned. One such operator was present in every daily paper, under the title "Theatrical Intelligence," for the theatre distilled the social forces of imperial life in London and presented it on a nightly basis. Because of the temporality of performance, the mélange of stock plays and new productions that made up a typical season not only reactivated past representations but also put forth new representational paradigms to explore present social problematics. Productions of stock plays frequently allegorized present power relations, whereas new productions attempted to capture the fleeting topicality of the present and posited possible futures for the nation and the empire. On any given night, events in the transformation of British imperial society were brought to the stage, often mediated by the sexual and commercial relations that accompanied all class interactions in the metropole at this time.

The theatrical analysis of these social transformations must be understood as a nightly laboratory in social manners that ultimately addresses the question of virtue that Pocock identifies as the decisive locus of Anglophone political thought. Plays might draw relations between inappropriate sexual behavior and instances of colonial mismanagement, or turn the end of the slave trade into compensatory performances of whiteness. In other words, the theatre tends to bridge the conceptual gap between realms understood to be explicitly political or economic and those understood to be specifically private and social. In so doing, it goes beyond the adjacency presented in the papers and actively takes part in the supplementation of juridical governance by more pervasive forms of subjectification. Theatre, a governmental mechanism whose target is manners, allows us to observe precisely how governmentality put the crises of sovereignty that swept through the British Empire in the 1770s and 1780s in abeyance. The plays on the London stage allow us to understand how a new form of citizen emerged, one suited to furthering the emergent form of empire inaugurated by the destabilizing loss of the American colonies and by the East India Company's disturbing flirtation with insolvency and absolutism.

After these events, and in reaction to the sense of national vulnerability they occasioned, Britons became heterosexual, and white, and came to possess private lives, all in ways they had not done before. Although these elements of individual identity and social relations existed before, they changed both their signification and their functionality. And it is not enough to argue that these emergent significations were indicators of relative privilege or derogation, which says little more than that power operates by forms of inclusion and exclusion. These changes in signification and function opened new possibilities in the realm of the social that not only allowed for the production of future life-forms but also actively rewrote social history to fit these emergent forces. I use the term life here advisedly because what we see during these reorientations of the social is a complex combination of discipline and regulation of the body as a crucial tactic in the consolidation of middle-class hegemony. That consolidation has proved to be extremely difficult to pin down, in part because it makes more sense to speak of multiple strands of embodiment and behavior that can be understood only retroactively as components of middle-class sociability. As Dror Wahrman has demonstrated, imagining the middle class was, and is, an extremely complex matter not only because the middle ranks were themselves a discontinuous field but also because their representation, both politically and discursively, was often highly contested.[12]

Wahrman argues that the period following the French Revolution saw the mobilization of the social middle in the political imaginary of Britain, and the final two chapters of this book track a similar activation in the theatrical representations of British policy in India in the 1790s. But my readings in chapters 6 and 7 build on arguments regarding the deployment of class in the imperial crises that beset the British Empire in the 1770s and 1780s. A significant portion of my argument focuses on how certain practices and social dispositions became signs not only of the cultural and national degeneration of social climbers in the colonies but also of the decline of metropolitan society, especially as it is exemplified by aristocratic dissipation. These two forms of degeneration are often figured as mutually constitutive developments reminiscent of the social breakdown that attended the decline and fall of the Roman Empire and, thus, as symptoms of impending imperial doom. Against this figural assemblage, one can discern a number of prophylactic or hygienic gestures that mobilize characters, tropes, and behaviors that are not necessarily referred to as middle-class inventions, but which ostensibly emerge from the social middle. On one side of this struggle, we have caricatures of both aristocratic and lower-class life, and on the other, we have an amorphous social entity that, as E. P. Thompson has argued, is not visible in the structures of power in the late eighteenth century.[13] If we understand the latter lack of visibility as a sign of the emerging normativity of the middle ranks, then what we are faced with are representations of the social that swing between an excess and a paucity of representation.

Frequently, in this book I use the excessive representation of aristocratic or lower-class figures to reflect on the representational lack of the middle ranks. The assumption here is not only that the middle ranks are thoroughly enmeshed in the power relations that are driving imperial self-fashioning, but also that much of the normative force of these middling dispositions relies on their vagueness, if not their outright invisibility. In fact, their normativity requires not actual or fully consolidated practices and identities but only some momentary consensus, perhaps elicited by a certain performance in a certain setting, that such a social disposition is potentially operative: in other words, the class does not have to have emerged as a definable entity for the forces surrounding its unconsolidated elements to effect social change. Thus when I speak about the middle class in this book I am using the phrase to capture a plurality of difficult-to-discern activities and identities that are still very much in flux, yet which are nevertheless exerting pressure on social relations. To put the problem metaphorically, the middle class operates more like a quantum than a particle in the analyses that follow: I tend to make it visible by giving a detailed account of its discursive and performative frame.[14] At times, this requires a great deal of specificity about the excessive figuration of the upper and lower ranks: as we will see in chapter 6, there is a key moment when critiques of aristocratic excess become more specific and focus on the specious dichotomy between landed and fashionable gentry and thus require a more refined critical idiom. At other moments in the argument, I opt for a level of nominalism, much as Foucault does, in order to locate polemically the emergence of regulatory transformations in the social.[15]

The transformations in the bodies of people in the middle ranks completed the middle-class revolution that spanned the long eighteenth century: aristocratic manners came to be coded as deviant mores, and lower-class sociality was represented as a form pathological excess. This revolution involved a fundamental alteration in the function of the family not only as social operator but also as figure for governance. In his account of the shift from the deployment of alliance to the deployment of sexuality, Foucault provided a heuristic for understanding the instrumentalization of reproductive heterosexuality in the Malthusian couple, the regulation of active female desire and the careful charting of sexual deviance as a threat to racial and class supremacy.[16] We encounter ample evidence supporting the emergence of these sexual deployments in the analyses that follow, and I argue that these questions of sexuality are fundamentally linked to problems of imperial performance. Their importance cannot be underestimated, for they are intimately tied to the beginnings of a new concept of race that makes it something essential rather than local and contingent. This new concept directly impinges not only on the emergence of biological state racism in the mid-nineteenth century but also on the beginning of a "deep" understanding of character and the rejection of surface meaning that will have an enormous impact on the representation of subjectivity.

These beginnings are all tied together and evident in the performances I discuss. What is perhaps less evident and no less important is that these deployments of sexuality, class, race, and subjectivity are themselves a new form of political economy that infiltrated the conventional sites of political and economic transaction during the constitutional and economic crises of the period. Of key importance in the British case is the decline of the Whig oligarchy. Edmund Burke, Charles James Fox, and Richard Brinsley Sheridan inhabit these pages like characters in a novel. The various constitutional crises precipitated by Whig attempts to deal with the economic messes of the East India Company on the one hand and George III's perceived absolutism on the other are evidence of a decline of Parliament as the figure of eternal and stable Britishness. The performative contradictions evinced by these events indicate precisely where sovereignty is supplemented, for as we shall see, the cracks where conventional definitions of sovereign politics start to fracture are filled by regulatory fantasies and tactics whose dynamics are primarily sexual. Thus the state's juridical control of its subjects is integrated with the institutional management of bodies and populations. This decline in the state as a figure for stability is compensated for by the very deployments outlined earlier, such that the mystification of the constitution initiated largely by Edmund Burke in the 1790s operated as a veil for the collusion of juridicality, disciplinary institutions, and regulatory tactics that we have identified as governmentality. What eventually emerges from this collusion is the state in a heightened form that will ruthlessly preside over the species being of the nation and the various peoples, now rendered as species, that are either incorporated into or ejected from the empire.

The seven chapters of this book are grouped into three sections, each of which works through a particular problematic associated with the precarious performance of imperial culture in metropolitan London. I have explicitly left questions pertaining to the Atlantic empire for another project, in order to focus on Anglo-Indian problematics, but, as we will see, the disruption of imperial activity in the Atlantic exerts pressure on the reception of Indian crises. The questions posed by the loss of the American colonies and the complex politics of antislavery have been frequently addressed, but they tend to revolve around questions of race and identity. It is my sense that many issues regarding performance in the circum-Atlantic remain undiscussed. My concern here, however, is more with the broader question of how the empire in Asia emerged as a compensatory imperial fantasy and how this impacted on the constitution and regulation of metropolitan society. Each chapter focuses either on specific theatrical performances or on the performance and reception of political events. Despite the popularity of the plays discussed in the book and the extraordinary level of public interest in the politics of imperial governance, many of these cultural events remain beyond the purview of conventional literary and theatrical scholarship.

Part of my critical strategy throughout the book has been to present the material in detail in order to give the reader a sense not only of the discursive parameters of imperial representation but also of the reception and discussion of performance materials in both the theatre and the press. Much of the argument of the book travels via the newspapers and this methodological decision means that the book's theoretical gestures regarding governance, racialization, and the sex/gender system exist in what I hope is a revealing tension with the ebb and flow of everyday life in the period. Many of the theoretical moves speak to present problematics in social relations that have their roots in this period, and many of the readings that support my argument are embedded in the muddle of life's mundane elements as they are represented in the papers. By playing both registers simultaneously, the argument demonstrates the dialectical relation between past and present social relations as exemplified by these particular archives in an attempt to perform a critical ontology of ourselves.[17]

Without moving into an excursus on the modulations of print culture, it is important to stress the tight fit between theatrical performance, political life, and the print media of late eighteenth-century Britain. Newspapers reported on the political news of the day, dutifully advertised and reviewed plays, discussed the world of business, and tracked down social scandal. At times the blend of information is purely disjunctive, and at other times it self-consciously ties together social and cultural spaces that contemporary scholars tend to separate. Most important for our purposes is the extraordinary mediation between scenes of entertainment, such as the theatre, and areas of public life, such as Parliament, which tend to be studied by scholars separated by disciplinary boundaries. The sheer topicality of the plays discussed in this book prevents such a distinction. As the newspaper evidence demonstrates, audiences were extremely curious about their reactions to performances, not because they were obsessed with the aesthetic merit of a particular play, but because plays at this historical moment were negotiating and presenting the transformations in British society on a nightly basis. It is this sense that the theatrical experience in this period can be understood as autoethnographic.

Domestic and Dramatic Reorientations: Theatre as Autoethnography

One of the working assumptions of this book is that a trip to the theatre was as much about the social experience of audience interaction as it was about the consumption of a particular performance. This is most obvious when the theatre erupted into violence either aimed at the production itself or, more routinely, among the audience. Such moments of social performance serve to remind scholars of Georgian theatre that the entire house, and not merely the stage, operates as a performance space. The public space of the theatre had become a site not only for modeling but also for regulating social practice. The Theatres Royal in this period were engaged in a form of autoethnography because so much of theatrical practice turned on the recognizability of character. The complexity of this kind of theatre lies in the relationship between the performance of character on stage, the enactment of character in the boxes and the pit, and the ensuing analysis of character in the newspapers, whose breathless scrutiny of the theatrical intelligence played no small role in the stylization of class and gender identity in this social crucible. Character in each of these instances means something slightly different, and the calibration and adequation of these differences arguably drive the social and cultural forces of the theatre at this time. This stylization impinges not only on the racialization of class and gender performance in this period but also on the very function of colonial materials in these autoethnographic acts. Charting and adjudicating the limits of social interaction, the theatre, perhaps more than any other form of cultural production, offers a glimpse of how change swept through a culture in the midst of fundamental social transformation both at home and abroad.

This sense that massive social change was afoot suffuses British culture in the late eighteenth century and can be recognized both by the anxiety it produced and by the emergence of a series of tropes that attempt to depict and hence to contain cultural transformation. One of these figures is that of the barometer. As Kathleen Wilson has argued, the 1770s sees the sudden figuration of women as barometers of the historical progress of nations. Citing William Alexander's *The History of Women, from the Earliest Antiquity to the Present Time* (1779), Wilson demonstrates that claims for Britain's national and racial superiority were supported by its supposed deference and protection of the female sex.[18] Wilson's key recognition is that these self-congratulatory indicators not only deform the actual historical state of women but also render them pawns in a larger game regarding the preeminence of cultures over which they have little control. An anonymous contributor to the *London Magazine* makes a similar gesture with regard to the theatre: "To know the state of the Theatres is certainly a matter of consequence, because it is a kind of barometer from which we may determine the rise or fall of publick taste."[19] With its subtle invocation of the fall of the Roman Empire, the barometric figure implies that "publick taste" and, by extension, the sociality of the public behave much like the weather: full of chaotic flows and counterflows that are difficult to predict and often quite dangerous. Most frequently the barometric figure is deployed to capture the degradation of the public by aristocratic dissipation and, hence, the insinuation that these practices constitute a symptom of imperial or national collapse.[20] Understanding the hybrid interactions of various social forces in the audience of Covent Garden and Drury Lane is a matter of anthropological concern in the late eighteenth century not only because each performance allows for an incremental surveillance of the public by itself but also because the entire assemblage of theatrical entertainment figures as a form of currency whose value directly impinges on Britons' self-evaluation in the economy of world history.[21]

Throughout this book, this combination of self-presentation and self-evaluation, which drives the relationship between audiences and the material culture of the theatre, is understood as a form of autoethnography and is the defining principle of the book's first section. The first two chapters demonstrate the relationship between two very different representations of British imperial adventure and the emergence of middle-class critiques of aristocratic vice. I argue that this linkage forms a crucial set of discursive and performative parameters that inflect all subsequent imperial representation on the London stage. Although both chapters work toward mutually supporting arguments, they focus on radically different works and operate as discrete case studies. The distinction between chapter 1's discussion of Samuel Foote's *The Nabob* and chapter 2's engagement with Loutherbourg's and O'Keefe's pantomime *Omai; or, A Trip round the World* can be superficially reduced to one of space. Foote's play is set exclusively in England and works through the impact of colonial economics on the social transactions of metropolitan life. Loutherbourg's extravaganza is set partially in Britain, but its primary objective is to bring the South Seas to London audiences. As Greg Dening has argued, *Omai* is explicitly ethnographic, but what I demonstrate is the degree to which the pantomime's protoanthropological description of people and picturesque representation of places in the Pacific is superseded by complex self-representations that further the racialization of class identity.[22] The chapter on Foote is less interested in racialization than in the way sexuality is deployed in what amounts to a detailed analysis of the relationship between the City and the Town at a moment when the imperial economy is undermining historical notions of aristocratic supremacy. The sexual fantasies mobilized by Foote surface in *Omai* and are sutured to a series of racial fantasies. This phantasmatic conjunction is crucial to the emergence of self-regulating middle-class bodies and plays a key role in the remarkable moment of imperial self-scrutiny occasioned by the impeachment of Warren Hastings.

Before turning to these arguments, we should have a general sense of a night in the theatre at one of the patent houses. Following the Licensing Act of 1737, the options for an evening's entertainment in London were severely constrained. Public theatrical performance, with some exceptions, was limited to Covent Garden and Drury Lane, with summer productions at the Haymarket. All productions in these houses were regulated by the Office of the Chamberlain who censored all new plays. In addition to these venues for legitimate theatre, the late eighteenth century also saw the pro-liferation of illegitimate forms of entertainment that evaded the scrutiny of the Licensing Act by presenting musical entertainments or other forms of spectacle that did not rely on the spoken word of actors.[23] These entertainments exerted considerable influence on dramatic practice in the patent houses, but for the moment I want to look in detail at a specific play in order to give some sense of the complex forms of sociability that traverse the production and reception of a licensed theatrical event: in this case, Elizabeth Inchbald's first and highly successful afterpiece *The Mogul Tale; or, The Descent of the Balloon* (1783). What I want to demonstrate is the dynamic relationship between audience and production that defines theatrical practice in this period and which makes the theatre such an important space for considering transformations in the social relations of imperial London. The notion of virtue, which plays such a crucial role in eighteenth-century political theory, infuses not only the play itself, but also the paratextual materials that surround the play—its theatrical precursor, the print satires of contemporary political debates regarding Indian governance, and a chain of newspaper commentary stretching back to an important theatrical and social scandal.

Inchbald started her career in the theatre as an actress and went on to become one of the most successful and innovative playwrights of the late eighteenth century. Ellen Donkin has argued that much of her success can be attributed to her lateral move from performer to playwright, an experience that gave Inchbald an intimate understanding of the dramaturgical elements of productions in the patent houses.[24] A typical night at the patent theatres of the late eighteenth century offered a range of entertainments for the audience. Aside from the main piece of comedy or tragedy on the bill, managers also staged afterpieces, which were often much lighter forms of entertainment, such as farce, pantomime, or various kinds of naval or military entertainment. These afterpieces were often highly topical, sometimes explicitly patriotic, and almost always designed to incorporate as much music, singing, spectacle, and low comedy as possible. The main work and the afterpiece were also separated by musical interludes and/or dance performances, and it was not uncommon for audiences to flow in and out of the theatre to catch a portion, if not all, of the evening's entertainment. The dynamic between main piece and afterpiece is sometimes difficult to ascertain, but it is clear that the afterpieces were often staged to direct audience opinion, or to reinvigorate ticket sales for a main production that was waning in popularity.

The Mogul Tale was first staged at the Haymarket on 6 July 1784 as an afterpiece to *Fatal Curiosity*. It was the first of Inchbald's many plays that associate an Oriental career, especially one funded by the East India Company, with sexual, familial, and economic irregularities. As with the later plays, the analogy between political and domestic authority provides both structural and rhetorical coherence to the comedy. Susan Staves has discussed how the late seventeenth-century stage explored the changing relations between sovereign and subjects through the relations between husband and wife.[25] Inchbald, I would argue, reinvigorates this analogy between state and family for the Georgian period, but with crucial reversals and modifications. It is now the family that is reconfiguring itself. In Foucault's terms, the familial relations formerly defined by imperatives of economic alliance were being transformed by the deployment of sexuality.[26] In Inchbald's plays, this reconfiguration is broached in terms of state governance, but the analogy is far more complex than on the Restoration stage because governmentality is in the midst of a fundamental rearticulation. As Foucault suggests in "Governmentality," from the mideighteenth century onward the family "becomes . . . the privileged instrument for the government of the population and not the chimerical model of good government."[27]

This shift from model to instrument is palpable in all of Inchbald's plays, for good governance is not modeled on the patriarchal aristocratic family, but rather functions via the construction of heteronormative identities that retain gender hierarchy without visible forms of coercion.[28] In short, what was posited as an analogy on the Restoration stage is here collapsed such that the family and the state are now mutually constitutive. The emergence of political allegories for the naturalization of bourgeois heteronormativity depends on a constitutive and threefold ejection. For Inchbald's reconfiguration of heterosexual relations to unfold as suggested requires, first, the ejection of suspect forms of masculinity; second, the reconstruction of the Orient as a site of threatening forms of *European* sexual and class identities; and, third, the reorientation of theatrical spectacles of the Other from exotic display to domestic rigor. As the following case study demonstrates, this triple reorientation, in which one set of cultural others is erased, reduced, and reconstituted in order to generate an emergent set of social norms, is crucial to *The Mogul Tale*'s critical relation to the representational economy of eighteenth-century theatre.[29]

All of *The Mogul Tale*'s action unfolds from a spectacular contravention of the harem walls. Capitalizing on the enthusiasm for ballooning following various demonstrations of the new technology in Britain, the play opens when a balloon carrying a doctor of music and a "Cobler" named Johnny and his wife Fanny crashes into the harem of the Great Mogul. The Mogul, who decides to "have some diversion with them," commands his Eunuch to "[a]ggravate their fears, as much as possible, tell them, I am the abstract of cruelty, the essence of tyranny; tell them the Divan shall open with all its terrors. For tho' I mean to save their lives, I want to see the effect of their fears, for in the hour of reflection I love to contemplate that greatest work of heaven, the mind of man."[30] The speech is unusual because the conventional despotic stereotypes of Orientalist discourse are here registered as conscious theatrical effects produced for the entertainment of not only the Mogul but also the audience.[31] After a stream of jokes on the Doctor's impotence and Johnny's rampant yet deviant desires, the farce closes when the Mogul underlines that his "despotic" behavior is little more than a dramatic pretense assigned to him by Europeans: "You are not now before the tribunal of a European, a man of your own colour. I am an Indian, a Mahometan, my laws are cruel and my nature savage" (19). But the instruments of torture and execution strewn around the stage are literally props both in Inchbald's and the Mogul's play. The Mogul's play is a theatrical experiment in the practice of othering that turns into a biting historical critique both of British imperialism and its self-consolidating cultural productions. Rather than confirm the English fear of him, he draws attention to the horrors they have perpetrated:

> You have imposed upon me, and attempted to defraud me, but know that I have been taught mercy and compassion for the sufferings of human nature; however differing in laws, temper and colour from myself. Yes from you Christians whose laws teach charity to all the world, have I learned these virtues? For your countrymen's cruelty to the poor Gentoos has shewn me tyranny in so foul a light, that I was determined henceforward to be only mild, just and merciful.—You have done wrong, you are destitute—You are too much in my power to treat you with severity—all three may freely depart. (19–20)

This critical turn depicts British colonial activity as an instructive counterexample to just governance. The Mogul's performance of tyranny becomes a representation of the governmental strategies of the East India Company. Therefore his performance not only enacts the way he has been culturally constructed but also the way his people have been colonized.

This amounts to a crucial cultural reversal: the Mogul figures as the exemplary Christian, and the English characters display stereotypical signs of Oriental excess and dissipation. This is most clearly seen in the second act when Johnny the Cobler, bearing the Mogul's handkerchief, roams through the harem. Behaving as he imagines the Mogul to behave, Johnny selects the most desirable woman. When she turns out to be Fanny, Inchbald effectively analyzes the representation of ostensibly non-English women on stage. The desire ascribed to Johnny's Oriental gaze reveals itself to be a hypersexualized desire not for otherness but for the same. However, it would be naive to argue that these gestures constitute an anticolonial strategy. Rather the play destroys a historically specific instance of the imperial gaze only to replace it with another form of colonial representation.

Inchbald's farce specifically restages Isaac Bickerstaff's *The Sultan; or, A Peep into the Seraglio,* such that a specific form of cultural consumption of the East is being ridiculed and ejected in much the same fashion that Bickerstaff himself was ejected from English society. *The Sultan* is a very close adaptation of *Soliman II* by Charles Simon Favart, who, in turn, based his play on a story from Marmontel's *Contes Moraux.*[32] With suitable changes in the nationality of the chief female character, the plot is consistent through all three versions: Roxalana, the pert English slave girl, replaces Elmira as the Sultan's favorite, and then, despite the opposition of other women in the harem and of Osmyn the Eunuch, she converts the Sultan to her ideas of English love and liberty (246). After his political and sexual conversion, the Sultan breaks Islamic law and convention by drinking wine, freeing his harem, and marrying Roxalana. Bickerstaff's farce revels in the Sultan's inability to govern Roxalana and attributes it to her Englishness. As is typical of mid eighteenth-century Orientalist discourse, all the comic business revolves around the usurpation of the Sultan's sexual and political power, for it is difficult to ascertain whether the repeated humiliation of the Sultan is a result of Roxalana's defiant national identity or her emasculating coquetry. The involution of sexual and political power simultaneously disables the myth of Islamic despotism and the sexual economy attributed to it by Christian Europeans. The farce ends with the Sultan and Roxalana married according to English aristocratic norms of sexual behavior.

The Sultan was Bickerstaff's last successful comic opera and was composed in exile after Bickerstaff was publicly denounced for sodomy. The controversy surrounding Bickerstaff, like that which consumed Samuel Foote a few years later, was a crucial moment in the regulation of homoerotic desire both on and around the London stage.[33] Bickerstaff played a prominent role in the construction of "effeminate deviance" in the 1770s because his flight to France after his sexuality hit the newspapers opened David Garrick, his manager, to a series of libelous poems.[34] The insinuation that Garrick and Bickerstaff were engaged in "unnatural acts" backfired on Garrick's enemies, but it effectively destroyed Bickerstaff's career. There are accounts of near rioting when it was suspected that a Bickerstaff play was being staged under a pseudonym.[35] Nevertheless, three years after the controversy, *The Sultan* was staged largely because Frances Abington, for whom it was written, pressured Garrick into producing it. Charles Dibdin and J. C. Bach provided music, and it was a monetary success.

Inchbald was intimately familiar with Bickerstaff's farce because she played the role of Elmira opposite Frances Abington's Roxalana exactly four months prior to the premiere of *The Mogul Tale* on 6 July 1784.[36] According to James Boaden, Inchbald was "constantly sifting over plots for farces" during the early 1780s.[37] She submitted a manuscript called "A Peep into a Planet," which Harris accepted under the new title *The Mogul Tale*. Aside from the replication of Bickerstaff's subtitle to *The Sultan—A Peep into the Seraglio*—Inchbald's farce employs precisely the same complement of characters. Both farces share a sultan, a eunuch, and three ladies of the harem. In the 1784 season, Inchbald herself played Elmira in *The Sultan* and Irena in *The Mogul Tale*.[38] But *The Mogul Tale* is far from a plagiarism of Bickerstaff's text. Rather, she takes the characters of *The Sultan* and puts them into contact with the primary agents in the production of Bickerstaff's farce. Thus the play critiques both the production and consumption of a particular staging of Orientalist fantasy in London at a specific historical moment. When the balloon descends into the seraglio—and into Bickerstaff's play—the audience is confronted with a doctor of music; a coquette named Fanny; and a cobler named Johnny, who represent Charles Dibdin, the composer of the music for *The Sultan;* Frances "Fanny" Abington, who owned the copyright to the play and was directly associated with the part of Roxalana; and Isaac Bickerstaff himself, who was famously named the "dramatic cobler" by Francis Gentleman in *The Dramatic Censor*.[39]

The metatheatricality of Inchbald's farce would have been immediately recognizable to regular theatregoers. Once we recognize the identity of the balloonists, a series of otherwise cryptic speeches becomes highly significant. Of chief import is the emasculation of Johnny in act 1. When the character played by Inchbald tells the balloonists that they have landed in the seraglio of the Great Mogul, Johnny's response is telling: "Eunuchs! Lord madam they are of no sex at all—we have often heard madam of the

Great Mogul. Why Lord he can't be jealous of me, and as to the Doctor there he is nobody—it is all over with him, he has no longer any inflammable air about him, either in his balloon or himself, its all gone, isn't it Doctor?" (4–5). The Mogul has no reason to be jealous of Johnny because, as Bickerstaff, he is a sodomite. Notably it is Johnny/Bickerstaff who proclaims the ferocity of the Mogul, so a link is drawn between his sexual deviance and the practice of othering in *The Sultan*. This gets amplified throughout the act, first, when Johnny asks if the eunuchs "are a good sort of gentlemen" and, second, when the Eunuch first appears (5). Upon his entrance, Johnny decides to say "he is a woman in men's clothes," but Fanny dissuades him, worried that the Great Mogul will fall in love with him. Instead of impersonating a woman, Johnny establishes a relationship with the Eunuch by asking him to "love an Englishman." Ironically, it is the Eunuch that prescribes firmness, boldness, and fortitude when Johnny comes before the Mogul. Johnny's impersonation of the pope rounds out the homophobic discourse of act 1.

The conjunction of Johnny and Bickerstaff is merely a continuation of the much earlier assassination of Bickerstaff in the popular press. Feminizing Bickerstaff at this point is hardly innovative, but it implies that Inchbald expects the audience to be well versed in the widely reported scandal. The second act, however, forgets Bickerstaff the sodomite and focuses rather on dissipated colonial desire. Johnny now emerges as the lustful lower-class drunkard who has been set loose in the harem. The fact that Inchbald can link the feminized sodomite and the hypermasculinized class other in one character should give us a clue to the cultural work achieved in their codeployment. I would suggest that both sexual threats, homosexuality and sexual promiscuity, are being attached to a specific form of Orientalist representation, here exemplified by Bickerstaff's *The Sultan*. This clearing operation opens the way for a different form of colonial discourse that not only ascribes normative heterosexuality to the cultural other but also ridicules the sexual practices of lower-class British subjects who are attempting to rise through the class structure during their colonial career.[40] The deployment of homophobic discourse for class consolidation involves the negation of a specific form of feminine identification. In *The Mogul Tale*, a great deal of attention is focused on the child of Johnny and Fanny, which I can't help but read as the "monstrous" child of Bickerstaff and Abington—that is, *The Sultan* and its principal character Roxalana. Embedded within Inchbald's critique is the regulation of active feminine desire, which made Abington famous in the role. What we are witnessing here is the ejection of feminized men and masculinized women—of gender liminality—from both the stage and the domestic theatre of the middle classes.

However, Inchbald's clearing operation, both in the realm of Orientalist representation and middle-class self-stylization, also engages directly with debates on Indian governance. The farce's most spectacular element—the descending balloon—ties the play directly to a series of satirical prints published throughout December 1783 that figured the fate of both the East India Company and Fox's East India Bill as similarly troubled balloons.[41] The debate surrounding Fox's East India Bill is considered at length in chapter 3, but for the moment it is enough to recognize that some of Inchbald's key dramaturgical decisions incorporate the news of the day as filtered through the print market. Like the play itself, the anonymous *The Aerostatick Stage Balloon* of 23 December 1783 fused a satire on the attempts of the coalition government of Charles James Fox and Lord North to rein in the power of the East India Company with a broader critique of the sexual dissipation of Foxite society (fig. I.1). The balloon has three tiers, one of which contains Fox, Lord North, and the Duke of Portland. Fox's gambling comes under direct censure as he is about to cast three dice marked "Madras," "Bombay," and "Bengal." The three prominent members of the coalition are flanked not only by the actress Mary "Perdita" Robinson and other demireps associated with the Whig elite, but also sexual quacks such as Dr. Graham of "celestial bed" fame. The clear insinuation is that Fox's Indian policy is continuous with his predilection for gaming and whoring. The accompanying poem demonstrates the integration of vice and imperial policy:

> Who choose a journey to the Moon
> May take it in our Stage Balloon.
> Where love sick Virgins past their prime
> May Marry yet and laugh at time,
> Perdita— W—sley Fillies free,
> Each flash their Lunar Vis a Vis,
> There N—th may realize his Dreams,
> And F—x pursue his golden schemes
> And Father B—ke may still absolve 'em
> Howe'er the Devil may involve 'em.[42]

This concatenation of the stage, allegations of vice among prominent Whigs, prostitution, and "Fox's golden schemes" to take over control of the East India Company indicates how deeply integrated these issues were

FIG. I.1. Anonymous, *The Aerostatick Stage Balloon*, 23 December 1783 *(courtesy of the Department of Prints and Drawings, The British Museum, London; BM 6284)*

in the metropolitan imaginary. The sheer popularity of the balloon as a vehicle for satirizing Indian affairs would not have been lost on Inchbald's audience, nor would the incorporation of specific political scandals, such as the loss of the Great Seal after the defeat of Fox's India Bill, into the second act of the farce.[43] But, as we will see in chapter 3, the specific allegations presented in *The Aerostatick Stage Balloon* offer a key for understanding Inchbald's complex strategies not only in *The Mogul Tale* but also in *Such Things Are.*

The Mogul Tale is a helpful example of theatrical autoethnography not only because it weaves together so many of the concerns of this book but also because it demonstrates the high degree of topical knowledge routinely assumed of the audience. And the particular knowledges invoked are, I believe, symptomatic, for the papers and the satirical prints routinely interweave theatrical, political, and scandalous "intelligence." In the prints, these separate concerns are often fused as in *The Aerostatick Stage Balloon*. In the papers, remarks on events and performances in the patent houses are contiguous both with lightly veiled accounts of the scandals of the day and with reports, both satirical and serious, of parliamentary transactions. However, these same London dailies, which Benedict Anderson deployed so successfully as a trope for the consolidation of the imagined community of the nation, are arguably a sign of exactly the opposite social forces.[44] Extended engagement with the papers and the print satires of the late eighteenth century demonstrates that they are more accurately described as a disjunctive field in which contradictory and often spurious accounts jostle for the attention of the public. Anderson's trope of the newspaper landing on the doorstep in every house attempted to capture the simultaneity of ideological consolidation in the early nineteenth century, but this needs to be counterbalanced not only by the haphazard and often communal reading of the papers but also by the sheer proliferation of partisan accounts. This counterbalancing is important because during the period discussed in this book the generation of public opinion regarding the various imperial and constitutional crises that dominated the news was highly chaotic, in part because the papers and prints were themselves associated with the very political parties that found themselves in a state of reorientation. The *Morning Chronicle* could always be counted on to give the Whig interpretation of politics and culture, but Whiggism itself was a fractured and often contradictory field. This sense of political confusion is even more pronounced in the visual satires of the period. The fact that the most famous satirists of the day—Gillray, Sayers, and Dent—were regularly contradicting their own representation of political events, often from one day to the next, is a sign less of simple apostasy than of a more deep-seated alteration in the constitution of the political.

The fact that the dailies were not a zone of homogeneous nation making is important for this study because the press is the key link between the theatre of politics and politics of theatre. Throughout this book the press is understood to be a capricious operator that provided Londoners with information regarding themselves and the world but, in so doing, provided the material both for heterodox anxieties and for compensatory ameliorations regarding the social constitution of the empire. And these anxieties and ameliorations permeated audience expectations and the reception of theatricalized versions of the same issues. At the risk of stating the obvious, it is important to emphasize that the latter thirty years of the eighteenth century were a period of extraordinary economic, social, and political upheaval in the British Empire. Shortly after the cessation of the Seven Years' War, in which British global supremacy over the French was established, almost every aspect of the relationship between metropole and colony had to be reconstructed due to fundamental changes in governmentality. We will be looking at many of these in detail, but a brief outline of the various crises and adjustments helps to give a sense of both the urgency and the interconnectedness of the matters reported and analyzed in both the press and the theatre.

As Nancy F. Koehn has demonstrated, the ten years following the Treaty of Paris demanded a complex engagement with the economic and constitutional challenges posed by Britain's newly acquired global supremacy. That engagement was marked by a combination of almost unrestrained ambition and nagging trepidation that the British Empire would go the way of ancient Rome, sixteenth-century Spain, or seventeenth-century Holland.[45] At the core of both Britain's commercial confidence and its collective insecurity was the problem of how to bring the different economic and political systems of the Atlantic and Indian colonies into harmony with the fiscal military state of Great Britain. Resolving this problem was a topic of intense interest and endless frustration.[46] The 1770s was marked by the political and economic disaster of the American Revolution, the temporary financial collapse of the East India Company, and unforeseen military setbacks both in North America and India. Losing the thirteen colonies and failing to decisively overcome Haider Ali of Mysore seriously shook both the psychic and the material bases of British imperialism. Despite supremacy on paper, British corporations and armies were losing significant struggles on a global scale.

The pressure of these reverses cast a long shadow on the 1780s. Disaffection with George III's rule and a series of inept flirtations with absolutism on the part of the Crown brought about a series of constitutional crises each of which was intimately tied to questions of how to correct errant colonial administration. The constitutional crisis of 1784 was directly precipitated by conflict over Fox's East India Bill, which attempted to bring the East India Company under direct control of the Ministry; the

impeachment of Warren Hastings—the first governor-general of Bengal—
further deepened the sense that all was not well in the East India Company and raised questions about the nature of sovereignty during this
period of hybrid colonial governance; the Regency crisis was partly fueled
by Whig senses that George III mismanaged the American war; and the
pervasive wrangling over constitutional matters following the French Revolution continually refers to the threat posed either by constitutional reform to British colonial administration or by French colonial aspirations.[47]
Britain emerged from these constitutional, military, and economic crises
in the 1790s through a recalibration of imperial interests. This was partly
enabled by the disintegration of the oligarchical desires of the Whig opposition at home, and by the new emphasis on military domination of the
Indian subcontinent. These two developments were intimately tied to the
final transformation from a mercantile to a territorial empire, and this
transformation pervaded metropolitan and colonial societies. The emergence of the combined disciplinary and regulatory regimes that molded
middle-class life in the nineteenth century was in many ways a direct response to the potential breakdown in the empire made visible in the 1770s
and 1780s. It is precisely this pattern of anxious self-scrutiny, tentative self-
diagnosis, and triumphal self-projection that characterizes the analysis
of the emergent empire that took place in the imaginary space between
Parliament, the print media, and the theatrical world—a space that we
could refer to as that of everyday life.

The second section of this book is very much concerned with this imaginary space between the satirical world of the London newspapers and the
theatre, because it considers the politicization of theatre and the theatricalization of politics in the period leading up to and during the first season of the Hastings impeachment.[48] The three chapters that make up this
section operate less as case studies than as a continuous meditation on the
problem of bringing imperial governance into performance. However, the
entire argument is organized by women's perspectives on the spectacle
of governmentality. Gender becomes a key thematic not only because
women play such a controversial role both in the rhetoric and the scene
of impeachment, but also because some of the most incisive commentary on this unique moment of imperial self-scrutiny comes from Elizabeth Inchbald and Frances Burney. As we will see, women observers were
profoundly aware of the limits placed on the understanding of Anglo-
Indian relations by the homosocial structure of parliamentary sociability.
It is my contention that during the trial fundamental problems in the relationship not only between metropole and colony but also between po-

litical elites and the emergent bourgeoisie became visible in moments of gendered performativity. These women were witness to the performance of men who were working on an extremely precarious stage and who were caught between two divergent discourse networks: one prescribed by the history of Parliament and one prescribed by the common law.

These problems need to be understood not only in economic and imperial terms but also in terms of governance itself. One of the most remarkable things about the impeachment of Warren Hastings is that it marks one of the most dramatic and lasting incursions of the common law on the British Constitution. Unlike previous impeachments, the proceedings against Hastings were carried out not according to special parliamentary rules but rather according to the rules of evidence prescribed by conventional legal procedure. P. J. Marshall notes that "While complete separation of the judicial and political work of the House [of Lords] was not achieved until the middle of the nineteenth century, the monopoly of the law lords over legal business was not often challenged. . . . Within a week of the opening of the trial, the House of Lords made it clear that it intended to follow contemporary legal practice rather than seventeenth-century precedents."[49] This meant that the Lords had to hear the prosecution's evidence on all the charges before hearing the defense. This decision virtually guaranteed Hastings's acquittal and was met with acrimonious dissent from Fox and Burke. Accounts of Fox's response indicate that he recognized that the impeachment was diverging from the Constitution:

> He entered into a discussion of the *Lex et Consuetudo Parliamenti* (the law and usage of Parliament), and asserted, that it was coeval with our Constitution, and that it was, if rightly considered, of still greater importance than the common law of England, or even the written or statutory laws of the Realm. He explained this by stating, that the *Lex et Consuetudo Parliamenti* was superior to every other species of law, since it was paramount to all—it judged the Judges, and put those upon their trial who could not be otherwise tried at all.[50]

Fox would lose this argument, but it does signal a transformative moment when one vision of the state would be overtaken by a much more diffuse set of institutional practices.[51] Despite Fox's claim that the managers will convict Hastings under any set of rules, his widely reported private anger over this decision is intriguing because it demonstrates not only the managers' clear sense that their case against Hastings rested less on tangible evidence than on oratorical brilliance, but also their sense of impotence before the law. In this case, one can point to an explicit moment when the disciplinary effects of legal institutions infiltrated Parliament in a fashion that actually suspended procedures inherent to the theory of sovereignty built during the seventeenth century. Put in Foucauldian terms, sovereign power was permeated and reconfigured by the forces of the emergent legal institution, and thus the trial is an early example of a transformation of governmentality that leeched power away from the state to disciplinary regimes. The victory of the common lawyers in the House of Lords made one component of the British Constitution obsolete.

This incursion meant that politics had to operate through the extra-parliamentary medium of public opinion. The excessiveness of much of the impeachment's oratory can therefore be understood as a compensation for the managers' loss of political effectivity before the impassive face of the law. The extremity of the managers' performances has become mythic: both Burke and Sheridan suffered similarly dramatic collapses on the third day of each of their four-day speeches, as if to emphasize that the enormity of Hastings's crimes had damaged their own constitutions.[52] And all of the managers addressed the Lords as if the entire proceeding was an inquiry into Britain's moral pretensions in the realm of world history. Fox's apparently "involuntary" exultation on the proceedings themselves, which followed his castigation of the Lords for ignoring the sanctity of the *Lex et Consuetudo Parliamenti,* captures the tenor of the managers' own acts of self-mythologization:

> At such an effort [the impeachment], in the admiring view of surrounding Nations, it were impious, if not possible, to be calm!—Indifference were Insensibility—that prophaned each sacred influence in Heaven and Earth!—There was no collective virtue superior—in the history of England—in the History of Man! It sprang from MOTIVES, of all others the most High and pure—the GOOD OF OTHERS;—and it flowed to CONSEQUENCES, of all others, the most gratifying and enduring—the well-founded APPROBATION OF OURSELVES![53]

That such an utterance could be reported as both "involuntary" and "reasonable" speaks volumes about the cultural significance of the impeachment, for it seems to suggest that the ethical inquiry into imperial culpability erupts from and is channeled through the body of the orator himself. Even in the eyes of an unsympathetic viewer, the managers' performances were deemed to be signs of history and thus indicative of far more than Hastings's guilt or innocence.[54]

At the core of this book's second part, chapter 4 combines an analysis of specific oratorical acts by Fox, Burke, and Sheridan during the impeachment proceedings with the visual representations of the trial in the satirical print market in order to stress not only the problem of bringing British rule in India into representation but also the ancillary sexual fantasies that emerged when the managers attempted to enact their abhorrence of Hastings's actions. Chapter 5 extends this analysis of performance and sexual anxiety by attending closely to Frances Burney's analysis of Burke's and Fox's oratory. Burney's diary offers an analysis of oratorical practice that is as cognizant of oratorical theory as it is of crucial problems in imperial governance. In this sense, I go much further with the text than other commentators on the impeachment and accord it status as a rigorous theoretical engagement with the question of imperial self-fashioning. Chapter 3 is arguably the most complex chapter in the book and, like chapter 5's assertion of Fanny Burney's political acumen, it contends that Elizabeth Inchbald's early Orientalist comedies are deeply involved with fundamental problems in political theory. We have already seen how *The Mogul Tale* refashions Orientalist representation into a mechanism of sexual normativity. Chapter 3 returns to the political events satirized in that farce in order to offer a detailed account of the place of Montesquieu's thoughts on despotism not only in the debate on Fox's East India Bill of 1783 but also in Inchbald's extraordinary comedy *Such Things Are*. *Such Things Are* opened just before Hastings was called to the bar, and I argue that Inchbald's play uses Montesquieu's notion of governmental principle both to dissect the political culture of her day and to offer a radical solution to problems of governance highlighted during the constitutional crises precipitated by Fox's East India Bill. As the framing structure of this section suggests, the fantasies and anxieties that drive these performances are fundamentally tied to metropolitan problematics; therefore, the theatrical projection of metropolitan concerns into ostensibly distant spaces needs to be understood as epiphenomenal, as itself symptomatic of a need for temporary self-distancing to comprehend the historical transition that was engulfing British imperial society.

Warring against the Self: Transforming Entertainment

As we approach the final years of the eighteenth century, autoethnography is supplemented and eventually displaced by complex forms of phantasmatic projection that I would argue are far more actantial. In its autoethnographic phases, theatrical imperialism in London helped lay the ground for the embodied imperial subject of the early nineteenth century. In doing so, it became one of the forces that helped to instantiate what Michel Foucault, Paul Gilroy, and others have usefully defined as biological state racism.[55] This form of state-sanctioned deployment of codified racial difference as a tactic of social regulation did not fully cohere until the middle of the nineteenth-century and the various signs of racial difference did not fully congeal in the theatrical productions of the late eighteenth century.[56] The elements of racialization I trace in this book are still very much in flux, and only with a retroactive glance can we discern which elements will achieve later significance.[57] What is visible in the theatre of this transitional period is a simultaneous resignification of the racialized performer and a startling shift in the relationship between performer and audience that intervenes in the process of ethnic identification that defined previous theatrical practice. This shift from a drama focused on self-stylization and critique to forms of spectacle that enact cultural and racial supremacy can be most visibly traced in the development of illegitimate dramaturgy. But new tactics were also in effect in the patent houses and can be used as signs of important historical bifurcations that alter the meaning of long-standing figures and tropes for racial, national, and class distinction.

Throughout the eighteenth century, the borders between race, nation, and class were often extremely difficult to discern. As Kathleen Wilson reminds us, race referred not to "scientific sets of physical characteristics but to bloodline and lineage" and thus was not that distinct from prevalent definitions of the nation.[58] One of the most complex problems for historians of British identity is how to disentangle these intertwining meanings. In his highly suggestive treatment of the shifting meaning of blood that attended the emergence of middle-class bodies in the late eighteenth century, Michel Foucault offered an important model for how to think about the recodification of race. In his lectures at the Collège de France in 1975–76, Foucault supplemented his notion of disciplinary power with a technology of power that he described as regulatory. Disciplinary power was "essentially centred on the body, on the individual body . . . [and] included all devices that were used to ensure the spatial distribution of individual bodies . . . and the organization, around those individuals, of a whole field of visibility."[59] The notion of disciplinary power is a crucial expansion of Marx's notion of cooperation, which is marked as a precondition for capitalist production in volume 1 of *Capital* but which did not receive a full specification.[60] But it is possible to excavate a link between cooperation and racialization in Marx's mordant recognition that "when the worker cooperates in a planned way with others, he strips off the fetters of his individuality, and develops the capabilities of his species."[61] In supplementing Marx's analysis, Foucault gives us an important indication why the questions of individuation and visibility are so crucial to eighteenth-century culture, but his turn to the question of "biopower" and "governmentality" takes up a problematic explicitly beyond the purview of Marxism. Foucault's interest shifted to a technology of power aimed not at the individual body and its integration into the modes of production but rather at one aimed at the population or the species and its maximization:

> Now I think we see something new emerging in the second half of the eighteenth century: a new technology of power, but this time it is not disciplinary. This technology does not exclude . . . disciplinary technology, but it does dovetail into it, integrate it, modify it to some extent, and above all use it by sort of infiltrating it, embedding itself in existing disciplinary techniques. . . . Unlike discipline which is addressed to bodies, the new non-disciplinary power is applied not to man-as-body but to the living man, to man-as-living-being; ultimately . . . to man as species.[62]

The key conceptual leap here is that the second technology of power, termed biopower or regulatory power, acts not on the individual body but on the mass of bodies that constitutes a population. Foucault suggests that disciplinary power and regulatory power incorporate the body simultaneously and thus permeate one another. This notion of two series operating on the same set of signs offers a way of understanding what is otherwise a chaotic transformation. In the permeation of disciplinary by regulatory technology, we have a model for the resignification of the body itself that downplays the visibility of individual traits in favor of the mobilization of mass qualities.

Foucault uses this transformational dynamic to explain the shift from one notion of race—that based on bloodline and lineage as signs of political sovereignty—to another in which populations are considered in their phantasmatic racial totality. It is significant that these largely unsupported claims emerged from a consideration of governmentality, for Foucault was attempting to explain the fundamental shifts in the locus of governance that we have discussed earlier. Because sexuality lies at the intersection both disciplinary and regulatory power, it is a privileged site of inquiry. As Foucault states, "sexuality, being an eminently corporeal mode of behaviour, is a matter for individualizing disciplinary controls that take the form of permanent surveillance. . . . But because it also has procreative effects, sexuality is also inscribed, takes effect, in broad biological processes that concern not the bodies of individuals but the element, the multiple unity of the population. Sexuality exists at the point where body and population meet."[63] One of the primary arguments of this book is that the deployment of sexuality is crucial to the racialization of class relations, and this argument comes to its conclusion during my readings of Mariana Starke's *The Sword of Peace* and the complex reception of her subsequent play, *The Widow of Malabar*. But there is something else at stake here that impinges directly on the relationship between theatre and its audience, on what I would call theatre's specifically governmental effects.

This book contends that theatrical productions enact governance and, in so doing, both discipline and regulate their audiences. What we see during the primarily autoethnographic performances of the book's first section is a careful management of identification that relies on suturing the relationship between the performer and the audience member. Affiliation between audience members is therefore mediated by identificatory relations with specific theatrical roles. The analysis of the Hastings trial in the book's second part turns on the unraveling of these identificatory mechanisms and highlights the governmental vacuum into which regulatory power would rapidly expand. The third part of the book tracks a transformation in entertainment in which the object of the performance is the consolidation of the audience. The suturing processes of individuation that define earlier theatrical practice are integrated into new representational tactics that address not the relationship between performer and audience member but between the spectacle and the audience as a totality. That totality is figured in national terms, but the very meaning of nation has changed in the process of audience regulation such that the former ethnic definition of nationality has been superseded by a definition that either implies biological supremacy or asserts the existence of a unified racial population. In the period where a new form of British subjectivity was being consolidated, symptomatic misrecognitions emerged that were not unrelated to the performative contradictions encountered by Burke and Sheridan during the impeachment process. In the scene of impeachment and in ensuing theatrical representations of colonial affairs, acts of impersonation figure forth a new kind of subject whose instability requires compulsive reiteration and reconsolidation.

Two distinct yet connected strategies are used to put this instability in abeyance. The first concerns the resignification of whiteness on the stage in the late 1780s, and the second involves the transformation in audience-performance relations in the illegitimate theatre. Despite clear ethnographic gestures in the productions discussed, the two final chapters focus primarily on fantasies of governance that are secured not only by military and territorial expansion but also by explicit assertions of British military supremacy. Chapter 6 takes up the question of interracial desire and racial degeneration by looking at Mariana Starke's *The Sword of Peace* as a metropolitan version of Lord Cornwallis's policy of military reform in the late 1780s. Starke offers a scathing critique of the sexual and governmental practices of British colonial functionaries in India and argues that their ostensible Indianization will be rectified by the example of reformed military rule. Starke ties together all the concerns about character formation broached in the previous chapters and attaches them to anxieties occasioned by the Hastings impeachment. But her attempts to put the era of company mismanagement firmly in the past by positing a new governmental regime clearly based on the accession of Cornwallis to the post of governor-general generates a series of contradictions that undermine her chief repositories of normativity. The performance of normativity becomes a problem because there is a disjunction between her normative examples of military masculinity and the obsolete forms of masculinity exhibited by the customary leaders of the nation. This disjunction is a result of the transitional quality of imperial society at this historical moment, and into this metropolitan power vacuum she inserts fantasies of middle-class self-regulation. The play's fascinating prologue and epilogue, written by George Colman, take this entire problematic and bring it into the field of theatrical reception by equating moments of colonial degeneration in the play to degraded practices in the metropole. What emerges from these paratheatrical texts is an argument for the place of the woman playwright in the public recalibration of imperial relations that resonates with both Inchbald's and Burney's earlier critiques of public masculinity. However, I also discuss the co-optation of Starke's critical strategies in her subsequent play *The Widow of Malabar*. Again I make a more tenuous connection to Cornwallis's governmental policies in order to show that the same fantasies that undergirded the ill-fated notion of the Permanent Settlement in India animate Starke's attempt to reform aristocratic gender roles in *The Widow of Malabar*.

If chapter 6 is the culmination of much of the book's engagement with the deployment of sexuality, race, and class, then chapter 7 closes the project by tracking the place of spectacle in the consolidation of national and racial subjects at the end of the century. Unlike previous chapters, this chapter steps out of the legitimate theatre and into the turbulent realm of precinematic display in order to examine a host of productions that attempted to bring the long British war with the sultans of Mysore into performance. The martial tropes of the previous chapters are here transformed into modes of enactment such that military masculinity becomes much more than a normative example of proper governance: it becomes the catalyst for phantasmatic projections of national and racial supremacy. The actual practice of warfare infiltrates theatrical space, and audiences take on much more active roles in their own racialization. The chapter argues that the new forms of spectacular entertainment that flooded the market at the turn of the century fundamentally altered the economy of imperial representation. With the Hastings trial occluded by Cornwallis's triumphant victories in Mysore, India itself changes its function in performance and suddenly becomes a heuristic for understanding conflict in other colonial spaces. Of key importance here is the way Ireland and India are strangely aligned in James Cobb's comic opera *Ramah Droog.* The sexual fantasies documented throughout this book are here redeployed to intervene in the public reception of the Irish rebellion. And with this assertion of commutability, the book argues that a key phase in imperial representation has concluded to be superseded by a new form of performative regulation in which the audience is rendered not as a disparate collective but as a form of species-being.

PART ONE | *Ethnographic Acts*

SITTING IN ONE'S SEAT with family and friends, milling about the lobby and pit, or standing in the upper balconies, the theatregoer of the late eighteenth century was engaged above all in a complex mode of sociability whose political and cultural importance has been consistently undervalued and underexamined. This neglect is largely a result of the strength of arguments regarding the public sphere initiated by Jürgen Habermas and modified by a legion of scholars specializing in eighteenth century and romantic print culture. The heuristic value of *The Structural Transformation of the Public Sphere* is beyond doubt, but recent work on questions of sociability have emphasized critical blind spots in the largely heteronormative accounts of how the citizen-subject emerged through the cultivation of "audience-oriented privacy" and the "codification of intimacy" in genres such as the letter, the diary, and the novel.[1] As Gillian Russell and Clara Tuite have argued, sociability is often defined as a form of social interaction that exists for its own sake and is thus removed not only from the political power of the state but also from the rational communality of civil society.[2] This exclusion of a whole swath of social interaction from the purview of social theory rests on an analysis of the theatricality of sociability that understands social performance either as free play or the provenance of self-representation.[3] However, theorists of performance from a host of disciplines have demonstrated that because social performance always already incorporates history, it cannot be easily dispensed with. Judith Butler makes this abundantly clear when she argues "that performativity cannot be understood outside of a process of iterability, a regularized and constrained repetition of norms. And this repetition is not performed *by* a subject; this repetition is what enables a subject and constitutes the temporal condition for the subject. This iterability implies that 'performance' is not a singular 'act' or event, but a ritualized production."[4] The complex temporality of Butler's thesis should give us pause, for it implies that the subject is preceded by social norms, enacting and modifying them all in the same moment. In the moment of social performativity, the history and future of social relations are in a state of nonlinear negotiation whose outcome is not easy to specify. That specification requires careful attention to the historicality of performance itself.

But that historicality, as Joseph Roach has demonstrated in his analysis of performative surrogation in circum-Atlantic culture, often works through chaotic mechanisms, some of which generate flows of great cultural significance and some of which amount to little beyond themselves.[5] Significance in this context is largely a result of what remains culturally and socially operative—for example, much of the literary scholarship on eighteenth-century British imperialism is deformed by nineteenth-century understandings of race. This deformation, which has been recently anatomized by Roxann Wheeler, testifies not only to the continuing effectivity of racial categorization as a means of social control, but also to the necessity of paying attention to historical assemblages that became obsolete or occluded.[6] The emergence of social formations is often made possible by events, actions, and dispositions that have no place in the future, except as the hidden, but constitutive, past. Social performance, by virtue of its very messiness, offers a rich field for the genealogist, and theatrical sociability, by virtue of the interplay between representation and enactment, remains a locus from which to supplement and reevaluate the often static accounts of public and private generated by scholars of print culture. Paradoxically, scholarship on sociability and performance may provide a useful countermemory from which to refine, reconfigure, or even challenge accounts of late eighteenth-century public spheres.

In perhaps the most clear tabulation of modes of sociability in eighteenth-century Britain, Peter Clark describes social interaction in the Georgian period as "an intricate tessellation" of "private" sociability of the home, of an "old style" sociability based around the church, Parliament, court, and the street, and of a "new style" sociability brought on by the commercialization of culture.[7] In spite of the fact that this new style of sociability took place in venues such as the theatres, pleasure gardens, shops, and dancing assemblies, Clark's analysis models this "new style" on the male homosocial environments of the coffeehouse and the club.[8] Russell and Tuite have gone some distance in rectifying the limiting view of sociability inherent in this methodological decision, but I wish to retain the notion of style because it allows us to think about the myriad social practices that might converge on any given evening in the theatre as a question of style and thus susceptible to both historical and rhetorical reading.

As an audience and a set of players congregated, a range of styles and counterstyles of individual self-representation and social exchange unfolded both in relation to the entertainment on stage and in relation to the entertainment inherent to sociality itself. What this implies is that the audience was engaged in moral and aesthetic judgments about their own constitution and practice of sociability. Because the theatre audience incorporated men and women, residents of the Town, the City, and the Country, fashionable, commercial and more common spectators, and a host of ethnically distinct subjects, the social practices housed within the walls of Covent Garden or Drury Lane amounted to a rather less-exalted form of "spectatorial ethics" than perhaps Adam Smith had in mind.[9] And yet, exalted or not, what audiences were doing at this historical juncture cannot be separated from the consideration of modes of behavior and everyday life that were the subject of print journalism, philosophical disquisition, and theatrical representation. What is peculiar about the theatre in this regard, which separates it from the more conventionally defined venues of the bourgeois public sphere, is that mutually constitutive acts of ethical spectatorship and ethical enactment occur in a tight temporal loop. Without the delay inherent to the print media, this kind of sociability involves a level of volatility that is perhaps unparalleled in the period.

I have introduced the notion of "ethical spectatorship" advisedly because the imperative behind Smith's invocation of the "impartial spectator" recognizes that such spectatorship of the social has economic and political value.[10] Like many forms of Enlightenment, Smith's particularly visual metaphorization of social inquiry plays a complex role in the mediation of social change—in its representation and evaluation. This is nowhere more evident than in the practice of Enlightenment ethnography and natural history. As the commercial range of the European empires expanded in the eighteenth century, it became economically necessary to develop modes of sociability between highly divergent societies. Thus, understanding "human nature" became important not only for establishing the moral duties of citizen-subjects of Britain to each other and to themselves, but also for navigating the social interface with non-Britons in order to further the commercial aims of the empire's charter companies. As Kathleen Wilson has reminded us, "dividing the human species up into nations was arguably the most widely used category of difference in the period, and nation served to map, literally and metaphorically, the moral, philosophical, theological and historical debates over human diversity, human nature, and the impact of climate, government, language and laws on both."[11] With a largely racial understanding of the term nation, one could argue that one of the ubiquitous projects of the period was to incorporate the often contradictory evidence brought back to the metropole by explorers, merchants, and less-interested observers into emerging theories of human nature and sociality. This is most evident in the difficult assimilation of information gathered during the Cook voyages for as often as not the incoming empirical information diverged considerably from the abstract categories devised by philosophers and protoanthropologists.[12] Under the pressure of an ever-expanding repertoire of human diversity, eighteenth-century ethnography was forced into increasingly reductive and abstract levels of distinction.

Because the social and cultural mapping of the world by Enlightenment thinkers has been widely discussed, two issues need reinterpretation here.[13] Whether the models of racial and national diversity were based on polygenetic accounts, as in those based on the pre-Adamite theory of Isaac la Peyrère, or on the more-pervasive monogenetic accounts of Buffon, Montesquieu, Blumenbach, and Kames, these protoethnographic texts carry a governmental imperative.[14] The gradation of varieties of mankind was inevitably incorporated into a linear pattern of human progress. With "Caucasians" (Blumenbach's term) placed in preeminent position, the rest of the world's peoples were categorized by their proximity or distance from this normative example. Aside from allowing for a refinement of the Great Chain of Being, which could establish the relative maturity of societies and thus their susceptibility to rule, both monogenetic and polygenetic accounts of difference quickly incorporated notions of degeneracy.[15] Whether it was due to the influence of climate, intermarriage, or simply conduct, one could argue that societies, which should by "nature" be more advanced, were caught in a regressive slide. This type of argument was used not only to suggest that residents of the tropics were inevitably held back by the influence of climate but also that members of more "advanced" societies would also lose their physical and mental vigor if subject to similar environmental factors.

Regardless of the projected origins of difference or the wide range of possible factors that ostensibly segmented mankind, what remains most important in this period of vague racializations is the assumption of a natural humanity that acts as a norm against which various manifestations of human variety will be valued and judged. In Britain, this natural humanity was grounded not on physiological difference but rather on what was described by a wide range of commentators as "natural liberty," a point elaborated by Sudipta Sen:

> The authoritarian family and the authoritarian nation-state were both results of a profound search for order in a world of rapid material change and uncertainty. The anxieties of disorder that were reflected in the current doctrines of political economy also generated two inviolable and mutually dependent qualities in the conception of the civilized state of nations: liberty and property. In the age of British expansion, native populations brought under ethnological scrutiny were inevitably defined by the lack of these qualities. It was considered perfectly reasonable, for instance, to claim and annex territory where there were no "natural inhabitants," or inhabitants endowed with natural liberties.[16]

This meant that British forms of juridical governance and British understandings of property became the norm against which other cultures and societies were judged. In the absence of a recognizable sovereign government, as often happened in the case of North America, British merchants or soldiers would either declare their own sovereignty or abruptly nominate someone sovereign and deal with that leader as though operating according to modes of governance endemic to England.

In the case of the more recognizably organized social structure of India, British functionaries reconstructed indigenous modes of governance in terms of European political institutions and operated—at least nominally—according to codes of international law and alliance. These conscious misrecognitions played a strategic role in not only enabling but also veiling British rule. As Thomas Pownall explicitly recognized as early as 1773,

> Although the sovereignty of the native Government of the country within the bounds of the dominion of the East India Company is abolished and annihilated, yet the forms and orders, the offices, and ostensible officers of Government remain—the tenure of the lands remains as it did; the rents and revenues as they did;—the state of rights personal and political, the rule of government, such as they were; the sovereign power and direction however, the absolute military command, the absolute perpetuity of right in the revenues . . . is held under a very jealous and exclusive power in the hands of the Company: although it suffers the government to be exercised by the nominal officers of the state—yet it is the holder of the state in its own hands.[17]

This form of veiled sovereignty in which now obsolete or compliant potentates were accorded the status of nominal rulers and in which indigenous governmental practices were retained was of crucial strategic importance in India, for it lent legitimacy to a rather dubious form of domination.[18] But the fact that Britons felt the need to legitimize their governmental practices is itself notable, for it emerged in part from the fantasy of British governmental preeminence and in part from the very real, if rarely articulated, sense that their hold on power was tenuous. The precise ratio of arrogance to anxiety shifted back and forth during the late eighteenth century until the final military victories over the sultans of Mysore and the Marathas squelched organized resistance and paved the way for the Charter Act of 1813, which asserted the Crown's "undoubted sovereignty" over all of the company's territories.

Because it carried the burden of legitimation, much of the ethnographic writing of this period focuses on the relationship between native peoples and the mutually constitutive notions of governance and property. Regions as culturally diverse as Africa, North America, India, Scotland, and Ireland became the object of an emergent ethnographic imagination whose primary objective was to provide an alibi for colonial rule. Thus nations were characterized either as naturally subservient or unfit to govern themselves, as always already enslaved or hopelessly prone to despotism. These characterizations often came in pairs. For example, Robert Orme, in his extremely influential *Historical Fragments of the Mogul Empire and the Morattoes and of the English Concerns in Indostan,* offered one of the earliest ethnographic accounts in which "the natural history of Indians is directly implicated with the project of imperial dominion."[19] Orme divides India into the subservient, effeminate Hindu population and the ruling martial Mogul society and attaches these qualities to various physical features and modes of conduct. As Sen notes, this "initial dichotomy of the subject population, marked by the opposing attributes of domestic and unruly, settled and nomadic, effeminate and martial, can be seen in other parts of the colonial world as well" including in the distinction between Ireland and Scotland.[20] On either side of these dichotomies, the subject population is portrayed as having no conception of property or as having been corrupted by despotic rule such that any sense of liberty or property has degenerated beyond reclamation. Subservience therefore is either natural or the result of historical degeneration. In the former category, we have the fantasy of Friday from *Robinson Crusoe* or the natives of Otaheite in the various treatments of Cook's first voyage to the South Seas. As we will see in our discussion of Loutherbourg's production of *Omai; or, A Trip Round the World,* the question of the Tahitian relation to property is of critical importance for the adjudication of British sovereignty. In the latter category, we have the myriad fantasies of Oriental despotism whether culled from the pages of Oriental tales or projected onto the principalities of India.

In this way, in the words of Uday Mehta, the British Empire became a mirror of British political thought.[21] This is not to say that British institutions were simply transposed or transplanted, but rather that the empire became a place where the nature of appropriate governance and the nature of property were put into question. As Sen argues, liberty and landed property were at the heart of Whig principles of governance and political economy:

The faith in individual liberty was generated no doubt, through a profound historical relationship between property, patrimony, and patriarchal authority within the household. Many of these ideas were enshrined in legislation that reflected the intimate connections between liberty, private property, and law. By the eighteenth century, the gentry household had acquired a much sharper definition with the gradual decline of a wider clientage: retainers, servants, and tenants. The new patriarchal family was founded on a close adherence to property and the reinforcement of paternal authority.[22]

That both liberty and property were literally and metaphorically tied to paternal notions of the landed family is important, because as the households of Britain changed so too did the faith that secured the colonial conception of rule. The corollary of ethnographic arguments such as Orme's that subject populations are destined to subservience is that the ruling constituency must protect itself from degeneration. In the nineteenth century, that meant that a strict separation was enforced between ruler and ruled, but in the late eighteenth century things were much less clear. As William Dalrymple and others have recently demonstrated, the everyday social and economic lives of East India Company functionaries and of the Indians who traded with or served them were deeply intertwined.[23] The legacy of this intimate interaction throughout this period would have a significant impact on the largely segregationist social policy in the nineteenth century. In the period preceding the Permanent Settlement, however, one can discern not only the existence of arguments both for and against different levels of cultural, social, and legal integration but also a set of arguments that firmly locate the contaminating effects of colonial service in India in the prior social deterioration of the metropole.[24]

John Brewer has argued that the midcentury saw the crystallization of the gentry's "natural tendency" to rule.[25] Like the "natural liberty" of colonial emissaries, however, that "natural tendency" was susceptible to degeneration. By the 1770s the political efficacy of the gentry was called into question by the economic crises generated by colonial speculation, by a breakdown in the system of credit, and by increasing pressure on the paternal structure of the aristocracy. As the middle ranks became more skeptical about both the solvency of landed property and increasingly convinced by charges of dissipation and corruption, one can chart increasing anxiety about both liberty and property. Significantly, the same symptomatology used to derogate colonized societies was deployed in the diagnosis of British cultural and social degeneration. Chief among these signs was effeminacy, and in this context gender insubordination became a sign of a breakdown both in the gentry's manifestation of "natural liberty" and in the property relations that ostensibly guaranteed their economic interest in the health of the nation. Perhaps a no-less-important set of signs was associated with despotism—cruelty, volatility, deceit, and sexual dissipation. These signs all pertain to forms of errant masculinity that proliferated in a wide range of discourses, representations, and performances.

This proliferation is critical because it returns us to the question of sociability in the theatre. Because gender plays such a crucial role both in the ethnographic project required for the legitimation of colonial governance and in the autoethnographic project of evaluating the state of British society at any given time, the dialectical relation between the representation of sociality on stage and the performance of sociability in the audience is evident in the sexual economy through which social exchange operates in the theatre. As Kristina Straub has persuasively demonstrated, the eighteenth-century theatre was a kind of laboratory for testing and analyzing sometimes subtle, sometimes violent transformations in the sex/gender system.[26] This was especially the case with regard to the representation of the family, of effeminacy, and of violent masculinity, for all three of these concerns were figuratively and literally tied not only to the threatened security of the governmental fantasy of landed property, but also to the emergent discourse of political economy that would provide the discursive integration of governmental, economic, and social institutions required for the legitimation of middle-class ascendancy. The family, of course, changes its function in this transformation from that of a figure for governance in which the sovereign state is understood as a hierarchical relationship between patriarchal ruler and subject-children to that of an assemblage that retains the former figurative connotations but supplements them with actual sexual deployments. While these transformations suffuse all social relations, the theatre's strange negotiation of intimacy and publicity makes it an illuminating venue for examining the dubiously "ethical" spectatorship endemic to its autoethnographic function.

Thus intimate signs and practices became indicators of macrological tendencies pertaining to the success of the nation and the empire in "the right disposition of things."[27] When a power vacuum emerged due to a decline in the landed gentry's capacity for rule, the commercial classes, whose power was based less on property than on contract, not only found itself compelled to rule but also exercised forms of governmental function not yet prescribed by the conventional juridical manifestations of landed power defined by the British Constitution. Like the East India Company's practice of legitimizing its institutional power by ceding nominal territorial rule to those who no longer have it, the middle classes developed complex forms of self-legitimation that retained the nominal structure of a now mystified Constitution, but which exercised power in a supplemental fashion through the institutional control of intimate practices generally deemed below the purview of sovereign government. This is the problematic addressed by Samuel Foote's *The Nabob,* to which we now turn.

CHAPTER ONE

Empire's Vicious Expenses

Samuel Foote's *The Nabob* and the

Credit Crisis of 1772

BRITISH POLITICIANS, CITIZENS, and civil servants of all stripes were deeply ambivalent about the future of the empire following the extraordinary expansion of British imperial interests at the end of the Seven Years' War in 1763.[1] As Edmund Burke appraised the situation of the British Empire in 1769, "The orient sun never laid more glorious expectations before us. . . . You are plunged into Empire in the east. You have formed a great body of power, you must abide by the consequence."[2] Now in control of territorial and commercial interests all over the globe, Britons were simultaneously thrilled by their newfound commercial supremacy and puzzled by how to integrate the very different political and economic forces of their Atlantic and Eastern holdings into the workings of the nation. For some, the possibility of transferring revenues collected under the newly acquired diwani—the agreement which enabled the East India Company to collect revenue in the regions of Bengal, Bihar, and Orissa—to pay down the huge national debt incurred during the Seven Years' War or to alleviate the potential loss of the American colonies came at a moment when it looked as though the entire imperial enterprise might disintegrate.[3] For others, the constitutional problems posed by the East India Company's accession to sovereignty threatened not only to undermine the sovereignty of the King-in-Parliament but also to link the finances of the nation to the fate of notoriously unstable East India Company stock.[4] Perhaps because British thinking on empire in this period was suffused by historical examples of imperial ascendancy and fall, the papers and the parliamentary record were filled with ambition and trepidation.[5] Considering the relative disparity between British imperial holdings in America and India in the 1760s—America was by far and away more economically and politically integrated with Britain—the final three decades of the eighteenth century must have come as quite a shock. By the early 1780s the Atlantic empire would be in ruins and the governance of India would remain a vexed question.[6] The working through of that trauma is the concern of later chapters in this book, but this chapter is concerned with the period of social insecurity immediately prior to the American Revolution.[7]

The spring of 1772 was a season of unparalleled imperial, economic, and social upheaval. In addition to the almost daily indication that the situation in the American colonies was moving ineluctably toward crisis, the newspapers were filled with two related stories: Lord Clive's defense before Parliament of his actions in India and the collapse of a series of Scottish banks affiliated with the insolvent financier Alexander Fordyce.[8] As Nancy F. Koehn argues, the North Ministry had been avoiding state action on Indian issues, but the credit crisis sparked by Fordyce, which enveloped Europe and brought the East India Company to the verge of bankruptcy, forced the government to intervene.[9] From the summer of 1772 onward, the newspapers were flooded with accounts of parliamentary debates and editorials on the proper integration of the Indian colonies into the economy of the empire. These debates would eventually result in Lord North's Regulating Act of 1773, which for the first time brought a chartered company within the orbit of the state's power. But the stories of Clive and Fordyce were important beyond their immediate relation to the Regulating Act, for they became signs either of Britain's irreversible descent into vice or of the nation's salutary resistance to social decay. If it was the former, then both events were further symptoms of the widespread narrative of imperial decline of which Gibbon's *Decline and Fall of the Roman Empire* is exemplary; if it was the latter, then the events could be subsumed into narratives of the exceptional qualities of British liberty. Of course, which of these two options readers espoused had a great deal to do with their economic and political alliances, but their cohabitation in the print media allows us to sketch in a series of cultural anxieties that are woven together by Samuel Foote in *The Nabob* and which return in various guises on the London stage for the next thirty years. At the risk of distorting the long development of these stories I want to put them in context and to connect them to specific dates in order to give some sense of their temporal compression in the months leading up to *The Nabob*'s first performance on 29 June 1772.

Clive, Fordyce, and the Appearance of Luxury

On 30 March 1772, Laurence Sulivan, the autocratic on-again, off-again chairman and director of the East India Company, introduced a bill to the House of Commons for the self-regulation of the Company. The culmination of years of wrangling between Lord Robert Clive and the directors of the Company, the bill constituted a final effort on the part of the Company to avoid government regulation of its affairs. By the middle of the eighteenth century, the East India Company had become one of the most complex corporations in the world and a far cry from the fairly straightforward commercial operation envisaged by its charter in the late sixteenth century. Throughout the seventeenth and early eighteenth centuries, the East India Company was a purely commercial venture with factories pursuing highly profitable trade at various locations around the rim of the Asian subcontinent. However, by midcentury it became involved in complex military conflicts with the French and their military allies in India that ultimately transformed the Company into a territorial power. Lord Clive's victory over the Nawab of Bengal, Siraj-ud Daula, at Plassey in 1757 and the defeat of the Mughal emperor and the Wazir of Oudh at Buxar in 1764 resulted in the conferral of the diwani to the East India Company. The accession to the diwani meant that the Company now assumed the civil administration of Bengal and thus gained the right to extract revenue from the land and its 20 million residents.[10]

However, the hybrid nature of the East India Company—it was both a commercial entity and the agent of sovereign governance—and its disconnection from direct parliamentary control made it a topic of some anxiety. Part of that anxiety was directly tied to the sheer profitability of its new role as territorial power. In addition to the surplus value accrued through trade, the Company was amassing large amounts of revenue through the taxation of Bengal such that the stability of its territorial regime became a matter of great economic importance. Any threat to that stability threatened the solvency of the Company, and the economic interpenetration of colony and metropole was such that any such threat would "pull down the credit system on which public finance and trade depended. In 1773 it was being said that the loss of India would produce a national bankruptcy."[11] This fear was exacerbated by the fact that, despite territorial rule, much of the Company's operation still relied on economic relations with Indian bankers and rulers over which the Company did not have absolute control. This was especially the case in relation to the large volume of unregulated private trade—trade carried out by Britons working on their own behalf outside the control of the Company—that had been growing exponentially throughout the century.

These private relationships between Company servants and indigenous financiers or banians not only expanded the British economic infiltration into Indian life but also contributed to the political destabilization of both the Company and the principalities with which it operated. Often decisions of some Company officials were made with their private interests in mind to the detriment of that of the Company or the nation, a subject of intense concern in the metropole. That concern was concretized by the figure of the "nabob," a term applied to recently returned Company officials whose massive private fortunes were seen to be destabilizing the fabric of metropolitan life. In the early 1770s the East India Company, ruling over vast territories and huge populations, was involved in an immense volume of trade. Yet its strange hybrid role meant that it was no longer an autonomous commercial organ but rather an entity deeply enmeshed and reliant on economic and political alliances with Indian partners. This transition above all others meant that governance of the Company itself became not only labyrinthine but also largely disconnected from the metropole. Because of the importance of India to the British economy, that disconnection could not be tolerated and thus the next thirty years saw the inexorable transference of governance from the Company to the state.[12]

Thus, as a rearguard action to preserve Company autonomy, Sulivan's bill was doomed to failure in part because its version of the Company was effectively obsolete and under rigorous public scrutiny. Following the revelations of William Bolts's *Considerations on Indian Affairs* and Alexander Dow's *The History of Hindostan,* widely circulated in the press and published in book form earlier in the year, the public had become extremely impatient with charges of rapacious improprieties on Indian soil, as well as the consistently poor performance of East India Company stock.[13] It was highly unlikely that the Company would be allowed to self-govern under these circumstances. As Koehn argues, "By 1773 most metropolitan officials believed that Parliament—not the monarch, executive departments, or colonial governors—had the sovereign right to regulate the Indian and North American economies."[14] The Regulating Act was imposed almost one year later against much protest from parliamentarians such as Burke, who felt that it was an incursion on the sacred rights of property.[15] The Regulating Act severely prohibited private trade and was the first if somewhat faltering step in transferring control of Indian affairs from the Company to Parliament. It did not resolve the question of the state's right to a share of the Bengal revenues or the question of the Crown's right of possession of Company territory, but it did ensure ministerial supervision of the Company's affairs at home and of its administration of legal, commercial, and military actions in India.[16]

Sulivan's proposal of self-regulation, however, prompted two crucial events, both of which were marked by their theatricality. The first was Robert Clive's famous defense of his actions in Bengal. Clive's speech to the House of Commons was widely heralded as one of the most remarkable oratorical performances of the age and was deemed of sufficient interest to be recorded in its entirety in two succeeding issues of the *Gazetteer*.[17] His accounts of the temptations of fortune were the focus of much discussion and debate for the way in which they cast the problem of corruption both as a joint Anglo-Indian problem and as a symptom of British cultural immaturity:

> Now-a-days every youth possessed of any interest endeavours to go out as a writer to the company. No matter how ill qualified he is by education; writing and cyphering are thought sufficient. The same talents which were deemed necessary when the company was only a trading body, are required now that they have become sovereigns of an empire as large as all Europe. The same hands that flourished a pen, are held capable of swaying a sceptre; and accordingly no other questions are proposed at their examination, but "can you cypher, can you write and keep accounts?" A specimen of their penmanship is produced, together with a certificate from some writing-master, that they have under him learned the true art of book-keeping after the Italian manner. . . . Being equipt, they receive their lessons from friends and relations. My dear boy, says the father, I have done my part, I have set you in the way of fortune, and it will be your own fault if you are not a made man. See what a fortune has been made by this Lord, and that Lord, by Mr. such-a-one and such-a-one; what hinders you to be as successful? Thus are their passions enflamed, and their principles corrupted, before they leave their native country.[18]

As the speech moves from its insinuations about "the true art of book-keeping after the Italian manner" and the repeated satirical assertion that more is needed to govern Britain's imperial holdings than penmanship, Clive firmly establishes that the roots of corruption lie in the excessive desires of the young men's metropolitan connections. This suggestion that the writers for the Company leave the British Isles already inflamed by the desire for excessive returns emphasizes that the predilection for luxury is a preexisting metropolitan problem. In making this allegation, Clive is in part participating in a widespread critique of speculation and stockjobbing. However, the negative connotation of the term *speculation* was not yet in circulation, and for many Clive embodied precisely the kind of activity that would eventually meet with disapprobation under this heading. So oddly enough, as Clive stands before the House, it is only his oratorical performance of "maturity" that prevents him from becoming the embodiment of his own example.

Clive's account of metropolitan greed is a prelude to an argument that has Indian creditors, or banians, preying upon the already active class envy of the East India Company officials. The description of the credit scheme is also notable, for the "raw boys" are advanced money by the banian without present collateral:

> What is the consequence of their landing in Bengal? One of these raw boys walks out into the streets of Calcutta, for his income will not allow him to ride. He sees writers, who are not greatly his seniors, marching in state on fine prancing horses, or carried along at their ease in a palanquin. He comes home and tells his Banyan what a figure his acquaintance made. And what hinders you to equal him in splendour? returns the Banyan. I have money enough, and you have nothing to do but to receive, for you need not ask. Well, money is advanced by the generous Mussulman: the youth takes the bait, he has his horses, his coach, his palanquin, his haram; and, while in pursuit of one fortune, spends three. But how is the Banyan in the meantime indemnified? Under the sanction of the young man, who is rising in the state, and making a quick progress towards a seat in council, he rises likewise, and commits various oppressions with impunity, the practice being so general, as to afford him perfect security. I can assure you, that native Britons are not the persons that directly oppress, but the Indians who take shelter under them, and who have paved their way to all exemption from controul by pecuniary obligations. Human nature is frail, and the desire of wealth is as strong a passion as ambition. Where then is the wonder that men should sink under the temptations to which they are here exposed? Flesh and blood cannot resist them. An Indian comes to you with his bag of silver, and entreats you to accept it as a present. If your virtue be proof against this trial, he comes next day with same bag filled with gold. Should your stoicism still continue, he returns with it

stuffed with diamonds; and if, for fear of detection, you refuse even this temptation, he displays his bales of merchandize, a trap into which a trader readily falls. He takes them at a low price, and sends them to a distant market, where he gains 500 per cent. Hence a new plunderer is let loose upon the society; but he is a plunderer whom we owe to the badness of our own regulations. The servants of the Company yield only because they are men; presents are so common and so prevailing in India, that it is almost impossible not to be carried along by the torrent. Meer Jeffier told me, that in the course of a year he received three hundred thousand pounds in this way, and I might have received as much while Governor. Judge, then, how difficult it is for men of common minds to return with unpolluted hands.[19]

What Clive describes is a private credit arrangement in which the ingenuous British functionary is put under "pecuniary obligations," which are only indemnified by what amounts to influence peddling. According to Clive, the offer of credit without collateral is based on the young men's relation to the Company. This has significant ramifications because the very system of private credit, which by this time sustains the metropolitan British economy, works on similarly superficial qualifications. Of equal importance is Clive's insistence that it is their desire for luxury that makes them vulnerable to this kind of alleged extortion. What is interesting is that the signs of luxury Clive invokes, the harem excepted, would be recognizable to his audience as the signs of excessive consumption in London society just as much as in Calcutta. The rhetorical force of the horses and equipage lies in precisely this commutability. At the heart of Clive's defense lies an unrelenting assertion that the Indian problem is, first, the product of a particularly felicitous fit between the functionaries' class-based susceptibility to luxury and the banian's willingness to fulfill that desire in order to shield his own economic predations and, second, inextricably tied to the problem of private credit both in Britain and in India. The rhetorical gambit is significant because it ineluctably ties the process of corruption in India to the anxieties regarding credit that animate much of the popular press during this period.

Clive's speech was met with widely divergent reaction. His enemies focused on how the fabular qualities of the speech turn the enriched and corrupt functionaries into victims, while his friends focused on how his careful detailing of the inaccurate claims made by the Company called into question both its leadership and its motivations in the quest for self-regulation. The weeks following the speech saw repeated allegations of gross improprieties perpetrated by Clive and by other members of the Company. These allegations culminated in the formation of the Select Committee of 1772 headed by General Burgoyne, which put further public scrutiny on Clive, and then of the Secret Committee, which probed the financial operations of the Company in a more discreet yet no less effective manner.[20] Horace Walpole gives some sense of the unease that accompanied all discussions of Indian affairs in a letter to his friend Horace Mann:

> We beat Rome in eloquence and extravagance; and Spain in avarice and cruelty: and like both, we shall only serve to terrify schoolboys, and for lessons of morality! "Here stood St. Stephen's Chapel; here young Cataline spoke; here was Lord Clive's diamond house; this is Leadenhall Street, and this broken column was part of a palace of a company of merchants who were sovereigns of Bengal! They starved millions in India by monopolies and plunder, and almost raised a famine at home by the luxury occasioned by their opulence, and by that opulence raising the prices of everything, till the poor could not purchase bread!" Conquest, usurpation, wealth, luxury, famine—one knows how little farther the genealogy has to go! If you like it better in Scripture phrase, here it is: Lord Chatham begot the East India Company; the East India Company begot Lord Clive; Lord Clive begot the Maccaronies, and they begot poverty—and all the race are still living; just as Clodius was born before the death of Julius Caesar. There is nothing more like than two ages that are very like; which is all that Rousseau means by saying, "give him an account of any great metropolis, and he will foretell its fate."[21]

Walpole's apocalyptic tour of post-imperial London does far more than mobilize the conventional comparison between the British and Roman empires, for the genealogy of decline asserts a causal relation between Clive and the macaronis that is important for understanding the antinabob sentiment of the period. With a predilection for highly feminized dress and for libertine practices, the macaronis became for a short period the focus of social anxiety largely because their combination of gender insubordination, homoeroticism, and predatory heterosexuality seemed to herald a devolution of aristocratic masculinity akin to that of the late phases of the Roman Empire.[22] Clive himself was satirized as both a tyrant and a macaroni (fig. 1.1).[23] This characterization of East India

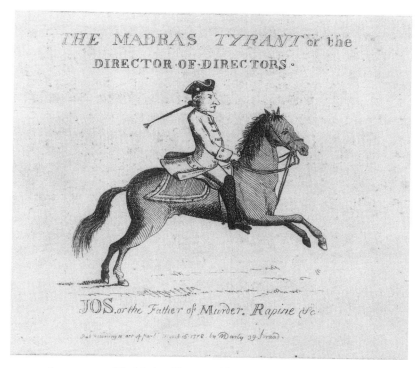

THE MADRAS TYRANT or the DIRECTOR·OF·DIRECTORS·

JOS.or the Father of Murder. Rapine &c

FIG. 1.1. Anonymous, *The Madras Tyrant or The Director of the Directors,* 1772 *(courtesy of the Department of Prints and Drawings, The British Museum, London; BM 5017)*

Company officials as macaronis infiltrated public discourse throughout the spring and summer of 1772. At a public meeting intended to forestall North's plan to regulate the Company, the Court of Proprietors of the East India Company found itself attacked on precisely these terms. One auditor rose and stated that "persons were sent out [to India] no way qualified, or initiated in mercantile affairs—mere Macaroni merchants—fit only for *capering in a lady's chamber*—with a view to plunder and increase their fortunes."[24] As we will see macaroni masculinity plays a vital role in Foote's satire, but its full complexity can only be appreciated when we turn to the related story of Alexander Fordyce.

On 9 June 1772 Alexander Fordyce, a partner in the banking house of Neale, James, Fordyce, and Down, fled to France after his fraudulent activities in the stock market were disclosed. The resulting bankruptcy of the firm caused a series of bank collapses throughout the month culminating in the closure of the firm of Glyn and Halifax on 22 June and the Ayr

Bank on 25 June. The shock waves of these closures were felt not only throughout banking houses both in Britain and the continent but also in the private accounts of many of Britain's foremost citizens.[25] Prior to intervention by the Bank of England, the credit crisis threatened to escalate into an international collapse. When the Bank of England did intervene, it did so selectively by bailing out the English firms and allowing the Jewish and Scottish firms to go bankrupt in what amounted to an act of financial ethnic cleansing.[26] The cascade of closures following the collapse of Fordyce's affairs precipitated the most serious economic and imperial crisis of the century. Most notably, the East India Company was plunged into liquidity problems that destabilized the value of East India stock.[27] Both the amount of money lost and the number of bankruptcies dwarf the consequences of the far more-famous South Sea Bubble. Some sense of the panic can be gleaned from the following notice in the *Gentleman's Magazine:*

> It is beyond the power of words to describe the general consternation of the metropolis at this instant. No event for 50 years past has been remembered to have given so fatal a blow both to trade and public credit. An universal bankruptcy was expected, the stoppage of almost every banker's house in London was looked for. The whole city was in an uproar; many of the first families in tears. This melancholy scene began with a rumour that one of the greatest bankers in London had stopped, which afterwards proved true. A report at the same time was propagated, that an immediate stop of the greatest must take place. Happily this report proved groundless; the principal merchants assembled, and means were concerted to revive trade, and preserve the national credit.[28]

However, it was not simply the magnitude of the collapse that caused alarm but its effect on credit. And although the concern expressed in this notice regards public credit, the primary problem was in the realm of private credit.

The Fordyce episode forcefully exposed the dangers of the expanding world of private credit to the stability of the national and imperial economy. A considerable portion of the financial and commercial affairs of the nation had their basis on paper instruments, "whose worth depended entirely upon the reputation of the person presenting them and the value attached to the signatures that appeared on them."[29] Thus, all manner of bills and bonds were guaranteed by something as vulnerable to obfuscation as appearance and personal reputation. Perhaps the best way to illustrate the import of these transactions is to take the example of Clive's own manipulation of bonds in his efforts to gain control of the East India Company. Bonds, in which one person's support is pledged in order to gain credit for another person, allowed someone with sufficient fortune to act anonymously through a series of agents. Clive did precisely this by entering into bonds with a range of agents who were all acting on his orders. As we will see, Foote translates this form of indirect acquisition in Sir Matthew Mite's financial dealings with the Oldhams.

Aside from providing shields for unethical business practices, private credit was in many ways as dependent on performance as more conventional theatrical representation. It is for this reason that invectives against private credit often mobilize antitheatrical discourse to construct an image of an economy corrupted by excessive layers of artifice. In an essay entitled "Of the Great Extent, Shameful Abuse, and Fatal Consequences, of Private Credit," one correspondent to the *Gentleman's Magazine* emphasized the unsettling level of social masquerade inherent in such instruments:

> The mischiefs from private CREDIT are innumerable. . . . It puts an end to all distinction between men, and enables those of inferior circumstances to view in appearance and manner of life with their superiors. . . . Surrounded as we seem by riches and plenty, we are actual bankrupts and starving. The most effectual step my poor imagination can suggest, "is to bring all sorts of people to live and appear as they really are; strip them of all false colourings; let them descend from their coaches to their pattens; and return to their stuffs, if they cannot pay for silks."[30]

The correspondent's concern with the difference between appearance and reality is more than an invective against class mobility, for it strikes right to the heart of private credit's susceptibility to fraudulent abuse. In the theatre of credit, it is precisely private credit's reliance on the performance of class identity that allows for its excessive extension. As long as one appears solvent, more credit can always be obtained.

The press was quite agitated about private credit in the months prior to *The Nabob*'s first performance, but when Fordyce's activities became public he emerged as an emblem for the entire system of extravagant speculation. Citing "the late failure of a considerable Banker" as an occasion for the remonstrance of "the spirit of extravagance and speculation, which at present prevails in the City," a correspondent goes on to lay out the situation thus:

Even the City . . . hath learnt the arts of ruin, and understands the use of money so perfectly that it employs it in a thousand destructive shapes. The sudden and rapid accumulation of fortunes in trade is a striking proof of that unbounded and dangerous extent of credit which at present prevails; and which enables a man to trade for twenty times his worth; or, in other words, prompts him to grasp at sudden affluence, by staking the fortunes of his friends and relations: If his desperate pursuits succeed, he alone reaps the profit and the glory; if they are defeated, he falls with all the dignity of an ancient hero, surrounded with the sacrifices of his dearest friends and companions.[31]

This amounts to a lightly veiled account of Fordyce's activities, for he made extraordinary amounts of money speculating on East India stock, pushed the speculation further in the Falkland Island affair, and suddenly lost everything, thereby pulling all of his financial associates with him.[32] In the aftermath of Fordyce's bankruptcy, slow and steady growth comes to figure not only as a sign of national economic stability but also of personal honor and integrity. In the post-Fordyce world, the widely accepted practice of private credit becomes a depredation on unsuspecting guarantors. This revision has important ramifications for how we understand the economic transactions in Foote's play. Before turning our attention to *The Nabob*, however, it is important to sketch one further set of tropes associated with Fordyce.

At the time of the collapse, Fordyce's activities were figured primarily in terms of gaming. Horace Walpole is typical of the contemporary reaction to Fordyce's fraud:

Will you believe . . . that one rascally and extravagant banker had brought Britannia, Queen of the Indies, to the precipice of bankruptcy! . . . . Fordyce is the name of the caitiff. He has broke half the bankers, and was very willing to have added our friend Mr Croft to the list. . . . He went on the same errand to an old Quaker; who said, "Friend *Fordyce,* I have known several persons ruined by *two dice;* but I will not be ruined by *four dice.*" As the fellow is a Scotchman, and as the Scots have given provocation even to the Bank of England by circulating vast quantities of their own bank's notes, all clamour against that country is revived, and the war is carried very far, at least in the newspapers.[33]

As Walpole emphasizes, the reaction to Fordyce was imbued with anti-Scottish sentiment. But in addition to Fordyce the gamester, the press was also propagating the image of Fordyce the class interloper. Fordyce came from a family of hosiers and the *Gentleman's Magazine* makes much of his rise:

> This success [in the stock market in the late 1760s] was fatal to Mr. Fordyce; for it induced him not only to speculate for still larger sums in the Alley, but in many other pursuits. . . . The capricious goddess still favoured him; and he seemed so infatuated with her kindness, as to think she was intirely at his command. He purchased a large estate, with a most elegant villa, at Roehampton, where he aimed at surpassing the Commissaries and Nabobs in grandeur and magnificence. . . . His ambition was now unbounded; he soared far beyond the line of mere mercantile splendour, and nothing less than nobility seemed equal to his wishes. . . . Failing in the present attempt to obtain a seat in parliament, he sought for honours in another channel, and paid his addresses to a Lady of quality, who, dazzled by his pomp and apparent fortune, consented to the marriage.[34]

The details of this account are significant because the chief signs of Fordyce's class aspirations—his conspicuous consumption, his machinations for a seat in Parliament, and his marriage to a lady of quality—are precisely those of Sir Matthew Mite in Foote's play.

Men of Commerce and the Vulnerable Gentry

It is a commonplace of both theatre history and British social history that Samuel Foote's *The Nabob* established the figure of the exemplary nabob and thereby encapsulated the anxieties of an entire nation. Most discussions of Foote's play argue that Sir Matthew Mite is a composite portrait of various East India Company agents who had returned to London fabulously rich and proceeded to destabilize both the domestic economy and the aristocracy's firm grip on fashionable society. There are allusions to General Richard Smith, a particularly profligate gambler whose father was a cheese monger; to Mr. Thomas Rumbold, whose perpetration of election fraud with the Christian Club was directly satirized in the play; and, of course, to Lord Clive, whose relation to the play is complex.[35] Clive himself may have prompted his inclusion after stating in the speech discussed earlier that the fact that Foote had not satirized him was evidence of his rectitude.

However, despite the long-standing historicization of Foote's satirical portrait, the full import of Foote's play remains unappreciated until one deals with the following puff from the *Morning Chronicle*, which appeared less than a week before the opening of *The Nabob:*

> A correspondent recommends to the consideration of Mr. Foote, the late crush amongst the Bankers, as he thinks it a fine subject for his genius to work upon; especially if he takes a certain character, and weaves it into his new piece called the Nabob, since from its title, it is imagined a looking-glass will be held up for some particular fortune-hunting gentlemen to see themselves in, at the same time that they are exposed to the world.[36]

The unnamed correspondent, who may well be Foote himself or one of his associates, opens another set of condensations that seriously complicates the play's interpretation and its legacy. At one level, it is far from surprising to see the correspondent call for weaving Fordyce into *The Nabob*. Foote's entire career was based on his ability to refashion the news of the day and represent it to his London audiences, and, as we have seen, the collapse of the Scottish banks dominated public opinion at the time. We have no direct evidence that the specific call was answered, although Foote's *The Bankrupt* of the following summer is explicitly about Fordyce. However, the fact that the correspondent could envisage Fordyce's activities as comparable with those of Clive and other former East India Company agents should give us pause.

The interweaving of Fordyce into *The Nabob* may be appropriate in order to explicate what I believe is the autoethnographic imperative in Foote's play. Put simply, Foote's excoriation of Sir Matthew Mite is intimately tied to a heretofore unrecognized critique of the vagaries of private credit. As the letter to the *Morning Chronicle* indicates, the suspect qualities of the Nabob are also those of the suspect creditor. The commutability of these two figures is underlined by charges of vice, which are worthy of scrutiny not least because they reflect behavior in metropolitan society. In other words, Foote's play operates much like Clive's speech in that it suggests a preexisting social pathology that is made visible by the Nabob figure. How Foote contains and redirects this social pathogen can be discerned from the play's rigorous treatment of space.

Little of the commentary on *The Nabob* recognizes the significance of the play's structure, and much of the criticism implies that the play is merely a jumble of episodes.[37] Like many of Foote's Haymarket comedies, it is divided into three acts, and key scenes such as the speech to the Antiquarian Society that opens act 3 appear to be little more than set pieces integrated into a negligible plot. If one attends to how the play deploys space, however, it becomes evident that the second act is fundamentally different than the first and the third. Set in two distinct interior spaces in Matthew Mite's hall, the second act can be described for all intents and purposes as Mite's divan. In the eighteenth century, the term *divan* has largely Turkish connotations and simultaneously refers to the sultan's private council of the Porte and to the cushioned interior space where such councils assembled. Mite's divan, true to this strain of Orientalist discourse, is an interior space that encloses fantasies of absolute power and of languorous sexual dissipation. The second act opens in a private chamber where Mite negotiates with a series of minions, including a waiter from Almack's gaming house, Crocus the flower girl, and Match'em the procuress. In each case, the focus of Sir Matthew's attention is on the acquisition and sustenance of libertine vices associated with the aristocracy. After resolving these private affairs, Sir Matthew enters an adjoining saloon where he engages in transactions first with the Christian Club regarding the purchasing of a seat in Parliament and second with Thomas Oldham regarding the extortion of a matrimonial alliance with the Oldham family. In both of these spaces, Mite operates according to long-standing tropes of Eastern despotism. The chamber and the saloon amount to spaces of private vice and public corruption respectively in that the scenes set in "The Chamber" give a detailed account of Mite's personal dissipation, whereas those in the saloon emphasize his threat to society at large. The way in which private vice and public corruption slide into one another in the second act is symptomatic; however, before considering the particulars of Mite's divan, it is important to recognize how it is framed by the first and third acts.

The Nabob opens and closes in the house of Sir John Oldham, who, as his name suggests, represents the landed gentry in the play. All of the action set in this space involves the negotiations surrounding Sir Matthew Mite's proposal to Sir John's daughter Sophy. This proposal amounts to an act of extortion because it comes complete with a promise to cancel Sir John's debts if he grants his daughter's hand and a threat to immediately recall them if he does not comply. The terms of the proposal and of Sir John's debt to Sir Matthew are presented to the audience in the form of a letter read by Thomas Oldham, Sir John's merchant brother:

THOMAS: To Sir John Oldham. Sir Matthew Mite having lately seen, at Lady Levant's rout, the eldest Miss Oldham, and being struck with her personal charms, proposes to her father the following treaty. . . . Upon a matrimonial union between the young lady and him, all hostilities and contention shall cease, and Sir John be suffered to take his seat in security. . . . Secondly, as Sir Matthew is bent upon a large territorial acquisition in England, and Sir John Oldham's finances are at present a little out of repair, Sir Matthew Mite will make up the money already advanced in another name, by way of future mortgage upon his estate, for the entire purchase, five lacks of roupees. . . . Or if it should be more agreeable to the parties, Sir Matthew will settle upon Sir John and his Lady, for their joint lives, a jagghire [annual income]. . . . And that the principals may have no cares for the younger parts of their family, Sir Matthew will, at his own expence, transport the two young ladies, Miss Oldham's two sisters, to Madras or Calcutta, and there procure them suitable husbands. . . . And as for the three boys, they shall be either made supercargoes, ships's husbands, or go out cadets and writers in the Company's service.[38]

For Foote's audience the very language of treaty would have invoked Clive's remarkable acquisitions in Bengal. Of crucial importance to how we understand this proposal is the fact that Clive's negotiations with Mir Jafar and others were subsequent to crushing military victory. In short, Mite's offers, like the offers of alliance between the Company and resident Nawabs, are all but impossible to refuse because Sir John has already been defeated, but here the victories are less martial than financial.

Thomas's reading of the proposal is repeatedly interrupted by Lady Oldham's objections to the "treaty," which insistently claim the privilege of aristocratic birth as sufficient insurance against the unsuitable match. But Sir John and Thomas recognize that that privilege has been undercut by Sir John's debts. Thomas's detailed description of the transaction not only establishes Mite as Sir John's creditor but also emphasizes that Mite's identity was shielded by transfer (10–11). What this means is that Sir John borrowed money from a third party whose credit was surreptitiously ensured by Mite. The significance of this detail is twofold: first, it was a mechanism employed by Clive in his failed attempt to buy up a controlling interest in East India Company stock; second, it affords Foote the occasion to fulminate on the dangers of private credit in which no one appears to be who they are.

However, it is hard to judge the precise tone of the final sentence in the foregoing passage because Thomas's sympathy for "the plain English gentleman" and "the innocent Indian" is compromised by the fact that he eventually replaces Mite as Sir John's creditor and brokers a marriage between his nephew and Sophy that was formerly seen as beneath the Oldhams' social standing. In this, Lady Oldham is an interesting indicator because her resistance to Thomas Oldham and Sir Matthew Mite is only one of degree. As she states early in act 1, when Sir John suggests that they ask for Thomas's opinion regarding the marriage proposal, Thomas's opinion is valuable "on the value of merchandize, or the goodness of a Bill of Exchange; But there is a nicety, a delicacy, an elevation of sentiment in this case, which people who have narrowed their notions with commerce, and considered during the course of their lives their interest alone, will scarce comprehend" (5). Her unwillingness to discuss the proposal with Thomas is based on the same class insularity that deems Sir Matthew's "treaty" unworthy of response. Sir Matthew Mite and Thomas Oldham are both men of commerce and, hence, threatening to the Oldhams' crumbling sense of social superiority. Interestingly, Foote emphasizes this relationship between Mite and Thomas late in the first scene:

LADY OLDHAM: Is it possible Sir Matthew can have acted from so infernal a motive, to have advanced the money with a view of distressing us deeper?

THOMAS: Sir Matthew is a profound politician, and will not stick at trifles to carry his point.

LADY OLDHAM: With the wealth of the East, we have too imported the worst of its vices. What a horrid crew! (13)

This passage is often cited as the argument of the play, but Thomas's correction of Lady Oldham indicates that this view is not only naive but also historically and economically unviable:

THOMAS: Hold, sister! don't gratify your resentment at the expence of your justice; a general conclusion from a single instance is but indifferent logick.

LADY OLDHAM: Why, is not this Sir Matthew—

THOMAS: Perhaps as bad a subject as your passion can paint him: But there are men from the Indies, and many too, with whom I have the honour to live, who dispense nobly and with hospitality here, what they have acquired with honour and credit elsewhere; and, at the same time they have increased the dominions and wealth, have added virtues too to their country. (13)

Thomas's defense of British colonial activity is interesting because it would have satisfied both sides of the Clive debate. For those who would equate Mite and Clive, he can be figured as an anomaly from which one should not generalize, whereas for those who would distance the two, Thomas's remarks simply reiterate those of Clive's defenders. What remains intact is the assumption that the influx of wealth from the East is not inherently vicious. In this light, Foote's satire recoils on the Oldhams themselves for they seem to be existing in a fantasy of aristocratic privilege. Their self-insulation from the material circumstances of imperial metropolitan life renders them not only naive but also passive in their own affairs. It is possible to hear a register of condescension in Thomas's comparison between a "plain English gentleman" and "an innocent Indian."

This sense of condescension has important ramifications for the overall structure of the play, because after establishing the vulnerability of the Oldhams in the first scene of act 1, Foote follows Thomas to Sir Matthew Mite's hall. The spatial transition involves a shift from a scene of aristocratic decay to one where the power of new money is everywhere evident. The second scene is dominated by a door guarded by Mite's minions Janus and Conserve and all of the action is aimed at setting up the difficulty of accessing Mite in his self-styled divan in act 2. As Janus's name indicates, Mite's servants act as janissaries who regulate access to the nabob. In the midst of the comic business of this scene, Thomas and Mrs. Match'em, Mite's procuress, find themselves among other supplicants asking for an audience with the sultanlike nabob. At one level, the scene seems staged only to give an occasion for the long joke on Sir Timothy Tallboy, which was ostensibly based on a real situation, but closer scrutiny indicates that something else is going on here as well.[39] After Match'em successfully makes her pitch for entry, Thomas makes his own case. Janus immediately mistakes him for "a Jew broker, come to bring my master the price of the stocks." When Thomas corrects this assumption, he is barred entry until he bribes his way in. Throughout the play, Mite is associated with Jewish moneylenders and is continually offering bribes to those who would block his entry into institutions such as the House of Commons or the Antiquarian Society. Here Thomas uses the same tactics to gain access to Mite. The fact that he is granted entry along with Mrs. Match'em is also significant, for a number of links are drawn between her trade in women's bodies and his financial dealings.

But first it is important to recognize how Foote mirrors the structure of act 1 in act 3. Again the act is divided in two, but the spatial order is precisely reversed. The third act opens with Matthew Mite attempting to gain access to the Antiquarian Society. Mite's disquisition on Dick Whittington's cat seems to stand out from the rest of the play and prompted Horace Walpole to renounce his membership in the Society of Antiquaries that Foote was satirizing. But the structural parallel to the second scene of act 1 indicates that Foote's satire works on two levels. The suggestion that Mite's attempt to enter the Antiquarian Society repeats Thomas's attempt to enter the Mite's divan effectively casts the officers of the Society as janissaries and demands that we compare the protected institutions. Within the terms of the satire, Foote is suggesting that the Society's invention of tradition is as morally suspect as Mite's self-invention as a displaced Eastern potentate.[40] The implication is that both institutions are grounded on suspect fantasies. Thomas and Mite, each in their own way, are supplicants before figures who wield a certain phantasmatic power. In the case of Thomas, he is searching for an audience with someone whose wealth may amount to little more than a web of paper instruments. In the case of Mite, he is searching for cultural capital that likewise may be grounded on similarly fraudulent documents. The suggestion that the nabob's wealth and the Society's account of England's origins are fundamentally suspect drives to the heart of the deep-seated cultural anxieties of the period. The sudden recognition that the nation's history, like the economy, is dependent on the reputation of the signatories of its paper instruments captures not only the unease occasioned by the bubble of 1772 but also the very anxiety that prompted the passion for collecting cultural artifacts.

The parallel between the first and third acts is even more evident in the final scene of act 3. As it was in the opening of act 1, the audience is again witness to a complex series of transactions, both financial and sexual, set in the house of Sir John Oldham.[41] The first act establishes that Oldham's financial dependence on Mite provides the leverage for Mite's proposal of marriage and his claim to Oldham's estate. Mite's threatened incursion into the aristocracy operates on the two defining characteristics of aristocratic identity: his proposal aims not only for alliance of blood but also for "a territorial acquisition." The play's denouement resolves this threat rather straightforwardly by eliminating Mite's financial leverage over the Oldhams. What is remarkable is that this elimination is actually a transfer of obligation, for in paying down Sir John's debt to Mite, Thomas becomes his new creditor. The *London Magazine*'s review of *The Nabob* is illuminating here because it specifies how this transfer was achieved on stage: "Mr. Oldham, seeing things thus far advanced, takes a bill out of his pocket equal to the value of the sum, exchanges it for the bond, and the Nabob is dismissed with disappointment and rage."[42] But in exchanging a bill of credit for Mite's bond, Thomas insists on quite specific terms for his loan:

LADY OLDHAM: Brother, what words can I use, or how can we thank you as we ought? Sir John! Sophy!

THOMAS: I am doubly paid, Lady Oldham, in supplying the wants of my friends, and defeating the designs of a villain. As to the mere money, we citizens indeed are odd kinds of folks, and always expect good security for what we advance.

LADY OLDHAM: Sir John's person, his fortune, every—

THOMAS: Nay, nay, nay, upon this occasion we will not be troubled with land: If you, sister, will place as my pledge my fair cousin in the hands of my son—

LADY OLDHAM: I freely resign her disposal to you.

SIR JOHN: And I.

THOMAS: Then be happy, my children! And as to my young cousins within, I hope we shall be able to settle them without Sir Matthew's assistance: For, however praiseworthy the spirit of adventure may be, whoever keeps his post, and does his duty at home, will be found to render his country best service at last! (70–71)

This exchange, the play's closing dialogue, posits key similarities between Mite's and Thomas's actions as creditors in order to establish subtle yet crucial distinctions. If Mite's attempt to gain Sophy's hand and her father's land is tantamount to extortion, then how are we to interpret Thomas's repetition of part of Mite's demand? Foote explicitly states that the marriage between Sophy and Thomas's son, which was previously barred due to perceived differences of rank, is granted as security for the loan. And it is important to remember that Mite's "treaty" is pitched as an act of assistance between friends. The frequent structural and rhetorical parallels between Mite and Thomas culminate in this scene, and what becomes immediately apparent is that the distinctions between Mites's extortion and Thomas's good business are subtle yet precise.

What we are presented with here are two competing models for solving a credit problem. The embarrassed finances of Sir John Oldham, here representing the financial decay of the aristocracy, render the family and the class susceptible to the demands of its commercial creditors. The two models of class accommodation, while quite similar, differ on four issues. First, both Mite and Thomas demand the hand of Sophy, but the former's proposal is solely a marriage of alliance aimed at securing Mite's place in society. Foote emphasizes that Mite and Sophy's acquaintance is limited to a sighting at Lady Levant's rout, whereas the relationship between Sophy and Thomas's son is a long-standing romantic involvement frustrated by class distinction. So while it would be inaccurate to suggest that Thomas's request of Sophy's hand for his son is not also aimed at an alliance between the City and the Town, the request is sanctioned by their prior companionate relationship. I would argue that the legitimacy of Thomas's demand is based in part on this adequation of alliance with sentimental love and that this legitimation has vital implications for the class politics of the play.

That said, it is crucial that Thomas's demand, unlike Mite's, has no designs on Sir John Oldham's estate. This second distinction means that, however much the aristocracy is indebted to its commercial benefactors, its claim to political and historical legitimacy remains intact. Within the terms set out by the play, Mite's "treaty" not only raises the possibility of interclass marriage but also culminates in the substitution of Mite for Sir John. This transgression of class hierarchy is quite distinct from that signified by Thomas's demand because the companionate marriage brings about an adequation of the classes rather than a substitution.[43] In short, Thomas's security is basically that of the English Constitution slightly recalibrated to accommodate the fact of the commercial class's growing wealth, whereas Mite's proposal reallocates political and social power to the highest bidder. It is for this reason that Thomas's closing speech in the third act emphasizes that his machinations "render his country best service at last!"

Folded into this nationalist problematic is the third and arguably the most important distinction between Mite's and Thomas's financial activities. Thomas's general defense of colonial trade in act 1 stands in marked contrast to his specific critique of Mite's financial and commercial activities in the third act. His critique is staged not as a correction to Lady Oldham's prejudice against new money as in act 1, but as a partial affirmation of the instability of rapid accumulation:

LADY OLDHAM: You will, Sir Matthew, pardon my weakness; but I would rather see my child with a competence, nay, even reduced to an indigent state, than voluptuously rioting in pleasures that derive their source from the ruin of others.

MITE: Ruin! What, you, I find, adopt the popular prejudice, and conclude that every man that is rich is a villain?

LADY OLDHAM: I only echo the voice of the public. Besides, I would wish my daughter a more solid establishment: The possessions arising from plunder very rarely are permanent; we every day see what has been treacherously and rapaciously gained, as profusely and full as rapidly squandered.

MITE: I am sorry, madam, to see one of your fashion, concur in the common cry of the times; but such is the gratitude of this country to those who have given it dominion and wealth.

THOMAS: I could wish even that fact was well founded, Sir Matthew. Your riches (which perhaps are only too ideal) by introducing a general spirit of dissipation, have extinguished labour and industry, the slow, but sure source of national wealth. (65–66)

This remarkable exchange performs crucial cultural work in the way that it combines two related but distinct anxieties. The importance of this section of the play is indicated by the fact that Lady Oldham's speech is directly cited in many of the reviews.[44] Her excoriation of Mite's thoughtless luxury and his insensitivity to the ruin of others participates in the antinabob discourse that surrounded all discussion of Clive's activities in the months prior to the opening of the play. But Thomas's slight redirection invokes the critique of indiscriminate private credit, which dominated the news in the three weeks that followed the collapse of Fordyce's affairs and immediately preceded the first run of *The Nabob*. The crucial details in Thomas's speech are his suggestion that slow accumulation is preferable to rapid speculation, his insinuation that quick gains foment vice, and, most important, his own supposition that Mite's fortune is "only ideal." As we have already seen, these three points are crucial to the critique of the abuses of private credit following the revelation of Fordyce's fraud. For an audience thoroughly steeped in this crisis, Thomas's aside signals that Mite's fortune is based not only on colonial violence but also on paper instruments whose value may be grounded on air. This linking of two similarly suspect forms of accumulation is the necessary precursor for Thomas's suggestion that "notwithstanding [Mite's] seeming security, perhaps the hour of vengeance is near!" (70).

In the post-Fordyce climate, Thomas's prediction of Mite's future insolvency would seem to be sealed, but Foote leaves Mite with the last word on this matter:

MITE: You must, Master Oldham, give me leave to laugh at your prophetic effusion. This is not Sparta, nor are these the chaste times of the Roman republic: Now-a-days, riches possess at least one magical power, that, being rightly dispensed, they closely conceal the source from whence they proceeded: That wisdom, I hope never to want. (70)

Concealed in Mite's response is Foote's own prophecy regarding the combined effects of rapacious financial dealings both in the colonies and in the metropole. The speech's subtle distinction between "the chaste times of the Roman republic" and those of the Roman Empire performs a double critique and marks the fourth and most subtle distinction between Mite and Thomas. First, it insists, not inaccurately, that colonial corruption and rampant speculation are too much a part of emergent imperial capitalism to disappear and that they will ultimately lead to a national decline. But it also states something about the deployment of the law, for Mite invokes the passing of the republic to counter Thomas's fetishization of the law. When Thomas has his audience with Sir Matthew, Foote is careful not only to show how Mite mobilizes the law to achieve his ends but also to show Thomas's recognition that Mite's designs are vulnerable on this count. Thomas defeats Mite's designs on Sophy and Sir John by anticipating the legal recall of Sir John's debt. When he pays down the debt, the lawyer Rapine succinctly states that "The law, Sir Matthew, always sleeps when satisfaction is made" (69). Mite's response is telling and historically resonant for he states that "Our practice is different in the Mayor's Court at Calcutta" (69). For Thomas, the law proves itself to be above its manipulators and hence is cherished as a national treasure. But Foote's reference to the Mayor's Court at Calcutta activates the ongoing debate concerning legal reform in Bengal, which lies at the heart both of the Select Committee's inquiry into Clive's affairs and the East India Company's resistance to direct government regulation. In this light, Foote is arguing that the British Empire will go the way of its Roman predecessor if it does not apply British law uniformly across colony and metropole—that is, that the imperial project will fail if it does not govern itself as a republic in this regard. It is perhaps Foote's most radical and hence carefully concealed intervention in the social climate of the early 1770s, especially in light of its resonances with unrest in the American colonies. It places him squarely in opposition both to the directors of the East India Company and to those who advocated for a strict separation of the state from the commercial affairs of the colony.[45] And it also implies that the play is not uncritical of Thomas's protectionism.

Foote's subtle distinction between the demands required of Mite's and Thomas's credit can therefore be summarized as follows. Thomas's credit is aligned with an almost protectionist investment in the slow acquisition of wealth through industry and labor at home; with an accommodation between the commercial classes and the aristocracy, which secures the financial power of the former and the historical legitimacy of the latter; with figures of companionate marriage as opposed to naked marriages of alliance; and with a phantasmatic investment in the law as the necessary check on the commercial and financial affairs of the nation. Mite's credit is aligned with images of colonial adventure and metropolitan speculation; with a replacement of the decaying gentry with the newly moneyed merchant class; with an understanding of marriage based solely on aristocratic notions of familial alliance; and with an understanding of the law as one of many mechanisms to be deployed in the maximization of profit and gain. These two assemblages are brought into contact in order to critique the latter positions, but this does not necessarily involve an absolute endorsement of the former. Rather, Foote's critique of Thomas's credit remains operative because he exerts a great deal of energy in generating the extraordinary figural economy that will come to dominate subsequent engagement with colonial problematics on the London stage. In order to comprehend that figural economy, we need to enter the divan of Sir Matthew Mite and consider the macaroni gambler.

The Divan of the Macaroni Gambler

The opening and closing acts of *The Nabob* present two similar but ultimately incommensurate solutions to the series of cultural and economic anxieties attendant upon the financial embarrassment of Sir John Oldham and thus set the stakes of the debate around nabobry and private credit. Because Mite's and Thomas's relations to Oldham are so similar, it becomes crucial for the politics of the play that the odiousness of Mite's activities be firmly associated not with his business practices but with his vicious motives. Act 1 ends with Thomas successfully bribing Mite's janissaries for an interview with the self-styled nabob. However, his business with Mite is delayed by three exchanges in Mite's private chamber that effectively translate the anxiety surrounding the system of private credit into easily deployed tropes of personal dissipation and vice. The translation is crucial because it is part of an overall strategy of cultural containment that has its counterpart in the actions of the Bank of England and the House of Commons in the wake of the crisis of 1772. The second act, which I have described as taking place in Mite's divan, is quite literally an anatomy of vice that is structured by the stereotypical dissipation of the Eastern potentate, but which relies on the careful suturing together of Clive and Fordyce for its precise details.

The exemplarity of Fordyce and Clive is crucial for interpreting *The Nabob* because Sir Matthew Mite makes his first appearance in act 2 dressed as a composite of the two figures. The second act opens with Sir Matthew in macaroni dress taking lessons in how to throw dice from a waiter from the famous gambling establishment of Almack's. It is clear from the *London Magazine* review that Mite is immediately feminized by his costume: "The second act discovers the Nabob sitting at a table in his gambling dress, the silk night gown, straw bonnet, &c. which the virtuous gentlemen of Almack's use when at play. The table is covered with dice, and several other implements of polite gambling, and a waiter from Almack's attends to teach him the profound art of throwing the dice with grace."[46] Everything in the staging of this scene is doubly significant, so it is important to work through its implications carefully. As we have already seen, both antinabob discourse and the discursive shaming of Fordyce draw links between these examples of dissipation and macaroni masculinity. Walpole's suggestion that Clive begot the macaronis is not uncommon, and many examples of contemporary cartoons portray either Clive or more composite nabob figures in macaroni dress. At one level this is not surprising because the very ostentation associated with these individuals is manifest in their indulgence in fashion. But the discomfort generated by the feminine apparel of the macaronis goes beyond a discomfort with luxury. The public criticism of macaroni style often interweaves a critique of luxury with images of aberrant masculinity. The macaroni, like the fop in Garrick's plays, is a suspect figure largely because his narcissism is seen to promulgate an excessive consumption not only of clothes but also of women.[47] In short, macaroni style is often associated with an aberrant form of heterosexual masculinity that involves insatiable desires that need not require the consummation of any particular liaison. This has important ramifications because eighteenth-century sexual practice is frequently figured in economic terms, and in this economy everything is about appearance and not actual production, about image and not actual value. Macaroni style, therefore, operates as a particularly apt signifier not only for the excessive consumption of the nabobs

FIG. 1.2. Anonymous, *The Macaroni Gambler*, 1772 *(courtesy of the Department of Prints and Drawings, The British Museum, London; BM 5016)*

but also for precisely the kind of fraudulent production associated with stockjobbing and private credit. It should therefore come as no surprise to find that the most famous image of Fordyce is of the banker dressed as a macaroni gambler (fig. 1.2).

The intense condensation of excessive consumption and fraudulent production in the costume of Sir Matthew Mite effectively joins the problems of colonial excess and metropolitan speculation in a fashion that I believe fully answers the call for Foote to "weave" Fordyce into his critique of nabobry. But it is important not to lose sight of how the scene of Mite learning to handle the dice—Fordyce again—mobilizes the same set of suspicions as those coded into his dress. In this scene, Mite's actions are a perfect translation of the cultural anxieties evoked by his clothing, for gaming was widely perceived to be a form of aberrant production that, like private credit, was based not on substance but on something as intangible as fortune. In fact, the two practices are figured as both interchangeable and causally related. For example, Fordyce's manipulation of bonds and his attempts to fix stock prices are consistently seen as nothing more than gambling with other people's money. Significantly, the waiter in this scene identifies the fundamental rule of this kind of gaming when he states that Sir Christopher Clumsy "got no credit by losing his money; was ruined without the least reputation" (29). A more succinct account of how private credit operates could not be imagined, for, as the Fordyce case indicates, significant numbers of the aristocracy and of the merchant class were happy to give him credit when he was making extraordinary gains in East India Company stock. The macaroni gambler both figures for credit and ultimately requires it.

Foote deploys the tropes of gaming and macaroni dress in a particularly cunning way, because he emphasizes that both Mite's actions and his clothes come from the waiter from Almack's. Mite must be trained in these particular styles of dissipation by one who is not only from the servant class but whose livelihood depends on the ongoing ruin of the gaming upper orders. This reiterates Thomas's echo of Clive in act 1 that the alleged vices of the nabobs are not a function of colonial contact but a symptom of metropolitan moral decay. It is tempting to read this gesture as a pathologization of the lower orders—that is, the waiter contaminates Mite—but such a reading needs to be modified by the recognition that the waiter outlives the destruction of many a gambler's fortune. I would argue that the waiter and the play's other working-class characters form a service economy that thrives entirely on the destruction of metropolitan wealth and hence is also entirely reliant on the influx of colonial fortunes, however questionably obtained. What this implies is that the servants are thoroughly integrated into an economy that is doubly unstable, due on the one hand to the volatility of markets for colonial goods and on the other to the abuse of paper instruments. Foote is highly specific about both forms of instability. In addition to the detailed account of Sir John Oldham's precarious credit relations and the insinuation that Mite's fortune is "ideal," Foote also refers directly to the surplus of tea brought on by the American boycott against the Townshend duties, which seriously encumbered the East India Company in the early 1770s (40–41).[48] Foote's deployment of this service class in the play allows him to suggest a causal relation between the abuse of private credit in the metropole and the abuse of power in the colonies. The high amount of risk involved in excessive speculation ultimately required the steady influx of capital from the colonies. As a diagnosis of British imperial and domestic policy in June 1772, Foote's position is not only apt but also prophetic, for one could argue that the Regulating Act of 1773 was passed in part because a regulation of the East India Company's affairs was necessary to prevent a repeat of the bank closures of the previous year.

The scene of dicing with the waiter indicates that Mite's interactions with his servants are more than simply set pieces for demonstrating his sultanlike despotism. The excess of macaroni dress and its implied sexual aberrations translates the conventional representations of dissipated Eastern masculinity into the social world of London's new money. As the second act unfolds, Foote extends this strategy of translation such that the sexualization of Foote's economic critique that opens the act is not only deepened but also consolidated by a corresponding racialization. Mite's next exchange is with Mrs. Crocus, who provides him with flowers. His dissatisfaction with her bouquets allows for a performance of the narcissism implied by his macaroni dress, but his objections reveal an anxiety about his skin. As he states, "You know my complexion has been tinged by the East, and you bring me here a blaze of yellow, that gives me the jaundice. Look! Do you see here, what a fine figure I cut? You might as well have tied me to a bundle of sun-flowers!" (31). In this scene, Mite not only performs the despot's haughtiness; he also suggests that he may have adopted the bodily signs of colonial disease or perhaps even racial difference. This insinuation of bodily contamination or hybridity is not uncommon in anti-Company discourse of the period.[49] But it is important to recognize that this moment implies that the macaroni dress and the flowers both represent his sexual narcissism and conceal his bodily decay and his racial hybridity. But this amounts to an overdetermination within the conventional othering strategies of Orientalist discourse, for sexual dissipation and racial contamination are often interchangeable.

The assemblage of Orientalist tropes is completed in the final interview in his private chamber with Mrs. Match'em. If the exchange with Mrs. Crocus allows Foote to perform the absolute sovereignty of the despot over his minions, then his dialogue with the procuress gives the audience a glimpse of the corresponding sensualist. Within the terms of Orientalist discourse, Mrs. Match'em manages the acquisition of women for Mite's satiation. What remains unclear in the scene is what the nature of his satiation might be. After Mite explores the possibility of "founding in this town a seraglio" and is informed that previous attempts failed because ladies in England tended not to consent to their confinement, the scene offers a detailed account of how Match'em attempts to acquire women for Mite (37–38). Almost their entire conversation focuses on the ready deployment of bills and other negotiables such as diamonds to pull women into relations of obligation to Sir Matthew. In other words, Mrs. Match'em operates as the shield enabling precisely the kind of extortion that Mite practices on Sir John, and it is hard to determine whether his object here is similarly an alliance and an estate or, conversely, sexual gratification.[50] Their combined designs are on ladies of quality whose finances have been embarrassed by gambling debts:

MITE: I have sent some rough diamonds to be polished in Holland; when they are returned, I will equip you, Match'em, with some of these toys.
MATCH'EM: Toys? how light he makes of these things!—Bless your noble and generous soul! I believe for a trifle more I could have obtained Lady Lurcher last night.
MITE: Indeed?
MATCH'EM: She has been pressed a good deal to discharge an old score, long due to a knight from the North; and play-debts, your honour knows, there is no paying in part: She seemed deeply distressed; and I really believe another hundred would have made up the sum.
MITE: And how came you not to advance it?
MATCH'EM: I did not chuse to exceed my commission; your honour knows the bill was only for five.
MITE: Oh, you should have immediately made it up; you know I never stint myself in these matters.
MATCH'EM: Why, had I been in cash, I believe I should have ventured, your honour. If your honour approves, I have thought of a project that will save us both a good deal of trouble. . . . That I may not pester you with applications for every trifle I want, suppose you were to deposit a round sum in my hands.
MITE: What, Match'em, make you my banker for beauty? Ha, ha, ha!
(33–34)

This lengthy passage demonstrates how explicitly the play deals with the mechanisms of private credit. All the discussion of bills and advancements, of recalled debts and female gaming, is exceedingly topical, and Mite's final joke ties together much of the argument thus far. By calling Match'em his "banker for beauty," sexual deviance and private credit are linked rhetorically by a trope on banking. Or one could argue that sexual deviance and banking are linked to represent the depravity of private credit. The commutability of the terms is revealing because by the time we leave Sir Matthew Mite's divan, the play has firmly established a set of ethnocentric arguments against both nabobry and stockjobbing that recasts their threats to economic stability as incursions on the sexual and racial norms of the nation.

In this light, the play's substitution of Thomas for Mite as Sir John's creditor takes on new significance because it amounts to a normalization of social relations that is both ethnocentric and deeply tied to a deployment of sexuality whose racial overtones are crucial to the self-stylization of the emergent middle ranks. Suddenly, the security Thomas demands for his loan—that is, the marriage of Sophy and his son—figures as the social accommodation required for the ejection of the catalog of vice associated with Mite's suspect sexuality. What is so unsettling in the broader view of the play is that this precisely allegorizes the actions of the Bank of England following the collapse of Fordyce's affairs. As noted earlier, the bank stopped the credit crisis by allowing Scottish and Jewish firms to collapse. Thomas, like the Bank of England, bails out the "plain Englishman" and predicts the collapse of Mite, who is everywhere throughout the play associated with either Eastern dissipation or Jewish avarice. And the security demanded is represented by the marriage of Sophy and Younger Oldham, between the daughter who has now learned of her father's aristocratic vulnerability in an age of commerce and the son who has acceded to a new sense of social legitimacy. It is security of a very particular kind because it reinforces the middle-class fantasy that its rigorous accession to normativity will "render his country best service at last!" (71). And it effectively ties the sexual self-regulation of companionate marriage to the bank's regulation of the abuses of private credit and the state's regulation of commercial affairs in the colonies. The establishment of this triad of norms and its corresponding recognition of who should be regulating each sphere is the ultimate legacy of Foote's intervention in *The Nabob*.

Foote's comedy couldn't be more explicit about the nominal power of the aristocracy. The Oldhams are accorded nominal power by leaving their claim to landed status intact, but the adequation of liberty and property has been undercut by two supplemental gestures that ultimately locate power in the commercial classes. The transferal of the Oldhams' debts to Thomas and the marriage of Sophy to Thomas's son undo the Oldhams' chief claims to political legitimacy. The former gives Thomas potential power over the Oldhams' landed property and the latter runs counter to the Oldhams' search for a marriage of alliance for their daughter. In short, Thomas, the figure of commerce, interrupts the Oldhams' claim to liberty through property or blood. Instead, their liberty is now secured by a contractual relation to Thomas and by the sexual deployments inscribed in companionate marriage. In short, one narrative of the decline and fall of Britain's social elite—and, by figural extension, the empire over which it is supposed to preside—is averted by the financial and sexual normativity of the middle ranks of metropolitan commerce.

As my reading of *The Nabob* indicates, the autoethnographic analysis of British society was obsessed by anxieties regarding the security of property. These anxieties were deeply intertwined with critiques of vice that saw dissipation as a sign of cultural and social decay. Because so much of British political thought in the period was focused on the necessity of virtue to counter the ubiquity of corruption, the theatre was replete with characters who have either lost their ability to secure property, or who have devolved into vicious practices that render them defective subjects. More often than not, these two forms of corruption together generated a portrait either of aristocratic degeneration in the figure of effeminacy or of the natural incivility or violence of the working class. As noted earlier, this same binary opposition between forms of passive and active degeneration was not only operative in quasi-anthropological accounts of non-European societies written during this period but also endemic to British claims to governmental legitimacy in the colonies. *The Nabob* allows us to see how specific figurations of vice were attached to particular economic problematics in the relationship between landed property and commercial interest, but we need to turn to the realm of imperial spectacle to examine how fantasies of racial and class supremacy deploying sexuality attempted to put the specter of governmental and economic instability to rest.

CHAPTER
TWO

"As Much as Science Can Approach Barbarity"

Pantomimical Ethnography in *Omai; or,*

A Trip round the World

IF *THE NABOB* OFFERS a glimpse of the economic and sexual anxieties that traversed metropolitan rule, then Philippe Jacques de Loutherbourg's and John O'Keefe's enormously successful pantomime *Omai; or, A Trip round the World* of 1785 provides an opportunity for testing many of the most pressing concerns regarding the representation of colonial space and colonized peoples.[1] Greg Dening's reading of *Omai* describes it as "a translation into entertainment of ethnographic moments in which the European strangers confronted the otherness of the Pacific island natives, tried to describe that otherness and in that description possess them."[2] But as Johannes Fabian has demonstrated, protoanthropological texts from the late eighteenth century understood the relationship between parts of the world as temporal relations: "Dispersal in space reflects . . . sequence in time."[3] Kathleen Wilson's recent survey of travel narratives and natural history texts from the 1770s and 1780s that attempt to deal with the knowledge acquired during the Cook voyages emphasizes that

> the four-stage version of human development articulated by Scottish social scientists, which had held that human society naturally developed over time through stages based on the mode of subsistence, was well established by Cook's time. But the current emphasis on empirical observation had shown that Pacific peoples were prone to exhibit contradictory characteristics that were not subsumable under earlier primitivist or social science models. Proponents of social evolutionism following the Cook voyages tended to envision a more complex configuration of development from savagery to civilization, one that was less mechanistic, unwilling to found explanations for

social differences upon a single cause such as climate or subsistence alone and more nuanced in the understanding of history, combining spatialized and progressive notions of time and simultaneity with the perception that economic and cultural growth entailed both progress and corruption.[4]

Omai thoroughly engages with these comparativist forms of protoanthropology, but my interest here focuses on how ostensibly historically less-developed peoples were deployed with degenerate metropolitan types to generate a fantasy of variable development in the metropole. Through a series of complex substitutions, Loutherbourg and O'Keefe draw equations between degenerate forms of sociability in London and specific sexual practices associated with Tahitian people that ultimately shifts the specter of aristocratic dissipation onto racialized figures of the underclass. My contention is that a crucial step in the consolidation of the middle classes requires a divagation through the combination of ethnographic fantasy and pantomimical excess that defines *Omai*'s particular protoanthropological project.

Omai was described in one opening-night review as "the stage edition of Captain Cook's voyage to Otaheite [Tahiti], Kamtschatka, the Friendly Islands [Tonga], &c, &c," but such a description fails to convey adequately the strange blend of spectacle, commedia dell'arte narrative, and ethnographic observation that constitutes the pantomime.[5] Of particular interest is the way in which two fields of representation—commedia dell'arte and ethnography—are carefully woven together because each field would seem to presuppose radically distinct mimetic registers. The lavish costume and set design were scrupulously overseen and at times prepared by Loutherbourg and John Webber. Webber was Cook's chief illustrator on the Third Voyage and everything about his participation in the production is aimed at generating the effect of ethnographic authenticity. Speaking of the pantomime's closing spectacle, one reviewer summarized *Omai*'s pedagogical imperative:

> A procession of the natives of the different islands and other places visited by Captain Cooke is here introduced. The music preserves the characteristic airs of the different people in the procession, as much as science can approach barbarity.
>
> The APOTHEOSIS of Captain Cooke closes this most admirable assemblage of curious views.[6]

Newspaper commentary on the pantomime emphasizes the innovative assemblage of "curious views" of distant Pacific islands and peoples, but a sizable portion of the pantomime focuses explicitly on metropolitan spaces. In addition to the marae of Tahiti and spectacular views of the Kamchatkan coast, *Omai* contains detailed views of Plymouth Sound, a lawcourt in London, Kensington Gardens, Margate, and street scenes from the City. Despite the pedagogical attention to the representation of the Pacific, much of the pantomime's action focuses on anarchic scenes of urban life in the metropole that represent the decay of British society.

The London presented to the audience of *Omai* allegorically depicts the metropole as a site of theft, avarice, corruption, and sexual vice. The specific scenes in London target legal officials, lawyers, aristocrats, Jew brokers, prostitutes, and various members of the laboring classes for pantomimic ridicule. In this representation, London is saturated with social pathogens whom we have already seen lurking around the private spaces of Foote's comedy. However, *Omai* also presents British activity in the Pacific as the paragon of soldierly virtue that actually operates as a hygienic device for curing social ills in the empire. Put simply, two styles of British subjectivity are contrasted through the performance, and the conventions of pantomime are deployed in an innovative fashion to offer both a critique of vice in the metropole and a consolidation of virtue in the figure of Captain Cook. In the process, the native inhabitants of the Pacific islands represented in the pantomime are subjected to a series of complex refigurations. At the level of narrative, Omai, Londina, and the other Tahitian characters are not only shadowed by familiar commedia figures, such as Harlequin and Columbine, but also perform roles proscribed by commedia types. Recent criticism of the pantomime tends to see these divergent mimetic registers as supplemental disjunctures, but I wish to argue that commedia dell'arte and ethnography are part of a continuous field and that their very continuity tells us a great deal about the process of racialization not only on the London stage, but also in the imperial imaginary.[7] This chapter demonstrates that there are nodal points where each representational field maps onto the other.

Despite Loutherbourg and O'Keefe's careful attempts to link these mimetic registers, the audience of *Omai* played a crucial role in their ultimate accommodation. Despite their acknowledgment of the pantomime's ethnographic merit, the critics and the audience demanded changes to the pantomime that altered its critique of metropolitan society. Loutherbourg responded to his critics by revising the pantomime on a nightly basis, and we are fortunate that a strong historical record exists for the reconstruction of these changes. As we will see, the additions of explicitly racist performances and the reorientation of the play's deployment of sexual deviance provide very precise indicators of how Britons were dealing with the economic and social uncertainty that beset the empire in the 1770s and 1780s. In the process of developing this argument, the chapter interrogates the kinds of viewing implied by the multiform modes of display employed by Loutherbourg. *Omai's* modes of display come together in a highly racialized triangle of desire whose ultimate aims are entwined with the emergent sexual economy of the middle classes. From this seemingly unimportant spectacle one can derive a set of propositions connecting middle-class self-stylization in the metropole to the knowledge practices that will come to define the second British Empire.

*Attractions on Display: Oberea's Arse, Mai's Kiss, and
Cook's Apotheosis*

Captain Cook's exploration of the Pacific took place over the three separate voyages of 1768–71, 1772–75, and 1776–80. At the risk of simplifying the history of the acquisition of ethnographic materials from the South Pacific and their subsequent dissemination in the metropolitan culture of the British, I want to isolate three separate yet entwined discursive assemblages that play a key a role in the articulation of this chapter's argument.[8] The first is the publication and reception of John Hawkesworth's *An Account of a Voyage round the World* in 1773. Hawkesworth's extraordinary text narrates the first voyage in a symptomatic fashion, and his accounts of contact between Cook's crew and the Tahitians were widely read and discussed.[9] The response to Hawkesworth's *Account* ranged from the quasi-scientific to the purely voyeuristic, but it is the so-called "philosophical" response to the text that most interests me. The startlingly frank representation of the sexual practices of the Tahitians and of the interracial sexual activity between British men and Tahitian women, most notably between Sir Joseph Banks and Pūrea, the ostensible queen of the island, generated streams of commentary, both learned and lascivious.[10] While the former took the form of fantasies of natural society, the latter took the form of biting satires aimed at Banks and other learned commentators on cultural difference, at Hawkesworth, and ultimately at the British aristocracy.

The anonymous "An Epistle from Mr. Banks, Voyager, Monster-hunter, and Amoroso, to Oberea, Queen of Otaheite" will serve as a helpful example of the satirical response to Hawkesworth's text, for it carefully incorporates all the typical targets. Framed by what at first appears to be learned commentary and copious textual annotation on Maohi, the Tahitian language, the poem is ultimately a burlesque on the entire ethnographic project. The poem restages—complete with citations—the key scenes of sexual practice from Hawkesworth as spectacles of Banks's pornographic desire. The reader is situated somewhere over Banks's shoulder watching Oberea having sex with Obadée, and on another occasion watching a public sex act between a young girl and an older youth that is facilitated by Oberea.[11] The following lines give some sense of the ambivalent presentation and reception of these scenes:

> The gallant sons of Britain's warlike land,
> In curious crouds around the beauty stand,
> While, as she turns her painted bum to view,
> With fronts unblushing, in the public stew,
> They search each crevice with a curious eye,
> To find exotics—where they never lie.
> O shame! were we, great George, thy gallant crew,
> And had we—damn it—nothing else to do,
> But turn thy great design to filthy farce,
> And search for wonders on an Indian's a—?[12]

I am interested in the theatrical metaphor that makes up the punch line. The suggestion that the great heroic project of exploration has degenerated into farce implies that George III's management of the theatre of the world's oceans has devolved into illegitimacy. This scene is accompanied by an engraving that deftly satirizes the advancement of knowledge as little more than a sexual spectacle. The engraving translates the entire scene to the metropole and satirizes the learned gentlemen and the women of fashion who gaze upon the tattooed markings that adorn the Tahitian woman's buttocks.[13] The moral imperative of this critique becomes evident as the poem suddenly turns to the effect of reading Hawkesworth:

> But then to print our tale! O curse the thought!
> Curse those who sold,—a blush for those who bought.
> Fine tales for misses!—charming table-talk!
> Delightful too in each meandering walk,
> Through Britain's ample plains!—the lustful squire
> With ease may quench his unsubdu'd desire:—

One page of *Hawkesworth,* in the cool retreat,
Fires the bright maid with more than mortal heat;
She sinks at once into the lover's arms,
Nor deems it vice to prostitute her charms;
"I'll do," cries she, "what Queen's have done before;"
And sinks, *from principle,* a common whore.[14]

The suggestion that Hawkesworth's *Account* circulates in metropolitan culture as an incitement to prostitution and libertinism is, of course, hyperbolic, but it highlights the degree to which some measure of prophylaxis was deemed necessary when dealing with sexualized figures such as Oberea. Pūrea's arse is a point of fascination: it is heavily marked and yet its signification is no less eloquent in the drawing rooms of London than in the dwellings and marae of Tahiti. It would however be absurd to argue that this arse communicates in the same way in both places. The distinction is precisely one between sexual farce and regal spectacle.

Oberea's arse is important because the set of sexual signs that adhere to Tahitian bodies in this period is also active in a less visible form in the reception of Mai, known to Europeans as Omai, into London society during 1774–76.[15] If Hawkesworth's *Account* is the cultural flashpoint of the first voyage, then the newspaper coverage of the daily encounters between men and women of society with a native of Raiatea named Mai operates in much the same fashion for the second.[16] Mai was brought to England on Cook's second ship *Adventure* by Captain Tobias Furneaux and placed under the care of the Earl of Sandwich and Joseph Banks. In their company, he circulated in society and was presented to the king. As Rudiger Joppien has noted, the impact of his visit was widespread:

> Omai was a curiosity, a visually striking personality, and a living experiment. His whole cultural background made him a provocation to Western society and a welcome test for those who believed in Rousseau's ideas about man's happy and morally superior existence in the state of nature; he was a perfect example of the "noble savage." Interest in Omai was shared by almost all quarters of philosophy and learning, and some of the leading artists of the day, including Sir Joshua Reynolds and Nathaniel Dance, made him the subject of their portraits.[17]

The exemplarity of this living "wonder," however, was the subject of a highly complex debate. The newspaper accounts of his stay are fascinated by every infringement of polite behavior and the following paragraph from the *London Chronicle* sums up much of the discourse: "In respect to mental qualifications, he seems to possess scarcely any, all his observations leading to immediate corporeal gratifications, in some of which, however, he shews himself to be a *sensualist* of the first kind."[18] Despite the occasional dissenting opinion that Mai exhibited a kind of natural discernment, the real debate concerned the interpretation of the sensuality ascribed to his every utterance and action.

An extensive letter to the same paper about a month later is typical in its blurring of the line between sensuality and sensibility, between desire and discernment:

> He evidently has an affable, as well as a tender disposition; he possesses likewise much discernment and quickness. A mark of sensibility he shewed very lately. He was observing some anglers fishing near Hertford, and was pleased to learn in what manner they were employed; but, when he saw the hooks baited with a live worm, he turned away to avoid a sight so disagreeable, and declared his antipathy to eat any fish taken by so cruel a method. An instance of his discernment and quickness he exhibited when he was introduced to the Duchess of Gloucester, previous to his going to Hertford. The Duchess not being prepared with a present proper for Omiah, it occurred to her, that a pocket handkerchief, embellished with her coronet, might be acceptable to him; it was presented to him. Omiah immediately kissed the coronet and made a most complaisant bow to the Duchess. As this mark of his attention, politeness, and quickness was unexpected, it gained him the good graces of all present.[19]

The evidentiary claims of these scenes are intriguing in part because Mai acts in a manner that perfectly accords with the class and gender fantasies swirling around the notion of a man of sensibility. When he kisses the coronet on the handkerchief, he performs precisely as his aristocratic observers—and the writer of the letter—would desire, for he effectively submits to the superiority of their rank.

But this bubble of class and gender fantasy was burst a few weeks later in an equally symptomatic response in the same paper:

> Politeness and sensibility, we are told, are his characteristics.—He was shocked at the idea of putting a live worm on a hook. . . . Excellent creature! who could think he had ever heard of the Aroey! (and

to which blessed society he very probably belongs) the Aroey, a society, which according to Hawkesworth, consists of two or three hundred of each sex of the Gentry of Otaheite, who live like rabbits in a warren, with this difference, that they murder every child that is born of their amours, that their refined mothers may suffer as little interruption of their pleasure as possible. Who could think Omiah had ever heard of the inhumanity of such an epicurean sty?[20]

At one level the letter writer is simply countering the fantasy of natural society with Hawkesworth's own description and condemnation of the Arioi.[21] But it is important to recognize that the animalization that concludes the passage encompasses more than the "Gentry of Otaheite." An implicit comparison is being drawn between "the principal people of Otaheite, of both sexes, [who] have formed themselves into a society in which every woman is common to every man"[22] and the British gentry. This critique of aristocratic vice is quite specific not only because of the subtle comparison between Tahitian infanticide and the common, and often fatal, aristocratic practice of sending infants to wet nurses, but also because of the more directly scurrilous attack on the interracial contact between Mai and the Duchess of Gloucester:

> He is wonderfully polite we are told; he bowed, and he kissed the coronet on the handkerchief given him by the Duchess of ——.
> All very clever indeed. But when Mr. B—— had his first audience of the principal Lady of Otaheite [Oberea], says the historian Hawkesworth, she tucked her petticoats up to her middle, and by way of salutation turned herself around and around. If therefore Omiah's ideas of politeness were formed in his own country, what must he have thought of the rudeness of her Grace, who did not deign to honour him with the polite salutation of Otaheite?[23]

In this curious moment of cultural leveling, the writer raises a key question regarding not Mai's social performance but rather that of the duchess. Is the presentation of the handkerchief simply a more refined—or rude, depending on one's notion of politeness—version of Oberea's gesture? Both actions promise intimacy and display rank, for the marks on Oberea's arse and the coronet on the duchess's handkerchief both indicate social superiority. Mai's response would suggest that he interprets the "gift" in precisely the same way as Banks interprets Oberea's visual "gift," for he focuses his attention on the coronet. That these gifts exist on the same continuum has important ramifications for it suggests that these cultural exchanges are inherently sexual and that their apparent distinction is akin to that between gold and paper money. In this sexual economy, Oberea shows the bullion whereas the duchess offers a form of legal tender that promises similar satisfaction. Much could be made of this because the largely middle-class assaults on aristocratic vice during the 1770s focus as much on sexual practice as on the system of economic and social credit, which not only facilitated the luxurious profligacy of the gentry but also threatened to corrupt the British economy.

The consistent deployment of Omai and Oberea in the complex debate on the dissipation of the aristocracy is crucial to a number of emergent cultural formations. As the middle classes begin to gel around fantasies of healthy bodies, racial purity, sexual rectitude, and commercial restraint, one begins to see a parallel phantasmatic investment in the sexual dissipation, disease, luxury, and racial degeneration of its class others. These negative fantasies are being applied both to British aristocrats and, in this case, to what were perceived as their social equals in the South Seas.[24] In this light, publications such as "Omiah's Farewell; Inscribed to the Ladies of London," in which Omai ostensibly details the charms of notable society women in rhyming couplets, operate as slightly naughty entertainment and as a subtle racialization of class relations. As we will see, this complex nexus of desire plays itself out in Loutherbourg's pantomime in Omai's pursuit of the fair Londina, who stands for London's women of fashion. But before exploring this sexual economy, I want to turn to another culturally significant moment in the reception of Cook's activities in the Pacific and approach the play from the arse-end as it were.

As has been extensively discussed elsewhere, the deification of Captain Cook following his death in Hawaii in 1779 involved a wide range of cultural interventions that ultimately played a defining role not only in the ideological consolidation of Britannia's imperial claim to the world's oceans but also in the reactivation of the specter of the primitive in British colonial fantasy. Along with the extensive newspaper accounts, the Admiralty's multiple publication of the official report of the Third Voyage in 1784 and John Webber's accompanying engravings generated a mythic figure whose importance to the formation of British national identity in this turbulent period cannot be underestimated.[25] Loutherbourg's *Omai; or, A Trip round the World* capitalized on the intense public interest surrounding Cook's death and it plays a fundamental role in Cook's deification. The famous image of Cook being borne to heaven by the allegorical figures of Fame and Britannia above a view of Kealakekūa Bay, Hawai'i, which circulated widely as an engraving attributed to Loutherbourg, was based on a monumental painting designed by Loutherbourg and painted by the Reverend Matthew William Peters for the final scene of *Omai*[26] (fig. 2.1). The image was first shown to the public as a part of Loutherbourg's pantomime, and the context of its presentation is revealing:

> The [last] scene [of the pantomime] . . . is a most extensive view of the great bay of Otaheite, the sun-set, with a view of ships at anchor, and a royal palace in front, and the people ready to receive and crown their king. A fine view offers itself of all the boats of the island entering the bay with ambassadors from all the foreign powers bringing presents, and a procession ensues, and salute Omai as an ally of Britain, and compliment him with an English sword. This is succeeded by dancing, wrestling, boxing, etc. The Clown wins one of the dancers by the present of a nail. Harlequin and Columbine, Omai and Londina, are united, and the entertainment concludes with the an *apotheosis* of Captain Cook, crowned by Fame and Britannia, with the medallions of several celebrated English naval officers in the background.[27]

So much is happening in this scene it almost defies analysis. At one level, the view of the bay, which was based on Webber's drawings, and the immense procession of representatives from various cultures in the Pacific all dressed in costumes designed from Webber's firsthand observations are intensely ethnographic. On another level, the union of Harlequin and Columbine, of the Clown and the dancer, and of the *inamorata* Omai and Londina brings the commedia narrative to its generic closure. And then we have the extraordinarily nationalist intervention of the descending painting, which radically disrupts the performance itself and suddenly reconstructs the theatre as an exhibition space.

Despite universal approbation of the painting's "*vrai semblance* of person, of ease and graceful disposition of figure, [and] of general effect," this transformation of the theatrical space was sufficiently disruptive to prompt critical commentary.[28] On the one hand, some reviewers regarded the painting as distinct from and superior to the pantomime in which it is presented: "Such a picture—in point of all that constitutes the sublime of the art—the drawing and disposition of the figure—the well-expressed countenance—the perfect colouring, and the attitude of *Cook* himself— such a picture will immortalize the author as well as the subject of it—and were there no other merit in the Pantomime—would hold forth the

The APOTHEOSIS of CAPTAIN COOK.

From a Design of P.J.De Loutherbourg.R.A . *The View of* KARAKAKOOA BAY
& is from a Drawing by John Webber. R.A *(the last he made)in the Collection of* M^r.G.Baker.

London. Pub.^d Jany 20. 1794. by J .Thane,Spur .Strat .Leicester Square.

FIG. 2.1. After Philippe Jacques de Loutherbourg and John Webber,
The Apotheosis of Captain Cook, engraving, 1794 *(courtesy of the
Department of Prints and Drawings, The British Museum, London)*

attractions of an EXHIBITION in itself."[29] But others reacted quite negatively
precisely because the painting failed to take advantage of the theatre as
a space for spectacle and performance: "The painting is admirable . . .
but though we consider this a beautiful picture, it did not answer our ideas
of an *apotheosis* or *deification*. We did not expect to see a *flat* painting—
we looked for magnificence—something in perspective that would have
occupied the whole scene."[30] The second reviewer's disappointment arises

from two aesthetic problems that run through the production. The first is the conflict between exhibition and enactment. In the context of the scene described here, the painting, however monumental, is less spectacular than the procession of eighty-two exotically costumed players (a substantial portion of whom are barely clad dancing girls), the physical comedy of the pantomime characters, the heroic singing of the Captain, and the ostensibly Tahitian ravings of a "mad prophet" that immediately precede the painting's descent. The painting quite literally brings the entertainment to a close and the solemn allegory suddenly reorients the audience experience from low and often lascivious comedy to reverent nationalist elegy.

The elegiac qualities of this gesture are accentuated by the fact that the pantomime presents the audience with two Britannias. The first is embodied by Mrs. Inchbald in the magical second scene in which the beauty and nobility of Londina are first disclosed to Omai by a genie figure. The second is exhibited in the picture, as though the living breathing embodiment of the nation is now only available as a portrait of its theatrical self. Significantly, the play also presents two captains, one living and one dead, one embodied and one painted. When Mr. Brett steps onto the final scene of the pantomime, his presence is perhaps no less disruptive than the descent of the painting because he has figured nowhere in the play. But he has a crucial role because he is the one who ultimately engages with the threatening Oberea, whose sexual aggressiveness has been transformed here into malevolent sorcery:

> Recitative—Captain
> Accept from mighty George our Sovereign Lord
> In sign of British Love, the British Sword
> Oberea
> Oh, Joy! away my useless Spells and Mystic Charms
> A British Sword is proof against the World in Arms.
> Captain
> Ally of Joy! Owhyee's [Hawai'i's] fatal Shore,
> Brave Cook, your great Orono [Lono], is no more!
> Chorus of Indians
> Mourn Owhyee's fatal Shore,
> For Cook, our great Orono is no more![31]

This declaration of shared peace and mourning represents something new in the discourse surrounding Oberea, for the transaction, although still sexualized, renders her passive. The phallic exchange represents the union between the King of England and the Queen of Otaheite, but everything in the prior accounts of Oberea's sexuality has been reoriented and she has been subsumed into a sea of gender normativity. This point is evident in the design of her costume, for unlike other native women in the pantomime, Oberea's dress conceals rather than exposes the contours of her figure (fig. 2.2).

This desexualization impinges on how we interpret not only the mythic figure of Captain Cook but also his nonappearance on stage. By working through a proxy captain, the play effectively separates Cook from Oberea and hence puts any hint of their prior association into abeyance.[32] If this can be seen as a prophylactic gesture, then the captain's song, which immediately follows the transfer of the sword, tells us a great deal about what is really at stake in this final scene because what emerges is a prescription for the art of living:

> Air—Captain
> Ye Chiefs of the Ocean your Laurels throw by,
> Or Cypress entwine with a Wreath;
> To prove your Humanity, heave a soft Sigh
> And a Tear now let fall for his Death!
> Yet the Genius of Britain forbids us to grieve,
> Since Cook ever honoured Immortal shall live
> > Yet the Genius, etc.
> The Hero of Macedon ran o'er the World;
> Yet nothing but *death* could he give.
> 'Twas George's Command, and the Sail was unfurl'd,
> And Cook taught mankind how to *live.*
> > Yet the Genius, etc.
> He *came* and he *saw,* not to conquer, but save;
> The Caesar of Britain was he;
> Who scorn'd the Ambition of making a Slave
> While the Britains themselves are so free.
> Now the Genius of Britain forbids us to grieve
> Since Cook ever honor'd Immortal shall live.[33]

The newspapers unanimously agreed that Brett's performance of the captain's song, which is widely reprinted everywhere except the printed version of *Omai,* was one of the play's highlights In her reading of *Omai,* Kathleen Wilson recognizes that this air incorporates the fantasy of the progress of nations that characterized much eighteenth-century natural

FIG. 2.2. Philippe Jacques de Loutherbourg, *Obereyau [Oberea] Enchantress,* watercolor, 1785 *(courtesy of the National Library of Australia, Canberra)*

history.[34] Wilson's arguments regarding the consolidation of national identity are no doubt accurate, but this consolidation is accompanied by the parsing of the nation into racialized class categories whose characteristics are most visible in their relation to sexual vice. This parsing establishes "a finer set of gradated exclusions" that open onto a new configuration of power.[35] Cook's death becomes a sign not only of the preeminence of British liberty and humanity but also of a new form of imperialism, distinct from that of Alexander and Caesar, which explicitly "teaches mankind how to live." That this lesson foregoes conquest and slavery is perfectly apposite as the mercantile impulses that defined the first British Empire, and the Atlantic slave trade, which seemed to crystallize what was wrong with British colonial activity to this point, came increasingly into disrepute. What we are witnessing here is a fundamental recalibration of the objectives of empire in which life—in all of its biological and ethnographic connotations—becomes a focus of intense cultural scrutiny.

This recalibration brings *Omai* within the purview of what Foucault described as the emergence of biopower as a mode of social regulation.[36] Foucault's analysis of the relationship of racialization and the regulation of populations makes only fleeting reference to coloniality, but Ann Laura Stoler argues that the full impact of this relationship can only be understood through an understanding of the negotiation between colony and metropole. Sudipta Sen's similarly expanded definition of the term "colonial" is useful because it focuses our attention on the play of normativity in the negotiation between metropolitan and colonial society that is represented in *Omai*:

> My usage of the term "colonial," . . . thus follows not necessarily the linear chronology of military conquest and expansion, but along the terms of a certain regime of political reasoning inherent to the mercantilist commercial drive, a whole ensemble of articulations, measures, and policies both eristic and faithful to a certain vision of power and authority (what Foucault might call a *dispositif*) whose directions are marked at both ends: the parliamentary process in England as well as the quotidian administrative routines of the first phase of rule in the Indian interior.[37]

Sen's focus on the Indian case is explicitly aimed at clarifying the relationship between metropolitan and colonial governmentality, but my sense is that Loutherbourg's involution of London and Tahiti in *Omai* requires a similar methodological gesture. There is a certain vision of power whose ensemble of racial and sexual fantasies is endemic to the nonlinear development of an emerging form of imperial thought and which makes itself felt in the relationship between English and Tahitian subjects. That relationship is mediated by two modes of representation, one ethnographic and one pantomimical, and I believe that the way these two modes are reconciled reveals a great deal about the bodily stylization of classed bodies at this historical moment, which resonates with Stoler's attempts to produce a genealogy of biopower in the expanded field of imperial culture.

This genealogy is vitally concerned with questions of sexuality. As Foucault states, "it is . . . the privileged position it occupies between organism and population, between the body and general phenomena, that explains the extreme emphasis placed upon sexuality in the nineteenth century."[38] As that which circulates between the disciplinary and the regulatory, sexuality offers a pivot from which to analyze transformations in the relationship between fantasies of class or rank and those tenuously associated with race and nation. In both the first productions of *Omai* and in its subsequent revisions, one can discern how the deployment of sexuality impinges on or enacts these transformations, but understanding their full significance requires equal attention to the space—both theatrical and geographical—in which these deployments are staged. We have already seen how the enactment of peace between England and Otaheite rectifies Oberea's aberrant sexuality. That rectification is matched by the disembodiment of both Cook and Britannia in the apotheosis painting. If Oberea is now a body corrected, then Britannia and Cook accede to the remarkable luxury of having no body at all. In the first instance, the libertine desire formerly associated with Oberea is put on display as a correctable malady, and in the second, desire itself is obviated and replaced by a flat allegorical display of national exemplarity. As the reviewer for the *Times* recognized, this amounts to a disavowal of triumphal magnificence in favor of a form of imperial display that perhaps can be best described as museological.

Museological Strategies and Pantomimical Tactics

A brief midrun notice from the *Morning Post* is typical of much of the newspaper response to Loutherbourg's *Omai:*

> To speak of it, as it now is, 'tis an assemblage of the most beautiful scenery taken from view, perhaps the most delightful in nature; it unites also the simple and the sublime, leading us from the plain Otahitean hut, to the superb mansion of enchantment. It presents us with characters so much heard of since the memorable voyages of the immortal *Cook,* and brings before us the manners and customs of the Southern world. It also gives us the most perfect resemblance of some of the finest views that Britain can produce, and for splendour and character, the dresses have not hitherto been equalled. Abounding as it now is with numerous beauties and attractions, the indefatigable manager has added more, for we are informed that the second part will this evening be enriched with many new pantomimical tricks, accomplished at a very great expence. Edwin will likewise contribute his share, by the introduction of some new songs.

FIG. 2.3. John Keyse Sherwin after a drawing by John Webber, *A Dance in Otaheite*, engraving from James Cook, *A Voyage to the Pacific Ocean (by permission of the Thomas Fisher Rare Book Library, University of Toronto)*

> The united beauties of this entertainment will probably be a rich treat to the holiday gentry, and a source of amusement and instruction to a higher class, and though "last, not least" we hope a mine of wealth to the spirited and liberal managers.[39]

Ubiquitously hailed as the most expansive and expensive assemblage of painted sets, theatrical machinery and elaborate costume, the pantomime needs above all to be considered as a visual experience perhaps unrivaled on the eighteenth-century stage.[40]

Loutherbourg's costume, prop, and set designs are profoundly influenced by two figures: John Webber and Sir Ashton Lever.[41] Loutherbourg's friendship with John Webber, Cook's chief illustrator on the third voyage to the South Seas, is evident in much of the design. The *Morning Post* explicitly recognized the importance of Webber's participation in the production: "*Mr. Webber,* who was with Capt. Cook in his last voyage, gave the information how to dress the characters in the new Pantomime of *Omai;* and it was from that Gentleman's drawings, done on the spot, that many of the scenes are taken. The moon light one particularly, which was much admired, we are informed, was wholly painted by *Mr. Webber.*"[42] Aside from participating directly in the painting of sets, Webber's drawings of Tahitian life, many of which were already in circulation as engrav-

FIG. 2.4. Philippe Jacques de Loutherbourg, *Dancer,* watercolor, 1785 *(courtesy of the National Library of Australia, Canberra)*

ings, provide clear models for many of Loutherbourg's drawings. As Joppien has carefully documented, the careful replication of Webber's landscapes also extends to his ethnographic illustrations. Webber's detailed representations of the ceremonial clothing of Tahitian women (fig. 2.3) are clearly the models for Loutherbourg's designs for the women's costumes in part 2 (fig. 2.4). The remarkable correspondence here underlines the degree to which Loutherbourg goes out of his way to represent the clothing of distinct populations with as much veracity and specificity as he can. The procession that closes the pantomime acts as a runway show of sorts for ethnically distinct fashion and demonstrates the continuing importance of clothing as an index for cultural, religious, and national identity.[43] This desire for cultural specificity was augmented by frequent recourse

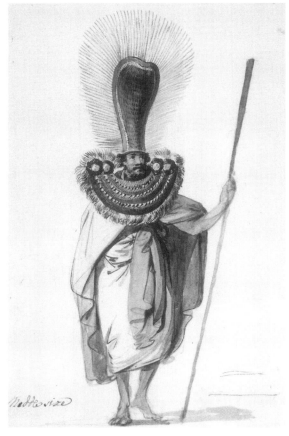

FIG. 2.5. Philippe Jacques de Loutherbourg, *Toha, Chief of Otaheite, Oedidee,* watercolor, 1785 *(courtesy of the National Library of Australia, Canberra)*

to Sir Ashton Lever's Museum, which was otherwise known as the Holophusicon. Lever's extensive collection of South Sea materials from the Cook expeditions was on display next door to Loutherbourg's workshop, and, as Joppien demonstrates, Loutherbourg almost certainly used various objects, vestments, and headdresses from the collection as models for his designs. For example, the neckpiece in Loutherbourg's design for Oedidee corresponds to a similar object in Lever's collection (fig. 2.5).[44]

If we were to look only at costume design, it would be tempting to argue that the pantomime's object was to replicate via first- or secondhand observation the distinctive dress of the various South Sea islanders whose cultures were outlined in Hawkesworth's *Account*. But there are key deformations not only in the visual material based on Webber's drawings but also in the harlequinade that indicate that the pantomime's representation of the "world" is far more complex than initial observation would suggest. First of all, the very collocation of commedia characters and historically based characters like Omai, Oberea, and Odidee should give us pause. What we are faced with are two different mimetic registers jostling in the same space. Joppien tends to see these conflicting modes as supplemental disjunctures in which naturalistic display gives way to harlequinade and vice versa. However, this implies a certain seriality, which does not arise either in the detailed newspaper accounts of the pantomime or in the published "text." Careful scrutiny of these materials indicates that the commedia elements interact simultaneously with the play's protoethnographic elements: Omai, Oberea, and other recognizable historical figures interact with Harlequin, Columbine, and other zanni in a field that is rigorously defined by the ostensibly scientific gaze of Webber and Lever. What this suggests is that these two mimetic registers are not disjunctive but part of a continuous field.

If we can imagine these mimetic registers as overlapping layers or overlapping transparencies, then the question becomes what ordinal signs are used to collate the layers. A clue to this complex process of collation lies in a subtle difference in set design that can be excavated by carefully comparing two surviving stage maquettes from the play's initial production. The first is from the sixth scene of part 1 and constitutes "A View of Kensington Gardens, from which Hyde-park is seen covered with horses gigs, &c in Rottenrow, and the coach road" (fig. 2.6).[45] The multiple paintings of trees in the wings allow for a remarkable illusion of depth and also act as frames not only for the action, but also for the parade of a series of caricatures including "an old thin city usurer, and the old dame his wife, two characters well known in London."[46] This London scene and the caricatures of London life that it contains are only as successful as they are recognizable. A similar comment could be made with regard to the preceding two scenes that stage "a view of Lord Mount Edgecumb's seat at Plymouth, and the sea-port at sun-rise" and a court of justice somewhere in the City of London, respectively. In all three cases, these scenes are the locus of extensive pantomimical trickery and of a series of projection effects. The characters ridiculed in these scenes constitute an anatomy of corruption. Scene 3, set in Plymouth, strings a series of transformation tricks targeting servants and a barrow-woman, which results in the theft of Omai's talisman. The corrupt legal officials of scene 4 to whom Omai applies for the return of his stolen talisman devolve into a chorus that

FIG. 2.6. Philippe Jacques de Loutherbourg, Scene model for Kensington Gardens in Omai *(courtesy of the Department of Prints and Drawings, Enthoven Collection, Victoria and Albert Museum, London)*

begins "sneezing, yawning, dancing, whistling, laughing and crying" such that it forms a composite portrait of insanity. Scene 5 depicts Omai, Harlequin, Londina, and Columbine dodging the elaborate displays of conspicuous aristocratic consumption in Kensington Gardens. In a touch reminiscent of Foote's critique of private credit, this scene's principal target is a Jewish usurer working among the parading coaches and strolling gentry. Scene 6 revolves around Londina's father's attempt to sell her to Omai's amatory rival, Don Struttolando, who is derided as both a fop and a class interloper. Taken together, these scenes mobilize all of the specters of metropolitan decay brought together not only in *The Nabob* but also in the daily papers.

However, the very recognizability of the scenes renders them stable envelopes for pantomime's stage magic, and this stability requires such visual spectacle to maintain audience interest in what would otherwise be little more than a routine satire of metropolitan vice. This is precisely not the case in the non-English scenes that dominate part 2. The second stage maquette is a case in point (fig. 2.7). This interior set corresponds to the Kamchatkan interior in the second scene of part 2, but it also con-

FIG. 2.7. Philippe Jacques de Loutherbourg, Scene model for inside a Jourt in Omai *(courtesy of the Department of Prints and Drawings, Enthoven Collection, Victoria and Albert Museum, London)*

flates three distinct interior scenes from Webber's engravings. The space presented is a fusion of Nootkan, Kamchatkan, and Hawaiian interiors. (figs. 2.8–10). This hybrid space is unusual in the pantomime and suggests two key distinctions. First, a fundamental distinction between the representation of picturesque exterior spaces and the representation of interior spaces corresponds to how one looks at nature and how one looks at culture. Second, non-English spaces, both interior and exterior are subject to layering and deformation in ways that the English spaces are not. The rendering of metropolitan space on stage is remarkably constrained by comparison, which will have important ramifications later in the argument, but for the moment I want to consider further the distinction between nature and culture in the non-English sets.

The process of layering is only activated in the realm of non-English culture, but it is the architecture of the London stage that structures the overlay of Webber's views. The structure of the Kensington and the "Kamchatkan" scenes are identical: each has a backdrop with two scrims fanning out on each side of the stage. The visual effect is the same, for the

FIG. 2.8. William Sharp after a drawing by John Webber, *The Inside of a Winter Habitation in Kamtschatka,* engraving from James Cook, *A Voyage to the Pacific Ocean (by permission of the Thomas Fisher Rare Book Library, University of Toronto)*

scrims give depth and allow for concealed entrances onto the stage. Joppien's discussion of Loutherbourg's knowledge of the Leverian museum is helpful here because it is clear that the Pacific manufactures painted onto the scrims and replicated as props are not presented in the form of a wonder cabinet or a rare show. Rather they are part of an integrated "view" similar to the view of Kensington Gardens. This is important because materials collected on Cook's voyages were divided into two types: "natural" and "artificial" curiosities. The former included drawings and specimens of the flora and fauna collected at each stopping point in Cook's expedition. The latter included objects and clothing manufactured by the people with whom Cook and his crew had contact during their journey. As Adrienne Kaeppler has shown, these human manufactures were considered of less scientific importance than the "natural curiosities."[47] Institutions such as the fledgling British Museum showed comparatively little interest in artificial curiosities, and it was up to private collectors like Lever to put these objects on display. In the Holophusicon, artificial and natural curiosities were displayed without distinction, so here the line between nature and culture was effectively blurred.

This was not the case in Loutherbourg's own museum venture, the Eidophusikon, which used all of his skill in stage mechanics and projection to replicate natural and specifically atmospheric phenomena. Loutherbourg's and Lever's museums were not only proximate but also

FIG. 2.9. William Sharp after a drawing by John Webber, *The Inside of a House, in Oonalashka,* engraving from James Cook, *A Voyage to the Pacific Ocean (by permission of the Thomas Fisher Rare Book Library, University of Toronto)*

operated at the same time. However, it is in *Omai* that Loutherbourg initiates a new museological strategy distinct both from his earlier practice and from Lever's example. If we think of *Omai* solely in terms of display strategy, then what we have is an expansion of the objectives of the Eidophusikon. Like the earlier venture, Loutherbourg expends a great deal

FIG. 2.10. William Sharp after a drawing by John Webber, *The Inside of a House in Nootka Sound,* engraving from James Cook, *A Voyage to the Pacific Ocean (by permission of the Thomas Fisher Rare Book Library, University of Toronto)*

of scenic and machined energy in replicating views and natural phenomena. At times the stage is showered in hail, thunder erupts, and various
projections are employed to imitate the movement of clouds and the sun.
However, he also breaks new ground by replicating artificial curiosities
as props, costumes, and interior scenes. In both cases, Webber is the primary source, but despite a tendency in Webber's images to separate the
quasi-ethnographic from the picturesque, the cultural from the natural,
Loutherbourg's design tends to make the former a subset of the latter.
Replicated cultural artifacts are subsumed into the all-embracing category
of "natural curiosity." Hence, the interior space in the "Kamchatkan" scene
is structured much like the exterior space of Kensington gardens, and religious objects in the former are viewed much like trees in the latter.

What I am describing here is a subtle form of dehumanization that had
an impact on the pantomime's reception and subsequent modification.
To render the Pacific islanders as natural objects designed for visual observation alone radically deprived them of agency and hence of the capacity to effect stage action. Reviews of the opening two shows of *Omai* were
abundant in their praise but also indicated that the second part was less
successful than the first because it was merely a series of views insufficiently tied together by pantomimical action. As the *Morning Chronicle*
reports, "The new Pantomime, as before, excited great admiration. The
comick business of it was somewhat altered and amended, but there is still
room for improvement in this respect. It is, if any thing, too much of a
shew, and not quite enough of a pantomime. At the same time, every spectator must admit that it is a splendid and exact representation of all that
is interesting in Captain Cook's voyage to Otaheite, the Friendly Islands,
&c."[48] The reviewer here is picking up on a fundamental tension between
two modes of spectatorship demanded by *Omai:* the picturesque views
and ethnographic replications associated with Pacific spaces and peoples
construct a fairly passive viewing position for the contemplative spectator, whereas the stage magic of pantomime and its heavy reliance on physical theatre associated with the metropolitan scenes seem to elicit a far
more direct bodily response. This is an interesting critique because the
second part takes place exclusively in Pacific settings whereas the first, with
the exception of the opening two scenes, is set in recognizable English
locales. It would appear that the audience's interest in the views was sec-
ondary to the visual and performative trickery that dominated part 1. This
tells us something about the effectiveness of Loutherbourg's museological strategy, for his rendering of the artificial as natural enables him to

bring cultural difference to the stage as visual spectacle; but it also prevents him from activating cultural difference in performance. This is especially notable in the performance of the main Tahitian characters, who are remarkably passive in comparison with the characters overtly drawn from commedia.

Loutherbourg's solution to this perceived problem is telling. To counteract the passivity inherent to the viewing experience of the picturesque, he introduced a series of modifications to subsequent performances, including the addition of more physical trickery for the Clown, played by D'Elpini; the incorporation of more singing and dancing; and, most important, the addition of a new character designed specifically for the talents of Edwin. This new character is identified in the *Morning Chronicle* as a "Travelled native of Tongataboo [Tongatapu]" and in the printed version of *Omai* as an "Otaheitean, supposed to have accompanied Omai to England."[49] The uncertainty regarding the geographical origin and the identity of this character is important because, unlike Omai, Oberea, Odiddee, and Towha, he does not correspond to a historical personage. His physical appearance on stage is also singular: "The introduction of Edwin's song last night in the new Pantomime had an excellent effect. He was introduced in the character of an Otaheitian, who had accompanied Omiah in his voyage, and had most whimsically and pantomimically dressed himself in a piece of the habit of each country he had met with in his several voyages."[50] A note to the print version attempts to argue for the ethnographic probability of his costume by cryptically stating that "The idea of his dress was taken from Cook's Voyages, where it is said, that Omai, to make himself fine on his introduction to a Chief dressed himself with a piece of the habit of each country he had been in his several voyages."[51] Dressed in scraps of clothes from all countries, Edwin is effectively a living and breathing embodiment of the hybridity evident in the layering of the Kamchatkan interior. Equal yet contradictory claims are made for Edwin's costume: on the one hand, it is seen as wholly befitting pantomime and, on the other, it is seen as a further example of the play's ethnographic veracity. Both mimetic registers are fully adequated in Edwin's costume, which allows us to comprehend more fully what is at stake in the racial fantasies that suddenly erupt from his performance. Before delving into the particulars of Edwin's song, however, we need to look carefully at Loutherbourg's other modifications to the pantomime and, specifically, to D'Elpini's performance as the Clown, in order to isolate the suture points between pantomime and ethnographic fantasy.

One of the most puzzling aspects of *Omai* is its explicit deviation from the pattern of the eighteenth-century harlequinade.[52] Conventional holiday pantomime involves a frame story, derived from either fairy tales or current events, which generates a blockage that must be resolved in the embedded narrative of the harlequinade. This blockage is usually sexual, and the main characters in the frame are usually transformed into Harlequin and Columbine by fairies or other magical creatures. *Omai* does not follow this pattern because, rather than transforming Omai and Londina into Harlequin and Columbine, the commedia figures function as servants to the central couple and occupy the same theatrical space. The relationship between frame and embedded narrative is generally akin to that between constricted society and anarchic green world. In a rather unusual reversal, *Omai* opens in Tahiti, where Oediddeo's threat to Omai's right of succession and the sexual blockage between Londina and Omai are established; magically transports the characters to England; and then follows them back to Tahiti. Tahiti, conventionally understood as the epitome of natural society, is figured as a zone of dynastic uncertainty and infecundity. Once the blockage is overcome, the pantomime shifts back to the newly rectified and revivified world of the frame narrative. In conventional holiday pantomime, the tricks are located primarily in the second part of the embedded narrative and are used to bring Harlequin and Columbine or the *inamorata* together. However, the first productions of *Omai* concentrated the tricks in the first section of the play, which is set largely in England. And the England it presents is remarkably unruly and disturbing. In the first scene at Plymouth, the theft of Omai's talisman as he tries to make his way through a throng of working-class characters parodies the alleged theft of British items by Tahitians in Hawkesworth's *Account*. The court seems to restore the rule of law by returning the talisman, but a constable engages in another theft as the court dissolves into sneezing and song. The sixth scene offers a view of Kensington Gardens in which "the principal characters . . . are an old thin city usurer and the old dame his wife, two characters well known in London." Other scenes involve Londina's incarceration in her father's house; in the second half, Londina's father attempts to sell not only feathers but also Columbine. Taken together, these details suggest that England is a land dominated by theft, avarice, and the moral depravity of the slave trade.

Harlequin and Columbine lead Omai and Londina through this anarchic and vicious world. What is remarkable is that the pantomime associates this anarchy with the metropole and asserts that Omai can only come to power through a "union with the British Fair." As Oberea claims at the end of the pantomime, Tahitian magic must give way to the magic of British might: "[A]way my useless spells and magic charms, / A British sword is proof against the world in arms." The spatial reversal in the pantomime has effected a replacement of magic with military might such that the saturnalian world of Tahiti is literally transformed into a space of imperial normativity, where Oberea blesses the English sword, Omai accedes to middle-class subjectivity, and Cook is elevated into a god of imperialism. *Omai*'s divagation from conventional harlequinade structure allowed Loutherbourg simultaneously to critique metropolitan society and yet to lay claim to Tahiti in a fashion that reconstructs it as the mirror of normative British society. In short, he gets to stage metropolitan corruption—located in officials of the state, in the aristocracy, and in working-class characters—and to project a middle-class fantasy of colonial governance through military domination. It is hard to tell if the plot structure is an exercise in ironic cynicism, but one thing is certain: the audience was extremely uncomfortable with the displacement of conventional pantomime trickery, and Loutherbourg undertook a series of symptomatic revisions to assuage their concerns. It may be that the original combination of critique and projection was simply too close to the truth of middle-class desire for social control and thus too open to direct scrutiny.

Loutherbourg's alterations to *Omai* over the weeks subsequent to its initial performance effectively recalibrated the relationship between ethnography and pantomimical action. The following notice from the *Morning Chronicle* gives a sense of the kind of equilibrium that the public seemed to desire:

> The new Pantomime of *Omai*, confessedly all-powerful in point of scenery, is now much more attractive and entertaining than at first, from the increased variety of its tricks and pleasantries. The second act is refitted, and presents more pantomime objects than before. Scarcely a scene is viewed, before which the eye is not diverted by some laughable incident, as well as interested by the true and correct exemplification of the customs and manners of the natives.[53]

With so much of the production's initial focus placed on the preparation of scenery and costumes, the responsibility for achieving this equilibrium fell largely to Edwin's singing, D'Elpini's clowning, and the eventual participation of "The celebrated *Monsieur Bouverie*, principal mechanist to his Majesty of France . . . [who was] engaged to prepare several humourous tricks and deceptions."[54] This increased attention to visual deception focused audience attention on the magic performed by Omai and his attendant Harlequin.

Throughout the pantomime, Omai's talisman and Harlequin's wooden sword transform objects and costumes in a fashion that consistently gets the better not only of Omai's rival Don Struttolando but also of his servant, the Clown. The following description of the scene set in Kensington Garden gives some sense of the stage action:

> A crowd assembles; the clown purloins a carrot, which takes a magic change; he tries a turnip, which produces a similar effect. Struttolando calls him, and a kind of confusion ensues, in which the barrow-woman loses her crutch-stick, which being taken up by Harlequin, it immediately transforms itself into the usual wooden sword for Harlequin. A song is here introduced by the barrow-woman, after which she retires, and the Clown enters, who being struck by Harlequin's sword, his dress is transformed instantly to pair of breeches, which, rising up, button about his neck. All this enchantment is supposed to arise from a talisman in the possession of Omai, which he had from the genii to protect him from harm.[55]

The tricks here are well worn, but the relationship asserted between Omai's talisman and Harlequin's sword has significant ramifications. Within the terms set out by the performance, the stage magic of pantomime and the spirit magic of Otaheitie are equated. This implies that the mythic envelope that imbues Tahitian life is for Loutherbourg and his audience a subset of visual wonder. And this wonder is of a specific kind: namely, that associated with the stage mechanics and the bodily training of a form of theatrical performance usually deemed suitable only for children and degraded tastes. Many of the reviews that praise *Omai; or, A Trip round the World* argue that it is remarkable to find such instructive material in what is otherwise a foolish genre. The most interesting of these ambivalent reviews feels compelled to mark its disapprobation of the genre in order to mark the specific pedagogical merits of Loutherbourg's production:

> Pantomime Entertainments, which are generally degraded, when put in competition with the construction of a classical drama, have frequently nevertheless very substantial claims to our respect and pro-

tection; . . . We are led into these contemplations by a retrospect of the dramatic entertainment of last night. Our imagination was excited, our understanding enlarged, and our veneration for Captain Cook was confirmed. . . . The general effects of the pantomime were instructive, interesting, magnificent, and characteristic.[56]

But if we are to see *Omai* as an example of imperial pedagogy, then we must also recognize that its objectives go far beyond the promulgation of ethnographic knowledge of non-European cultures. The audience was being trained in the complex art of class ascendancy in the metropole.

Two highly significant issues emerge from the assumed adequacy of myth and stage magic evinced in both the pantomime and its reviews. In an altogether different theatre, that of transcultural contact, Europeans had already developed a set of gestural signs and theatrical spectacles aimed at generating mythic qualities. If we turn specifically to the case of Tahiti, there are numerous accounts of performances staged for precisely this end. For example, in Bougainville's account, the sailors set off rockets and use their firearms in highly theatrical ways to literally stage their difference from the natives of the islands. This is nowhere more evident than in the careful manipulation of costume.[57] Clothing is always a focus for the performance of civility, and in accounts of Bougainville's voyage much is made of the native's response to the sailor's vestments. The natives seek to determine if these newly arrived creatures are the same as they are by looking underneath their uniforms. Similar scenes of performance are amply presented in Hawkesworth's *An Account of a Voyage round the World,* and it is amusing to consider what happens when the deployment of costumes, props, and tricks goes awry. The English obsession with the theft of their snuffboxes and other props of civility is intriguing in this light, for it is precisely the manipulation of less-valuable objects—trinkets and mirrors—that subtly renders the Tahitians as innocent dupes. When the Tahitians interrupt this theatrical economy of exchange by stealing valuable objects or clothes, the English sailors suddenly find themselves on the wrong side of performance. Interpreting the English concern over theft in this way sheds light on the proximity between the gestural economy of pantomime and that of transcultural communication in a scene where there is no shared language.

One could suggest that the tricks of colonial conquest are not unrelated to the tricks of metropolitan pantomime. In the former, visual spectacle is deployed to elevate European characters; in the latter, similar visual tricks are used to devalue the objects of Harlequin's wooden wrath. What this implies is that the relationship between the agents of colonial conquest and the native audience of their spectacles of civility is similar to that between Harlequin and his comic mark. In the case of *Omai; or, A Trip round the World,* this means that D'Elpini's performance in the role of the clown is crucial for understanding how the play intervenes in the theatre of colonial contact, in part because he is Harlequin's primary target, and in part because the relationship between the two zanni or clowns reverses the racial hierarchy suggested previously.

However, before turning to D'Elpini it is important to recognize how the adequation of stage and spirit magic performs a crucial piece of cultural inoculation. Rendering Omai's talisman and Oberea's enchantments in this way has a significant impact on how the audience constructs the spiritual and cultural life of the Pacific peoples represented in the play. Any suggestion that these are religious practices is effectively consigned to oblivion—crucially so, because there is a history of deploying Tahitian culture as a countermemory for European religious doctrine. This is especially the case in France where Bougainville's *Voyages* was quickly incorporated into an Enlightenment critique of society. Diderot's notoriously libertine *Supplement to Bougainville's Voyage* revels in the "natural" sexuality of the Tahitians and uses Bougainville's quasi-ethnographic observations to stage an assault not only on the customs of marriage but also on the moral teaching of institutionalized religion.[58] As we have already noted, a similar kind of critique of artificial society also emerged in Britain, but its libertine manifestations were simultaneously indulged and condemned as immoral often in the same publications. This type of double presentation, which leers as much as it condemns, is symptomatic of the surveillance of gender and sexual norms in the 1770s. At the time of the performance of *Omai; or, A Trip round the World* in the mid-1780s, the deployment of Tahitian figures as exemplary subjects of religious and sexual freedom has given way to a different form of exemplarity, whose terms are derived from commedia dell'arte.

Omai joins the seemingly disparate representational fields of ethnographic travel narrative and harlequinade by activating the triangle of desire at the heart of most commedia plots. Much of the action of the pantomime revolves around the *inamorata* Omai and Londina. Throughout the play Omai pursues Londina and competes with the braggart Don Struttolando for her affections. But typical of commedia narrative, the lovers are extraordinarily passive, and the primary rival is too much of a coward and a fool to push the amorous plot to a crisis. Omai and the women of fashion whom Londina allegorizes thus figure as passive sexual subjects. This figuration diverges from a significant portion of the satirical verse on Omai's desires in the 1770s and from the totality of anti-aristocratic discourse in the period. In true commedia fashion, the passivity of the lovers is of course compensated for by their attendants. Omai is shadowed by Harlequin, Londina is served by Columbine, and Don Struttolando is pushed and pulled around the stage by D'Elpini as the Clown. The relationship between lovers and servants replicates the class structure of commedia plots, and it is important to recognize the degree to which this distinction of rank parses subjects into sexually active and passive figures. Omai and Londina are desiring subjects in the play, but the enactment of their desire and its fulfillment are performed by Harlequin and Columbine. What this means is that the passive and idealized triangle of desire is contained within a larger triangle, which is constantly erupting with lascivious gestures and direct sexual jokes.

This containment has important ramifications for the racial and class politics of the pantomime. It is important to remember that the internal triangle of a Tahitian prince, an Italian *amoroso,* and an English woman of fashion is composed of figures who are all conventionally associated with suspect or dissipated aristocratic sexuality. The potential union of Londina with Omai or Struttolando involves the threat of transculturation or interracial sexual practice. This internal circuit, therefore, carries with it the combined signification of the sexual and racial degeneration of the aristocracy. However, the sexual and racial signs associated with the internal triangle have been separated from Omai, Londina, and Struttolando and projected onto their servants, Harlequin, Columbine, and the Clown. And the specificity of this twofold operation of separation and projection is notable. Perhaps because the representation of Londina has the possibility of being the most scandalous—she could easily be construed as a direct satire on English society women—its dynamic is the most restrained. But the Omai-Harlequin relation resonates with strange transferences. As we have already seen, Harlequin replicates Omai's spirit magic with conventional pantomimical transformations, so there is some degree of commutability in the characters. Of all of Omai's character attributes, this relationship to his talisman is the fundamental sign of cultural difference from the English characters. As the play unfolds, the power of Omai's talisman is superseded by Harlequin's clapper.[59] It is as though Omai's cultural and religious identity are subsumed into Harlequin's gestural economy.

But more important is the possibility that Harlequin actually embodies Omai's negritude. At the time of Mai's circulation in British society a

FIG. 2.11. J. Caldwell after William Hodges, *Omai*, engraving, 1777 *(courtesy of the National Library of Australia, Canberra)*

number of commentators speculated on what they considered to be his negroid features. Speculating on why Mai agreed to come to England with Captain Furneaux, one writer offered the following interpretation of his face: "[I]t is said, that a flatness in his nose, which indicated a mixture of the negro breed and his family, and made him less respectable in those islands, where blood is considered in the highest degree, contributed to make him more ready to undertake this voyage, that he might gain personal consequence from it, to compensate for this family disadvantage."[60] The racialization of Mai here is notable as much for what it reveals about the reading of bodily signs as for what it says about the relationship between race and "family" or aristocratic privilege. It is clear that Mai is being read as someone whose family was of the first rank—in historical fact he was not an elite subject—but whose privilege was undercut by miscegenation.[61] That this comes down to Mai's face speaks on the one hand to the extraordinary interest in painting Mai's portrait during his visit and on the other hand to his commutability with Harlequin who frequently appears with a black mask (figs. 2.11, 2.12). The color of Harlequin's mask—or even whether he was masked—in this production remains unclear, as does the relationship between mask color and racialization, but the question posed by these details is, I believe, important because the emergent practice of racialization in the late eighteenth century is beginning to read the face like a mask for typical signs that then stand for traits of character and mentality.[62] In this context, one is tempted to ask whether the mask plays a more active role in the history of raciological thinking than has been hitherto recognized.

As Omai's cultural and bodily specificity is leeched out of his character and deposited into Harlequin, he slowly emerges as something rather different from the figure that animated the newspapers in the 1770s. He suddenly becomes a suitable sexual partner for Londina, whose sexual ex-

FIG. 2.12. Sir Joshua Reynolds, *Omai of the Friendly Isles,* pencil drawing, circa 1774 *(courtesy of the Rex Nan Kivell Collection, National Library of Australia, Canberra)*

cesses have also been projected onto Columbine. This process, therefore, erases the threat of interracial desire and replaces it with an idealized yet bland fantasy of heterosexual monogamy.[63] But it does so not by eliminating the signs of racial otherness and sexual excess but rather by exaggerating them now as attributes of characters of low rank. So a double prophylaxis is effected—one that protects both racial and class identity—by taking the exemplary signs of excess and attaching them to figures already well worn in an economy of ridicule.

One Zanni for Another

Commedia is a particularly slippery medium for this kind of regulation of social norms, and its heavy reliance on physical theatre allows for all sorts of dissent in what has the potential to become an exercise in hegemony. This is why D'Elpini's performance as the Clown, servant to Don Struttolando, is so fascinating. Within the template of commedia types, Don Struttolando is typical of the captain figure in that he combines braggadocio and cowardice in such a way that his hyperphallic attributes reveal themselves to be a compensation for his foolish impotence. He shares a great deal with the fop in this period whose professed libertinism often acts as a front or a pretext for effeminate narcissism.[64] This helps to explain why Don Struttolando simply evaporates as a sexual threat to Omai when, as the *Town and Country* summary of the pantomime succinctly states, Struttolando is "brought over to Omai's interest" in the penultimate scene and does not figure in the sexual unions of the play's conclusion.[65] However, Struttolando's servant, the Clown, is very much present in the final scene and is the focus of the most highly sexualized cross-racial encounter in the play.

As I have already noted, this closing scene unites Omai and Londina, and Harlequin and Columbine in a rather chaste fashion, but these unions are preceded by the performance of dancing girls based on Webber's illustration of a Tahitian festival. At the conclusion of the dancing, "The Clown wins one of the dancers by the present of a nail."[66] All of the careful evacuation of interracial sexuality between Omai and Londina is abandoned here and the audience is presented with what is effectively a scene of prostitution. It is a key moment because it plays out two scenes associated with contact between Europeans and Tahitians following the publication of Hawkesworth's *Account:* one historical and one phantasmatic. The first, of course, is the scandal not only of sex between British men and Tahitian women, which is amply documented in Hawkesworth, but also the fact that much of this sexual activity involved the exchange of "meaningless trinkets" not that distinct from the Clown's nail. Nails were used by Cook's men as currency for sex, and these exchanges were used not only as signs of Tahitian sexual freedom—or depravity—but also as an indication of their heterodox interpretation of British notions of property, which was often read as a form of noncomprehension, and thus of their incapacity for sovereign governance over their territory.[67] In short, this particular exchange is loaded with ethnographic and political significance.

The second implication is the insinuation, already noted with regard to "An Epistle from Mr. Banks, Voyager, Monster-Hunter, and Amoroso to Oberea, Queen of Otaheite," that reading Hawkesworth will itself be an incitement to libertinism and prostitution. Indeed, the very title of that poem tells us a great deal, for Banks is himself being satirized as an "Amoroso" not unlike Don Struttolando. If we understand Don Struttolando as an idealized figure for Banks, then the Clown carries the negative qualities associated with his supposed libertinism. This not only transfers the sexual dissipation associated with the Banks figure onto the debased figure of the Clown, but also represents the Polynesian dancing girl as the "natural" embodiment of prostitution. If we look closely at the descriptions of D'Elpini's performance and the few speeches attributed to the Clown, what we discern is a consistent fascination with clothing and a relentless pursuit of Londina. D'Elpini's clothes are continually transforming and early in part 2, while dressed in the aeronautical gear of a "scientific" traveler, he comments that "the ladies with my dress would much be taken."[68] In the first part, these obsessions are conjoined when "During [Harlequin's] absence, the Clown enters in Omai's cloaths, and Londina imagining him to be Omai, she lies down beside him."[69] This moment of masquerade instantiates the Clown's desire for Londina, and he makes a series of ludicrous attempts to woo her in the second part.

Some sense of the lazzi, or comic business, involved here can be gleaned from the Clown's air in the sixth scene of part 2 that appears in the Larpent text, but which was excised midway through the pantomime's run and replaced by Edwin's drunken song alluded to earlier:

> Air 11th—Clown
> There Miss Londina lolls, how lazy!
> On the green grass take your rest;
> But ye Conjurors make me a daisy,
> Then will she slumber on my breast.

Was I the breeze these Branches rocking,
Longing her lily leg to Note
Without Offence to her White Stocking,
I'd puff about her Petticoat.[70]

The Clown's desire to become a daisy or a breeze to gain proximity to Londina's lily-white body is simultaneously suggestive and ridiculous, because it partakes of the same figural economy associated with fops such as Garrick's Daffodil.[71] Here the joke is quite literal because the Clown wants to be a flower and, typical of the critical presentation of fops in the post-Garrick era, his sexual predation is undercut by signs of effeminacy. As the song continues, he threatens to "win [Londina] by surprise," and yet the insinuations of sexual assault are countered by indications that his masculinity is more than suspect.[72] The subsequent air, also excised during Loutherbourg's revisions, emphasizes that the Clown understands erotic desirability to be equatable with a lover's dancing skills and his wardrobe:

Not Spanish Struttolando,
    Nor Indian Omai;
Can do what I can do
    To love you, oh, may I!
I can caper, ah, ah, [*capers*] I can quaver, oh! oh! [*runs a Cantible*]
And want but a Lady to make me a Beau;
I want but a Wardrobe to dress very fine;
To get roaring muzzy, I want but good Wine.
If I had but the Money, I'd rattle at hazard,
And want but a Barber to ponder my Muzzard.[73]

That the Clown's dancing is dubious at best and his wardrobe more imaginary than sumptuous makes him a figure of ridicule both for his theory of desire and for his erotic practice. The *Times* welcomed "the pruning away one of D'Elpini's songs, for though we think him an excellent pantomime clown, he has nothing of the *Italian* in his voice".[74] "Italian" has a double signification here for it refers both to his singing voice and to his capacity as an *amoroso*. Throughout the eighteenth century Italians are routinely associated both with libertine desire and effeminacy, so the reviewer here is picking up on the critique of the Clown and his master Don Struttolando, but he is also suggesting that D'Elpini makes a poor fop.

This burlesque of foppish libertinism was a primary element of D'Elpini's performance, and it is interesting to consider how it plays out the critique of Banks discussed earlier. Much was made of the fact that in his famous encounter with Pūrea in which he lost his clothes, Banks took on the costume of the Tahitians. Such a moment of ethnic cross-dressing carried with it a certain sexual frisson that makes its way into the verse satires of the 1770s. As we have already seen, male libertinism is often portrayed as the impersonation of Tahitian sexual custom, and such representations neatly deploy existing figures of prostitution to critique aristocratic women. In this light, the Clown's aggressive pursuit of Londina not only enacts these former scenes of promiscuity to recall the critique of aristocratic vice, but also reorients them because Londina consistently rejects the Clown except when she thinks he is the now sexually normative Omai. What this means is that a hygienic barrier is being erected between Don Struttolando and his alter ego, the Clown, on the one hand, and Londina, on the other, that effectively trumps libertinism and saves the women of London from allegations of sexual impropriety.

Significantly, this hygienic imperative, which was so crucial to Loutherbourg and O'Keefe's initial construction of the Clown's character and to D'Elpini's performance of the role, quickly became vestigial. Perhaps because D'Elpini was not suited to the burlesque of foppish behavior and perhaps because the critique of libertinism was less important than the racialization of class relations, his extended airs in part 2 were replaced with something much more disturbing and arguably more ideologically necessary. D'Elpini's rapturous pursuit of Londina was replaced by a set piece written specifically for Edwin in the character of the "Travelled Native of Tongataboo" who ostensibly travels with Omai in a coat composed of fragments of a range of native costumes. This song was singled out for praise in all of the London dailies and I would like to quote it in its entirety in order to explore thoroughly the rather different account of the career of this phantasmatic Pacific envoy:

> I.
> In de big canoe
> I o'er the ocean cummee,
> Jack and merry crew
> Give good liquor ti me;
> Over sand and rocks
> Teach me to sail no paddle;
> Teach me den to box,
> So to use my daddle.
>   Tol lol lol, &c.

II.

Oh! I suck'd de grog,
Brandy, gin and rummee,
Vid de jolly dog,
Den to London cummee.
Vat you tink of dat,
Rice my hair did powder,
Rub my head vid fat,
Dats to make me prowder.
    Tol lol lol, &c.

III.

Snug as littel mouse
From de vind and veather,
Dragg'd about in house
Made of trees and leather,
To de voman fair
Up de stair I trottee,
She did sit on chair,
On de floor I squattee,
    Tol lol lol, &c.

IV.

But dis lady fine
Call me ugly divil;
Guinea, glass of wine,
Den so sweet and civil,
In her spousy jump
As of kiss I beg her,
Give my head de tump,
Cry get out dam negar.
    Tol lol lol, &c.[75]

Each stanza offers a debased version of key details from the accounts of Mai's sojourn in London: for example, a number of papers drew attention not only to Mai's adoption of English attire but also to his lack of familiarity with the use of a chair or sofa. What we have here is a coarse parody of Mai's visit that provides overtly racist gestures that contrast quite violently with the representation of Omai elsewhere in the pantomime, but which also stage the same hygienic imperative noted earlier with regard to D'Elpini's performance.

This entire process, however, turns on the deployment of prostitute figures adjacent to the *inamorata* both in London and Tahiti. Rather than a subtle critique of the fantasy of interracial desire ostensibly at the heart of Banks's libertinism, Edwin's song first constructs a subhuman racial type who is drunk and on the prowl in London and then stages his repudiation by "de voman fair." That the "Travelled Native of Tongataboo" receives his lessons in civility from British sailors, and a London prostitute underlines how notions of class otherness are deployed in the formation of the "dam negar." Edwin's character's proximity to the London prostitute is matched by the only instance of sexual deviance in the otherwise normative closing scene. The prostitutional relationship established between D'Elpini's Clown and the dancing girl by the exchange of the nail effectively repeats this collocation of working-class depravity and interracial sexual practices. Significantly, all of Edwin's songs in the pantomime cast him as a lower-class figure involved in the propagation of vice. In his first song, in part 1, he is inciting the women of London to gambling and in the final song added to the play in early January 1786, he appears as a pimp, along with his prostitute Poll, fighting in pubs, interloping at a play, and finally toasting English seaman that they "May . . . always the ocean command."[76]

This eruption of racial and class fantasy into the overtly ethnographic pantomime was not only called for by the audience and the critics but also embodied in the performance of a character who ostensibly stands for all types of people from the Pacific. Wearing his fragmented coat and recounting his public shaming by "de fine lady," Edwin enacts a form of racial derogation that both sexualizes and infantilizes Britain's cultural others encountered by Cook on his voyages. But in his performance, Edwin also draws explicit lines of affiliation between depraved lower-class characters and ostensibly "primitive" Polynesian subjects. The lower orders and the racially distinct exist together at a distance from normative middle-class whiteness. In perhaps the pantomime's most telling moment, Omai is witness to Edwin's song and "is driven to great Distress, and to the Exercise of his Magic Power" to flee the scene in pursuit of Londina. It is as though the eruption of racist fantasy prompts Omai to separate himself from one with whom he might be confused.

In light of Edwin's hyperembodiment of racial otherness, the palpable disembodiment of Cook and Britannia in the apotheosis painting now becomes highly significant. It would appear that the gestural economy of D'Elpini's tricks and the minstrel-like tactics of Edwin's singing operate as the chief sites of bodily fantasy and projection necessary for the evacuation or the whitening of Cook and Britannia. Understood in this way, the leeching of almost all the sexual and racial signs from the central triangle of desire in the commedia plot implies that the threats of interracial sexuality, active female desire, and foppish masculinity embodied by Omai, Londina, Don Struttolando, and their zanni attendants are necessary as examples of potential, but reformed, alterity. Their newfound normativity is instructive for it exists adjacent to, but not part of, the apotheosis painting. In the final scene, Cook and Britannia require an altogether disjunctive form of representation to ensure that they are effectively separated from the swirling mass of sexual, racial, and class fantasy broiling on stage below them.

But if Cook and Britannia require a separate representational plane, then the seemingly opposite representational paradigms of ethnographic observation and commedia narrative do not, because, as the pantomime unfolds, ethnographic detail is carefully transformed into types not identical but rather akin to commedia types. So the careful ethnographic observation of Webber gives way to the racist posturing of Edwin. The critique of aristocratic libertinism, which was so important to early discussions of Cook's voyages and Mai's sojourn in England in the 1770s, gives way to fantasies of working-class degeneration so totalizing that they subsume signs of vice into emergent signs of racial difference. In this regard, *Omai; or, A Trip round the World* marks a signal transition in middle-class politics from the shaming of the aristocracy to the racialization of the lower orders. And hanging quietly behind all this are the quasi-scientific views of the South Seas, which allow this recalibration of racial and class fantasy to be staged as a thoroughly educational experience.

PART TWO | *Women and the Trials of Imperial Masculinity*

IN EARLY MARCH of 1788, while the impeachment of Warren Hastings was raging in the House of Lords, the recently divorced Lady Eglantine Wallace stepped into the gallery of the House of Commons dressed as a man.[1] While it was not uncommon for women to enter the visitor's gallery during this period, a woman's appearance in breeches was deemed sufficiently scandalous to warrant extensive press coverage. The following passage is typical of the reaction not only because it uses the event as an occasion for feeble sexual innuendo, but also because it ties the event to Lady Wallace's upcoming and ill-fated comedy *The Ton:*

> Lady Wallace's *gallery* frolic has proved fatal to the repose of the married Members,—many of their wives, encouraged by her Ladyship's success, having ever since been trying to *wear* the breeches.
>
> Lady Wallace, it is asserted, means to *dramatize* the late debate on the Declaratory Bill, and introduce some of the rising Members in her piece.[2]

The rising members joke, as lame as it is, took on a life of its own and the papers publicly scrutinized Lady Wallace's sexual morals over the next few weeks until her comedy was resoundingly damned after three fractious performances. I have written elsewhere about the relationship between Lady Wallace's gender insubordination and the disapprobation of her critique of aristocratic vice in *The Ton,* but the jokes regarding her visit to the Commons betray a certain anxiety about mixing two very different styles of sociability.[3] Adopting Peter Clark's terms, the "old style" of sociability endemic to Parliament was brought into contact with the "fashionable sociability" that is defined by the public presence of women. Lady Wallace's appearance in the gallery brought two conflicting modes of sociability together, and her performance of masculinity served not only to highlight her own transgression of social boundaries, but also to activate a certain confusion in the social performance of the parliamentarians. Is the honorable member's performance to be addressed according to the homosocial rules of conduct that define his governmental function or according to the sexual codes implicit in the performance of fashionable sociability? The confusion is captured perfectly in the double connotation of "rising member," and I would argue that this event has a certain heuristic value.

Both Parliament and fashionable society were traversed by complex forms of theatricality whose organizing principles are not easily reconciled. However, during the 1780s events such as the impeachment of Warren Hastings before the House of Lords brought these spheres together on a scale that had never been seen before.[4] The incursion of women and of new forms of sociability into Parliament was arguably the most spectacular instance of the incremental infusion of women into the public sphere more generally. As their spectatorial relation to governance became more immediate, women increasingly adopted positions ancillary to, but not disconnected from, the practice of social regulation, either through highly mediated forms of critique or as governmental agents in their own right. In the former category, we find women such as Frances Burney, Elizabeth Inchbald, Hannah Cowley, Mary Hays, and Mary Wollstonecraft, all of whom engaged with the political life of the nation through media suited to forms of sociability deeply tied to the commercialization of culture—the novel and the theatre. In the latter category, we find not only the wives and mothers presiding over the domestic sphere, but also theorists of education and social amelioration, such as Catherine Macauley, Maria Edgeworth, and Hannah More. The writings of these women focused directly on problems in the configuration of British masculinity, and it is important to recognize that for all of these writers masculinity and male homosociality had to be reconstructed not only to resolve problems in the sex/gender system but also to stabilize the class aspirations of the middle ranks.[5] What has perhaps been underappreciated is that women's ethical spectatorship of governance—even in its most juridical forms—comes during a period of unprecedented upheaval in the history of British governmentality. As new forms of social regulation begin to achieve their effectivity, old forms of juridically based power found themselves under intense and sometimes tortuous reevaluation. And that process was a direct result of challenges to the very notion of sovereignty posed by the expansion of the empire. It should come as no surprise, therefore, that women such as Inchbald and Burney would link analyses of governmental corruption in the empire to constitutive problems in masculinity itself.

As my reading of Foote's *The Nabob* emphasizes, conventional arguments regarding the landed class's interest in maintaining political liberty were beginning to be hollowed out by the incursion of commercial interests. As the 1770s unfolded, the very term "liberty," which secured so much of British governance, would prove to be an extremely powerful fulcrum for colonial resistance to imperial rule. Despite repeated attempts to isolate liberty as a trait of British national identity, it was mobilized by the largely Whiggish inhabitants of the thirteen colonies in contexts that were welcomed by such prominent Whigs as Edmund Burke and Charles James Fox. In his famous speeches on the American Revolution, Burke found himself in the curious position of arguing that the dismemberment of the British Empire was necessary to secure the very principles that define Whig imperatives for commercial expansion. The contradictions posed by this analysis are important because they point to a tension not only within the fusion of liberty and property but also in the commercial objectives of the state. And these contradictions open onto important instabilities in British identity. Dror Wahrman, Kathleen Wilson, Eliga Gould, J. G. A. Pocock, and others have offered detailed accounts of how the American Revolution forced Britons to distinguish themselves as somehow different from a constituency that seemed utterly British in origin and manners.[6] In addition to a recalibration of the relationship between the "sovereign monarchy" and the "extensive monarchy," the necessity of self-definition exerted intense pressure on British subjectivity, and its effects suffused the everyday practices of Britons such that subtle shifts in discourse came to carry significance beyond their local context.

Because the act of self-definition was spread across a range of seemingly unconnected discourses and performances, British discussions of America in the 1770s or the 1780s provide only a partial account the transformation of governance in this period. Localizing analysis in this way would be far too simple and would ignore the degree to which the events in the American colonies altered the overall world system of imperial exchange. Furthermore, this would assume that the threat posed to British subjectivity by the American Revolution was comprehensible to Britons in the mid-1780s, and such an assumption underestimates the traumatic effects of these events. Some sense of the breakdown in comprehension can be gleaned not only from Wahrman's documentation of internal contradiction around terms such as "brothers" and "foreigners" in this literature but also from Eliga Gould's thesis regarding the silence of British commentators after 1785. If we envisage the American Revolution as a historical bifurcation, then its sheer magnitude renders it incomprehensible. For this reason, the bifurcation remains pervasive, insistently operative, but unsusceptible to direct analysis. So we have to move by indirection or as-if presentation. One such movement would travel through the violent history of the Caribbean, but for the purposes of this book we can track the emergence of a post-American British imperial identity in the complex debacles over British affairs in India. In short, I think it is rather simplistic to argue that Burke's pursuit of Warren Hastings, for example, is only about imperial guilt in one colonial locale. The crises that beset not only the representation of the colonies, but also the performance of metropolitan masculinity during the impeachment are thoroughly intertwined with the recalibration of social strata in the metropole. Such a reading isolates new valences of imperial violence that need to be thoroughly considered—for instance, what does it mean for the Whigs to be exorcizing or exploring the wound left by the American war by means of a tropological romp through Indian atrocities. One benefit, of course— if we are thinking of Britain's Atlantic empire as a traumatic subject struggling to deal with a remarkable moment of automutilation—is that India is distant both geographically and culturally. So despite the attempts of Burke, Sheridan, and Fox during the Hastings impeachment to render India and England commensurable, one could also argue that the effort, doomed to failure, provides an occasion for thinking through British identity from the far rather than the near margin.

Sheridan's and Burke's difficulties before the House of Lords are instructive for they demonstrate the degree to which the breakdown in the representation of India that haunts the impeachment is only part of the story. As Nancy Koehn has argued for the period following the Seven Years' War, "In an order characterized by ideological realignment and parliamentary instability . . . imperial governance—the means for achieving the ends of empire—thus became a touchstone for political identity."[7] At the end of the line, it is the destabilization of the subjectivity of the parliamentary orator and the ensuing deployment of sexualized figures to shore up metropolitan identity that arguably become the trial's legacy. Much of the sexualized rhetoric that played a prominent role in the prosecution of Hastings reemerged in the *Reflections on the Revolution in France* in arguably more embarrassing forms. Early reception of Burke's diatribe was marked by widespread ridicule not only of Burke's panegyric to Marie Antoinette, but also of the specious deployment of sexual assault in his narrative of events in France. The early criticism of Burke is highly reminiscent of the visual satires of Burke's and Sheridan's chivalrous relation to the Begams of Oudh, which is discussed in chapter 4.[8] However, as the Foxite position on events in France became increasingly difficult to maintain, these same tropes became powerful political devices. They achieved political effectivity because the cultural distance between Britain and France was sufficient to allow for xenophobic consolidation, but insufficient enough to allow for the underlying assertion of similitude necessary for its articulation.

This resituation of the Hastings trial also allows for a reconsideration of the function of the French Revolution in this stabilization of British identity. Burke's *Reflections on the Revolution in France* is helpful here for it is clear that much of the analysis of appropriate government that informed that book and prompted the meltdown in Whig identity had its origins in the Hastings impeachment.[9] If in the impeachment we see Burke examining what is constitutive of British government from the far side of the world, then one can argue that the *Reflections* brings the therapy a little closer to home. What changes, of course, is that Burke has a tangible history of French otherness with which to gird his emergent self and is absolved of the responsibility of having to create and specify Indian alterity. If this runs counter to conventional wisdom—that is, that the East functions as the self-consolidating other for the West—then what I am describing here is a relation to empire that is specific to the 1780s and subject to complex modulation and recalibration during the subsequent fifty years. The argument of *Orientalism* is appropriate to the nineteenth century, but even a cursory reading of the Hastings trial indicates that the alterity of India is far too vague and does not have sufficient critical mass in the cultural imaginary of metropolitan Britons to function as a consolidating agent for the traumatized British subject of the 1780s.[10]

If it sounds strange to be speaking of trauma and vulnerability at a moment when Britain remains globally dominant, then we need to reconsider a few key problems in the history of British imperial hegemony. The 1770s were characterized by cataclysmic economic and military reversals not only in the Atlantic empire but also in the Indian colonies.[11] Aside from the humiliating military losses in America, British forces acting under the direction of the East India Company, sometimes quietly and sometimes quite spectacularly, failed to quell resistance by ostensibly weaker Indian armies. These setbacks in India arguably had more impact on the assumption of supremacy that characterized British imperial fantasy than on the actual flow of power in the region. As Linda Colley and Kate Teltscher have argued, British losses at Pollilur and the spectacle in print culture of the emasculation of captive British prisoners in Mysore had a deep impact on the imperial psyche.[12] These military problems revealed a great deal about the mismanagement of both the American and Indian colonies, and India's first governor-general, Warren Hastings, would become the focus of widespread criticism of British military and commercial policy. Often military and commercial problems went hand in hand, and the sense that the military was unable to decisively put down colonial resistance was exacerbated by the growing sense that economic supremacy was also in a precarious situation. As we have seen, the collapse of numerous banks both in Britain and on the continent in 1772 was directly tied to the fraudulent manipulation of East India stock and to unresolved problems in the organization of colonial markets. With speculation rampant in the metropole, a situation emerged in which bills of credit far exceeded the actual value of goods being imported from the colonies. Into this precarious situation, the American tactic of boycotting British tea not only was a blow against the ability to extract taxation but also laid bare the mismanagement of the East India Company.[13]

The newspapers of this period are overwhelmed, as one might expect, by reports of American anticolonial activity and by ever-intensifying scrutiny of East India Company affairs. As my reading of *The Nabob* demonstrates, a third discourse accompanied these explicitly colonial matters that not only blends them together, but also goes forward to become, I would argue, one of the most important elements of the traumatic fantasies that beset imperial thought in this period. This is the extraordinary outpouring of texts critiquing aristocratic vice. At roughly the same time that the imperial economy is being readjusted to prevent a second credit crisis, middle-class Britons latched onto the twin signs of luxury and sexual dissipation as symptoms of social decay that threaten to undermine the stability of the British constitution. It is not uncommon to see letters to the editors of the daily papers in the early 1770s weave together the American threat, the Indian mismanagement, and the dissipated character of the gentry into one seamless fantasy of national, social, and economic vulnerability.[14] It is for this reason that so many discussions of the state of imperial relations either get figured in terms of gender insubordination and sexual deviance, or deploy sexuality as a means of correcting errant forms of masculinity.

When the events of the American war confirmed this fantasy of vulnerability, questions of social and cultural legislation in the colonies and in the metropole become especially pointed. But legislation needs to be considered in its broadest possible signification because we begin to see an impulse to regulate excess at almost every level of social organization and often in the same sphere of action. In other words, the attempts to regulate the East India Company are not divorced from the persistent efforts to regulate the body that Foucault isolates as the harbinger of middle-class sexual self-stylization. That these forms of bodily regulation eventually result in the racialization of class identity should not escape our notice because the seemingly disconnected tributaries of middle-class sexual identity and governmental affairs in the Asian subcontinent not only respond to the same social turbulence but also quite frequently share the same channels.

The purpose of the three chapters that make up this section is to examine the way two related sites of instability and hence anxiety—the state and the sex/gender system—found themselves entwined in the legislative attempts to deal with the East India Company in the 1780s. Unlike the American problematic, in which the demands for sovereignty operated according to principles almost indistinguishable from the British Constitution, the East India Company seemed to embody a form of sovereignty not only divergent from, but also threatening to, the careful accommodation of King-in-Parliament. As Bowen, Sen, and others have argued, the constitutional relationship between the state and the Company and its possessions was never established.[15] Koehn has demonstrated that "Adherence to the principles of the Glorious Revolution demanded that the supremacy of the legislature thus of the King-in-Parliament be upheld. . . . But metropolitan statesmen continued to argue . . . over how and to what extent that authority was to be exercised."[16] As Sen argues, this lack of clarity was a source of palpable unease: "There was in general a great deal of anxiety about what rightfully belonged to an individual and what belonged to the state. Possessions of the East India Company as the monopoly of a chartered corporation, according to some political commentators, were in essence public property and reverted to the state either in the case of a national crisis or need, or naturally with the termination of the Company's charter."[17] However, others argued that any claim on the Company's possessions amounted not only to a contravention of the laws of property but also to an incursion on the royal prerogative and thus on the Constitution. These positions were often held by the same persons at different historical moments: during his work on the Secret Committee and during the debate on the Regulating Act in 1772, Burke staunchly defended property rights, but during the debate on Fox's East India Bill in 1783 and all through the Hastings impeachment, he called for direct parliamentary regulation of Company affairs. These conflicted claims regarding the relationship between the state and the Company and its property were all tied to anxieties regarding the nature of the Company itself. And from the earliest phases of his analysis of Indian problematics in the 1770s right through the Hastings proceedings, Burke figured these anxieties in terms of gender and sexual violence:

In the year 1767, [the] administration discovered that the East India Company were guardians to a very handsome and rich lady in Hindostan. Accordingly, they set parliament in motion; and parliament, (whether from love to her person or fortune is, I believe, no problem), parliament directly became a suitor, and took the lady into its tender, fond, grasping arms, pretending all the while that it meant nothing but what was fair and honourable; that no rape or violence was intended.[18]

Burke recognized quite early in his engagement with Indian affairs that the East India Company was neither a commercial nor a governmental agency, but rather a hybrid of both. At times it behaved like a corporation operating according to mercantile imperatives, and at times it behaved like a nation-state mobilizing armies and signing territorial treaties. This hybridity had the potential to operate as a counterexample to the adequation of commerce and governance practiced by the British state. This was because the form of territorial sovereignty practiced by the East India Company was contractually based. As such, it constituted a state form that seemed to operate without the notion of landed property. In a sense, it exemplified a form of governmentality that threatened to make visible the obsolescence of the oligarchical social formations still lingering in the new imperial nation. This is why—despite its penumbra of moral justifications—Burke's critique of the East India Company was both pressing and self-interested, for it spoke directly to the fate of Whig governance. During the debates on Fox's India Bill of 1783 and during the impeachment of Warren Hastings, Burke advocated an elimination of the Company's governmental hybridity by bringing it within the orbit of the British state and the reassertion of oligarchical patriarchal order to which he had been committed since the Rockingham era. This attempt to protect an increasingly obsolete governmental mode reached its culmination in the period leading up to the Permanent Settlement, when attempts were made to refashion the contractual relations between indigenous landlords and their tenants according to British models of landed property.[19] In both cases, modes of sovereignty that were themselves in a state of transformation in the British Isles were projected outward in what amounts to a form of self-consolidating nostalgia for a Britain that was rapidly mutating into a capitalist imperial power.

That mutation was accompanied by new forms of regulation that supplemented conventional notions of sovereign juridical power. Micrological forms of social control, located primarily in emerging discourses regarding the family and the racialization of class relations, began to play a vital role in the constitution and regulation of laboring populations. What is so striking about this period in the history of Anglo-Indian affairs is that the constitutional struggles precipitated in part by the East India Company's unwieldy hybridity and in part by internal pressures on the relationship between king and Parliament found themselves put on display before a fashionable audience. Because the impeachment of Warren Hastings brought both Houses of Parliament and the cream of fashionable society under the same roof, women became witnesses and commentators on the trials of imperial sovereignty. All of the issues that preoccupied the autoethnographic practices of theatrical sociability were activated not only on the edges, but also at the center of debates on British governmentality in India. Questions of effeminacy, the decline of landed families, and the figuration of despotism as errant masculinity suddenly emerge as the substance of the Whig case against East India Company's flirtations with disturbing modes of sovereignty. It is as though the social frame that surrounded the impeachment infiltrated it to such an extent that the distinction between frame and picture, between new styles of sociability and old styles of governmental practice, began to dissolve in a fashion that revealed the overall composition of the social at this moment of regulatory transformation.

CHAPTER | *Inchbald's Indies*

THREE | Meditations on Despotism circa 1784

FOLLOWING HIS TRAVELS in the 1780s, Major John Taylor observed that "The enervation of the Sultans, from the period that they ceased to head their armies in person, and shut themselves up in the haram; the indolence, ignorance and selfish sensualities of the great officers of state; the insubordination of the Pachas; the disaffection of the Provinces . . . announce . . . the subversion of the Ottoman throne, and that the Eastern empire is soon to become the grand theatre of contention among the predominant powers of Europe."[1] At first glance, Taylor's remarks on "the enervation of the Sultans" amount to little more than a British commonplace about the sexual proclivities fostered by Eastern despotism. Taylor can simply invoke the sexual excesses of the sultan because his remarks were supported by an entire century of representations fascinated with the sexual practices of the Levant. However, the link between the sultan's "enervation" and "subversion of the Ottoman throne" should give us pause for it implies not only that a careful regulation of sexuality is fundamental to stable imperial governance but also that the body of the ruler is a viable locus for a theory of the state. Taylor is able to collapse the distance between micrological and macrological power, between the desiring body and the state, because he understands the sultan as the embodiment of absolute power. In a sense, his remarks are similar to critiques of monarchical or aristocratic excess that weave their way through the revolutionary politics of the late eighteenth century and that linger in the reformist politics of the early nineteenth century. Taylor's discussion of imperial decay strikes me as significant for its silence on the alternative to the subversion of the throne. After all, offering a coherent articulation of sexual regulation and state governance when sovereign power has been dispersed over legislative bodies and institutional formations is far more difficult than simply invoking a self-consolidating other. Taylor's patholo-gization of the Turkish other stands in lieu of a panoply of emergent prac-tices and disciplinary regimes that deploy sexuality in a fashion aimed at stabilizing British interests both at home and abroad.

Taylor's statement provides a useful entry point for examining the way in which Elizabeth Inchbald deploys India and related spaces through-out her work as part of a complex critique of late eighteenth-century British masculinity and statecraft. Unlike Taylor, however, Inchbald is less concerned with pathologizing native populations than with developing precisely those sexual deployments required for stable British governance that remain unspoken in Taylor's derogation of the sultan's sensuality. Five of Inchbald's twenty plays are either set in India or involve characters with conspicuously Indian careers.[2] "India" should perhaps be placed in quo-tation marks because key elements of these plays are modified versions of earlier representations of the Levant. This chapter examines the deploy-ment of the fantasy of despotism not only in the constitutional debate sur-rounding the death of Fox's controversial East India Bill, but also in Inch-bald's most important play from the mid-1780s, *Such Things Are.* Inchbald's career as a playwright began with an extremely complex farce entitled *The Mogul Tale; or, The Descent of the Balloon,* which used the fig-ure of the despot to meditate on deviant practices both on and off the stage. As I have already argued in the introduction, *The Mogul Tale* is a sus-tained critique of sexual deviance that parodically restages Isaac Bicker-staff's *The Sultan; or, A Peep into the Seraglio.* Inchbald's critique of the-atrical practice in this afterpiece was aimed at circumventing the "enervation" of British subjects involved not only in the colonial enter-prise but also in the complex reconstruction of the bourgeois family. And thus it targeted the very audience that consumed Bickerstaff's earlier play. However, we also saw how *The Mogul Tale* engaged with the satirical as-sault on the ill-fated Indian policy of the Fox-North coalition in 1783 and 1784, and, as we will see, the regulation of gender and sexuality that played such an important part in Inchbald's farce becomes a fundamental com-ponent of her more-developed critique of imperial governance in *Such Things Are.*

Running at roughly the same time as Inchbald's afterpiece, a rather dif-ferent farce was unfolding in the Houses of Parliament. Allegations of des-potism were leveled both at Charles James Fox for what was seen as an ex-plicit incursion on the prerogatives of the Crown and at George III for his clandestine campaign against Fox's East India Bill. A close reading of how Montesquieu's notion of despotism was deployed in the debate that ultimately killed the bill reveals a crucial ideological problem facing the British state at a time when the mercantile economy was in transition. The conflict between the mercantile bourgeoisie and the aristocracy was staged as a screen for a much more unsettling scene of domination, one that points toward the emergence of a new kind of imperial economy and ultimately of a new social order. In *Such Things Are,* I believe that Inchbald, herself an able theorist of the state, picks up on key aspects of Montesquieu's theorization of monarchy to offer a critique not only of the constitutional crisis of 1783 and 1784 but also of the proceedings against Warren Hastings. And she does so by taking key gestures first broached in *The Mogul Tale* and reorienting them once again to explore the notions of virtue, honor, and fear, which lie at the heart of Montesquieu's theorization of democracy, monarchy, and despotism, respectively. By working through the principles that ground these governmental forms, Inchbald is able to intervene in the controversy surrounding the governance of Indian affairs without appearing to be of any party.

Montesquieu's Monsters: Fox's East India Bill

The Mogul Tale was on the stage at the same time that one of the most important constitutional crises of the century was enveloping the coalition government of Charles James Fox and Lord North. Throughout 1783 Whig politicians, led by Fox and working on a template of action developed by Edmund Burke, attempted to rein in the power of the East India Company. Building on North's Regulating Act of 1773, which Burke had formerly opposed, Fox's East India Bill insinuated that the Company was teetering on bankruptcy and asked whether such an operation should be in the hands of a chartered company.[3] The bill was controversial not because anyone doubted the necessity of regularizing Company affairs but because it placed the management of the Company in the hands of a body of commissioners, all of whom would have been nominated by the coalition. The bill was immediately satirized by James Sayers as *A Transfer of East India Stock* (fig. 3.1). "The image of Fox carrying on his shoulders the great prize of East India House was a skillfully wounding accusation that he had wrested from the directors and shareholders for the enrichment instead of his own nominees."[4] The allegation was effective in part because East India Company stock was the object of such long-standing peculation and corruption. The insinuation that the ostensibly noble motives of Burke were but a cover for both his own and Fox's avarice is long-lived, and there

FIG. 3.1. James Sayers, *A Transfer of East India Stock*, 25 November 1783 *(courtesy of the Department of Prints and Drawings, The British Museum, London; BM 6271)*

are frequent references to Burke's dire financial situation, Fox's gambling debts, and Sheridan's insolvency well into the Hastings proceedings three years later.

Less sensational critics of the bill saw it not only as a Whig attempt to gain direct access to the financial power of the East India Company but also as an incursion against the sacred rights of property. Burke's eloquent speech on Fox's East India Bill and the pervasive sense that something had to be done in Leadenhall Street propelled the bill through the House with a heavy majority of 229–120.[5] When the bill went up to the Lords, however, a series of clandestine actions emanating from George III ensured its defeat. The king's dislike of Fox was widely known, and during December 1783 he and Pitt developed a scheme for breaking the coalition. In the second week of December, Pitt's cousin, Lord Temple, circulated an open letter from the king that clearly indicated that anyone who voted for the bill would be henceforth treated as George III's enemy. Such interference with the legislative process was extraordinary, even more so because the machinations operated as an open secret.

Nevertheless, on the evening of 15 December 1783, Fox was stunned when the Lords defeated the East India Bill by eight votes and the king requested the seals of office from North and Fox later that night. A contemporary report of the defeat of the bill crystallized the event in one theatrical scene:

> C. Fox was behind the throne during the whole time of the business yesterday, and seemed in great agitation. . . . I am told, that his countenance, gesture and expression upon the event were in the highest degree ludicrous from the extremity of distortion and rage, going off with an exclamation of despair, hugging G. North along with him and calling out for Sheridan—So Caliban, Stephano and Trinculo reeled off upon the disappointment of their similar project.[6]

The intertext here is William Davenant's and John Dryden's Shakespearean adaptation *The Tempest; or, The Enchanted Isle* (1667), and a brief digression on the politics of that play is illuminating.[7] Dryden's invention of a sister for Caliban named Sycorax generates a pair of incestuously coupling racial and sexual monstrosities, both of whom claim aboriginal title to the island. As Bridget Orr has argued, "Prospero's establishment of patriarchal governance [is] a reenactment of the original masculine usurpation which removes the island from the state of nature."[8] Caliban and Sycorax's threat to Prospero's civilizing patriarchal usurpation is augmented by the interference of Stephano and Trinculo, who attempt to overturn Prospero's rule by proposing marriage with the abhorrent Sycorax and by secretly scheming to geld Caliban. This parody of aristocratic marital alliance is ruthlessly ejected, but it raises a shadow economy of sexual and racial deviance that must be suppressed to ensure Prospero's rule.

From this outline of the interlocking sexual, racial, and political tropes in Dryden's adaptation, a series of observations can be made about Orde's theatricalization of politics. First, it is part and parcel of a fairly consistent figuration of Fox during this period both as a monstrous animal and as a sexual deviant. The former rhetorical gesture was grounded largely on his name, but the latter was very much based on the dissipation of Foxite society in the 1780s. Crucial to this denigration of Fox was a corresponding assault on Sheridan, as well as on the Duchess of Devonshire, which reached its highest intensity in the 1784 election.[9] Within the political milieu of the early 1780s, there is a certain logic to depicting Whig society as an incestuous milieu bent on challenging the patriarchal authority of the island's nonindigenous sovereign—that is, the Hanoverian kingship of George III. This rhetorical move in Orde's remark is key because George III emerges as the spectral Prospero whose foundational usurpation has moved the island of Great Britain from a state of nature to a civil society. So the debate over the despotism of George's actions and of the ensuing constitutional crisis is here refigured as competing forms of usurpation. The king's usurpation of Parliament, like Prospero's magic, is a clandestine affair but is legitimized on the grounds that it is favorable to the monstrosity of Whig desires. As Orde details the distortions of Fox's countenance, gesture, and expression, George III's body recedes from view in part because his presence is only ever implied. Like Prospero's magic, the king's body and the power ascribed to it operate in the realm of abstraction and thus he is preserved from precisely the set of tropes used for the despot.

Fox was not so fortunate. The printsellers were busily promulgating images of Fox in a turban, a sign that carries the double connotation of sexual dissipation and political ruthlessness typical of eighteenth-century accounts of despotism. Sayers's famous *Carlo Khan's Triumphal Entry into Leadenhall Street* of 5 December 1783 mobilized antinabob sentiment to attack the East India Bill, and this image more than any other gave the putative Whig desire for nabob status its full visual expression (fig. 3.2.).[10] To say that Fox had taken on the garb of the sultan suggested that Parliament had usurped the king and replaced monarchy with despotism. But in Whig circles, the figuration of George III as a despot was also routine. From the American war onward, George III appeared frequently in print satires wearing a turban (fig. 3.3). And following the defeat of the India Bill, Whigs were buoyed by the king's flouting of the constitution because it demonstrated what Fox and others had been saying for more than two decades: namely, that George III not only desired but also actively attempted to reverse the Glorious Revolution.[11] With Pitt now installed as prime minister, Fox and other key Whigs assailed the king as anticonstitutional and the Ministry as merely obscuring the despotism of the Crown. The representations of George III in a turban and the repeated allegations of despotic rule in early 1784 are linked to a long-standing critique of despotism and monarchical corruption that has its roots in Mon-

FIG. 3.2. James Sayers, *Carlo Khan's Triumphal Entry into Leadenhall Street*, 5 December 1783 *(courtesy of the Department of Prints and Drawings, The British Museum, London; BM 6276)*

tesquieu's *The Spirit of the Laws.* Already well known as the author of *Lettres persanes,* Montesquieu had profound influence on British thought in the decades after this masterwork of political and legal theory was first published, and its analysis of the British Constitution can be tracked both in the everyday practice of politics and in the theorization of governance.[12]

The Spirit of the Laws was mobilized by all sides in the debate over the East India Bill: Montesquieu's account of the British constitution was explicitly deployed by those wishing to kill the bill on the king's behalf, and his figuration of despotic rule underlay Whig attempts to counter the king's interference. What interests me here is that both Fox's supporters

FIG. 3.3. Anonymous, *The Patriot, George III (courtesy of the
Department of Prints and Drawings, The British Museum,
London; BM 5544)*

and supporters of the king were fighting with such similar weapons, and
that the success of the latter in part arose not only from a delegitimation
of the figural economy of despotism, but also from an enactment of one
of its chief signs. This chapter demonstrates why Montesquieu's theorization of despotism was available to opposing political camps and, with
the help of Louis Althusser's and Alain Grosrichard's readings of *The Spirit
of the Laws,* articulates how this struggle over Fox's East India Bill veils a
more widespread social upheaval that is directly connected to the fate of
mercantilism.

When Fox's East India Bill was introduced by Lord Abingdon to the
House of Lords,[13] he explicitly presented the bill as a threat to the British
Constitution and established two key tropes that were to be repeated
throughout his remarks: first, that Fox, like Cromwell, is after the king's
head and, second, that the British Constitution, as explicated by Mon-

tesquieu in chapter 11 of *The Spirit of the Laws*, established the House of Lords to prevent such a depredation. Later in the speech's peroration, Abingdon states that the nobility or the Lords have "the capacity of being the mediator between the king and the people, and of rendering justice to both, by opposing as well the encroachments of the Crown upon the liberties of the subject, as the encroachments of the subject upon the just prerogative of the crown" (136). In the terms set forth by Montesquieu, the nobility is here understood as both the social force and the political organ by which monarchy is protected, on the one hand, from its natural tendency to devolve into absolute tyranny and despotism and, on the other hand, from revolution and the despotism of the "people." According to Montesquieu, "The most natural intermediate, subordinate power is that of the nobility. In a way, the nobility is the essence of monarchy, whose fundamental maxim is: *no monarch, no nobility: no nobility, no monarch;* rather, one has a despot."[14] As we will see, how one defines the "people" is of signal import in the debate, but for the moment it is enough to understand the rhetorical function of what Althusser calls the myth of the separation of powers.

Althusser argues vigorously that the notion that the British Constitution exhibits a separation of powers is "almost completely a historical illusion."[15] According to received wisdom, Montesquieu's ideal state is composed of an executive (the king and his ministers), the legislature (the upper and lower houses), and the judiciary (the body of magistrates), each of which operates separately in its own rigorously defined sphere of action. As Althusser demonstrates, however, such a separation simply does not exist in Montesquieu's account of the British Constitution: through the power of veto, the executive encroaches on the legislature; through its right of inspection of the application of the laws, the legislature encroaches on the executive; and, finally, through its self-appointment as tribunal in cases of impeachment, for instance, the legislature encroaches on the judiciary (89). Recognizing that the separation of powers is in fact a calculated division of *pouvoirs* between determinate *puissances*—that is, the king, the nobility, and "the people"—Althusser asks "to whose advantage is the division made" (91). The answer is instructive:

> [T]he nobility gains two considerable advantages from this project: as a class, it becomes directly a political force recognized in the upper chamber; also by the clause which excludes royal power from the exercise of judgement and also by that other clause which reserves his power to the upper chamber, where the nobility is concerned, it

becomes a class whose members' prospects, social position, privileges and distinctions are guaranteed *against the undertakings of either the king or the people.* As a result, in their lives, their families and their wealth, the nobility are safe both from the king and from the people. How better to guarantee the conditions for the permanent survival of a decadent class, whose ancient prerogatives are being torn from it and disputed by history? (93)

With these remarks, Althusser both summarizes Montesquieu's desire to reconstitute the social and political power of the nobility and opens the door for an argument regarding political misrecognition. As the final question suggests, Althusser understands Montesquieu's investment in the nobility as a form of nostalgia that occludes a clear vision of what is really at stake not only in the placement of the nobility between the people and the king, but also in the historical forces that generate this accession to power. What he says about this misrecognition is, I believe, applicable to Lord Abingdon's speech with some qualifications.

After reminding us that much of the eighteenth-century discussion of monarchy imagines not only a conflict between the king and the nobility but also a supposed alliance between absolute monarchy and the bourgeoisie against the feudal lords, Althusser carefully separates the industrial bourgeoisie of the early nineteenth century from that which emerged from the mercantile economy in the early part of the eighteenth century and argues that the mercantile bourgeoisie was integrated into the feudal system:

All the economic activity which then seemed to constitute the vanguard (commerce, manufactures) was indeed concentrated on the State apparatus, subordinate to its profits and to its needs. . . . The great navigation companies were created first and foremost to bring into the country, and always more or less to the advantage of the royal administration, spices and precious metals from overseas. *In its structure the economic cycle of this period is thus orientated towards the State apparatus as its goal.* And the counterpart to this orientation is the fact that the "bourgeois" who at one moment or another give life to these economic operations have *no other economic or individual horizon than the feudal order that this State apparatus serves:* on becoming rich, the merchant does not, *with a few rare exceptions,* invest his gains in private production, but *in lands,* which he buys for their title and for an entry into the nobility; *in offices* that are functions of the administration, which he buys so as to enjoy their revenue as a kind of rent; and *in State loans,* which guarantee him large profits. The aim of the "bourgeois" enriched by trade thus consists of *directly entering the society of the nobility,* by the purchase if lands or the refurbishing of a family whose daughter he marries, or of *directly entering the State apparatus* via the gown and offices, or of *sharing in the profits of the State apparatus* via rents. This is what gives this upstart "bourgeoisie" such a peculiar situation in the feudal State: it takes its place inside the nobility more than it fights it, and with these pretensions to enter the order it seems to be fighting, it supports as much as it undermines it: the whole cycle of its economic activity and of the careers of its members thus remains inscribed *in the limits and structures of the feudal State.* (100–101)

I have cited this passage in full because it resonates so profoundly with the anxieties swirling around nabobry detailed in chapter 1. What the nabob makes visible is not the conflict between the mercantile bourgeoisie and the aristocracy but rather their inseparable integration in a state apparatus whose real constitutive "outside" is the lower orders. It is precisely this relationship that Foote dramatized in *The Nabob.* As Althusser summarizes, "the fundamental antagonism at that time did not counterpose the absolute monarchy to the feudal lords, nor the nobility to the bourgeoisie which was for the most part integrated into the regime of feudal exploitation and profited by it, but the feudal regime itself to the masses subject to its exploitation" (103). This helps to explain why Montesquieu's analysis of the three forms of government was accessible not only to those who sought to shore up the power of the aristocracy but also to those who wished to devolve more power to the emergent commercial powers. In other words, it is not cynicism but corresponding misrecognitions that allow both Lord Abingdon to cite Montesquieu against Fox and prominent Whigs to invoke Montesquieu against George III and Pitt. The anti-Foxite position presupposes the integral relation of mercantile charters with the state apparatus, and the Whig position indulges in a fantasy of aristocratic reconsolidation, which nevertheless assumes a mercantile vision of empire that is already in the process of becoming obsolete.[16]

When we turn back to the debate of 15 December 1783, what we discover is that the two ostensibly opposed positions are separated by very little indeed. Abingdon and those intimidated or bought off by the king's letter were content to cite Montesquieu and to demonize Fox as a monster worse than Cromwell, whereas the Duke of Portland, and Fox after him in the House of Commons, focused on the king's figurative despotism.[17] Abingdon's attack succinctly states that the "Bill that has for its subject-matter propositions as fatal to the just prerogative of the crown, by their adoption, as by their effects they will be found ruinous to, and subversive of, the rights, liberties, and properties of the subject: propositions as unique in themselves, as they are unmatched in the annals of our history" (136–37). With the invocation of English history, the oratory quickly capitalizes on comparisons between Cromwell and Fox in which Cromwell is held to be the more reasonable character. The characterization of Fox not only asserts his despotism but also questions his relation to the "people." Abingdon declares that Fox "does not shrink back from declaring, that he is not the king's minister, but the minister of the people; who glories in the distinction, who fortifies himself under it in the House in which he acts," and thus argues that Fox has blurred the line between the executive and the legislature (137). Hence, Abingdon can bring down the full force of Montesquieu's analysis of the separation of powers on Fox:

[T]he very ingenious and learned author of the Spirit of Laws; who, speaking of the English constitution, says "that the executive power ought to be in the hands of the monarch; because this branch of government, which has always need of expedition, is better administered by one than by many; whereas, whatever depends on the legislative power is oftentimes better regulated by many than by a single person." Again, "but if there was no monarch, and the executive power was committed to a certain number of persons selected from the legislative body, there would be an end of liberty, by reason the two powers would actually sometimes have, and would moreover be always able to have, a share in both." (140–41)

With Fox established as a threat to liberty, Abingdon can sketch in a very specific account of Fox's despotic ambition that manages to incorporate important documents in Whig policy. Pointing first to a series of minor bills introduced by the coalition to contain the king's influence and then to Burke's *Thoughts on the Cause of the Present Discontents,* Abingdon describes Whig actions as the "influence of an Aristocracy" defined as an "Oligarchical Junto in the two Houses of Parliament"; the bill becomes "a proposition to wrest the reins of government out of the hands of the executive power, and to place it in the hands of a self-created demagogue, supported by a factious and desperate cabal" (137). The gesture has political teeth because his actions point to the formation of an aristocratic elite that effectively enslaves the people in its own name. Both the people and the king are enslaved, and Fox rules by fear and fear alone.

However, if Abingdon and his allies are content to cite Montesquieu and suggest that Whig incursions on the prerogative have paved the way for a despotism of the "people" with Fox as its fearsome face, Fox's allies in the House of Lords countered with a strategy equally indebted to *The Spirit of the Laws*. Fox's chief ally in the Lords was the Duke of Portland, and his intervention in the debate counters the incessant citation of Montesquieu by mobilizing one of Montesquieu's fundamental tropes for characterizing the despot. Portland was extremely disconcerted by the rumors that Lord Temple was circulating a threatening letter in George III's name. As Amanda Foreman notes, a letter between Lord Frederick Cavendish and the Duchess of Devonshire indicates that Portland "confronted the king in his closet about rumours of a conspiracy" and that the king "fixed his glassy stare on him and ignored the question."[18] According to Grosrichard, the gaze and the letter are "the two key terms, the two driving elements, of [Montesquieu's figuration of] despotic power in the Orient. . . . the gaze and the letter, and the intertwining of imaginary and symbolic registers which maintain their interplay, assume a paradigmatic value in this world of silence and transparency."[19] The combination of the king's glassy stare and the letter appears to fulfill all the phantasmatic dimensions of the despotic scenario, and Portland chooses to mobilize them to full effect when he rises in the House of Lords. But Portland's strategy is hobbled by two key problems: George's despotic gaze is confined to the closet, and the letter does not operate openly but rather in the form of an open secret. Confined to the shadows, they do not figure themselves forth as evidence of despotic rule, for, as Grosrichard emphasizes, it is the public enactment of these signifiers that instantiates the fear that is despotism's activating principle.

The lengthy divagations that Portland must employ to establish George's despotism end up concealing it in the realm of rumor:

> [H]e begged their lordships most serious attention, since it materially concerned the constitution of the country. A rumour had prevailed for the last three days, that had given him very great alarm indeed. . . . Among other arts, rumours of different kinds had been circulated with the most sedulous industry; and among others, one of a very extraordinary nature indeed. In that rumour, the name of the most sacred character in the kingdom had been aspersed, and the name of one of their lordships, he hoped, abused; but certainly

such was the complexion of the rumour, that he should be wanting in regard to his own character, wanting in that love and zeal for the constitution, which, he trusted, had ever distinguished his political life; wanting in the duty he owed to the public as a minister, if he did not take an opportunity, if it turned out to be true, of proposing a measure upon it to their lordships, that would prove they felt the same jealousy, the same detestation, and the same desire to mark and stigmatize every attempt to violate the constitution as he did. (152)

Portland pretends to speak on behalf of the king's good name by threatening to propose a motion condemning the rumor of the king and Lord Temple's machinations, which he knows to be true. So in response to Abingdon, he does not charge the king with an unconstitutional incursion on the rights of the legislature, but rather calls the Lords to condemn the rumor, knowing full well that such a condemnation would bring the letter into the public and thus establish the king's despotic actions, and construct the Whigs as protectors of the Constitution from the actions of a particular king. This latter move effectively takes up Abingdon's call for the nobility to "oppose the encroachments of the crown upon the liberties of the subject" without threatening the notion of the monarchy itself. This is crucial because, as we have seen, the king's supporters explicitly argue that the Whigs are attempting to form an "Oligarchical Junto" or what Montesquieu would euphemistically describe as an aristocratic democracy. Portland therefore must fight two battles at once: he must materialize the rumor and, in so doing, demonstrate that the Whigs are protecting the Constitution from George III's absolutism.

However, Portland's strategy is countered by a remarkable moment of performance. The Duke of Richmond, a supporter of the king, immediately stands and obviates Portland's proposed motion by presenting a surrogate text—a text that specifies what is in the letter and yet conceals its materiality. After attacking Portland for vagueness, Richmond pulls out his prop: "A newspaper, which he had in his pocket, his grace said, contained as indecent and as scandalous a paragraph as ever he had met with; perhaps the noble duke alluded to the facts there stated. He would read it to the House. His grace then read the following article from an evening paper of Saturday" (152–53). The article repeats Portland's suggestion that the rumor is libelous but lays out the contents of the letter in detail, specifying not only the king's intimidation but also Lord Temple's involvement.[20] Richmond, who explicitly declares his opposition to the bill later in the discussion, performs an act of inoculation here, because, although the details of the conspiracy are introduced, they are now part and parcel of commercial print culture and can be dismissed as mere scandal-mongering for profit. His closing remarks are telling: "He would acquaint his grace [Portland], if he did not already know it, who was the author of these rumours; it was some hireling fellow, equally undeserving of his grace's patronage and their lordships' notice" (153–54). The double edge here is especially biting because it not only suggests that the rumor is nothing but scandal and hence immaterial, but also insinuates that the "hireling" is operating under Whig patronage unbeknownst to Portland. So the letter, initially introduced as a sign of the king's despotic actions, is turned around into evidence of Foxite despotism. By mobilizing the letter, Portland and the Foxite "hireling" are attempting to execute the king. In short, what started as a figural attack on behalf of the Whigs returns to bite Fox.

This reversal highlights a fundamental impediment to Foxite attempts to figure George III as a despot. As Althusser suggested about the nobility in Montesquieu's analysis of the English Constitution, the Whigs are fighting, this time in the name of the people, for the same ground as the king's supporters. Both the Whigs and the supporters of the king work to consolidate the integrated economic and social power of the aristocracy and the mercantile bourgeoisie. In a sense, the allegations that the India Bill would concentrate the economic power of the East India Company in the hands of Whigs simply states what the bill makes explicit: namely, that the health of the "Oligarchical Junto" depends on a specific form of class integration in which the mercantile bourgeoisie is willing to aspire to the condition of the aristocracy. The bill, while offering itself as a corrective to Company mismanagement, can also be read as a defensive measure against the future supersession of the influence of landed power by the industrial bourgeoisie. What terrifies the supporters of the king is that Fox may choose to act in a fashion that favors "connexion" over rank. So we are dealing with competing fears and a choice between despotic regimes: one threatened and surreptitiously enacted by the king's letter, and one threatened and frankly enacted by the bill itself. In this light, the very materiality of the bill, as opposed to the immateriality of the king's letter, tips the scale against Fox. This is why citation is such a vital strategy for Abingdon: by citing Burke's *Thoughts on the Cause of the Present Discontents*, he can hide the actions of what amounted to a lettre de cachet from the king, by parading a "letter" of Whig despotism. As evidence we need only look at how the bill is described during debate. Abingdon refers to it as "ambitious" and "violent" and suggests that it "seizes upon charters by force and violence" (137, 142). The Whig attempt to depict George III as a despot is effectively trumped by a citational strategy that ultimately understands the figural economy of Montesquieu's account of despotism to the letter, for it is not the substance of the despot's letter that matters but rather the fact of its material existence.

The sad fate of the Whigs following the defeat of the bill is instructive, because it indicates both a strategic blindness and a historical misrecognition. Fox extended the figural assault on George's alleged despotism but slowly lost his majority. Fox apparently welcomed the loss of the bill because it seemed to confirm the presence of the king's letter, and he strove in the weeks following the loss to initiate an inquiry into the material effect of the letter. However, from the outset Fox's handling of Lord Temple's role in the dissemination of the king's threat moved in a slightly different direction. After rehearsing the story of the letter and the threat such an action poses to the Constitution, he attacked the secrecy of the letter head on:

> [H]e took notice of the effect the rumours had produced, and declared, that if such an alarming instance was to prevail, it was not only more dangerous than any other, but that no one could venture to take the government of the country upon him. A Minister might be found bold and spirited enough, to look at the real condition of it, and adopt such measures as would effectually relieve it, but if after all his trouble, after his personal risque, the risque of his situation, and of his character, after he had got it through the House, the measure was to be *whispered away* by the prevalence of secret influence, by back stairs Statesman, by men who stole upon the private hour of the Prince, and came, like thieves, who rob in the night, to pilfer and poison, who would undertake the task of government, or stand the hazard of such a situation.[21]

With the specter of secret influence in his audience's mind, Fox embellishes the despotic scenario in what I believe is a symptomatic fashion. As his speech unfolds, he refigures Temple, Pitt, and other supporters of the king both as future victims of the despot and as potential usurpers:

> Mr. Fox very naturally expatiated on the conduct of the Lords of the Bedchamber, and talked of the miserable situation of a Minister who held his place at their volition; he said it brought to mind a saying of the late Mr. George Grenville [that] . . . "he never would again take

the command, while a band of Janissaries, like the Pretorian band of old, surrounded the person of the Prince, and were ready to strangle him on the order of a moment."[22]

The scenario is a familiar one from Montesquieu. The Oriental despot surrounded by his janissaries is able to execute his capricious will with lightning speed. And no one feels this as forcefully as his prime minister or vizier. One of the primary features of despotism according to Montesquieu is the elevation of any subject to the office of grand vizier. But the elevation comes at a cost for the vizier, for he

> is torn by a dilemma which seems irresolvable, since he is compelled both to be reckoned with and to obliterate himself, to be and not be the despot, to exercise all power alone and to exercise none. . . . This is an impossible situation, one which ought to discourage all ambition. But this is not so: "This office is a very hard one, and a Grand Vizier has very little time of his own, yet all aspire to this office with great fervour, although they know almost for certain that within a short time they will die."[23]

Fox quotes Grenville not only to emphasize that he will be no one's vizier, but also to critique Pitt as one who will happily obliterate himself in order to channel the power of the king. For Fox that way is full of danger because it renders the state vulnerable to internecine strife in the royal household. Fox's utterance is extremely subtle on this point, because it is quite unclear who is going to be strangled in the final sentence. One reading suggests that the minister of such a prince lives in perpetual fear of execution by the janissaries, but the reverse is also true: the prince himself may become the victim of his own guards if they prove to be more loyal to the minister.

In a sense this reciprocal relation between vizier and despot most terrifies Montesquieu and, by extension, Fox. Despotic states are not prone to civil war but rather to serial assassinations. Montesquieu's analysis of despotism is staged to teach two primary lessons aimed at preserving the social and political power of the nobility. First, because the despot needs to clear the field of all great personages, the nobility has the most to fear from this form of government. Second, the obliteration of the nobility "is the sure road to popular revolutions" because the violent passions of the people will eventually destroy those who pretend to absolute tyranny.[24] So what emerges in Fox's speech is a subtle suggestion that Pitt's willingness to serve George III is based on a misrecognition where Pitt both is and is not the despot. The undecidability of this phantasmatic identification is for Fox inherently dangerous and constitutive of despotism itself. Already working in opposition, Fox has sized up Pitt as one who derives pleasure from masquerading as the king, and Fox's fear—which perhaps arises from his own ambition—is that Pitt will one day figuratively execute the monarch in a fashion that excludes those whom Fox represents.

Despite the subtlety of Fox's deployment of the tropes of despotic power, however, it is not that distinct from Abingdon's use of citations from Montesquieu against him. And perhaps this is the most salient issue emerging from the constitutional crisis ensuing from the defeat of the India Bill: namely, that the monarchy was already in a state of corruption and that the real political struggle of the day was a household struggle regarding the relationship between the vizier and the nobility. It is possible to narrate the events up to and following the bill's defeat in a fashion that is entirely in keeping with Montesquieu's fantasy of the despotic state. On the one hand, Fox acted in connection with a portion of the nobility (here understood as the body of landed gentry and mercantile subjects bound together by the bonds of Whig principles) in a fashion that sought to counter George III's absolutist tendencies. In so doing, Fox refused to operate as the king's vizier, and hence he was effectively assassinated by the king's "guards." The execution was so effective that the Whigs never again came into power. On the other hand, there was Pitt, conspiring with the king to "execute" Fox and establish himself as the new vizier. But it would be naive to suggest that this is any less of a resistance to the king. Only through his ascension to ministerial status can Pitt partake in the king's absolute power and channel it for his own ends. One has to become notable in the janissaries' field of vision to eventually turn them on the king.

The paradox here is captured by Grosrichard because both positions accept that ministerial authority partakes of a figurative death: "[I]n the despotic State, either one lives and counts for nothing, or one counts, but on the condition of giving one's life. In these terms, freely offering his head to the despot when he demands it is not the vizier's failure. It is his triumph."[25] This paradox sheds light on why the Whigs initially exulted in their defeat but then found themselves in perpetual opposition. The loss of the bill and the death of Fox's Ministry confirmed the king's despotism, but the Whigs overestimated the advantage to be derived from this recognition because they failed to realize that the connections that ensured their parliamentary majority depended on the life conferred by the king's gaze. With Fox dead in the eyes of the despot, parliamentarians slowly drifted over to the new vizier because he was politically alive.

As a heuristic device, this fable helps us to understand two crucial issues that would haunt the Whigs for the next decade. The first is the question of the "people" and their role in the Whig schism in the early 1790s. Acting as a good vizier must to keep his head, Pitt ruthlessly ensured that Fox could not reengage the notion of a noble resistance to George's absolutism by acting in the interests not only of the king but also of those who would otherwise make up Fox's real constituency. This meant that Fox's phantasmatic constituency, the "people," slowly transformed from the propertied and mercantile interests of Whig society to the very commercial orders that Whiggism had putatively adopted but resisted throughout the 1760s and 1770s. This transformation hollowed out the party from within, until the French Revolution brought the party's self-definition into crisis. In this light, Fox's early support for the French Constitution becomes a testimony to his desperate desire to resuscitate himself, which paradoxically has its roots in a nostalgia for Whig oligarchy but which operates through a misrecognition of Whig principles that ultimately separates him from his past.

Such is Burke's point both in the *Reflections on the Revolution in France* and in the *Appeal from the New to the Old Whigs* when he breaks into his famous panegyric to none other than Montesquieu.[26] What we see when Burke crosses the House and takes up against the concept of the "people," as it is mobilized not only by Paine but also by Fox in the early 1790s, is a more consistent response to the same nostalgic desire. What has happened is that Pitt has effectively separated the notion of the "connections" between mercantile and landed interests that formerly defined Whiggism from specific individuals and adopted it as his own base for resisting both the "people" and the king. Burke can cross the House because Pitt's party is not that different from the Whig oligarchy as it defined itself prior to the defeat of Fox's India Bill. This reading of Whig disintegration through Montesquieu clarifies the vexed question of Burke's apostasy, for it indicates that Burke does not move from left to right but rather that left and right transform into one another. It is the dead man, Fox, who, forced by the hand of the despot, diverges from his political roots and finds himself ultimately with the common people. This, of course, implies that Fox shifts from one who played with and deployed Montesquieu's phantasmatic scenario of despotism to one who was able to see what Althusser describes as its real objectives: namely, the preservation of the political power of the affiliated interests of the mercantile bourgeoisie and the landed gentry against the twofold threat of the emergent industrial bourgeoisie and the ever present mass of exploited laborers.[27]

A second issue that the fable clarifies is the Whigs' obsession with Hastings and the place of India in their slow march into political oblivion (see chapters 4 and 5). If we understand the defeat of the India Bill as precipitating the death of Fox and, by extension, his party, then the relentless pursuit of Hastings, especially by Burke, can be understood profitably as an act of mourning, one that predicts the death of Whiggism. Everything Burke mobilizes against Hastings not only attempts to reverse Fox's assassination but also works through the death of his own view of party in *Thoughts upon the Cause of the Present Discontents* that was effectively killed by Abingdon on the night of 15 December 1783. This negotiation with dead versions of their former selves is locked in political language whose parameters are defined by Montesquieu's *Spirit of the Laws*[28] and gets irresolvably intertwined with Hastings's depredations. The performances of Burke, Fox, and Sheridan reveal their attempt not only to indict Hastings but also, literally, to give life to the statesman's body. This hoped-for resurrection shows why the trial's theatricality was of such vital concern.

The Spirit of the Laws: Such Things Are

Elizabeth Inchbald's *Such Things Are* was most likely written in the middle of 1786 and opened on 10 February 1787, three days prior to the opening of the impeachment proceedings against Warren Hastings. Because the rhetoric of despotism played such a prominent role in the Whig analysis of the East India Company, Inchbald engages with the Hastings problematic by focusing on the constitutional crisis generated by Fox's East India Bill in 1783 and 1784. Her meditation on despotism has developed from her initial intervention in *The Mogul Tale* to a complex analysis of the political theory, which everywhere animated the rhetoric of despotism during the constitutional crisis. Inchbald decides to approach the problem of despotism neither through its figuration in Montesquieu nor through citation of *The Spirit of the Laws*, but rather through the principles that distinguish governance.

The fundamental innovation of Montesquieu's theorization of the forms of government lies in the totality of the nature and the principle of action of each discrete form: "There is this difference between the nature of the government and its principle: its nature is that which makes it what it is, and its principle, that which makes it act. The one is its particular structure, and the other is the human passions that set it in motion" (21). In Montesquieu's famous tripartite division, democracy depends on virtue, monarchy on honor, and despotism on fear. Althusser argues that the relationship between nature and principle in each form of government is put to the test when governments are corrupted. Book 8 of *The Spirit of the Laws* opens with the contention that "The Corruption of each government generally begins with that of the principles," and Althusser's gloss offers a helpful starting point for a discussion of *Such Things Are*:

> Corruption . . . constitutes a sort of experimental situation which makes it possible to penetrate the indivisible nature-principle unity and decide *which is the decisive element of the opposition.* The result is that it is definitely the principle that governs the nature and gives it its meaning. "When once the principles of government are corrupted, the very best laws become bad, and turn against the state: but, when the principles are sound, even bad laws have the same effect as good."[29] . . . Thus it really is the principle which is, in the last resort, the cause of the development of forms and their meanings. (52–53)

Montesquieu says this explicitly in the clause following the one cited by Althusser for he states unequivocally that "the force of the principle pulls everything along" (119). This means that laws and constitutions not only cannot protect the state but actually can contribute to its downfall in times of corruption. Principles ultimately protect the state and its inhabitants. Thus, all the wrangling over the constitutionality of Fox's East India Bill or of the king's response is beside the point if the principles of government are corrupted. In the particular case of George III's monarchy, if the principle of honor has been corrupted, then constitutional arguments are actually part and parcel of the devolution of the monarchy into a state of despotism. Inchbald mobilizes this recognition in her sentimental comedy, but to understand the depth of her analysis, we need to clarify what precisely Montesquieu means by principle.

Montesquieu's signal innovation in political theory is his conviction that the nature of government is not purely formal. As Althusser succinctly summarizes,

> The *principle* takes us into life. For a government is not a pure form. It is the concrete form of existence of a society of men. For the men

subject to a particular type of government to be precisely and lastingly subject to it, the mere imposition of a political form (*nature*) is not enough, they must also have a disposition to that form, a certain way of acting and reacting which will underpin that form. As Montesquieu puts it, there has to be a specific *passion*. Each form of government necessarily desires its own passion. (45)

A theorist of government has to be as finely attuned to the social interactions of a particular constituency as he or she is to the history of its laws. Again Althusser's analysis provides the formulation necessary for understanding the opening Inchbald finds for a theatrical theorization of government:

> Considered not from the viewpoint of the *form* of the government, i.e. of its political exigencies, but from the viewpoint of its *content,* i.e. of its origins, *the principle is really the political expression of the concrete behaviour of men,* i.e. of their manners and morals, and spirit. Of course, Montesquieu, does not say in so many words that the manners and morals or spirit of a nation constitute the very essence of the *principle* of its government. But he does set out from principles as the pure forms of government: their truth appears in their corruption. When the *principle* is lost, it is clear that *manners and morals effectively take the place of principle:* they are its loss or salvation. (56)

In a time of political corruption, when monarchy has devolved into despotism, the playwright, not the politician, finds herself in an auspicious situation, for she is the arbiter of manners and morals, and thus of the spirit of the nation. In this light, sentimental comedy, Inchbald's preferred mode of composition proves to be generically appropriate to such a calling, for it turns on the representation of manners and the correction of morals. We have already seen Inchbald's willingness to accede to the regulation of concrete social relations through theatrical representation in *The Mogul Tale.* However, her ambitious comedy *Such Things Are* builds on the strategies of the earlier farce to provide a critique not only of private desires but also of the desires that drive the state. Montesquieu's analysis opens the door for Inchbald to collapse both levels of desire into a totalizing critique of a political culture that is caught in the thrall of its own nostalgia for a type of society and a type of empire that is rapidly becoming obsolete.

Inchbald strategically sets the play on the "island of Sumatra, in the East

Indies." At the time of the play's production, the East India Company was extending its influence in the island, but very little was known of Sumatra in the metropole.[30] It is in a sense terra incognita for London audiences and thus can act as a laboratory of sorts for staging governance. Its status as an island is important, because, like Robinson Crusoe's island, Sumatra is a symbol for Britain itself. However, the island never fully figures for Britain; rather it functions as a heuristic scenario for examining specific matters of principle that are clearly applicable to Britain on the eve of the Hastings trial. It is the burden of the first two acts to establish the spirit of the nation of Sumatra.

Inchbald's portrait of British society in the East Indies is scathing. Act 1 opens in a parlor at Sir Luke Tremor's, with Sir Luke and Lady Tremor trading insults. They are both social climbers and are attacked in a manner that is by now well worn. Sir Luke describes his wife as a woman without character who at the time of their marriage was "without one qualification except [her] youth—and not being a Mullatto."[31] The indication of her whiteness is important, for despite her lack of education and her faults, she represents a certain kind of colonial English identity that is not beyond repair. In this regard, Inchbald's satire on British subjects in the East Indies is not reduced to simple antinabob sentiment. Sir Luke, we discover, is both an idler and a coward, but he is cognizant that his social milieu is corrupted by despotic rule. As his name suggests, he is the embodiment of despotism's key effect: fear has beaten down his courage and extinguished even the slightest feeling of ambition.[32]

Fear infuses all of the play's social relations. The Sultan rules by fear, and Sumatra is itself an extensive prison.[33] But despite the ubiquity of terror in the play, all is not as it seems. The Sultan, for instance, turns out to be a surrogate sultan and a closet Christian. His Christianity arises from his love for the Christian Arabella, who was "sent in her youth by her mercenary parents, to sell herself to the prince of all these territories. But 'twas my happy lot, in humble life, to win her love, snatch her from his expecting arms and bear her far away" (40). During a rebellion against the "true" prince, the sultan-to-be takes the side of the rebels in part because such a position pits him against the very figure who would subjugate his lover in the harem. In the midst of the battle, the "young aspirer" is killed and the sultan-to-be is pressed to stand in for him because he "bore his likeness." He takes to the role because he believes that the "true" prince has abducted and murdered Arabella. In a remarkable speech, the Sultan reveals that his political character is defined by his erotic loss: "Frantic for her loss, I joyfully embraced a scheme which promised vengeance on the enemy—it prospered,—I revenged my wrongs and her's, with such un-sparing justice on the foe, that even the men who made me what I was, trembled to reveal their imposition; and they find it still their interest to continue it" (40). The Sultan therefore rules by fear, but he does so in the name of resistance to the erotic desires of the former prince. In fact, all of his actions prior to and following the rebellion show him to be acting against the imputed sexual slavery of the harem, in favor, first, of monog-amous seclusion and, second, of his nostalgia for his lost conjugal bliss.

As in *The Mogul Tale*, Inchbald presents her audience with a despot, but one who is disconnected from its conventional sexual tropes. Never-theless, the Sultan's interlocutor, Mr. Haswell, who figures explicitly for the prison reformer John Howard, still regards him as mentally diseased and sets himself up as the Sultan's potential physician. This gesture places strict limitations on the Sultan's despotism. His rule is corrupted not by the sexual deviance of Oriental polygamy but rather by an excessive man-ifestation of monogamous love for Arabella. And this excess exists in spite of his Christianity: what Haswell recognizes is that the Sultan's Christian-ity arises from his desire for Arabella and not from any adherence to the principles of Christian virtue. Haswell's task therefore is to rein in that ex-cess and demonstrate that excessive desire even for one lover makes one blind to the love of others. As Haswell explains in the final scene when the Sultan and Arabella are reunited: "Dread her look—her frown—not for herself alone, but for hundreds of her fellow sufferers—and while your selfish fancy was searching, with wild anxiety, for her *you* loved, unpity-ing, you forgot others might love like you"(66). By tightly knotting the Sultan's practice as a ruler to the errant assumptions of his erotic desire, Inchbald effectively collapses the public and private dimensions of his character. This implies that the correction of his private excesses will al-ter the nature of his government and, by extension, the social relations of all who are subject to it.

This rectification of despotic rule via the inculcation of private restraint is further elucidated by Inchbald's other primary intervention in the fig-ural economy of despotism. The Sultan's rule is defined not, as Gros-richard's analysis of Montesquieu would suggest, by the combined power of the letter and the gaze, but rather by blindness. The Sultan's gaze is lit-erally occluded by the apparatus of his power, for he holds Arabella in prison for fourteen years because he cannot see her. The very darkness of the prisons that represent the extent of his tyranny conceals the sup-posedly lost object of his affections. And his decrees are unable to bring her into the light because his very ability to issue decrees is founded on her absence. This is Inchbald's key recognition: that the loss of Arabella, of the object of desire, is a constitutive misrecognition. All of the Sultan's violence arises from his distorted attempts to regain something that he thought was killed by his sexual and political rival. At the heart of his tyranny lies a homosocial conflict regarding the proper exchange of women. As an enemy of the imputed prostitution of the harem, the Sultan is on the side of sexual normativity, but his attempts to reconstitute his former monogamous relationship are so immured in a combination of nostalgia and vengeance that they make him blind to the present: a present in which his lover exists just beyond his field of vision. As a political device, his gaze is fearsome because it sees all but one thing.

Inchbald's analysis here of despotic rule in Sumatra amounts to a rigorous critique of the homosocial rivalry that drives not only British masculine self-stylization but also the day-to-day flow of British politics. Just as the homosocial conflicts in Parliament seem disconnected from everyday life, the Sultan's pathological desires appear to be separate from the rest of the play; however, as Montesquieu would suggest, the fact of their existence inflects all the characters' manners and morals. The Sultan, although only intermittently seen in the play, is in fact ubiquitous. And his adverse effect on Sumatran society is intimately tied to forgetfulness: "A corrosive, self-deceiving and treacherous amnesia pervades both public and private life. The Sultan's tragic acts of forgetting—his failure to remember, as Haswell explains, that others might love like you (5.3)—is represented as a primary cause of the contagious misery which characterizes this inhuman state."[34] Throughout the play, the repression of past materials generates symptoms of a social pathology. In the case of the Sultan, unresolved homosocial rivalry generates a form of excessive desire, which has led him to take on the violent character, if not the sexual proclivities, of the former prince.

The Tremors, like the Sultan, seek to exist in a perpetual present, which is in fact defined by an excessive investment in the past. For example, Sir Luke's desertion of his regiment in the midst of battle deforms his character such that he not only feels threatened by Twineall's mistaken praise of his military accomplishments but also moves to seek vengeance against him. Sir Luke's unresolved cowardice has developed into a species of deviant gender identity that impinges on his national character. His inability to accede to the role of soldier has rendered him an impotent husband and a servile colonial subject. Similarly, Lady Tremor's concealment of her low rank has developed into a complementary form of nonnormative sexual identity, for she seems always on the verge of entering into an adulterous relationship with the treacherous Lord Flint. In the manuscript version of the play, this proclivity carries a further insinuation of national insubordination: Lord Flint was originally a French ambassador named Count Misprision who attempts to seduce English women. As Sir Luke states, "he was sent hither from Tripoli to settle a treaty of Commerce with our Court—instead of which—he is trying to carry on an illicit one with every Englishman's Wife in the Island."[35] Lady Tremor responds that the count's attempts at seduction would fall on deaf ears if the husbands paid proper duty to their wives.

The manuscript confirms that the insistence of repressed past materials has generated symptomatic forms of sexual and political deviance in these characters. It should come as no surprise that the correction of the Sultan through his reconciliation with Arabella is immediately followed not only by Sir Luke and Lady Tremor's repentance for their persecution of Twineall but also by a public disclosure of their respective secrets. In keeping with Inchbald's deployment of sexual symptoms to mark social decay, the play closes with a resuscitation of the Tremor's marriage and the all-important inauguration of a new marriage between Elvirus and the Tremor's daughter Aurelia. Within the figural economy of social health that thoroughly imbues this portion of the play, it is as though the cure of one marriage guarantees the reproduction of marriage itself as a bulwark against the devolution of society into a state of despotic terror.

However, if this hygienic impulse takes up much of the play's latter acts, it is clear that Inchbald is just as concerned with a careful delineation of the governmental problems posed by figures such as Lord Flint and Twineall. Lord Flint is the play's self-appointed vizier and the development of his character from manuscript, to submission text for the chamberlain, to the printed text is extremely revealing. As noted earlier, Lord Flint starts off as a French seducer in the manuscript version, but by the time the play is submitted to Larpent he has become an Englishman perverted by his contact with despotic rule. As Sir Luke states, Lord Flint was "Sent from his own country in his very infancy, and brought up in the different courts of petty, arbitrary Princes here in Asia; he is the slave of every great man, and the tyrant of every poor one" (3–4). Flint's forgetfulness only superficially mimics the Sultan's forgetfulness, for there does not appear to be a constitutive loss at the heart of his inability to remember: forgetfulness is simply a political device. As Sir Luke emphasizes, Lord Flint forgets nothing, but he pretends to forget the everyday in order to render himself inscrutable. The following passage reconstitutes in italics the material deleted from the Larpent text:

SIR LUKE: . . . do you suppose he is as forgetful as he pretends to be? no, no— but because he is a favourite with the Sultan, and all our great men at court, he thinks it genteel or convenient to have no memory—and yet I'll answer for it, he has one of the best in the universe, *and is the most circumspect and careful in all his dealings of any man living, yet he is perpetually making blunders—presuming to be absent, and to remember nothing at all, and his character he supports so well, that some of his friends are weak enough to pity him for it, as a constitutional defect, while it is merely the result of art.*

LADY: I don't believe your charge—*all his mistakes and forgetfulness, I am sure are the effects of Nature.* (3)

The distinction between constitutional and natural defects is the setup for a much more biting satirical move, which incorporates Lord Flint's political artifice with his sexual deviance. After listening to Sir Luke rant about how Lord Flint never makes a mistake to his own disadvantage, Lady Tremor counters with an account of their shared experience of his sexual indiscretions, for he has clearly made passes at Lady Tremor in front of Sir Luke:

LADY: *I have known him forget himself so far, as to pay his addresses to a Lady even before her own husband—I have known him forget himself so far, as to make such promises.—*

SIR LUKE: *Of which, when he was reminded, he'd forget himself so far, as not to be able to recollect a word he had said.*

LADY: *And that's all very natural to some constitutions.—*

SIR LUKE: *It may be natural in a political constitution, but never in a civil one.*[36]

Inchbald's double play on the words *constitution* and *civil* indicate that more is at stake here than Lord Flint's servile adherence to the Sultan. The suggestion is that Lord Flint's behavior arises out of a constitutional defect understood in both political and bodily terms.

Somewhat later in the scene, Sir Luke summarizes his allegations against Lord Flint by suggesting in a fleeting aside that he does "no great honour" in mentioning his name (5). But Lord Flint, while certainly without virtue, is in Montesquieu's terms a man of honor. Early in *The Spirit of the Laws*, Montesquieu argues that virtue is an unnecessary attribute in a monarchy:

Ambition in idleness, meanness in arrogance, the desire to enrich oneself without work, aversion to truth, flattery, treachery, perfidy, the abandonment of all one's engagements, the scorn of the duties of citizens, the fear of the prince's virtue, the expectation of his weaknesses, and more than all that, the perpetual ridicule cast upon virtue, these form, I believe, the character of the greater number of courtiers, as observed in all places and at all times. (25–26)

The catalog of traits here reads like the dramatis personae of Inchbald's play, suggesting that the despotic state of Sumatra may well be a monarchy in a state of corruption. Sir Luke's account of Lord Flint's self-interest resonates with Montesquieu's presentation of monarchy, for it is the nobles' selfish preservation of their own interests that paradoxically ensures the moderation of the state. In Montesquieu, honor is the passion of the nobility and enables the nobles to act as a check on the absolutist tendencies both of the king and the people. Paradoxically, Lord Flint is in Montesquieu's terms constitutionally necessary to the health of a monarchy; however, in a corrupted state his very constitutionality works against the state. He is not only the Sultan's minion; he actually maintains and furthers the corruption of Sumatra. Inchbald emphasizes this in a brilliant leveling gesture that appears in the Larpent text but not in the print version of the play. As we will see in the next chapter, Sir Luke's allegations against Lord Flint culminate in an indictment of colonial rule that is not that distant from Burke's indictment of Warren Hastings:

SIR LUKE: . . . you know how all this fine country is harassed and laid waste by a set of Princes, Sultans, *Nabobs, Vice-Roys, Governors*—and I know not what—who are for ever calling out to each other "that's mine," and "that's mine;"—and "you have no business here"—and "you have no business there"—and "I have business every where;" [*Strutting*] then "give me this,"—and "give me that;" and "take this, and take that." [*Makes signs of fighting*] (4)

Flint may be necessary to some political constitutions, but he is alien to what Sir Luke calls a civil constitution. If one reads only the political implications of this joke, this implies that civility and monarchy, whether degraded or moderate, are mutually exclusive. But if one also factors in the concept that marriage is a civil union, it also implies that Lord Flint's openly adulterous and predatory overtures are similarly uncivil. What links the two forms of incivility is their frequent deployment in bourgeois critiques of the aristocracy. Taken together, Inchbald is taking a withering glance at the place of the aristocracy in the government of the state and in the deployment of sexuality that ultimately points toward the necessity of a form democratic governance that is regulated from top to bottom by the introduction of forms of normative sexual and class relations.

It may be that the material presented here from the Larpent text that was excised prior to the printing of the play was simply too inflammatory for publication. But her presentation of Lord Flint carefully separates her from a range of factions fighting over the impeachment of Warren Hastings. The collocation of sultans, nabobs, and governors indicates that she shares some of Burke's analysis of Hastings's accession to "arbitrary power," but her indictment of Lord Flint's character separates her both from Whig nostalgia and from the servility evidenced by those who engineered the defeat of Fox's East India Bill. As a supplement to Betsy Bolton's suggestion that Lord Flint represents Lord Chesterfield, I would argue that he is just as persuasively a symbol for Lord Temple or even for Pitt himself.[37] As evidence we need only remember that he operates in a clandestine fashion as the Sultan's vizier and exercises his power by carrying around letters that declare characters such as Twineall to be enemies of the Sultan.

If we understand Lord Flint to be the embodiment of aristocratic and monarchical corruption, then Twineall's function in the play becomes more palpable. Twineall, like Lord Flint, is well suited to both monarchical and despotic government, for he is a flatterer who works continually for his own advancement. This perhaps explains why the play's most violent conflict is staged between them, because Lord Flint recognizes that Twineall aspires to his condition proximate to the Sultan. Hence, as one could predict from Montesquieu's account of the vulnerability of the vizier, Flint protects himself by suggesting that Twineall is a threat to the Sultan and arranges for a state-sanctioned assassination of the foppish flatterer by mobilizing the Sultan's guards. Sir Luke and Lady Tremor become complicit because they fear not only Lord Flint's retribution but also Twineall's revelation of their secrets. Significantly, just as with Lord Flint, Sir Luke also jokes on Twineall's ambivalent relationship to honor when the Sultan's guards arrest him for crimes against the state:

TWI: But if they have left out *honourable,* it can't be me—I am the Honourable Henry Twineall.
SIR LUKE: Aye, that you are to prove before your judges. (57)

That judgment turns on the attribution of seditious meaning to what Twineall believes are intentionally ambivalent and inconsequential remarks regarding the Sultan. What he does not understand is that in the despotic state the content of the utterance is less important than the fact of its performance and that to the guards any utterance regarding the Sultan's legitimacy is by definition a threat.

Like Lord Flint, Twineall is raised in the world of politics. His father and his uncle are both in the House of Lords, but when Haswell asks him about specific political issues before Parliament, Twineall's speeches devolve into the combination of elision and circumlocution that Twineall declares is in fashion at this moment in London (11). This fashionability is directly tied to Twineall's foppish dress, and his clothes are a convenient figure for his deviance. This is especially notable in the manuscript version of the play: when Haswell mistakes Twineall for a woman, Twineall takes it for a compliment. What exists as an explicit remark in the manuscript is maintained via Twineall's feminine costume in the play's performance. Twineall's excessive femininity plays the same role as Flint's excessive masculinity: both are variations from the norm that suggest their social and political deviance. Likewise, his artificially telegraphic speech is the linguistic analogue to Lord Flint's contrived lapses in memory. He is the embodiment of the foolish man of fashion who, bereft of virtue, finds his way through society by flattering those as vacuous as himself. Unfortunately, Twineall's flattery has the reverse of its intended effect because it is based on faulty information, and he finds himself facing execution. However, all that separates Flint and Twineall are degrees of palpable deniability: because Twineall is a flatterer, he can be held accountable for his words, regardless of how vague and misleading they are, whereas Flint always seems able to disown his opinion by pretending to forget the meaning of his utterances. The political analysis here is prophetic because it suggests that the real political danger in the despotic state lies in the dissemination of political utterances.[38] As the Sultan emphasizes to Haswell, the men who serve him "fill my prisons every day with wretches, that dare to whisper I am not the real Sultan, but a stranger. The secret, therefore, I myself safely relate in private: the danger is to him who speaks it again" (41).

It is with this sense of the danger of political speech that Haswell remonstrates both Twineall and his persecutors. As the play unfolds, flattery becomes the object of Haswell's chief pronouncements on vice and social decay. Late in act 5, Haswell interrupts Twineall's torrent of praise and offers a critique of flattery that defines Englishness in terms of verbal performance:

HAS: Hold! Hold!—This, Mr. Twineall, is the vice which has driven you to the fatal precipice whereon you are—and in death will you not relinquish it?

TWO: What vice, Sir, do you mean?

HAS: Flattery!—a vice that renders you not only despicable, but odious; *nor are you alone the sufferer, but the poor wretches who listen to your praises, are betray'd, and become even more odious than yourself.*[39] (70)

The unpublished version establishes a reciprocal relation between the flatterer and the one being flattered. This has an important resonance with Montesquieu's despotic scenario that Grosrichard describes as the paradox of the vizier:

> How can one be loved by a despot while being ignorant of his wishes, yet certain of responding to those wishes? The despot's subject answers: by giving him the opportunity to love himself through me. In a world where there are those who have nothing and are nothing, while the Other is and possesses everything, after the gift of life the spontaneous form assumed by the gift of love is *flattery;* it is the giving of an image which offers the despot more than he has, but supposes in exchange that he will accept that he is not everything, since you cannot be flattered except by someone who matters in your eyes. . . . the logic of flattery demands that it be carried always to excess, to inflation, to extravagance.[40]

Grosrichard's remarks indicate the narrowness of the field of action accorded to Twineall and Lord Flint. They flatter themselves into existence but, in so doing, partake of the odiousness of absolute tyranny. And from Grosrichard's analysis one can glean the figural connection between flattery and sexually suspect economies of excess.

Perhaps the play's most telling moment occurs immediately after Haswell, empowered with the signet of the newly reformed Sultan, releases Twineall from prison. No sooner does Twineall launch into a series of encomiums on Haswell's benevolence and compassion than Haswell orders the guards to "Seize him—he has broken his contract already" (71). Twineall corrects himself by insulting Haswell, and Haswell declares that he'll "forgive *that* meaning, sooner than the other—utter any thing but flattery—Oh! never let the honest, plain, *blunt* English name become a proverb for so base a vice" (71). The invocation of plain English discourse as the bulwark against a vice associated in both Montesquieu and Inchbald with the corruption of monarchy into despotism has extraordinary political implications, not least of which is the assertion of a relationship between virtue, Englishness, and honest, plain speech. As we will see in chapter 5, this becomes for Frances Burney a crucial problematic in her analysis of the oratory of Burke and Fox during the Hastings trial.

This latter conjunction brings us straight to Haswell himself, for he is the embodiment of virtue in the play. The tactical advantage of such a construction should be by now obvious, because Haswell can walk through the play as both the example of virtue and the patient assailant of vice. But it would be naive merely to assume that Inchbald mobilizes Haswell and John Howard to critique the fantasy of Oriental despotism. From a perspective steeped in Montesquieu's *Spirit of the Laws,* such a valorization carries with it an incipient critique of monarchy in favor of republican governance because virtue is the defining principle of democracy. The deployment of Howard is ultimately aimed at reengaging the very issues that precipitated George III's resistance not only to Fox's East India Bill but also to Whig notions of party. By attending to Howard, one can evoke Burke's spectral presence in this play and suggest that, like the Sultan, his passion for vengeance against Hastings and his royal supporters arises from an earlier misrecognized loss.

When *The Spirit of the Laws* focuses on the imposition and enactment of law in the various forms of government, Montesquieu argues in no uncertain terms that the law's enactment and the penalties conferred on its subjects operate as signs of the state's spirit:

> Severity in penalties suits despotic government, whose principle is terror, better than monarchies and republics, which have honor and virtue for their spring.
>
> In moderate states, love of the homeland, shame, and fear of blame are motives that serve as restraints and so can check many crimes. The greatest penalty for a bad action will be to be convicted of it. Therefore in moderate states civil laws will make corrections more easily and will not need as much force.
>
> In these states a good legislator will insist less on punishing crimes than on preventing them; he will apply himself more to giving mores than to inflicting punishments. (82)

It is therefore possible to assess the moderation and to examine the form of a government by attending to the severity of its punishments. As is well documented, the reign of George III was arguably the most punitive in the eighteenth century. The hallmark of moderation is difference in penalties—that is, making the punishment fit the crime—but precisely this lack of differentiation characterizes British jurisprudence in this period. Furthermore, even a cursory glance at the Hastings trial records indicates that the managers attempted to demonstrate not only the sanguinary nature of Hastings's governance but also a symptomatic leveling in the application of punishment. In both regimes—which many observers felt were mutually supporting—crimes against persons and crimes against property were often accorded the same punishment.

Such Things Are conducts its allegorical analysis of both George III's and Hastings's governance by attending closely to both the frequency and arbitrariness of the state's punitive mechanisms and offers middle-class reform as the only solution. To do so, Inchbald conscripts John Howard, in the form of Mr. Haswell, to explore the Sultan's prisons. This tactic separates her from Whig critics of George III's absolutism and of Hastings's imputed rapacity, and thus her critique is mobilized from a space outside of conventional parliamentary political discussion. In short, Howard offers her an avenue of critique that is indirect enough to protect her from simple charges of party alliance at a time when the conflict over Hastings's impeachment utterly polarized the political world. The importance of this indirection is captured in her prefatory "Remarks" to the 1808 edition of the play:

> The writer of this play was, at the time of its production, but just admitted to the honours of an authoress, and wanted experience to behold her own danger, when she attempted the subject on which the work is founded. Her ignorance was her protection. Had her fears been greater, or proportioned to her task, her success had been still more hazardous. A bold enterprise requires bold execution; and as skill does not always unite with courage, it is often advantageous, when cases are desperate, not to see with the eye of criticism: chance will sometimes do more for rash self-importance, than that judgement, which is the parent of timidity.[41]

This retrospective account of the play's composition and production is carefully coded because the recognition that "a bold enterprise requires bold execution" indicates that she was fully aware of the play's political volatility. A Whiggish indictment of Hastings would not make it through the chamberlain's office, but a play whose political critique of imperial governance travels at an oblique angle disguised as a tribute to John Howard's humanitarianism and as a satire on Lord Chesterfield operates with sufficient buffers to ensure production.[42]

For all their ignorance about the island of Sumatra, the audience would have been highly cognizant of Howard's reputation regardless of whether they had read his *The State of the Prisons,* for his inquiries were widely discussed throughout the 1770s and 1780s. To a reader of Howard's account of British jails, however, certain scenes would have clearly demonstrated that Sumatra was not at all unlike Britain in the treatment of its prisoners. Howard made this same connection in the reverse direction when he compared the lack of air in most British jails with that of the infamous Black Hole of Calcutta. Howard's work was in general not a philosophical inquiry into the rights of the prisoner and the state but a review of the material conditions of prisons themselves. It was the evidentiary quality of his work that allowed him to be deployed in more sweeping enlightenment critiques of statecraft. In this regard, Inchbald's play shares a great deal with the French praise of Howard's findings, but her deployment of Howard uses the materiality of the theatre to effect a similarly materialist critique.

Act 1 is divided into two types of spaces. The play opens in Luke and Lady Tremor's drawing room; as we have seen, this opening scene offers a portrait of a society whose internal dynamics are utterly deformed by despotic rule. The second, third, and fourth scenes of the opening act are set in the prison. And it is Haswell who links the two spaces. The division of the prison scenes into two separate types of space is notable, because, as Howard reported, British jails were typically divided between a common ward and more comfortable "masters apartments."[43] Movement between these two wards was regulated by fees paid to the warden. Act 1, scene 2 is clearly a common ward: as the stage directions state, Haswell and the Keeper interact with "Several Prisoners dispersed in different situations" (20). When they move to "Another part of the Prison" via a damp passageway, the scene changes to a single space with "A kind of sopha with an old man sleeping upon it—Elvirus sitting attentively by him" (20). The Keeper explicitly states that prisoners situated in this more hospitable inner chamber pay for less harsh treatment: "In this ward . . . are the prisoners, who by some small reserve—some little secreted stock when they arrived—or by the bounty of some friend who visit them—or such-like fortunate circumstance, are in a less dismal place" (20). In terms of the physical aspects of the stage, the sofa becomes the very sign of class distinction that defines the architecture of the British prison. One of the stock props of Orientalist representations of the East becomes the figure that equates Britain and Sumatra. In this allegorical economy, the sofa, normally associated with the decadence of the Sultan, emerges as a figure for what Howard saw as the naked power of rank in the British penal system and thus it operates as a kind of icon of aristocratic corruption in both imperial spaces.[44]

Further attention to the prison scenes of act 1 reveals that this architectural equivalence signals a more specific critique not only of spirit of the laws of the British state under George III but also of Burke's self-identification in the pursuit of Hastings. This latter point is quite complex and requires that we attend both to the specifics of the prison scene and to the historical legacy of Fox's East India Bill in the conception of party unity. In the printed version of the play, the Keeper's tour of the common ward focuses on two prisoners, one "suspected of disaffection ... sentenced to be here for life, unless his friends can lay down a large sum by way of penalty, and another who was tried for heading an insurrection and acquitted, but who remains incarcerated because of 'Fees due to the Court'—a debt contracted while he proved his innocence" (20). The latter prisoner's predicament conforms to one of the principle tenets of Howard's *The State of Prisons* and some of the legislation arising from its publication. Howard discovered that many of those incarcerated were often declared innocent but were held because they could not pay various fees incurred during their imprisonment. Innocent prisoners found themselves indefinitely confined because they were unable to pay fees to the jailers and to the courts. An entire economy of fees and bribes ensured that being charged was often sufficient to effect punishments, which, considering the dangers of prison life, were often fatal. Howard's position on the ills of confinement is summarized in Haswell's first meeting with the Sultan:

HAS: The prisoner is your subject—there misery—more contagious than disease, preys on the lives of hundreds—sentenced but to confinement, their doom is death.—Immured in damp and dreary vaults, they daily perish—and who can tell but that amongst the many hapless sufferers, there may be hearts, bent down with penitence to Heaven and you, for every slight offence—there may be some amongst the wretched multitude, even innocent victims. (38)

Inchbald's representation of the prison spaces emphasizes their unhealthiness, and most of the prisoners that Haswell encounters are in the process of dying of jail fever.

Howard's analysis of the prison system vividly portrayed the unhealthiness of the prison confines, but his account of corruption and excessive punishment made his text more than a catalog of atrocities. What he demonstrated was that the problems he described were symptoms of broader social ills, and nowhere was this more apparent than in his discussion of debtors. In addition to discovering that many prisoners were incarcerated in spite of their innocence because of a system of fees, Howard also revealed that the bulk of those imprisoned were not convicts, who were for the most part executed, transported, or branded. More than half of those confined in Britain's jails were debtors, and considering the virulence of the prison spaces themselves, this meant that by their confinement they were effectively executed. Significantly, in the manuscript and the Larpent text of *Such Things Are,* Inchbald includes a debtor in the common ward. After turning from the prisoner suspected of disaffection to the Sultan, and prior to encountering the prisoner accused of insurrection, the Keeper presents "a Debtor, a youthful prodigal, whose ancestors were rich—his father left a charitable donation to this prison, and now a pennyworth of bread a day (his dying father's bounty to poor Prisoners) is all that [is] left him of his parental legacies." This version of the play effectively places debt, disaffection, and insurrection on the same plane, and thus a civil offense is deemed to be no different than a crime against the state. One cannot argue conclusively for why the debtor does not appear in the printed version—it may have been suppressed by the chamberlain, or the manager, or a combination thereof, or it may have been deemed incidental—but in light of the larger argument of this chapter, its presence in the manuscript and the Larpent text opens the door for advisedly tentative conclusions.

First, the collapse of the difference between the civil offense of debt and the treasonous crime of insurrection is the most extreme symptom of a society corrupted by despotism. Such a state exhibits no moderation, and thus the prison scene is the most tangible instance of Inchbald's enactment of Montesquieu's analysis of legal penalties as indicators of the nature and principle of government. In this light, Howard/Haswell's critique of the prison is deployed as the thin edge of an overall critique of the spirit of the laws, which ultimately turns on the character of Haswell himself, for like Howard in Inchbald's prefatory remarks, he is praised for his virtue. As act 5 unfolds, Haswell corrects and unites all the characters, and the play closes with a series of encomiums to Haswell's virtuous qualities. Twineall suggests that these encomiums are another form of the very flattery that Haswell has so rigorously exorcized, but Elvirus closes the play with the following defense: "[T]here are virtues, which praise cannot taint—such are Mr. Haswell's— for they are the offspring of a mind, superior even to the love of fame—neither can they, through malice, suffer by applause, since they are too sacred to incite envy, and must conciliate the respect, the love and the admiration of all" (74). Haswell's Christian virtues here are literally incorruptible: they are not susceptible to flattery and they do not incite envy. Elvirus—and, by extension, Inchbald—is suggesting that Haswell's actions and his character have conciliatory effects within the social body and, as such, are the spring of social cohesion. When one recalls that the play deploys Twineall and Lord Flint to perform a devastating critique of the complicity of principles of honor in the demise of moderate monarchy, it is clear that Inchbald is arguing for virtue over honor as a corrective social passion. In light of the pervasive influence of Montesquieu on the staging of the problem of government, this means that Inchbald is deploying Howard to make a radical argument for some form of democracy to supersede a period of monarchical corruption.[45] It is no wonder therefore that Inchbald looked back on the play as a hazardous enterprise.

This gesture toward democracy, however, does not take place at the formal level of governance but rather at the level of its guiding principle—that is, the manners and morals of the subjects governed. As my earlier reading of *The Mogul Tale* and this reading of *Such Things Are* demonstrate, the management not only of the social and governmental relations between subjects but also of subjects' relations to themselves turns on very particular understandings of virtue. The sexual regulation that lies at the heart of the earlier farce has been expanded into an overarching vision of middle-class ascendancy in the later more mature play. In this light, the sexual deviance of Twineall and Lord Flint can be understood as the incorporation of *The Mogul Tale*'s critique of aristocratic and theatrical dissipation into a radical analysis of the British state on the eve of the Hastings impeachment. In doing so, Inchbald mobilizes sexual fantasies already at work in Montesquieu's fantasy of Eastern despotism but turns them toward an argument directly counter to Montesquieu's own desire to reconstitute the place of the nobility in monarchical government. This latter turn is, I believe, crucial because it demonstrates how Howard and Montesquieu are deployed not only to critique the absolutist tendencies of both George III and Warren Hastings, but also to circumvent the nostalgia that characterized Whig critiques of both leaders' abuses of power.

The latter circumvention is particularly visible when one considers the place of Burke in the entire drama of Indian affairs from the debate on Fox's India Bill to the impeachment of Hastings. As noted earlier, Burke's understanding of Whig identity plays a vital role in the assassination of Fox's East India Bill in the House of Lords. Lord Abingdon alleged that

Fox's bill operated according to the exclusive gestures prescribed by Burke in *Thoughts on the Cause of the Present Discontents* and threatened to place the wealth of the East Indian Company into the hands of the Whig oligarchy. This is a tendentious reading of the bill, but it nevertheless undermined public confidence in Whig actions to the point that more than a decade later the indictment of Hastings could still be lampooned as an attempt to line Whig pockets.[46] The insinuation of Whig conspiracy was long-lived because it was based on a palpable and arrogant desire first exhibited by the Rockingham Whigs and then furthered in Foxite society to occupy a privileged place between the king and the people. Burke was the primary Whig theorist of that arrogant balancing act, and I want to briefly suggest how Inchbald's deployment of Howard and the question of punishing the debtor may have been aimed directly at him.

One of the most important panegyrics to John Howard came from none other than Burke in his famous "Speech at the Guildhall, in Bristol, Previous to the Late Election in that City" of 1780. Burke's speech upon the loss of his Bristol seat argues in no uncertain terms that a representative does not simply do the bidding of his constituents but is rather an independent subject elected for his ability to withstand the fleeting desires of the moment. As David Bromwich notes, many political commentators of the day recognized that "Burke's vaunted independence of local prejudices was lamentably consistent with the arrogance of the Rockingham party."[47] One of the issues on which Burke disagreed with his constituents was his advocacy of Lord Beauchamp's legislation to reform the "law-process concerning imprisonment" for debt (225). Defending his support for this bill, Burke argues in terms that are reminiscent of Montesquieu regarding the danger of a penal system that does not distinguish civil infractions from criminal acts: "There are two capital faults in our law with relation to civil debts. One is, that every man is presumed solvent . . . and thus a miserable mistaken invention of artificial science, operates to change a civil into a criminal judgement, and to scourge misfortune or indiscretion with a punishment which the law does not inflict on the greatest crimes" (227). This analysis is augmented by evidence culled from Howard's documentation of prisons in Britain and Europe regarding the reform of the punishments for debt in Holland. Burke's self-defense closes with an encomium to Howard's "humanity" and "charity" that resonates with the way he is praised in *Such Things Are* (229). It may well be that Inchbald's and Burke's shared regard for Howard and their desire for the reform of the law surrounding debt are coincidental. But one could also argue that Inchbald mobilizes Howard precisely because he figures so prominently in Burke's public self-stylization as a statesman in the Rockingham party. The invocation of Howard may well be a haunting.

If Burke is acting according to principles learned from Howard, then one can postulate a potential affiliation between his politics and those presented by Inchbald in *Such Things Are* that is forestalled or obviated by his later affiliation with Fox. In this light, Burke becomes a figure whose political adherence to the Whig oligarchy distorts the very analysis needed to separate himself from the obsolescence of his party's self-definition. Such a gesture would allow Inchbald to align herself with Burke against Hastings while at the same time marking a specific line of demarcation between her critique and that of the Whig opposition. This has specific implications for the Hastings impeachment because so many of the primary charges against Hastings revolve around cases that replicate the excessive punishment for debt described by Burke. For example, Hastings's alleged extortion of the Begams of Oudh and the violation of the zenana of Panna, Rani of Benares, mother of Chait Singh, operated on the presumption that they were secreting funds in the zenana so as not to pay their debts.[48] It is not an exaggeration to state that the punishment of the debtor haunts the impeachment proceedings in much the same way that it haunts *Such Things Are*. The suppressed lines on the prisoner confined for debt are a poignant elision not only because they circuitously point to the fleeting possibility of democracy as a solution to the state's descent into despotism, but also because they highlight the very limits that prevent Burke's pursuit of Hastings from coming to anything but acquittal. His commitment to the social and economic interests of an amalgamated aristocracy and mercantile bourgeoisie means that his political opposition to Hastings ultimately does not differ materially from those supporting Hastings. In this scenario, Howard, in the guise of Haswell, represents a political road not taken, a road not contaminated by Foxite economic and sexual dissipation, not corrupted by absolutism or by debt and excess, but whose principles are based on Christian virtue and middle-class restraint—a road where, in Inchbald's eyes, such things ought to be.

CHAPTER

FOUR

The Raree Show of Impeachment

At Westminster, where next I go,
Except that cold the wind is;
A novel sort of raree-show,
Reflects our Eastern Indies.

For lo! the Com—ns of G——t B——n,
Bring forth a man ill-fated;
Whom rising Speakers try their wit on,
And so the Bull is BAITED.

"What has he done," as there we sat,
I ask'd a knowing neighbour,
"He stole, he said, the RAJAH'S PLATE,
"And eke his DIAMOND SABRE.

"Dire plunder, massacre, and rape,
"He proudly sought his fame in;
"Yet, fear'd Religion might escape,
"So made his Groom, a BRAMIN

Surely, I cried, his hapless fate
No other scarce can equal;
He never had the SWORD or PLATE,
And so I doubt the sequel.

God bless, our Sov'reign Lord the K——g,
May no nice points perplex him;
No Patriot's roar, nor Pindar sing,
Nor Peers protest, to vex him.

"LONDON; OR, THE MORNING LOUNGE.
ODE THE FIRST," *Morning Post*, 7 MARCH 1788

FOLLOWING THE DISINTEGRATION of the Fox-North coalition in 1784, the long process of bringing Warren Hastings to trial was staged from the opposition side of the house. Hastings was the first governor-general of Bengal appointed according to the strictures outlined in the Regulating Act of 1773 and remained in power until he was recalled in 1785. During that period, Hastings's interpretation of the Regulating Act and the powers conferred to him resulted in ambitious acts of military and diplomatic conquest in the Asian subcontinent that greatly enhanced the opportunities both for the consolidation of the East India Company's profits and for the pursuit of private gain. As Rajat Kanta Ray states, "for the civil and military officers of the Company it was a question of 'whether it should go into a blackman's pocket or mine.' Warren Hastings's opponents in Council found upon inquiry that 'there is no species of peculation from which the Honourable Governor-General has thought it reasonable to abstain.'"[1] However, despite the potential for increased revenue, the Company did not fare particularly well during this period and the state of Bengal became increasingly impoverished. In contrast, Hastings amassed a conspicuous private fortune during his tenure and thus opened himself to charges of corruption. But it was Hastings's often disruptive pursuit of military conquests against the Maratha confederacy and the sultans of Mysore that generated the fiercest metropolitan criticisms because these military operations seemed to be at variance with the East India Company's commercial charter.

> Henry Dundas, the rising Scottish politician who was becoming an expert on India, observed in the House of Commons in April 1782 that, "As matters stood, military exploits had been followed till commercial advantages were in danger of being lost." With Warren Hastings in mind, he then reminded the House that no Company servant had the "right to fancy he was an Alexander, or an Aurengzebe, and prefer frantic military exploits to the improvement of trade and commerce of the country."[2]

Dundas failed to have Hastings recalled in 1782, but the pursuit of Hastings was taken over in earnest first by the Fox-North coalition and then the Whig opposition under the strategic guidance of Edmund Burke.

Burke became a master of the labyrinthine affairs of the East India Company and schooled himself on all aspects of Indian society. From his initial involvement in the Secret Committee, which inquired into the actions of Clive and the Company directors in the winter of 1772–73, his response to the economic problems of integrating Indian trade into the empire was filtered through a constitutional lens. By the early 1780s his earlier reluctance to regulate the Company during the debate surrounding the Regulating Act transformed into a desire to bring the Company under direct parliamentary control. His close association with Hastings's archenemy Philip Francis not only gave him access to a great deal of information regarding the internecine warfare within the East India Company but also colored his interpretation of Hastings's actions.[3] He quickly reached the conclusion that British misrule was a species of despotism that not only "destroyed the very fabric of the Indian economy and society" but also threatened to contaminate the British Constitution.[4] This recognition that colonial corruption would eventually destroy metropolitan governance fit well with Burke's and Fox's already existing conclusion that George III's advocacy of Hastings was a further sign of an absolutist threat. Setting himself up both as a guardian of Indian peoples from the extortion and oppression fostered by Hastings's rule and as the moral protector of the British Constitution, Burke slowly introduced evidence against Hastings into the parliamentary record until the Commons, against extraordinary odds, initiated impeachment proceedings against Hastings in the House of Lords by a strong majority. This was the first time an opposition party forced a formal impeachment in the history of the English parliament, and many observers understood the entire affair as a Whig assault on both the Ministry and the Crown.

The Whig campaign against Hastings generated some of the most important oratory of the period, but the printsellers consistently countered these efforts with images that rendered the entire affair either as a skirmish in the party or as theatre of the lowest order. The anonymous *The Common Stage Wagging from Brooke's Inn* of 1 April 1786 (fig. 4.1) translates Whig tactics into itinerant theatre. Burke's strategy for the parliamentary session of 1786 aimed to "spin out proceedings and delay a decisive vote on which they could be summarily terminated. He would not introduce his charges immediately and call for a vote of impeachment on them as precedents suggested, but he would ask the House to receive evidence first in the form of papers laid before it."[5] The traveling troupe of impoverished comedians hauling their props marked "India Papers" are under the direction of a demon from Brooke's Inn, the seat of Whig stratagem. The asses which pull the stage coach of evidence have the faces of Burke, Fox, Sheridan, and North. A poster on the right of the composition advertises that "For a Few Days will be Performed a COMEDY called IMPEACHMENT by a Ragged Company (late) of His MAJESTY's Servants. . . .

FIG. 4.1. Anonymous, *The Common Stage Wagging from Brooke's Inn*, 1 April 1786 (*courtesy of the Department of Prints and Drawings, The British Museum, London; BM 6939*)

Laughing between the acts to conclude with ALL in the WRONG." The print questions the legitimacy of the Whig's actions, for the performance of impeachment is undertaken by actors no longer working by sanction of the Crown. This is reinforced by the explicit invocation of Sheridan's and Fox's financial embarrassments so that the entire campaign is recast as an elaborate ploy to resolve the debts of prominent Whigs. What had lain dormant in the earlier print battle over Fox's East India Bill in 1783 returned to undercut the seriousness of the Whig's allegations by figuring them as at best poorly performed comedy or at worst vulgar farce.

The impeachment before the House of Lords started with great fanfare in the winter of 1788 and concluded with Hastings's acquittal in 1795. Despite a steep falling off in public interest as the trial progressed, the opening season from January to June of 1788 was the most widely reported event in the London papers. Of Burke's original nineteen charges against Hastings in the House of Commons, only six were pursued before the House of Lords.[6] Unlike the campaign against Hastings in the House of Commons, the impeachment was to follow the rules of evidence proscribed by the common law. This decision severely disabled the manager's case because the charges themselves were drafted not with an eye on legal protocols, but rather with a sense of their capacity to figure forth Hastings's inhumanity.[7] And the managers themselves were not lawyers, but politicians. Saddled with Burke's rhetorically excessive charges and confronted with the Lords' decision to hear all the charges before asking for Hastings's defense, the managers found themselves in a situation where everything turned on their limited capacity to circumvent legal procedure through the sheer power of oratory. After Burke's bristling four-day opening speech, the first season of the impeachment commenced with Fox's masterful speech on the Benares charge, which dealt with Hastings's extortion of Chait Singh, and concluded with Sheridan's extraordinary summation of the charge pertaining to Hastings's treatment of the Begams of Oudh.[8] These three oratorical moments and their reception are the primary focus of this chapter and are handled as perfomative events whose significance goes far beyond the immediate concerns of the impeachment.

For these few months in early 1788, the trial became a public sensation like no other. Much has been made of the theatricality of the impeachment of Warren Hastings.

> In keeping with the *Enquiry [into the Origin of our Ideas of the Sublime and the Beautiful]*'s definition of the functioning of "real sympathy," the impeachment at Westminster Hall became the most spectacular stage in London: as one of the managers, Gilbert Elliot described it, "[The audience] will have to mob it at the door till nine, when the doors open, and then there will be a rush as there is in a pit of the playhouse when Garrick plays King Lear. . . . The ladies are dressed and mobbing it in the Palace Yard by six or half after six, and they set from nine till twelve before the business begins. . . . Some people and, I believe, even women—I mean ladies—have slept at the coffeehouses adjoining Westminster Hall, that they may be sure of getting to the door in time."[9]

Elliot's remarks are typical of representations of the impeachment both in the popular press and in the multitude of satirical prints that were published prior to and during the proceedings. Despite the ubiquity of correlations between the impeachment and the theatre, there has been little sustained discussion of why theatrical tropes dominate not only the contemporary print media but also more recent analyses of the event. Even Elliot's description contains intriguing but largely ignored points of entry into the trial's significance. The only antecedent to this kind of "mobbing" of a trial was for the scandalous proceedings against the Duchess of Kingston for bigamy and adultery a few years earlier. Whereas in that case the interest was principally voyeuristic, the Hastings trial promised scandal and entertainment of a different order. This distinction is marked in Elliot's comparison of the trial to Garrick's performance of Lear. If, as Elliot suggests, the audience throngs to Westminster for a cathartic performance of tragic hubris, then he clearly projects the audience's desire not only for the humbling of a great man but also for a working through of colonial guilt. But his supplemental remarks indicate that something else is at stake in London society's heated desire for tickets to the impeachment.

Elliot's fascination with the presence of women in Westminster Hall is shared by virtually all accounts of the proceedings. The day after the trial's opening, the *Times* "Bon Ton" column reported that

> Yesterday the great *World* attended the trial of WARREN HASTINGS, Esq.—and whether he be convicted, or whether he be acquitted, his accusers are entitled to the thanks of the ladies mantua-makers and milliners.
>
> They have raised many a fair one from her drowsy pillow to snuff the morning air; but many a fair one they have deprived of rest. About twelve at night *hair-dressing* commenced. What an hour for *hair-dressing!* and the operators continued *twisiting of curls* till nine the next morning. . . . Above, and all around, there was a blaze of beauty. The stile of dress was more gay and less brilliant than when *Kingston's* Duchess stood at the bar. There were few feathers, and these very low—but a profusion of artificial flowers ornamented the ladies heads—Many wore chains, and strings of pearl, or of beads of various colours from their ears—there were a few of cut steel— Bracelets adorned every arm.—There were no hoops, and the bosom, which formerly projected out of all symmetry, nearly retreated to the proportion of nature.—The gowns were full and flowing, with long trains—the fabric mostly of sattin—the colours dark or white.[10]

Both the *Times* and Elliot recognize that the presence of women in the hallowed halls of the state make for a spectacle of gendered performativity that is rivaled only by London's pleasure sites: Vauxhall Gardens, Raneleagh, and the Theatres Royal. This has significant implications because the styles of gender performance through which Elliot and others understand the presence of women at the trial are modeled on those exhibited in the theatre. As is well known, women's roles in the audience of Covent Garden and Drury Lane were proscribed by their styles of visibility, for these were sites equally suited to aristocratic display and prostitute performance. This distinction is registered in Elliot's remarks on the audaciousness of women sleeping in coffeehouses to ensure their seats. His slip between "women" and "ladies" indicates that there is something vaguely improper about their desire to see the public shaming of Hastings. Elliot's description and the *Times* catalog of sartorial display subtly indicate that the impeachment proceedings, like all theatrical events, are traversed by their own specific erotics.

This chapter and the following clarify these axes of desire and articulate why they are so important to our understanding of this unprecedented moment in the history of imperial self-scrutiny. However, a full appreciation of this issue requires a prior meditation on the politics of visuality both in the managers' performance of the trial and in the trial's satirical reception. The importance of the obsessive displacements of self and other on display in the theatre of Westminster Hall lies less in its inherent inability to render satisfactory judgment of the historical processes of colonial and commercial conquest than with its ancillary productions—the racialized and sexualized countertheatres offered by the satirical prints. The three sections of this chapter roughly follow the chronology of the trial's first season, but each handles a different aspect of theatricalization. The first section looks at how tropes of theatrical illegitimacy were deployed to raise questions about the devolution both of the state and of the impeachment's audience. The second section examines how tropes derived from precinematic display captured how the trial's representation of imperial relations produced phantasmatic projections and mystifications of sovereignty. And the final section deals specifically with the troubled performance of imperial statesmanship in Burke's and Sheridan's oratory.

The Raree Show of Precedence: Space and Legitimacy

A party of Horse Guards, under the command of a Field Officer, with a Captain's party from the Horse Grenadiers are ordered to attend daily during the trial.

A body of three hundred Foot Guards have also orders to keep the avenues clear, and a considerable number of constables are to attend for the purpose of taking offenders into custody.

From the scarcity of accommodation at every part of the West end of the town, the trial of Mr. Hastings is supposed to have drawn more people to London than have visited the metropolis at any one time for several years past.

Times, 13 FEBRUARY 1788

From the trial's outset, the newspapers and printsellers were obsessed with how the scene of impeachment literalized the power relations that defined not only the state but also fashionable society. Newspapers published the order of precedence in the realm so that observers would be better able to interpret the room's spatialization of power.[11] These lists were helpful keys to the widely circulated nonsatirical representations of Westminster Hall at the time of the impeachment. These images emphasize the crowd and the spectacle of the event, but the way that they organize space is illuminating. In most cases, the architecture of the hall is used to define the axes of power in a fashion that emphasizes the relationship between Lord Chancellor Thurlow, who presided over the proceeding and who was widely believed to be in the pocket of both the king, and the defendant. T. Prattent's *A View of the Court Sitting on the Trial of Warren Hastings* of 1 May 1788 offers a typical view of the hall in two-point perspective from the Lord Great Chamberlain's Box for the Ladies (fig. 4.2). In fact, most of the illustrations of the impeachment put the viewer in the position of the women observers. At the center of the composition is the seat of Lord Chancellor Thurlow and along the vertical axis running through his chair at equidistant points are the empty Throne and "Warren Hastings, Prisoner." This distorts space to emphasize the links between these three personages. It should come as no surprise that views of the proceedings that deviate from this strict axis between the state and Hastings are confined to satirical attacks on Burke, Fox, and Sheridan. A similarly subtle visual device is used in the famous map of the proceedings published in the pro-Hastings *History of the Trial of Warren Hastings, Esq.* (fig. 4.3). Both literally and figuratively, the empty spaces of the map designate types of people and their distance from the throne. What remains unclear, despite the generally exonerating quality of the text, is the relationship between the generic figure representing Hastings and the empty chair of George III. The hyperembodiment of Hastings in the image underlines the contradiction implicit in prosecuting one man for the crimes of empire,[12] but the cancellation of George III's body, and indeed of the bodies of the entire legislative apparatus, also crystallizes a fear regarding precedence: namely, that Hastings and not the king is the real ruler of the empire.

FIG. 4.2. T. Prattent, *A View of the Court Sitting on the Trial of Warren Hastings*, 1 May 1788 *(courtesy of Peel Collection, The Pierpont Morgan Library, New York; no. 81)*

If these nonsatirical mappings of state power are subtly realized, then the bulk of the visual representations of the trial are not. The anxiety regarding George III's subordination to Hastings was given ample treatment in prints such as *The Bow to the Throne* (fig. 4.4). An entire subgenre of prints presents Hastings buying his acquittal from Thurlow and the king with Indian plunder (see fig. 4.5).[13] As Dorothy George notes, this print and Dent's *The Surprising Stone Eater* of 28 March 1788 satirize Hastings's gifts of diamonds to the king and queen by comparing the royals to a much-advertised performance of a stone eater in London in 1788.[14] This deployment of visual tropes derived from the theatre and from less-exalted forms of performance is a recurring satirical device during the impeachment. And no single print compares with William Dent's *The Raree Show* of 25 February 1788 for understanding the representational strategies for dealing with the crisis of imperial self-scrutiny instantiated by the trial (fig. 4.6). The print was published less than two weeks after the commencement of the proceedings and it superimposes the full range of visual tropes employed to ridicule the theatricality of the trial. As Dorothy George summarizes, "the Trial of Hastings in Westminster Hall is trav-

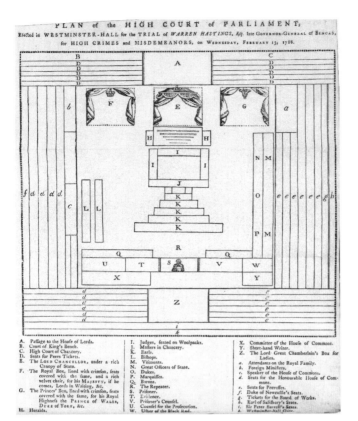

PLAN of the HIGH COURT of PARLIAMENT,
Erected in WESTMINSTER-HALL for the TRIAL of WARREN HASTINGS, Efq. late GOVERNOR-GENERAL of BENGAL,
for HIGH CRIMES and MISDEMEANORS, on WEDNESDAY, FEBRUARY 13, 1788.

A. Paffage to the Houfe of Lords.
B. Court of King's Bench.
C. High Court of Chancery.
D. Seats for Peers Tickets.
E. The LORD CHANCELLOR, under a rich Canopy of State.
F. The Royal Box, lined with crimfon, feats covered with the fame, and a rich velvet chair, for his MAJESTY, if he comes, Lords in Waiting, &c.
G. The Princes' Box, lined with crimfon, feats covered with the fame, for his Royal Highnefs the PRINCE of WALES, DUKE of YORK, &c.
H. Heralds.
I. Judges, feated on Woolpacks.
J. Mafters in Chancery.
K. Earls.
L. Bifhops.
M. Vifcounts.
N. Great Officers of State.
O. Dukes.
P. Marquiffes.
Q. Barons.
R. The Repeater.
S. Prifoner.
T. Evidence.
V. Prifoner's Counfel.
U. Counfel for the Profecution.
W. Ufher of the Black Rod.
X. Committee of the Houfe of Commons.
Y. Short-hand Writer.
Z. The Lord Great Chamberlain's Box for Ladies.
a. Attendants on the Royal Family.
b. Foreign Minifters.
c. Speaker of the Houfe of Commons.
d. Seats for the Honourable Houfe of Commons.
e. Seats for Peereffes.
f. Duke of Newcaftle's Seats.
g. Tickets for the Board of Works.
h. Earl of Salifbury's Seats.
i. Sir Peter Burrell's Seats.
k. Weftminfter-hall Gate.

FIG. 4.3. From Anonymous, *The History of the Trial of Warren Hastings, Esq. Late Governor-General of Bengal, before the High Court of Parliament in Westminster-Hall, on an Impeachment by the Commons of Great-Britain for High Crimes and Misdemeanours* (London: Debrett, Vernor and Hood, 1796) *(by permission of the Thomas Fisher Rare Book Library, University of Toronto)*

estied as a raree show in a booth."[15] A raree show or rare show is an early form of the peep show that could be transported and exhibited throughout the city. As a form of entertainment it constitutes the lowest form of spectacle and is often considered a subtheatrical form of display.

In Dent's print, the fashionably dressed audience that dominates the foreground of the illustration struggles to gain access to the rather temporary-looking booth in the left of the frame that stands for Westminster Hall. The mob of gentlemen and ladies outside refers directly to the

FIG. 4.4. James Gillray, *The Bow to the Throne—Aleas—the Begging Bow*, 6 May 1788 (*courtesy of the Department of Prints and Drawings, The British Museum, London;* BM 7312)

excitement during the early phases of the trial. The bills on the front of the booth refer to specific speeches and sketch in the spatial deployment of the managers and the prisoner in the hall. The bill on the left is headed with a pair of spectacles and is inscribed "From the left side of the booth may be seen Alexander the Little." As the previous illustrations of Westminster Hall indicate, the managers' table is situated to the left of the hall's central axis; therefore, looking from the left, one sees through Burke's spectacles. If one looks from the right one takes the viewpoint of Hastings's defense team and hence, as the bill indicates, "from the right may be seen Alexander the Great." In contrast to the shortsightedness signified by Burke's spectacles, this bill is headed by an opera glass that allows the viewer to have a long-range prospect. But the opera glass is also a metaphorical device linking the defense to George III, who is frequently caricatured holding an opera glass.

These two opposing optical devices are trained on the same object, and Dent's reference to Alexander the Little and Alexander the Great invokes

Fox's speech on the Benares charge of 22 February 1788. In a digression on making the punishment suit the crime, Fox refuted Thurlow's comparison between Hastings and Alexander the Great:

> Mr. Hastings had lately been compared to a conqueror, whose fame filled the universe;—a character [Thurlow] so exalted as to dispute PRECEDENCE with the *second personage* in the kingdom [the Prince of Wales] had assimilated Warren Hastings to Alexander the Great. But if any resemblance were found, it could not be to Alexander when his mercies and his victories kept an equal pace;—it could not be to the generous or forgiving conqueror;—the likeness must be meant to Alexander the maddened after a debauch; to Alexander in petu-

FIG. 4.5. Anonymous, *The Diamond Easters, Horrid Monsters*, March 1788 *(courtesy of the Department of Prints and Drawings, The British Museum, London; BM 7288)*

FIG. 4.6. William Dent, *The Raree Show*, 25 February 1788 *(courtesy of the Department of Prints and Drawings, The British Museum, London; BM 7273)*

lant wantonness setting temples on fire—to Alexander when his follies and his crimes had excited horror and contempt sufficient to obscure the radiance of former glories.—In the first points of the comparison there was not a shade of resemblance; in the latter part of
the parallel there was all the justice that could be required.[16]

The bill above the door of the raree booth in Dent's print operates as a
highly condensed sign for the political allegiance between Thurlow,
George III, and Hastings. Fox's insinuation regarding Thurlow's claim to
precedence is visualized in the extreme foreground of the print. As part of
the crowd, one finds the Prince of Wales in a fit of rage and Thurlow cast
as a devil riding on the shoulders of George III, asking that the prince
"Make room for precedence." The king's garter ribbon is inscribed "Bulse"
in recognition of his susceptibility to Hastings's bribes.

The chief satirical elements of the bottom half of the image are structured by the passage from Fox's speech that took place three days prior
to the publication of Dent's print. But beyond the quick turnaround time
in image production, there are other aspects of *The Raree Show* that warrant careful attention. By depicting Westminster Hall as a raree booth,
Dent not only diminishes the proceedings but also allows for the spectacle to be visually contained. But it is a containment that paradoxically
allows for an exponential increase in the theatricalization of the trial. The
rare booth is actually a prop in a much larger performance that includes
the audience, the street, and, most important, the antics of Burke, Fox, and
Sheridan now rendered as three clowns or zanies performing on a balcony.
The clowning of the principal managers and the banners that dominate
the top third of the image draw the entire print into the theatrical economy of what Jane Moody has recently designated "illegitimate culture."

The significance of these banners requires a brief digression on the legislation of different kinds of entertainment during the eighteenth century.
As Moody summarizes, following the Licensing Act of 1737 "Any individual performing an 'Interlude, Tragedy, Comedy, Opera, Play, farce or other
entertainment of the stage' not previously sanctioned by letters patent
or licensed by the Lord Chamberlain . . . would now be liable to punishment as a rogue and a vagabond."[17] This criminalization of the nonli-
censed performer is crucial to the print's attack on the managers, but
Dent's street theatre invokes a more complex set of tropes. The Licensing Act also generated a system of textual censorship for the patent theatres that left a wide range of bodily performance including ropedanc-
ing, acrobatics, music, and singing unregulated by the lord chamberlain.

In 1752, legislation was introduced to curtail "the spectre of political radicalism, the promotion of plebeian immorality and the uncontrollable reproduction of urban criminality" that was ostensibly associated with these forms of performance.[18]

> This legislation unwittingly established an enduring division in the regulation of London theatre. The Act of 1752 was based on the assumption that the public entertainments offered at Sadler's Wells and other unlicensed theatres within a 15–mile radius of Westminster represented a non-dramatic sphere of bodily performance utterly distinct from the drama staged at Drury Lane and Covent Garden. No provision was made for the textual scrutiny of political subversion but rather the moral and social pollution spilling out from plebeian pleasure.[19]

From this strange distinction, a series of strategies, often shared with legitimate pantomime, were developed for introducing text into productions for which it was legally assumed there would be no text. Foremost among these strategies were the deployment of text on banners and the accompaniment of text with music. As long as words were not spoken, then the productions were not subject to the political censorship of the lord chamberlain.

This form of regulated but uncensored production, with all its inherent potential for political subversion, lies at the heart of Dent's theatricalization of the trial. The raree booth is a small part of a larger form of bodily performance of which Burke, Sheridan, and Fox are the central musical performers. The banners present versions of Hastings's activities that clearly could not receive royal sanction. On the left-hand placard, a ravenous Hastings devours an Indian woman and tramples the prostrate bodies of women and children. The central placard features Burke half-submerged in the tears he has elicited from his audience. In a reenactment of Mrs. Sheridan's fainting fit during Burke's opening speech, a man is applying smelling salts to a fainting lady. And the right-hand placard, inscribed "Dancing on the Tight-Rope," portrays Hastings the "ropedancer" hanging from a gibbet. All three placards indicate that the production is traversed by the managers' view of the case. In this light, the tussling crowd and the foot guards attempting to control them gain a new significance, for the emotions elicited by the managers' performance are understood to be not only plebeian but verging on the criminal. In other words, the raree show and the spectacle within which it is contained occasion a devolution in the cultural and social life of the city. With aristocrats fighting in the street, Dent insinuates that the antics of Burke, Sheridan, and Fox and the multiple shows they are peddling transform polite society into a mob in need of forcible restraint. It is a complex satirical gesture, for it allows Dent to simultaneously attack the managers and visually render Hastings as the unequivocal exponent of evil.

By rendering the trial as illegitimate performance, Dent not only diminishes the managers' oratory, but also attacks the audience itself. For example, the print presents two Burkes. Despite the fact that the Burke on the placard is perhaps more realistically rendered, it is the second Burke on the scaffolding that Dent proffers as the more accurate portrayal of the trial's chief agent. Cast in a hybrid of Jesuitical and Oriental costume, this second Burke's vaunted oratory is rendered as a species of musical performance. Burke's costume, his pose, and his horn are based on Sayers's famous caricature of Burke in *Carlo Kahn's Triumphal Entry into Leadenhall Street* (see fig. 3.2), but Dent's alteration of the banner hanging from the horn is instructive. In the earlier print the banner shows a map of Bengal whereas the later print is simply inscribed "Sublimity." This captures one of the most famous elements of Burke's Indian sublime—namely, his rhetorical invocation of the map of India in the speech on Fox's East India Bill discussed in chapter 3. Suleri's argument that Burke's method of exemplification devolves into a repetitiveness that tends "to dissolve rather than consolidate the image of India that Burke seemingly wishes to create"[20] is here anticipated by Dent's print, for one is forced to ask how much of Burke's "music" can be heard in the cacophony of represented sound. As if in dialogue with Burke's account of the sublimity of sound, Dent's print, seems to suggest that Burke's audience cannot "forbear being borne down, and joining in the common cry, and common resolution of the crowd."[21] Contrary to his intentions, Burke's sublime oratory in this analysis fails to consolidate his audience because it lacks the "temper" to resist this devolution.

If Burke's music is marked by its repetitiveness, then the caricature of Fox as Punch captures both the violence and the perceived indebtedness of Fox's speech on the Benares charge.[22] Because so much of the knowledge regarding Indian affairs resided with Burke, it was a common conceit throughout the trial that Fox was merely mouthing the words of his colleague. It is therefore not surprising to find Fox portrayed as a puppet whose clothes are inscribed "Argument," "Wisdom," and "Knowledge." He is literally wearing the erudition in which Burke the puppeteer has clothed him. What Fox contributes to the proceedings is not knowledge

FIG. 4.7. James Sayers, *For the Trial of Warren Hastings,* circa February 1788 *(courtesy of the Department of Prints and Drawings, The British Museum, London; BM 7276)*

but style, and here the characterization as Punch gains its resonance. Commentary unsympathetic to the managers' cause characterizes Fox's performance as less skilled than Burke's and emphasizes its combination of violence and repetition: "For individual passages, separable from their novelty, or their original importance, in idea or diction, Mr. Burke is the mighty master. This speech of Mr. Fox was not so distinguished. It abounded, however, in distinctions of its own kind, of which the best was vehemence; the worst, unnecessary repetition of preliminary words."[23] These backhanded compliments suggest that Fox, like Punch, has little to offer beyond repeated violent outbursts. This allegation has its visual counterpart in two parodies of the tickets for the proceedings by Sayers

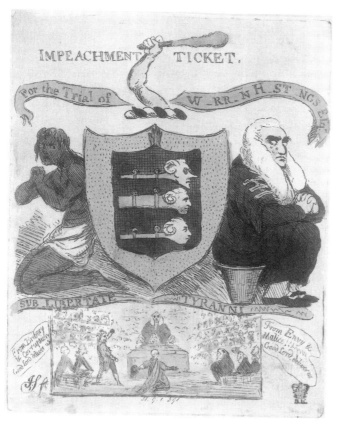

FIG. 4.8. James Gillray, *Impeachment Ticket,* circa February 1788 *(courtesy of the Department of Prints and Drawings, The British Museum, London; BM 7277)*

and Gillray that were circulated roughly at the same time as *The Raree Show* (see figs. 4.7, 4.8). The images are pro-and anti-Hastings, respectively, but they both feature Fox waving a clenched fist over Hastings head. These tickets refer explicitly to Fox's angry response to the Peers' decision to follow the rules of common law in regard to the hearing of evidence.[24] Fox's profession of allegiance to the *Lex et Consuetudo Parliamenti* in the face of this decision is satirized as merely an oratorical posture.[25] Whether figured as Punch or as the embodiment of vehemence, Fox becomes a grotesque figure able to perform, but not feel, Burke's combination of sympathy and outrage.

Dent's caricature suggests that such oratory can only sustain the interest of audiences of the most vulgar or childish taste and this implies that the taste of the aristocracy has degraded into that of the mob. At the heart of this figuration of impeachment as illegitimate theatre lies a fascination with the relationship between the audience and the space of performance. The presentation of the aristocracy mobbing Westminster Hall in *The Raree Show* makes explicit the specter of mob violence that haunts much of Burke's political thought both prior to and following the impeachment. Dent makes visible the class politics that flow beneath the surface of the managers' oratory, for the Whig commitment to oligarchical fantasies of British society discussed in chapter 3 infused much of Burke's analysis of Hastings's governance and became operative in the figural economy of his speeches. As we will see, there is a complex relationship between the excessively figured Indian multitudes and the underrepresented specter of the metropolitan laboring classes who silently threaten Whig fantasies of political legitimacy that can be excavated not only from Burke's dramatic theory of politics but also from the print satirists' tropological investment in the distorting qualities of Burke's spectacles.

Burke's Spectacles

Foreigners are extremely affected by the magnificent solemnity of Mr. Hastings trial; but they, at the same time, cannot avoid expressing their surprise, that the first women should be the last to add to it. A Spanish gentlemen enquired on Friday last of the person who sat next to him, whether the Peeresses were privileged to laugh as loud in Westminster Hall, as they do at the playhouse?

Times, 5 MARCH 1788

As mentioned at the outset of this chapter, much of the reception of the Hastings impeachment explicitly engaged with the Whig attempt to rein in the East India Company four years earlier. This engagement derived from a widespread recognition that the impeachment was a continuation of political and constitutional battles that remained unresolved despite Pitt's attempts to put them to rest. From the political struggle over Fox's East India Bill of 1783 there emerged two sets of tropes that exerted heavy influence on the Hastings impeachment. The first has been admirably explicated by Sara Suleri in her discussion of Burke's famous speech on Fox's East India Bill:

The paradigm that he establishes can be schematized as follows: India as a historical reality evokes the horror of the sublimity, thus suggesting to the colonizing mind the intimate dynamic it already shares with aesthetic horror; such intimacy provokes the desire to itemize and list all the properties of the desired object; the list's inherent failure to be anything other than a list causes the operation of sublimity to open into vacuity, displacing desire into the greater longevity of disappointment.[26]

In Burke's theorization of tragedy in *A Philosophical Enquiry into the Origin of Our Ideas of the Sublime and the Beautiful,* the individual and society form different moments of the same assemblage. As Burke states, "most of the ideas which are capable of making a powerful impression on the mind . . . may be reduced very nearly to these two heads, self-preservation and society."[27] Because he attaches these ideas to the sublime and the beautiful respectively, the aesthetic as such in Burke's account preserves the self, in the instance of the sublime, *and* ties these selves together, in the passions associated with the beautiful. But below or behind this assemblage there flows another relationality that melts individuals into masses that cannot be named "society" but rather must be designated as the crowd. In this undifferentiated mass one can locate that which must remain the constitutive outside of Burkean aesthetics and politics. What is crucial for us to recognize is that the representational distance that Burke introduces in his theatricalization of politics is necessary not only to constitute both society and the individual but also to put the melting crowd in temporary abeyance. In this particular case it is the "Indian millions" that surface momentarily to consolidate both Burke and the nation he represents and then disappear into compensatory tropes.

In Burke's related discussions of sympathy and tragedy, the primary link that joins individuals in "the great chain of society" swings back and forth between two examples of our pleasure in sympathy—public execution and tragedy. Burke argues that the sympathy for the plight of others elicited both by tragedy and execution varies only in degree, and that the passion felt for others is constitutive of our humanity.[28] He also emphasizes, however, that whatever pleasure joins us in this common humanity relies on a representational distantiation: "When danger or pain pass too nearly, they are incapable of giving any delight and are simply terrible; but at certain distances, and with certain modifications, they may be, and they are delightful, as we everyday experience."[29] This distance preserves the immanence of the individual and establishes mediate spacings between individuals in the social. But it also installs fundamental, yet almost unmentionable, distinctions between these social individuals and their rhetorically constituted class and colonial others. These other constituencies enter Burke's discourse as subsocial or extrasocial entities, which are either too proximate or too distant to fit comfortably into Burke's largely visual examples of the sublime scene.

Burke's discussion of the sublimity of sound and loudness presents an instance where this minimum representational distance is contravened. Instead of the spectacle of execution, Burke invokes another mass formation that haunted the imagination of community in the eighteenth century: "[T]he shouting of multitudes has a similar effect; and by the sole strength of the sound, so amazes and confounds the imagination, that in the staggering, and hurry of the mind, the best established tempers can scarcely forbear being borne down, and joining in the common cry, and common resolution of the crowd."[30] This passage indicates that there is an experience beyond that of the sublime when one confronts the roaring mob. If a proper distance is maintained, if one's temper is resolute, the loudness of the crowd will open onto an aesthetic experience of the sublime and the self will be preserved. However, the passage also recognizes an inclination to give up one's self-preservation and melt into the mass. One's experience in this case is no longer aesthetic or political in Burke's terms—one enters into a relationality in which neither individuality or society signifies, in which one is "borne down" out of humanity. And the specificity of Burke's example is resonant, for it is precisely in the acoustic, rather than the visual, that representational distance is difficult to stabilize. As we will see, Burke's specular instruments come under attack as the trial unfolds.

The class relations encoded within these two political scenographies are extremely important. Public execution in the eighteenth century was primarily occupied with killing the laboring poor.[31] Likewise, mob formation has historically been aligned with the underclass, as can be seen in Burke's spatialization of crowd melting—that is, one is borne down into the common cry. The distinction between the aesthetic experience that posits the individual in society and the "communal" experience of melting into the crowd can be polemically stated as the difference between killing the underclass for one's self-consolidation and becoming the underclass. It is also the difference between killing the body of the other and becoming embodied. This is why, when Burke gives us an example of execution, he specifies the person to be executed is "a state criminal of high rank."[32] This elevation of the hanged facilitates the analogy between tragedy and execution by focusing on the sympathy elicited by the plight of an uncommon individual. It is via this analogy that Burke introduces the representational distance required for his theatricalization of the political. One could argue that the analogy between the tragic hero and uncommon criminal is one of the limits of Burke's political thought. This misrecognition enables Burke to erase all sympathy between the emergent bourgeoisie and the abjected laboring poor, thereby allowing him to consolidate the great chain of society by excluding the threatening fluidity of the crowd.

This misrecognition both deforms and informs the theatre of the impeachment. It is clear from Burke's earliest engagement with the Indian question, that he recognized that the triadic relationship between the British state, the East India Company, and the Indian principalities it controlled was beset with structural problems that often put the interests of the state in opposition to those of the Company. In the impeachment, Burke chose to filter these structural critiques through a series of exemplary dramas between Hastings and selected Indian victims of his "arbitrary power." This not only focalized colonial relations through the actions of one man; it also drastically reduced the number of Indian characters in the drama. For example, the two most spectacular charges, the Benares charge, which was handled by Fox, and the Begams charge, which was handled by Sheridan, quickly resolved into conflicts between Hastings and Chait Singh and between Hastings and the Begams of Oudh, respectively. With a limited number of supporting players, the managers radically simplified the complex relations of treaty, taxation, rebellion, and commerce into tragic intrigues between noble subjects. This involved a controversial equation of caste and rank in Burke's discourse that is crucial for his aestheticization of politics, for it simultaneously ejects the mob and the largely Hindu peasantry. In both cases, this ejection is carried out at the level of figuration, as in the famous resolution of the sublime vastness of the Indian subcontinent into the figure of a hungry mouth: "Through all that vast territory there is not a man who eats a mouthful of rice but by permission of the East India company."[33] With this ejection, the relationship between the managers of the impeachment, the narratives they tell, and the audience in Westminster Hall is carefully circumscribed in order to maximize identification between the audience and the victims of Hastings's alleged tyranny. And this narrowing of purview is aimed at consolidating the Peers and the Commons against Hastings in a fashion that nevertheless avoids the question of unequal distribution of wealth both in the colony and the metropole. In short, the placement of the laboring poor and the colonized peasantry is carefully maintained while all attention is focused on Hastings's style of governance.

The act of historical simplification described here was counterbalanced by the oratorical excess of the managers, which frequently mobilized sensational description to consolidate opinion against Hastings. Perhaps most instructive is the famous description from Burke's "Speech on Opening of Impeachment of Warren Hastings" of the tortures promulgated by Hastings's minion Devi Singh at Rangpur. The extraordinary violence of the account was packaged to maximize its emotional effect. In reading the following passage it is important to consider how the controlled delivery of such material operates in the theatre of impeachment:

> The innocent children were brought out and scourged before the faces of their parents . . . This was not all. They bound the father and son face to face, arm to arm, body to body; and in that situation they scourged and whipped them, in order with a refinement of cruelty that every blow that escaped the father should fall upon the son, that every stroke that escaped the son should strike upon the parent; so that where they did not lacerate and tear the sense, they should wound the sensibilities and sympathies of nature. . . . But Lords, there was more. Virgins whose fathers kept them from the sight of the sun, were dragged into the public Court, that Court which was the natural refuge against all wrong, all oppression, and all iniquity. There in the presence of the day, in the public Court, vainly invoking its justice, while their shrieks were mingled with the cries and groans of an indignant people, those virgins were cruelly violated by the basest and wickedest of mankind. It did not end there. The wives of the people of the country only differed in this; that they lost their honour in the bottom of the most cruel dungeons, where all their torments were a little buried from the view of mankind. . . . Here in my hand is my authority. For otherwise one would think it incredible. But it did not end there. In order that nature might be violated in all those circumstances where the sympathies of nature are awakened, where the remembrances of our infancy and all our tender remembrances are combined, they put the nipples of the women into the sharp edges of split bamboos and tore them from their bodies. Grown from ferocity to ferocity, from cruelty to cruelty, they applied burning torches and cruel slow fires (My lords, I am ashamed to go

further); those infernal fiends, in defiance of every divine and human, planted death in the source of life.[34]

I have quoted this passage at length to emphasize not only Burke's careful use of repetition but also his physical performance of horror. Contemporary accounts of the trial indicate that Burke had to pause because he was overcome by his own description and we know that at least one audience member, Mrs. Sheridan, had to be revived after this passage. One could well argue that the crucial distance needed for aestheticizing these events was contravened in these moments and paradoxically the full force of the violated colonial multitudes suddenly erupted into the theatrical space of impeachment only to be displaced by acts of metropolitan revivification. Burke continued his discourse after a pause and after the smelling salts were applied to Mrs. Sheridan. As in the substance of the speech, Hastings becomes the occasion for a bodily enactment of natural humanity and of sympathy for these unnamed virgins and mothers.

But regardless of Burke's performance of this material, the necessity of "a criminal of high-rank" for the containment of more threatening multitudes both at home and abroad introduces a theatrical element outside of Burke's control. Within the visual space of the trial, Hastings too is an actor and his impassivity at the bar was the object of much discussion. As both the *Times* and the *Public Advertiser* observed early in the trial, "Whatever perturbation of mind Mr. Hastings may inwardly suffer pending this business, his exterior deportment is allowed, on all sides, to be very becoming—affecting no levity on the one hand, nor discovering any marks of confusion or embarrassment on the other."[35] His lack of emotion was interpreted as a sign both of guilt and innocence, but it also needs to be considered as a derealization of the tragic economy mobilized by the managers. By refusing to react, to show emotion, the central figure becomes an enigma. This evacuation of emotion is key because the passions are such a fundamental part of Burke's understanding of the subject. To be affectless is in a sense to be outside the realm of the human but not in the sense that Burke, Fox, and Sheridan would like. Far better for the managers if they could demonstrate an unnatural expression of emotion. Rather than an "infernal fiend," Hastings sits in Westminster Hall as an impassive cipher. As the criminal of high rank, Hastings is necessary to the aestheticization of the political, but he has to exhibit some particularity or his very exemplarity will ultimately defuse or subvert the political efficacy of the impeachment. It would have been far better for the managers if Hastings could be provoked somehow to contradict the laws of natural sympathy.

We can get some sense of the strategy behind Burke's oratorical performance by looking briefly at the way in which *Reflections on the Revolution in France* frequently mobilizes the power of emotion by conforming historical events to the form of sentimental tragedy.[36] His representation of Marie Antoinette as the threatened woman prepared to defend her honor attempts to evoke an emotional response similar to that drawn by Sarah Siddons's performances at Drury Lane. The theorization of emotional affect that follows Burke's presentation of the crowd scene in Marie Antoinette's boudoir insinuates that the failure of Dr. Price and the Revolution Society to be drawn into sympathy with the queen's distress is a sign of their perversion. Defending his own tears, Burke argues that he feels for the queen

> because it is *natural* I should; because we are so made as to be affected at such spectacles with melancholy sentiments upon the unstable condition of mortal prosperity, and the tremendous uncertainty of human greatness; because in those natural feelings we learn great lessons; because in events like these our passions instruct our reason. . . . We are alarmed into reflexion; our minds (as it has long since been observed) are purified by terror and pity; our weak unthinking pride is humbled, under the dispensations of a mysterious wisdom.[37]

This litany of justifications insists that Burke's feelings regarding the queen's vulnerability and his judgment of the French Revolution itself are natural. Significantly, this double naturalization insists that "in events like these our passions instruct our reason." The key gesture in Burke's political analysis is to declare the normativity of specific passionate responses in order to pathologize those who do not share his feelings of sympathy.

This famous passage in the *Reflections* has its precedent in Burke's sudden expression of emotion during the account of torture. As the violence of the passage accelerates, so too does the figural despecification of the victims. At the beginning of the passage, Burke is speaking about the torture of a recognizable category of victims—that is, the men, women, and children of Rangpur—but as the passage unfolds Burke moves to the more general category of mothers and then finally ventures forth on his description of what amounts to a crime against the breast. This simultaneous focalization and generalization leads to a fetishization of the breast as the signifier of maternality "where the sympathies of nature are awakened, where the remembrances of our infancy and all our tender remembrances are combined."[38] This important gesture allows Burke not only to enact the "natural" response to such acts before his audience in Westminster Hall in a manner that attributes normative masculinity to himself while at the same time denying it to Hastings, but also to re-territorialize the breast itself, which plays such a vital role in Burke's theorization of the social. As Frances Ferguson has observed, the breast is Burke's iconic sign of the beautiful, and for Burke the beautiful is precisely that which elicits those passions which bind individuals together in society.[39] It is not an exaggeration to assert that a crime against the iconic breast is for Burke a symbolic violation of the sympathy that defines human society. As we will see, the breast becomes a crucial sign that ties together much of the first season of the trial: from Burke's opening speech to Sheridan's apostrophe to filial piety in the summation of the Begams charge, the social bond implied by the relationship between mother and nursing child figures for civilized humanity.

What we see in both the *Reflections* and the "Speech on Opening of Impeachment of Warren Hastings" is the centrality of the enactment of a moment of spectatorship to both Burke's analysis and his presentation of historical events. As an orator, Burke performs as someone who has seen atrocity—albeit at second hand—and who carries the responsibility of making both the Peers and the audience "see" Hastings's depravity. And yet in Burke's visualization of the atrocities at Rangpur what we discover is that the very medium of oratory forces him to rely on figurative substitutions that despecify and hence distort the view of events in India. The tortured breasts of the women of Rangpur, like the threatened figure of Marie Antoinette, both exemplify and occlude the historical events that Burke is trying to bring into presentation. The illuminating effect of figurative exemplification, therefore, also distorts or conceals these historical events.

This entire problematic was captured by the visual satirists in the recurring trope of Burke's spectacles. These spectacles or extensions thereof make frequent appearances in the satirical prints either as impediments to vision or as mechanisms of phantasmatic projection. The former is most vividly figured in Johann Heinrich Ramberg's *Sublime Oratory—a Display of It* of 5 March 1788 (fig. 4.9). As Robinson notes, "the sublimity of Burke's oratory is jeered as deriving from the street filth which, like Fox to his right, he hurls at Hastings."[40] But it is Burke's black glasses that prevent any of the hurled charges from hitting Hastings whose extraor-

FIG. 4.9. Johann Heinrich Ramberg, *Sublime Oratory—A Display of It*, 5 March 1788 (*courtesy of the Department of Prints and Drawings, The British Museum, London; BM 7270*)

dinary Oriental costume is conspicuously unmarked by dirt. The correlation between Burke's blindness and the ineffectiveness of his oratory is intriguing because it suggests that the failure to inflict damage on Hastings derives not from a profusion of words but rather from their misdirection. Burke's sublime oratory, quite literally, is off the mark.

As the trial dragged on, Burke's spectacles were deployed in an increasingly complex fashion. The rather blunt trope of blindness is replaced by a much more troubling and subtle set of visual tropes that emphasize varying degrees and kinds of projection. Optical mechanisms begin not only to proliferate in the prints but also to be applied to Hastings. In *No Abatement* of 31 May 1791, William Dent reapplies the trope of the glasses, but now five years later the satire, like the composition itself, is far more convoluted (fig. 4.10).[41] Burke holding a cross marked "Charge" is the largest figure in the print and effectively divides the visual field in two. To the right of him are images corresponding to key scenes from the oratory of the trial's first two years. Along with emblematic figures of mutilation, starvation, and death, Dent has provided images of the Begams of Oudh shown chained with wasted dugs, Nandakumar hanged, Chait Singh holding another hangman's noose, and, at the center of it all, a female figure with mutilated breasts that corresponds to Burke's sensational description of the atrocities of Rangpur in his opening speech to the impeachment. All of these images are framed by clouds indicating that they are delusional and only visible through the enlarged spectacles which Philip Francis places before Hastings's eyes in the extreme left of the composition. Before Hastings are caricatures of Pitt, Sheridan, Fox, and Grey, each of whom offers a different choice of death. The dislocation of Burke's spectacles from his own eyes to those of Hastings is glossed by the caricature of Burke himself: "Ay, now you are my good Spirits, Black, White, Blue and Grey torment him with a choice of deaths, let him not rest night or day, whilst I raise up those Shades, and those my chief Spirit F[ranci]s, Source of the Charges, thou Imp of Envy strip him of his Plumage and hold my Spectacles to his Eyes, that he may See as I do, confess, die and be dam'd for hoarding his Riches."[42]

Aside from the long-standing suggestion that the Whigs are after Hastings for "hoarding his riches," the key phrase here is "that he may See as I do," for it invokes the Burkean notion of sympathy almost to the letter. The entire scene amounts to a visual rendering of the theory of sympathy: only the optical mechanism of the spectacles introduces a distortion, which underlines the spurious naturalization of such a notion as the commutability of spectatorship. In making Hastings see as Burke does, Dent insinuates that Burke is promulgating versions of events that not only further his own political subject position but also erase those of his enemies. The reductive quality of Burke's model of reception, which too quickly generalizes audience response, is captured vividly by the dislocation of the spectacles. Such an insinuation strikes to the heart of a politics based on the affective demonstration of sympathetic feeling, for it indicates that the ostensibly "natural" feelings shared with others in response to political or aesthetic events are subject to mechanical distortion and psychic projection. The managers' repeated assertion throughout the first year of the trial that the Peers only need be shown Hastings's crimes to convict him is here undercut by the double assertion that vision is not only perspectival but also subject to artificial manipulation. Dent's print also carries the further connotation of desperation on the part of the managers for it seems to suggest that if they can't convince the Peers to convict Hastings, then maybe Hastings can be convinced to execute himself. In other words, the spectacles, dislocated from Burke, lead whoever looks through them to summary judgment.

But what precisely are we to make of the suggestion that the events Burke forces Hastings and the English nation to see are phantasmatic con-

FIG. 4.10. William Dent, *No Abatement,* 31 May 1791 *(courtesy of Peel Collection, The Pierpont Morgan Library, New York; no. 236)*

structions arising from the shortsightedness of his own political identity? At one level, Dent and others are simply arguing that the managers' account of Hasting's activities are biased by party. There is no shortage of prints that make precisely the same claim with regard to Hastings's defense: especially the large number of prints that depict Hastings bribing the king, the queen, and Lord Thurlow with diamonds and ruppees. But by invoking spirits "White, Black, Blue and Grey," Dent equates Burke's actions with Hecate's invocation of the spirit world in eighteenth-century versions of *Macbeth.*[43] In this context, Burke becomes not only a diabolical accessory to the murder of the rightful king, but also one who deals in phantoms and prophecies. In spite of the critique of the managers inherent to this figuration, Burke's magic here conjures scenes of violent depredation that haunt the trial, and the entire scene focuses attention on the problem of figuring forth Indian atrocity.

The question of how to present persons and events in the Indian subcontinent is a continuing problem in the managers' case for a variety of reasons. First, in his opening speech Burke argued that the conduct of Mr. Hastings "had been distinguished for an adherence, not to the general principles which actuate mankind, but to a kind of GEOGRAPHICAL MORAL-

ITY—a set of principles suited only to a particular climate, so that what was peculation and tyranny in Europe, lost both its essence and its name in India."[44] In countering Hastings's "geographical morality," Burke and the managers were committed to a model of governance that operated according to European values, here understood as universal principles of morality, by refiguring Indian social institutions as somehow equivalent to English traditions. By taking the position that colonial rule required different strategies of governance, Hastings's initial defense before the House of Commons forced the managers to demonstrate forms of similitude that were at best rhetorical and, more often than not, highly strained. As Anna Clark states,

> Neither Burke nor Sheridan believed that Indian men could enjoy the same rights as British men. Burke argued for a notion of natural rights, by which he meant the right to be governed by laws, to enjoy liberty, to have one's customs, traditions, and inherited privileges respected, but not the right to participate in politics. Sheridan declared that the instinct of liberty was "less active in the Indian than in the Englishman," so someone had to save them.[45]

Second, their audience, with the exception of the East India Company agents and functionaries, had little or no experience or knowledge of Indian affairs. This is evident from the outset of the trial, for Burke found it necessary to discuss at length the broad historical and cultural features of Indian society prior to and during Hastings's term as governor-general. Third, at the level of evidence many of the key players were either dead or, like Hastings's Resident at Lucknow, Mr. Nathaniel Middleton, unable or unwilling to remember key events necessary for establishing Hastings's legal culpability. For this reason, oratory came to play a more central role in the managers' strategy than the evidence, making, as P. J. Marshall argues, Hastings's acquittal inevitable.

But Sara Suleri is more to the point when she discusses how Burke sees the inability to understand the Indian situation as a problem of representation itself. In Burke's "Speech on Fox's India Bill 1 December 1783" he states that

> All this vast mass, composed of so many orders and classes of men, is again infinitely diversified by manners, by religion, by hereditary employment, through all their possible combinations. This renders the handling of India a matter in an high degree critical and delicate.

... It is an empire of this extent, of this complicated nature, of this dignity and importance that I have compared it to Germany and the German government—not for an exact resemblance, but as a sort of middle term, by which India might be approximated to our understandings, and, if possible, to our feelings, in order to awaken something of sympathy for the unfortunate natives, of which I am afraid we are not perfectly susceptible, whilst we look at this very remote object through a very false and cloudy medium.[46]

Burke's recourse to this visual trope is crucial because it simultaneously recognizes the inaccuracies generated by the remoteness of the "object" and the distortions endemic to the very mechanisms used to see the "object" more clearly. As Suleri goes on to argue, India's supposed sublimity renders it epistemologically inaccessible except through the distortions of the sublime's retroactive consolidation of the object. At the heart of Burke's own rhetoric is a recognition of the inevitability of the "truth" being replaced by distorting figurations.

As the first season of the impeachment wore on, the visual satirists specified these conceptual shortcomings in the presentation of evidence in terms of the mechanical distortion of optical information. Like Dent's satire of the trial as illegitimate performance in *The Raree Show,* other satirists invoked the nebulous world of precinematic display. The most extraordinary examples of this specification are to be found in a pair of related prints by Sayers and Gillray. James Sayers's *Galante Show* showed Burke as a showman manipulating a magic lantern (fig. 4.11).[47] The composition places the viewer behind Burke and members of the impeachment audience watching them watch the projection. Projected on the sheet draped in the background from left to right are an elephant labeled "A Benares Flea," Mount Ossa labeled "A Begum Wart," four eyes half-submerged in their own tears labeled "Begums Tears," and a spouting whale labeled "An Ouzle." In the foreground to the right of the lantern "are the heads of two spectators in back view who are applauding; one says 'finely imagined'; the other 'poor Ladies they have cried their eyes out.' The *profile perdu* of Lord Derby appears on the extreme right, saying, 'very like an Ouzle [weasel],'" quoting Polonius from *Hamlet* 3.2.[48] Leaving the Shakespearean quotation aside for a moment, the satirical attack turns on the optical distortion of scale. By magnifying objects out of all proportion, Burke's lantern exercises a persuasive force on the unidentified audience members, but the effect on the viewer of the print is precisely the opposite. By providing a viewpoint behind the lantern, Sayers makes the

FIG. 4.11. James Sayers, *Galante Show,* 6 May 1788 *(courtesy of the Department of Prints and Drawings, The British Museum, London; BM 7313)*

apparatus of distortion visible. Of perhaps equal importance is the subtle conversion of the space of the impeachment itself, Westminster Hall, into the space of projection. This transformation of the space from that of the state to that of the theatre is exemplified by the audience's aesthetic response to the show.

Sayers's print was brilliantly parodied a few days later by Gillray in his *Camera Obscura* of 9 May 1788 (fig. 4.12). The composition and viewpoint of the print precisely replicates that of *Galante Show,* but Gillray casts Hastings as the showman manipulating a camera obscura. The substitutions are grounded on the same questions of scale that provide the logic of Sayers's satire, but subtle distinctions push the parody away from simple reversal. In *Galante Show*, the optical mechanism takes small objects in the foreground and magnifies them on a clearly marked screen in the background. In *Camera Obscura*, the images in the background directly correspond to each of Sayers's visual tropes: from left to right Gillray represents

(1) an "Elephant" chained to a British flag devouring an Indian and trampling on the body of another; (2) "Mount Ossa," a conical mountain. (3) "Begums in Tears": a British officer raises his sword to smite a kneeling Indian woman whom he holds by the hair; other women kneel at his feet; on the ground is a decapitated infant. A wagon, with a British flag, inscribed "Plunder" drives off in the background. (4) a "Whale" spouting.[49]

But now the optical mechanism takes these large images, inverts them, and contains them within a box. In the process, the extraordinary violence of the large images is filtered out and the audience, now facing the viewer of the print, is presented with a flea, a wart, skin'd mice, and an ouzle. The inversion inherent to the camera obscura mechanism is deployed by Gillray to figure the erasure of atrocity. Beyond the simple optical inversion, which insinuates that Hastings is reducing events of extreme import into trivial matters, the redeployment of the audience is crucial because we are now able to identify the viewers as Lord Thurlow; Queen Caroline, bedecked in the jewels given to her by Hastings; and George III, manipulating an opera glass or telescope. Thurlow's response to Hastings's show emphasizes the charm of Hastings's diminishment, and Queen Caroline states that she shall cry her eyes out for the poor mice. In both cases, the responses emphasize the beauty of reduction as opposed to the sublimity of magnification in Burke's magic lantern show. At this level, Gillray argues not only that Hastings counters Burke's show by bribing those most in power over his fate, but also that he does so by resorting to a different form of aestheticization. Within the terms set forth by Burke himself in *A Philosophical Enquiry*, the depicted Hastings counters the sublime consolidation, so crucial to Burke's vision of Indian affairs, with an aesthetic tactic of miniaturization aimed at preserving the bonds of society here figured by the corrupt royal couple and its chief minion.

But something else happens in Gillray's parody that may be of even more significance. Despite its careful mimicry of composition, Gillray's image demarcates a fundamentally different space than that of Sayers's *Galante Show*. In Sayers's image, Burke's magic lantern show is staged in

Labels within the image:
an Elephant — Mount — Ofsa. — Begums in Tears. — a Whale

Charmingly diminish'd — Poor Miss. I shall cry my Eyes out — very like an Ouzle

CAMERA-OBSCURA — a Flea. — a Wart. — Shind Mice. — An Ouzle. — Minor fuit infamia Vero

J.S. ft — Tuesdays Wednesdays & Thursdays

52. 9. 1. 403 Pub.d May 9.th 1788 by S.W. Fores N.o 3 Piccadilly

FIG. 4.12. James Gillray, *Camera Obscura*, 9 May 1788 *(courtesy of the Department of Prints and Drawings, The British Museum, London; BM 7314)*

the interior space of Westminster Hall and the placement of the optical mechanism, screen, and audience are all clearly demarcated. This spatial containment confines the satirical import of the image to a critique of Burke's alleged exaggerations. But Gillray's image does not inscribe such an interior space except for that of the camera obscura itself. The violent images in the background and the images of Hastings, the camera, Thurlow, and the royal couple in the foreground appear suspended in abstract pictorial space. This suspension is of singular importance because it means that the atrocities figured in the background are not understood as distorted images but rather as merely remote. The overall pictorial space of the print figures the space of empire itself and the background images operate as signs of world historical events. Thus, the foreground witnesses are involved in an altogether different scene of viewing than in the *Galante Show*. Gillray presents Hastings, Thurlow, and the royal couple observing the trial from outside the scene of impeachment. This is significant because the king was never present at the proceedings, but the fact of his external interest in the trial was everyday emphasized by the centrality of his empty throne. In Gillray's scenario, the enclosed space of the camera obscura itself figures for Westminster Hall. The shift is subtle but activates a crucial set of allusions regarding the role of the king and the visualization of guilt.

As we have noted, both prints allude to a seemingly cursory speech from act 3, scene 2 of *Hamlet* shortly after the performance of "The Mousetrap." The allusion is both complex and instructive, for in this scene Hamlet watches Gertrude and Claudius in order to read culpability in their response. After the royal couple demands the cessation of the performance, Hamlet feels that he has evidence of guilt. Eventually, he is summoned by Polonius to see his mother. The following dialogue ensues:

POLONIUS: My lord, the queen would speak with you, and presently.
HAMLET: Do you see yonder cloud that's almost in shape of a camel?
POLONIUS: By th' mass and 'tis, like a camel indeed.
HAMLET: Methinks it is like a weasel.
POLONIUS: It is backed like a weasel.
HAMLET: Or like a whale.
POLONIUS: Very like a whale.
HAMLET: Then I will come to my mother by an by. [*aside*] They fool me to the top of my bent.—I will come along by and by.[50]

Within *Hamlet* this brief moment indicates Polonius's utter corruption in the face of power—in the process of bending to Hamlet's princely status, he will see things as Hamlet presents them—and his strategy for dealing with Hamlet's supposed insanity. In *Galante Show*, the allusion is deployed to figure Lord Derby as a foolish toady. But the implication is that he is also going along with Burke's either real or feigned madness. This wrinkle suggests that Burke's oratorical magnification is part of a larger strategy of entrapping not only Hastings but the administration and the king that support him. This subtle undercurrent carries with it the implication that Hastings and his royal supporters are tainted like Claudius and the added recognition that Burke's strategic manipulation of events is aimed at real corruption at the highest levels of the state.

In Gillray's hands the *Hamlet* allusion takes on less hyperbolic significance, but its deployment illuminates the anxiety generated by Hastings himself. In *Camera Obscura*, George III misquotes Polonius and thus suddenly emerges as both subservient and confused. This complex gesture refigures the relationship between Hastings and the Crown. In this recasting, Hastings becomes the royal prince and the real king is degraded into his subservient employee. Like many of the prints that show the king, queen, and Thurlow accepting bribes from Hastings, Gillray aims to uncover corruption, but the suggestion that the king is Hastings's servant implies that the seat of the king, both literally in Westminster Hall and figuratively at the head of the nation, is empty. The emptiness of the throne and the subtle elevation of Hastings to princely status activates the ubiquitous anxieties regarding not only Hastings's near sovereign status while in India but also his extraordinary wealth. The fear expressed here helps to explain why Gillray's print eschews a representation of Westminster Hall for the theatre of world history. From this wide-angle view, Hastings becomes a dangerous threat because of a power vacuum in the British state. He is excessively visible because the British monarch is everywhere missing. In Gillray's view, there may be some anxiety that the "body" of Hastings is more visible than the body of the king. In a single image, Gillray captures both the uncertainty regarding imperial sovereignty at this historical moment and the anxious perception that the East India Company is exhibiting a form of hybrid sovereignty beyond that defined by King-in-Parliament.

Thus far in my discussion of the trial, the specter of theatrical illegitimacy and the distortion endemic to precinematic display have come to figure for the devolution of the audience and the mystification of state and Company power, respectively. These figurations have both attempted to control the reception of the managers' oratory by recasting it as something other than an embodied speech act. As we have seen, diminishing the trial into visual spectacle still allows for a substantial engagement with the impeachment, but it also obviates the complex problem of acting. In the following section, my analysis of the theatrical relationship between the impeachment and its audience shifts from the visual incorporation of the audience in Westminster Hall to the oratorical performance of Burke and Sheridan in various speeches pertaining to the Begams charge—that is, from the spectacle of imperial sovereignty to the much more troublesome performance of imperial statesmanship.

The Begam's Tears: Performing Imperial Statesmanship

> While Mr. Sheridan was animadverting on the conduct of Sir Elijah
> Impey, the countenances of some of the East India Nabobs, who
> were present, strongly depicted the anticipating fears of Charles, in
> School for Scandal, "If they talk thus to *morality* and *sentiment*, what
> will they say when they come to me?"
>
> *Times,* 5 JUNE 1788

After the highpoints of Burke's and Fox's speeches of February, the trial
devolved into a miasma of incomplete testimony provided by largely hostile witnesses. The daily newspapers dutifully reported the events and
managed to generate some interest in Nathaniel Middleton's tendency to
forget any important details that might incriminate Hastings. In their in-
terrogation of witnesses, the managers often lost control of the testimony
and, as the trial moved toward recess, both the managers and the public
eagerly awaited Sheridan's summation of the evidence of the Begams
charge. The former group hoped that Sheridan would consolidate opinion against Hastings in much the same fashion that his earlier speech on
the same topic in the House of Commons pushed the inquiry into Hastings's activities to a formal impeachment. The latter group's anticipation
of Sheridan's speech undoubtedly had much more to do with the desire
for a reprise of what was arguably his most famous theatrical role.

In the period between Sheridan's first delivery of the Begams speech on
7 February 1787 and its second performance during the trial proper, however, a number of things happened to the popular representation of the
Begams that altered both the speech's reception and its role in the theatricalization of imperial culpability. Sheridan's famous deployment of the
family in the Begams speech involved a suspect sexualization that was
the grounds for a far more disturbing racialization of both the Begams
and Nawab Wazir of Oudh in the print media. The foundation of this
counterhistory of the Begams' plight was reinforced by material brought
forward by the managers themselves and filtered through emergent fantasies of interracial sexuality, which can be traced back to the dissemination of Oriental tales in both print and theatrical culture.[51]

The Begams charge focused on events in 1781 leading up to and including the seizure of the property of Sadr al-Nissa and Bahu Begam, the
grandmother and mother of the Wazir, Asaf al-Daula. The two Begams
were the mother and wife of Shuja al-Daula whose amity with the East India Company had resulted in a prior agreement guaranteeing the pro-

tection of lands and treasures to the widows. After the uprising of Chait Singh, Hastings and his primary agents in the affair, Nathaniel Middleton and Sir Elijah Impey, accused the Begams not only of supporting the uprising, but also of promulgating rebellion in their own territories. The managers of the impeachment argued that this accusation was contrived as a pretext for plundering the Begams' fortune. As Sheridan famously put it in his great speech to the House of Commons, "their treasure was their treason."[52] However, in part because so much of the evidence necessary to prove conclusively a breach of treaty between Hastings and the Begams was missing and in part because of the difficulty of proving Hastings's foreknowledge and direction of Middleton's and Impey's actions, Sheridan's speeches on the charge emphasize the criminality of Hastings's violation not of contract but of "filial piety." This tactical move alleged that Hastings forced the Nawab Wazir to resume the jaghires of his mother and grandmother, seize their treasure, and divert the funds collected from both actions to Hastings and eventually to the Company. In this context, Hastings's compulsion of Asaf al-Daula became a crime against human nature. This crime was aggravated by a detailed account of the violation of the sanctity of the zenana, but on this issue the comparison between the Begams and English ladies, which was so crucial for the elicitation of sympathy for the Indian women, fractured in a fashion that demands careful scrutiny. What emerged in this moment of fracture was a crisis in the representation of the violation of both sexual and social mores that impinged on the precarious definitions of feminine propriety and masculine violence that ultimately engulfed the actions of the managers.

The complex rhetorical gambit at the heart of the Begams charge had its foundation in Burke's "Speech on Fox's India Bill 1 December 1783." The published version of the speech, which is no doubt quite distinct from what actually transpired in the House of Commons, nevertheless records two crucial moments where Burke folds the response to his argument into his own discourse. In both cases, Burke's remarks on the extortion of the Begams of Oudh and on the similar confiscation of property of Panna, the mother of Chait Singh, provoked the laughter of "some young members." In the first instance, Burke's account of the plunder of the Begams is interrupted and his rebuke is only cursory:

> The *instrument* chosen by Mr. Hastings to despoil the relict of Sujah Dowlah was *her own son*, the reigning Nabob of Oude. It was the pious hand of son that was selected to tear from his mother and grandmother the provision of their age, the maintenance of his

brethren, and of all the ancient household of his father. [Here a laugh from some young members]—The laugh is *seasonable,* and the occasion decent and proper.[53]

But when he is interrupted a second time, the earlier moment becomes a setup for a symptomatic interweaving of colonial and metropolitan affairs. The scene is instructive as much for what it shows about the British assumptions regarding Indian femininity, as for what it demonstrates about Burke's tactics:

> This antient matron, born to better things [a laugh from certain young gentlemen]—I see no cause for this mirth. A good author of antiquity reckons among the calamities of his time, *Nobilissimarum faeminarum exilia et fugas.*[54] I say, Sir, this antient lady was compelled to quit her house with three hundred helpless women, and a multitude of children in her train; but the lower sort in the camp it seems could not be restrained. They did not forget the good lessons of the governor general. They were unwilling "to be defrauded of a considerable part of their booty, by suffering them to pass without examination."—They examined them, Sir, with a vengeance, and the sacred protection of that awful character, Mr. Hastings's maitre d'hotel, could not secure them from insult and plunder.[55]

This narrative of Hastings's sanction of the insult and plunder of Panna and the women of her zenana made its way into the Benares charge, but what interests me about this scene is the degree to which it encapsulates both the substance and the style of Sheridan's later oratorical rendering of the Begams charge.

It is of key strategic importance that the audience be able to recognize the Begams—or, in the preceding passage, the mother of Chait Singh—as women of quality worthy of the same respect as an English lady. Yet, as in the earlier interruption, precisely this claim provokes the laughter of the "younger" members. The age of these parliamentarians is significant because all through the speech Burke, like Clive in his earlier account of the Company's shortcomings, focuses on the immaturity of the East India Company functionaries:

> The natives scarcely know what it is to see the grey head of an Englishman. Young men (boys almost) govern there, without society,

and without the sympathy of the natives. . . . Animated with all the avarice of age, and all the impetuosity of youth, they roll in one after another; wave after wave; and there is nothing before the eyes of the natives but an endless, hopeless prospect of new flights of birds of prey and passage, with appetites renewing for a food that is continually wasting. . . . There is nothing in the boys we send to India worse than the boys whom we are whipping at school, or that we see trailing a pike, or bending over a desk at home. But as English youth in India drink the intoxicating draught of authority and dominion before their heads are able to bear it, and as they are full grown in fortune long before their heads are ripe in principle, neither nature nor reason have any opportunity to exert themselves for remedy of the excesses of their premature power.[56]

Burke's castigation of the young members of Parliament partakes of a similar charge of immaturity and suggests that their lack of sympathy and respect for the "antient lady" and her household makes them comparable with the birds of prey that are laying India to waste. Both the trope of the predatory bird and the transference of it to the laughing parliamentarians effectively establish that metropolitan support for Hastings's government is already tainted by the same lack of humanity.

The allegation is sustained by the allusion to Tacitus, which invokes the specter of Rome's decline, and is reinforced by a digression on the degradation of metropolitan economic and political life by precisely the returned East India Company employees with whom one assumes Burke's adversaries are associated:

> In India all the vices operate by which sudden fortune is acquired; in England are often displayed, by the same persons, the virtues which dispense hereditary wealth. Arrived in England, the destroyers of nobility and gentry of a whole kingdom will find the best company in this nation, at a board of elegance and hospitality. . . . They marry into your families; they raise their value by demand; . . . there is scarcely a house in the kingdom that does not feel some concern and interest that makes all reform of our eastern government appear officious and disgusting; and, on the whole, a most discouraging attempt. . . . [I]t is an arduous thing to plead against abuses of a power which originates from your own country, and affects those whom we are used to consider as strangers.[57]

So the laughing interruption becomes an occasion for Burke to mobilize an antinabob discourse that focuses on precisely the sites of cultural anxiety marked by Foote ten years earlier. The double specter of nabobs marrying into aristocratic families and of their destabilization of the domestic economy is evoked as the cause of the degradation of metropolitan culture whose proof is manifest in the laughing young men seated across the House from Burke. In short, the interruption is turned into a sign of why Fox's India Bill is necessary not only for the alleviation of Indian oppression but also for the reclamation of the virtues of the British Constitution and the national character.

After the failure of Fox's bill and the fall of the Fox-North coalition, the pursuit of Hastings unfolded according to a different set of tactics. The evidence against Hastings was laboriously introduced into the House piecemeal until Sheridan's speech on the Begams of Oudh ensured the impeachment. As the editor of Sheridan's speeches states,

> Every prejudice, every preposession were gradually overcome by the force of this extraordinary combination of keen, but liberal, discrimination; of brilliant, yet argumentative wit. So fascinated were the auditors by his eloquence, that when Mr. Sheridan sat down, the whole house, the members, peers, and strangers, involuntarily joined in a tumult of applause, and adopted a mode of expressing their approbation, new and irregular in the house, by loudly and repeatedly clapping with their hands.[58]

This account of both specific and general responses to the speech emphasizes a sudden spatial transformation in which the seat of government momentarily takes theatrical shape. This account of Sheridan's speech shows us something about the effectivity of oratory itself that resonates with Gillray's *Camera Obscura* print. At the height of its enactment, oratory has the capacity to take its audience out of the spatial and temporal constraints imposed by the state's legislative and legal apparatus and effects an abstraction which obviates precisely that which stands in the way of convicting Hastings—namely, the particularity of English common law. The "irregularity" of the outburst of applause marks a rupture in the decorum of the venue that is matched by a perceived historical rupture in the remarks of Burke, Fox, and Pitt:

> Mr. Burke declared it to be the most astonishing effort of eloquence, argument, and wit, united, of which there was any record or tradi-

tion. Mr. Fox said, "all that he had ever heard—all that he had ever read when compared with it dwindled to nothing, and vanished like vapour before the sun." Mr. Pitt acknowledged, that it surpassed all the eloquence of ancient or modern times, and possessed every thing that genius or art could furnish, to agitate and controul the mind.[59]

All three politicians take the speech out of its present moment and evaluate it in relation to the entire record of Western civilization. Such a gesture is fitting because part of Sheridan's strategy was to hold Hastings accountable not only for specific breaches of contract with the Begams but for acts against humanity itself, here defined by the sanctity of filial piety.

Julie Carlson and others have noted that indicting Hastings for crimes against the family was a tactical move aimed at avoiding key evidentiary problems in the managers' case.[60] But it also involved a restaging of material first articulated in Burke's "Speech on Fox's India Bill." The fact that Sheridan was able to take the same material that prompted laughter from Burke's audience in 1783 and refashion it to evoke sympathetic tears and universal admiration in 1787 and 1788 can be understood as a strategic refashioning of Burke's earlier interchange. One could argue that Dent's *The Long-Winded Speech* of 4 June 1788 is visualizing precisely this form of discursive indebtedness (fig. 4.13). But, unlike Dent's caricature in which the phrases of the impeachment spew out of Sheridan's mouth as unconnected syntagms from the pressure of Burke's and Fox's ministrations, Sheridan's refinement of the material is anything but random. Burke's reverence for the "antient lady," his figuration of the laughing parliamentarians and the East India Company functionaries as impetuous children corrupted by premature power, and his image of the bird of prey laying waste to the land all make their way into Sheridan's speech, but in his hands these gestures take on different connotations. Sheridan characterizes the testimony and actions of Impey, Middleton, and Hastings as childishly amateur. Impey's inconsistent affidavits, collected after the fact of the plunder to establish retroactively the Begams' rebellion, are presented as embarrassments to the judiciary. Middleton's lies and lapses of memory are sarcastically presented as those of a schoolboy. And Hastings's arrogance, avarice, and, above all, the inconsistency, both in his dealings in India and in the management of his own defense, are symptoms of interrupted development.[61] Sheridan's satiric reduction of these three figures elevates Parliament into a site of venerable wisdom and hence constructs it as an embodiment of the very gravitas that Burke himself was trying to perform in the India Bill speech. It is a crucial reversal because it sub-

The words on the banners in the image read: Plunders Omrahs, Sacrificed, Begums, Filial duty, wantonly destroyed, Shackled Enriches, Treaties violated, Sustenance forbid !, Mangled, Rebellion Nominal, Cruelties confirmed, Incontrovertible, Monsters, Nature annihilated, Evidence, Jaghire, Elephant, Oude, Bambou, Jags, Begums, Begums, Begums, Family, Rapine, Defence, Denies

THE LONG-WINDED SPEECH,
Or the oratorical organ harmonized with
sublime and beautiful inflation.
Sold by W. Dickie, Strand & W. Moore Bond Street Jun 4. 1788

FIG. 4.13. William Dent, *The Long-Winded Speech*, 4 June 1788
*(courtesy of the Department of Prints and Drawings, The British
Museum, London; BM 7330)*

tly corrals the force of laughter and mobilizes it against Hastings, Impey,
and Middleton while emphasizing the connection between present parliamentarians of whatever age and the tradition of the state they represent.

With this established, Sheridan then activates Burke's bird-of-prey
trope to indicate that such immature instruments of governance, unless
corrected, develop into deformed characters that undermine the respect
due to British colonizers. On the last day of his four-day speech, after his

sudden theatrical collapse on the previous day, Sheridan wound the audience up for the climactic apostrophe to filial piety. In the process, he once again invoked the same set of tropes and allusions that had animated much of Burke's earlier rhetoric:

> This was British justice! this was British humanity! Mr. Hastings ensures to the allies of the company, in the strongest terms, their prosperity and his protection; the former he secures by sending an army to plunder them of their wealth and desolate their soil! His protection is fraught with a similar security; like that of a vulture to a lamb; grappling in its vitals! thirsting for its blood! scaring off each petty kite that hovers round; and then, with an insulting perversion of terms, calling sacrifice, *protection!*— an object for which history seeks for any similarity in vain. The deep searching annals of Tacitus;—the luminous philosophy of Gibbon;—all the records of man's transgressing, from original sin to the present period, dwindle into comparative insignificance of enormity; both in aggravation of vile principles, and extent of their consequential ruin! The victims of his oppression were confessedly destitute of all power to resist their oppressors; but that debility, which, from other bosoms, would have claimed some compassion, with respect to the mode of suffering, here excited but the ingenuity of torture![62]

By applying Burke's image of birds of prey desolating the land specifically to Hastings, Sheridan not only figures him as a predator, but he also constructs the Begams as docile victims. This ancillary construction of the Begams as passive led to a series of contradictions in the oratory because the evidence demonstrated both women to be able politicians and rulers in their own right, and because conventional British fantasies of the power structure of the seraglio were transferred to the zenana and, hence, to the Begams themselves.[63] Since these fantasies thoroughly intertwined despotic governance with sexual and gender identities outside British norms, Sheridan's and the managers' attempts to construct the Begams as passive victims were always already compromised.

Most discussions of Sheridan's speech focus on how Hastings's crimes against the family substitute for the less provable crimes against contract. There is no question regarding this aspect of Sheridan's performance, but I want to draw attention to a different set of substitutions that effectively erase the Begams from the scene altogether. In a seemingly cursory move, Sheridan directs the audience's attention to Hastings's counsel's attempt to prevent a private letter between Hastings and Middleton from being introduced as evidence "because it was manifestly and abstractedly private, as it contained in one part the anxieties of Mr. Middleton for the illness of his son."[64] In a gesture that replays Burke's deployment of the laughing parliamentarians as the sign of inhumanity during the India Bill speech, Sheridan uses this attempt to suppress evidence of Middleton's parental concern as a sign of Hastings's, if not Middleton's, lack of respect for the parent-child bond. The attempt to suppress the private letter, which no doubt was intended to prevent other more material evidence from being admitted, is brought forward as a repetition of the earlier disregard for filial tenderness in the act of compelling the Nawab Wazir to plunder the Begams. Sheridan's segue is stunning for the way it transports the crime from its colonial venue to a present metropolitan locale—literally, the site of the impeachment itself:

> This was a singular argument indeed; and the circumstance . . . merited strict observation, though not in the view in which it was placed by the counsel. It went to shew that some at least of those concerned in these transactions, felt the force of those ties, which their efforts were directed to tear asunder;—that those who could ridicule the respective attachment of a mother and a son;—who would prohibit the reverence of the son to the mother who had given him life;—who could deny to *maternal debility* the protection which *filial tenderness* should afford;—were yet sensible of the *straining* of those *chords* by which they were connected.[65]

This subtle gesture illustrates some of the key problems faced by Sheridan in the Begams charge. By suggesting that Middleton was sensible in contravening the parent-child bond, Sheridan can argue that Hastings's actions against the Nawab Wazir and the Begams were not a particular example of what Burke had earlier called "geographical morality" but rather the manifestation of a universal principle. In other words, what Hastings did to the Nawab Wazir, his counsel was effectively doing in the impeachment proceedings. Furthermore, it suggests that the Nawab and Middleton were similarly compelled to pervert their natural sense of justice. Acting for Hastings, both men are significant to Sheridan as examples of corrupted human nature. In this light, the Nawab Wazir's seizure of the Begams' property and Middleton's incomplete and biased testimony become examples of former rectitude that is perverted by association with Hastings.

This comparison between the Nawab and Middleton is forced because both the evidence and Sheridan's speech indicate that the relationship between the Nawab Wazir and his family was far from a model of filial tenderness. Sheridan acknowledges that there was standing enmity not only between Sadr al-Nissa and the Nawab Wazir but also between Asaf al-Daula and his father. These facts were damaging to Sheridan's overall strategy because they reintroduced the question of social and cultural difference which the invocation of the family was supposed to override.[66] The speech therefore activates a set of tactical displacements, only some of which were successful. The substitution of Middleton's concern for his son for the Nawab Wazir's concern for the Begams is one of these tactics and it works primarily by deploying one set of expressions, Middleton's letter and his faulty testimony, as a model for interpreting another—that is, Asaf al-Daula's own letter stating his reluctance to do Hastings bidding and his subsequent capitulation. Middleton's actions in Westminster Hall reductively stand in for the Nawab Wazir's complex actions in Oudh and hence the foreign is made comprehensible by a present example. But this substitution is only secure in the enactment of Sheridan's oratory. As P. J. Marshall states, "Sheridan . . . played havoc with Hastings's embarrassments, but his own version of events was so over-simplified that it cannot have carried much conviction after the effect of the oratory had worn off."[67]

A similar and even more powerful displacement emerges as Sheridan enters his apostrophe on filial piety. What is crucial to recognize in the following passage is how the address and the deixis turn his present audience into those wronged by Hastings's actions:

There was something connected with this transaction so wretchedly horrible, and so vilely loathsome, as to excite the most contemptible disgust. If it were not a part of his duty, it would be superfluous to speak of the sacredness of the ties which those aliens to feeling,— those apostates to humanity had thus divided. In such an assembly as that which I have the honor of addressing, there is not an eye but must dart reproof at this conduct;—not a heart but must anticipate its condemnation. "FILIAL PIETY! It is the primal bond of society—it is that instinctive principle, which, panting for its proper good, soothes, unbidden, each sense and sensibility of man!—it now quivers on every lip!—it now beams from every eye!—it is an emanation of that gratitude, which softening under the sense of recollected good, is eager to own the vast countless debt it ne'er, alas! can pay, for so many long years of unceasing solicitudes, honourable self-denials, life-preserving cares!—it is that part of our practice, where duty drops its awe!—where reverence refines into love![68]

Although the apostrophe continues a good deal longer, its crucial moment occurs when Sheridan first draws attention to the audience itself and then states that the sensibility of the primal bond of society is evident "now" on every lip and in every eye in that same assembly. It is important to think through this deictic moment as a performative act through which the speaker mobilizes the feelings of his audience in a fashion that equates its response to the situation of those wronged on the other side of the world. The entire rhetorical assemblage turns on a very specific familial trope: not simply the parent-child bond is being invoked, but the bond between mother and son. The Begams are being depicted first and foremost as mothers, and Sheridan implies that the Nawab Wazir, like each of the parliamentarians before him, is naturally indebted to his mother for her maternal care, and that Hastings forced him to renounce that relationship. But this specification also erased the women in the audience, and this failure to recognize the gendered qualities of his address generated significant problems before a mixed audience. Sheridan's treatment of this renunciation of the maternal takes us back to Burke's invocation of the damaged breasts of the women of Rangpur as signs of Hastings's depravity, but Sheridan's deictic gestures incite the audience to reconstitute the signs of damaged maternality with their own sympathetic familial emotions. What had elicited horror at the outset of the impeachment has been reactivated to generate sentimental identification. In short, the Begams' tears, so distant and so difficult to bring forth as evidence, are replaced in the oratorical moment by the self-evident tears of Sheridan's audience.

Rather than a straightforward expression of the shared humanity of Indian and British subjects, the apostrophe offers a figuration of the former by the latter that effectively erases the key distinctions between them. Furthermore, the transience of the oratorical bonding of listening subjects poses significant problems for Sheridan's strategy of displacement. Because of its performative qualities, each displacement must be superseded by another in order to keep the differences between Islamic and Christian society and culture in abeyance. It is precisely this insatiable need for figuration that makes the speeches so voluminous and so prone to recoiling on themselves. The most vivid and instructive examples of the unraveling of audience consolidation revolve around Sheridan's attempt to figure the violation of the Begams' zenana as rape. The discourse of rape is pervasive through the speech and is aimed at eliciting tears in a fashion akin to that of she-tragedy.[69] The only difficulty is that Sheridan, despite all his oratorical skill, is not Mrs. Siddons, and hence must describe violation rather than enact it. Unlike the instance of filial piety, Sheridan's performance of affect can generate sympathetic feeling, but it cannot enact the substitution of present for distant humanity. If the audience identifies with the "great feeling" expressed by Sheridan on this point, then its identification is not with the experience of violation but rather with an observer's pity for the violated.[70] This is a direct result not only of his performance of sentimental masculinity, which ensures that he is at best an observer of the violated woman's suffering, but also of the culturally distinct understanding of feminine propriety and normative sexuality that interrupts direct identification between the women in the audience and the women of the zenana, a point noted by Julie Carlson:

> Special difficulties accrue around the effort to gain sympathy for the Begums, either as elderly women or persons whose private quarters have been invaded. As a way of linking Hastings's invasion of the zenanas with rape, Sheridan emphasizes testimony regarding the sanctity with which the "sequestration" of Indian women is viewed, especially by the women themselves who elect to retire from the public eye because they view being viewed as "profanation." . . . This was gross miscalculation according to the court recorder who observes that "the female part of the audience did not seem to feel his distress."[71]

What this indicates is that conflicting understandings of gender and sexual propriety short-circuit the speech's intended effect or, more precisely, divide the response along gender lines. The implication of the court recorder's observation is that Sheridan's performance of distress established a homosocial bond between himself and his masculine auditors but alienated him from the ladies in the audience. This alienation suggests that for the women in attendance a boundary between Indian and English femininity had to be maintained in part because it was so effectively dissolved in Sheridan's paternalistic gaze.[72]

Of course, the boundary being enforced carries all the significance of cultural difference because it is the very different definitions of public and private, and the fantasies of sexuality projected onto each category, that animate this distinction. For Sheridan's imputation of rapacity to resonate, he carefully distinguishes the zenana from the widely held notion of the seraglio:

> The confinement of the Turkish ladies was in a great measure to be ascribed to the jealousy of their husbands; in Hindostan the ladies were confined, because they thought it contrary to *decorum* that persons of their sex should be seen abroad: they were not the victims of jealousy in the men; on the contrary, their sequestration from the world was *voluntary;* they liked retirement, because they thought it best suited to the dignity of their sex and situation: they were shut up from liberty, it was true; but liberty, so far from having any charms for them was derogatory to their feelings; they were *enshrined* rather than *immured* . . . . Such was their sense of delicacy, that to them the sight of a man was pollution; and the piety of the nation rendered their residence a *sanctuary.* What then would their lordships think of the tyranny of the man who could act in open defiance of those prejudices, which were so interwoven with the very existence of ladies in that country, that they could not be removed but by *death?*[73]

Sheridan's closing question draws his audience into the ethical scene in much the same fashion as the filial piety passage, but here the address to "their lordships" carries a number of connotations that alienate the women viewing the trial. As Julie Carlson emphasizes, women attending the trial "may also have experienced the testimony as fighting words aimed at their interest in seeing and being seen at the trial."[74] As we have already noted, the visibility of women at the trial and in the street outside Westminster Hall was the site of some anxiety. Sheridan's hyperbolic assertion of the purity and delicacy of the inhabitants of the zenana seems to cast aspersion on the far more public lives of the women in the audience. As attendees, the foremost women in London were exposed to accounts of sexual violence and sexual practices that were outside the realm of polite conversation.

But more important, this view of the zenana is counterintuitive to the audience, because their sense of the sequestration of women is grounded, as Sheridan himself acknowledges, on the prevalent notion of the Turkish seraglio as a site not only of sexual dissipation but also of gender insubordination. This is a problem because a significant portion of the contemporary representations of the seraglio emphasized the power of the foremost women over the sexually dissipated sultan, and hence any correlation between the zenana and the seraglio short-circuits the construction of the Begams as passive victims by reasserting their political agency. Sheridan's attempt to ignore the seraglio and all of the sexual fantasies associated with it relies on the desexualization of the Begams and the inhabitants of the zenana. But this desexualization of the Indian women, like Sheridan's representation of their passivity, was subject not only to internal but also to external contradictions. In the space between Sheridan's first speech on the Begams of Oudh in the House of Commons and his summation of the Begams charge at the impeachment, the managers' opponents resexualized the Begams and their zenanas in a fashion that arguably disabled this section of the speech for part of his audience at least. And this symptomatic breakdown in the rhetoric of the charge was facilitated by none other than Edmund Burke.

In one of the strangest moments in the entire trial, Burke introduced as evidence a passage from Prince Demetrius Cantemir's *History of the Turks* to prove the respect with which feminine modesty and maternal status are held in Moslem society. On 22 April 1788, Sheridan and Burke were introducing written evidence largely aimed at establishing the invasion of the zenana by East India Company soldiers as a species of rape. Sheridan brought forth testimony from Sir Elijah Impey—Hastings chief judicial official and a key player in the transactions at Oudh—that "nothing could be more sacred than the character of a woman, nor more venerable than that of a mother, in India," and Burke bolstered Sheridan's position with the following passage from Cantemir:

> The Sultans have always treated their mothers with great respect, in compliance with the divine precepts, and those of the Koran. They can not only introduce and change many things at pleasure in the Seraglio, but also the Sultan is forbid by the laws to lie with any of the women kept there, without his mama's consent. Every day, during the Feast of Bairam, the Sultan-mother presents a *beautiful virgin,* well educated, richly dressed, and adorned in precious stones, for her son's use. . . . If the Sultan has a mind to chuse a concubine unknown to his mother, he may indeed do it without opposition; but he is reckoned to act contrary to the rules of the Seraglio, and against his *mother's honour!* Very often, the Sultan communicates to his mother the affairs of state, as Sultan Mahomet is known to have done.[75]

The *Morning Post* reports that Hastings's counsel Mr. Law objected to the "*reveries* of Prince Demetrius Cantemir . . . unless it could be proved that

the customs of Musselmen all over the world were the same as at Constan-
tinople," but it is hard to imagine anything better for undercutting Sheridan's claim of sexual propriety both here and in the subsequent version
of the speech on the Begams charge.[76] The *Morning Post*'s account of the
reaction to this text is telling:

> The part of the passage, which related to the blooming virgins pro-
> vided for the Sultan, was not worded by Prince Cantemir in the
> manner in which he probably would have written it, if he could have
> foreseen that it would ever have been read before most ladies of Eng-
> land. Whether they were pleased or displeased at it, they can best tell;
> but their *blushes* shewed, that they felt the force of the moving de-
> scription of the Sultana's authority.[77]

For Burke's audience, the sultana both emerges as the bawd for her own
son and accedes to a position of authority over not only his state but also
his desire. Considering the fact that one of the connotations of the word
"mother" during this period is proprietor of a brothel, a whole series of
connections adverse to the managers' containment of the erotics of the
scene start to proliferate. If we transfer this narrative to the Begams charge,
then the former implication essentially constructs the zenanas as brothels
and the latter implication suggests that the Nawab Wazir's willingness to
plunder the Begams is due less to Hastings's coercion than it is to the Bahu
Begam's private but no less excessive power over him. In this scenario,
the Nawab Wazir's invasion of the zenana becomes a liberation from his
mother's excessive control over his public and private affairs.

Burke's tactical error was quickly satirized four days later in Sayers's
A Reverie of Prince Demetrius Cantemir, Ospidar of Moldavia of 26 April
1788 (fig. 4.14). This image of Burke's supposed fantasy life is the precursor to Dent's *No Abatement* discussed earlier, both in its figuration of the
elderly Indian woman and its suggestion that Burke's pursuit of Hastings is delusional. But Sayers's illustration, framing and embellishment
of the events of 22 April, not only probe the sexual fantasies that everywhere threaten to undermine the Begams charge, but also enforce a sense
of "geographical morality" by emphasizing signs of sexual, social, and
racial difference. Sayers's ascription of desire to Burke does not mobilize
the spectacles trope seen elsewhere in the satirical prints. The visualization of Burke's oratory as a species of optical distortion or magnification
gives way to a dream image whose broad contours conjoin the "facts"
drawn from the public reading of Cantemir's text and the fantasies prom-

FIG. 4.14. James Sayers, *A Reverie of Prince Demetrius Cantemir, Ospidar of Moldavia,* 26 April 1788 *(courtesy of the Department of Prints and Drawings, The British Museum, London; BM 7307)*

ulgated by Oriental tales. If the latter were not already active enough in the reception of the evidence, Sayers adds a number of crucial details. Burke sleeps next to his speaking notes, which place Cantemir's text above the following commentary: "Note Begum—The Viziers Mother frequently procures one of the most beautiful Virgins whom she adorns with Pearls and precious stones and brings to the Vizier whom she calls her Lion and desires him to take her to his Arms, this he most religiously performs and she is afterwards consig[ned] to the Zenana with 200 others whom he never sees a second Time."

Sayers's additions to Cantemir are symptomatic for he attacks Islamic social mores, here figured by the bust of Mahomet, the lamp, and the image of the Koran and by emphasizing the sexual profligacy of the sultan. It is a tired trope, but one that is adorned in this instance by a rather scurrilous pronoun slippage which makes it unclear which woman calls the Sultan "Lion and desires him to take her to his Arms." The suggestion is that by procuring virgins for her son, the mother, in this case Bahu Begam, not only acts out of displaced incestuous desire for her son but also identifies with the two hundred discarded wives. Over and against Burke's and Sheridan's deployment of the maternal as an icon for the sympathetic bonds of society, Sayers constructs not only a bad mother but also a nonmaternal relationship between mother and son. In a single xenophobic gesture, Sayers constructs the domestic life of the sultan as one of multiple perversion, undercuts the purity of the Begams, and counters the managers' protection of filial piety as a displaced form of incestuous desire. What is crucial to recognize is that both the "facts" introduced by Burke and the sexualized Orientalism of the discourse of the seraglio are equally damaging to the managers' presentation of the Begams charge.

However, what remains equally unclear both in Sayers's print and in the introduction of Cantemir's text to the trial is Burke's relation to the depicted scene. In the Sayers print, is Burke identifying with the sultan and hence with the sexual coercion of the conspicuously white virgin brought for his pleasure, or is the relationship that of a voyeur to a particular sexual transaction? And what are we to make of Burke's flowing robes and his pasha-like slipper? The costume both orientalizes and feminizes the great orator and seems to draw him into the scene of the dream. In terms of the trial, the passage from Cantemir was introduced as evidence of veneration for the mother, and it would seem that Burke favored a reading of the seraglio scene that focuses exclusively on the power dynamics of the transaction rather than on the sexual nature of the exchange. The effectivity of the Cantemir evidence, like Sheridan's later attempts to depict the sanctity of sequestration, relies on an abstraction of the scene that desexualizes the mother and, by extension, the entire zenana. What Sayers's print allows us to see, in its blunt ethnocentric gestures, is the degree to which the managers' handling of the Begams charge relied on a discursive containment whose fragility owed as much to sexualized fantasies of the East as it did to equally volatile fantasies of widowhood.

This latter problematic becomes evident in the more direct representations of the Begams in prints and in the press. If the relationship between Burke and the sexual transaction of his dream is unclear in *A Reverie of Prince Demetrius Cantemir,* then subsequent images are much more precise in their ascription of desire. In subsequent prints such as Sayers's *The Princess's Bow Alias the Bow Begum* of 1 May 1788, the managers are portrayed as suitors or obeisant subjects of Bahu Begam (fig. 4.15). The undecidability of their relation to Bahu Begam is itself important because it is precisely this combined desire for and subservience to women that marks the dissipation of the sultan's—and the managers'—masculinity for the European audience. But the image does more than refigure the managers' case as a symptom of Oriental profligacy that resonates with other allegations of Foxite excesses. The fact that Sayers retains the image of Burke with his eyes closed and basically reworks his image of the procuring sultana as a withered hag from the earlier print suggests that Burke's respect or desire for the Bahu Begam is grounded on his inability to see her. With his spectacles off and his eyes closed, Burke is blind to her palpable undesirability. The suggestion that desiring Bahu Begam is itself somehow odious is underlined by the subtitle "Bow wow wow," which puns on the Anglicization of her name, and more subtly by Fox's half-bow which arguably represents a certain reluctance. In all subsequent visual representations of the Begams of Oudh, this combination of decrepitude and racial difference is deployed to insist on the cultural difference between Indian and British society. Burke's inability to see here stands in for an inability to distinguish between a bawd and a reputable lady, between the violation of a space and the violation of a body, and ultimately between Indian and English subjects. And this failure to distin-

FIG. 4.15. James Sayers, *The Princess's Bow Alias the Bow Begum*, 1 May 1788 *(courtesy of the Department of Prints and Drawings, The British Museum, London; BM 7309)*

guish is presented as symptomatic of aberrant social and sexual relations. Throughout the satirical images of the Begams, intersexual relations between English men and widowed Indian women are signs of the managers' departure from normative sexuality, but what remains unstated is the relationship between British men and young Indian women. It is crucial for his critique that Sayers's emphasis on the age of the Begums remain at the forefront of their representation because it allows for the fetishization of young Indian women in the zenana to remain operative. And as we have seen the presence of the desirable, yet sacrificed woman is crucial to the critical ascription of Orientalized desire to Burke and the other managers.

These visual images of the widows' undesirability are counterbalanced by no less sexualized textual representations that imply that the Begams have more in common with the demireps of London society than the sequestered nuns of Sheridan's speech. The most remarkable of these is a faux newspaper report of a "Masquerade Extraordinaire" published in the *Times* during the recess just prior to Sheridan's summation of the Begams charge. The masquerade joke is a fitting place to conclude our discussion of the theatricalization of the trial because it renders political theatre as mock social theatre and offers some perspective on the representational strategies of both the managers and their satirists. The "Masquerade Extraordinaire" extends through two issues of the paper, and its detailed accounts of the costumes of prominent personages are the occasion for sometimes mild, sometimes bristling satire on contemporary London society. The passage relevant to the Hastings trial sexualizes the relationship between the Begams and the primary male actants in the trial according to the tale of Daniel and Susanna from the Apocrypha:

> Mr. Hastings and Sir Elijah Impey, as the two elders in the Apocrypha, charging one of the Princesses of Oude, who is habited like Susanna, with adultery. Mr. Burke, in the person of a *Daniel,* as the Lady's council. The arguments and cross questions were inimitably well supported, and afforded fine entertainment. How the Princess of Oude got over to this kingdom in a manner unknown to the public, is a mystery yet to be unravelled. Certain it is, however, that she was at this Masquerade, and in such a habit as Susanna wore before she undressed herself to bathe. Daniel had spectacles on his nose and though the event represented a time long antecedent to the christian aera, yet he often crossed himself and seemed to look, with a friar-like leer, on the beauties of Susanna.[78]

Casting Hastings and Impey as the elders from the Daniel and Susanna story simultaneously captures their combined efforts to accuse the Begams of rebellion and the contradictory quality of their testimony.[79] In the process, the allegory refigures Hastings's and Impey's avarice as lust and thus turns the breach of contract into an act of sexual violence. The masquerade enacts the managers' tropological strategy almost to the letter, except that it eroticizes rather than desexualizes the Begam. And the moment of eroticization is telling; by casting the Begam as Susanna on the verge of undressing herself, the text presents her not only at the height of her desirability to the elders but also at the point of her most intense vulnerability. The text implies that Burke's arguments, like those of Daniel, will succeed, but focuses the reader's attention on the sensational moment prior to both her refusal of sexual relations and her subsequent vindication from the elders' calumny. In short, she is simultaneously hypereroticized and endangered.

Significantly, the masquerade scene suggests that Burke's gaze—once again figured by his spectacles—is not all that different from that of Hastings and Impey, for he too "leers . . . on the beauties of Susanna" through his spectacles. The image of Burke as a leering friar plays on both the conventional satirical representation of Burke as a Jesuit and Sheridan's portrayal of the zenana as a sacred sanctuary akin to a monastery or a convent. The entire gesture intersects with the popular anti-Catholic satire of convents as sites of libertine excess and "unnatural" practices.

This ascription of "leering" desire is clarified by the subsequent invocation of Fox and Sheridan:

> Mr. Fox and Mr. Sheridan, as Neptune and Boreas, planning a general shipwreck by a convulsion of the elements. These were two capital masks—Neptune's trident and Boreas's face displaying what their intentions were. Mrs. Armstead, in a *mask* of Venus, stood close to *Neptune*—and in truth she had much need of the mask, for when she shewed her real face at supper, she looked more like Neptune's mother than a daughter of the sea.[80]

The throwaway line on Fox's lover—the celebrated demirep Mrs. Armstead—invokes a different kind of widow for the reader's consideration.[81] In the context of what we have seen thus far, an implicit comparison is being drawn between Fox's relationship with Armstead and the fantasized relationship between Burke and Bahu Begam. In this light, the portrayal of the Begam before being accused and vindicated of adultery is significant because it places her in a different place than Armstead. She is eroticized, not sexualized, and despite—or perhaps because of—her visual fetishization, she becomes a wife to be protected, not a widow to be propositioned. And the eroticization and dematernalization of the Begam turns on the contrast with the aging Armstead.

Oddly enough, this complex assemblage of attributes allows us to isolate the rhetorical problem faced by Sheridan in his oratorical attempt to render the violation of the treaty between the Begams of Oudh and the East India Company as a sexual violation. The Begams need to be figured as eroticized, yet innocent, subjects in order to activate them as possible victims of rape; but this figuration is blocked not only by the countervailing figuration of the Begams as desexualized mothers that is so crucial for the allegations regarding Hastings's neglect of filial piety, but also by the hypersexualization attendant upon the long-standing equation between Eastern women and courtesans like Mrs. Armstead. This points to a fundamental inability even among the managers to imagine the Indian women of the zenana as wives. As we have seen, Sheridan attempts to manage the erotics of modesty in his description of the zenana, but the centrality of the crime against the family to both the speech and the overall charge intervenes and forces a retroactive rhetorical containment of the sexual fantasies of Orientalism that effectively cancels this erotics. In a sense, this failed containment only points the way for the satirists to move in and literally dismantle the Begams charge by hyperbolically rendering the managers' desire for conviction as a displaced sexual fantasy. In this light, the rendering of Hastings's and Impey's avarice as lust in the "Masquerade Extraordinaire" has its counterpart in the satirists insinuation from the earliest phases of the Hastings affair that the managers' lust for conviction was a displaced form of avarice. And, in the end, it is this complementarity, so vividly captured in the faux masquerade, that makes the performance of imperial self-scrutiny at the trial so instructive.

As P. J. Marshall and Sara Suleri argue, the trial's attempt to see the crisis in imperial policy in a fashion that could generate an accommodation between national, commercial, and colonial governance was doomed from the outset by the fact that such historical processes cannot be visualized in such reductive terms. But of equal importance to this epistemological rupture at the heart of colonial relations is the proliferation of intertwined tropes aimed at suturing the social fabric of the metropole. The satirical prints that have been the focus of this chapter, with their crude diminishments of the oratorical feats of Burke, Fox, and Sheridan, indicate that the question of imperial culpability, even in the most pro-Hastings prints, is always already answered in the affirmative. It is hard to imagine that anyone following Nathaniel Middleton's incoherent testimony or at all cognizant of the manipulation of East India Company stock could believe that British activities in India were benign. There were too many indicators in the metropole that the opposite was true. The real contest being played out in Westminster Hall was whether, in the face of such culpability, it was possible for metropolitan society to continue to operate according to the rules that had structured social interaction since the Glorious Revolution. At the heart of Burke's attack and Hastings's defense was a complex argument about the performance of honorable masculinity at home and abroad, about the deployment of femininity in the scene of politics, and about the volatile sexualization of metropolitan and colonial spaces. What the satirical prints indicate is that in spite of the elevated oratory and august surroundings, the audience in Westminster Hall was witness to a conflict that worked according to many of the same tropes as the lowest forms of theatrical presentation and the tactics of everyday scandal. And this conflict generated a concatenation of racial and sexual figures that allowed the process of metropolitan self-consolidation to continue apace, but in a mode different than that defined by earlier forms of governmentality. It is from this recognition—that the trial produced styles of imperial subjectivity in spite of its failure to convict Hastings—that I wish to turn to Frances Burney's complex critique of the proceedings.

Molière's Old Woman

Judging and Being Judged with Frances Burney

WHAT ARE WE TO MAKE of Frances Burney's detailed and complex account of the impeachment proceedings against Warren Hastings? Both Sara Suleri and P. J. Marshall recognize the importance of Burney's *Diary* for understanding the theatricality of the impeachment, but perhaps because of the private qualities of the document—the diary entries are written for Burney's sister—neither scholar reads her text as a sustained critical intervention. Suleri's deployment of Burney is most interesting because she aligns Burney's reservations regarding Burke's role in the impeachment with her own analysis of the trial's excess. Citing Burney's inability to look at either Hastings or Burke, Suleri states that

> her difficulty is no mere gentility, but points to the colonial specta-
> tor's implication in a circuit of guilt far too amorphous to be con-
> tained in the body of one man. To be unable to look at either the ob-
> ject of prosecution or the prosecutor himself is to record a moment
> in which the colonial gaze is forced to retreat into blindness: such
> complicated acts of unseeing mark both Burney's and the *History*'s
> narratives of the trial as testaments to their guilty recognition of the
> intimacies of colonial violation.[1]

In Suleri's analysis, Burney's "unseeing" is used as a lever to critique Burke's deployment of figures of gendered violence in his rhetorical as-sassination of Hastings's character. Perhaps because Suleri is primarily concerned with Burke's role in the process and with the elaboration of the Indian sublime, key aspects of Burney's intervention that I believe point to a much more elaborate and thoroughgoing engagement with colonial guilt go unnoted. This chapter reads Burney's *Diary* as a sustained meditation on public affairs that carefully analyzes the theatricality of the trial. Burney pays close attention to her own role in this particular political theatre, for she is careful to emphasize that her physical presence, her conversation, and her range of actions in Westminster Hall are thoroughly deformed, or proscribed, by gendered fantasies of her situation in relation to the political. As a feminine witness to a masculine drama, her interventions raise crucial questions not only about the separation of spheres, but also about how the constitution of public masculinity itself impinges on any theorization of colonial guilt. Part of the difficulty of performing this reading of the *Diary*, however, is the degree to which seemingly trivial details, descriptions of domestic engagements and conversations, are accorded the same status as events of highest concern to the state. In short, the text almost invites one to overread, to construct the entire account as a carefully coded critique whose most biting moments are those which seem most innocuous. In order to demonstrate this problematic, I start this discussion with her account of an evening at the theatre immediately preceding the Hastings trial. As we will see, the passage resonates with much of the preceding chapter and seems to give some instructions for how to think about the theatricality of the impeachment.

Hath Not a Jew Eyes?

On Friday, 1 February 1788, Burney and other members of the queen's household went to see Sarah Siddons play Portia in *The Merchant of Venice*. In addition to stating that Siddons didn't seem at her best, Burney notes that the play was accompanied by "'The Humorist:' a thing without plot, character, sentiment, or invention; yet, by means of ludicrous mistakes and absurd dialogues, so irresistibly comic, for one representation, that we all laughed till we were almost ashamed of ourselves" (39).[2] It is precisely the kind of passing remark that confirms one sense of the occasional quality of the *Diary*. But when one returns to it after reading her account of the trial, this incidental remark is doubly activated. Is *The Merchant of Venice* invoked as some kind of coded preview of the Hastings trial? She would not be alone in making such a gesture. James Hook's *The Trial* of 17 May 1788 renders the impeachment as a specific moment from the trial scene in *The Merchant of Venice* (fig. 5.1). The space of Westminster Hall is distorted into a thrust stage, and a semitic Fox grasping a knife utters Shylock's response to Portia's famous speech regarding the quality of mercy: "My deeds upon my head. I crave the Law." The print

FIG. 5.1. James Hook, *The Trial,* 17 May 1788 *(courtesy of the Department of Prints and Drawings, The British Museum, London; BM 7321)*

puns on Law because Hastings's leading counsel, Mr. Law, is cast as Portia, adjudicating between Fox and Hastings. This suitably casts Hastings as Antonio and Thurlow as the Duke of Venice, and in the terms set out by the play, Law interprets the law in lieu of the state. The print therefore visualizes the incursion of the common law on "the Law and Usage of Parliament" that so disabled the managers' case. Fox's desire to kill the "Law" therefore, figures both for his personal animosity and for the managers' frustrated desire to operate according to parliamentary rather than legal rules. It is a subtle gesture, but one that is by now familiar from other satires of the trial, for the print emphasizes the close relationship between Thurlow, the king, and Hastings. George III hides behind Thurlow's seat, watching the drama through an opera glass, and thus Hook marks both the absent presence of the Crown and his barely veiled commitment to Hastings's acquittal. In a lovely detail, we find that the king is contemplating not the struggle between Law and Fox but rather the tiny crown on Hastings's turban—perhaps a subtle indication, seen elsewhere in the prints, that it is really the imperial merchant, not the sovereign, who wears the crown.

But this subtle lampoon of the state's corruption is, of course, overshadowed by the print's attack on the managers. The image of Fox the Jew depicts him and, by extension, the managers as agents of vengeance, not justice. Read through the Shakespearean script, the impeachment is thus a perverse manipulation of the law to enact revenge. But rendering Fox as Shylock also activates a series of connotations already in contemporary circulation. First, it calls up the repeated assertion that the managers' resentment hails from a combination of greed and personal enmity. Second, if we integrate the characterization into the narrative of *The Merchant of Venice*, it suggests that Hastings broke his bond with the managers, but the enactment of the forfeiture is impossible to effect without destroying themselves. This implication is complex, however; in the play Antonio finds himself in a precarious position because he is acting for Bassanio. I believe that Hook is insinuating that by acting for and enriching Thurlow and the king through the charter of the East India Company, Hastings has broken a contract with the Commons of England, whom the managers technically represent.

In this light, the figuration of Fox as a Jew casts aspersion not only the managers but also on the people they represent. This gains some resonance when one recognizes that the print portrays the moment immediately following Portia's soliloquy on the quality of mercy, which reads rather differently in this context:

> The quality of mercy is not strained;
> It droppeth as the gentle rain from heaven
> Upon the place beneath. It is twice blest;
> It blesseth him that gives and him that takes.
> 'Til mightiest in the mightiest; it becomes
> The thronèd monarch better than his crown.
> His sceptre shows the force of temporal power,
> The attribute to awe and majesty,
> Wherein doth sit the dread and fear of kings.[3]

Put in the mouth of Hastings's counsel, the speech becomes a critique not only of Fox's vehemence but also of his consistent attempts to rein in the power of the sovereign. For this reason, the print, which comes well after Fox's most active moments in the trial, focuses on Fox, for he is being depicted as a threat to the monarchy. But his threatening posture is undercut by his denial of mercy. The print seems to be arguing that Fox's long-term political goal of restraining the power of George III would be better served if the managers, unlike the king, demonstrated Hastings's forfeiture of his responsibilities both to those who govern him and to those whom he governs, and then offered Christian forgiveness. As a strategic commentary, Hook's print attacks in two directions at once, for it argues not only that the king should not simply overlook Hastings's misgovernment, but also that the punishment sought by the managers is neither likely nor politically efficacious. And here the ethnic slur already active in the invocation of Shylock becomes most acute, for it suggests that Fox's violence, whether understood as a treasonous assault on the Crown or as an interested assault on the riches of the East India Company, is contrary to the interests of an ethnically defined Christian Britain.

I have worked through the implications of this print's satire in some detail because its argument is not at all distant from Burney's own discussion of the political implications of the trial. The subtle critique of George III's position in the whole affair is lacking in Burney's account—she is after all part of the queen's household—but the sudden appearance of a woman in public vestment mediating in the conflict between Antonio and Shylock resonates with Burney's own self-placement between Hastings and the managers of the impeachment. Perhaps Burney's dissatisfaction with Siddons's "entrance into the character" of Portia is in fact a subtle indication of her own desire to play the judge in the drama about to unfold.

If the allusion to Siddons in *The Merchant of Venice* offers a subtle hint as to Burney's own self-construction in relation to the impeachment proceedings, then her more extended remarks on the evening's afterpiece, James Cobb's *The Humorist,* provide vital clues for understanding how this Portia is deployed in the theatrical space of Westminster Hall. On the day following the trip to the theatre, Mr. Wellbred comes to visit the royal household and proceeds to tell Burney which scenes of *The Humorist* he found most amusing. Foremost among these was the representation of the servant Pompey, and her response helps to specify the shame she felt at enjoying the piece:

> I owned the charge, but asked how he had discovered it. Instead of answering me, he picked out another part which had particularly amused me—then another and another that had struck me—then almost every part almost, through the five acts, with which I had most been pleased in the play.
>
> I was quite amazed at his seeing thus distinctly, and with such discernment, across the house. (40)

It is difficult to assess the precise register of these remarks, but Burney is clearly embarrassed for her laughter, either because the play was insipid, or because it was evoked by low caricatures. What is important for our purposes is the scene of being seen, especially that of being seen watching a play that ridicules the lower orders. Burney emphasizes that the entire scenario opens onto an evaluation of the characters of the audience according to their response to the staged drama. When Wellbred states that "I take[s] great delight in watching for thoughts and opinions at particular passages during a play: 'tis at least half my amusement. I think that then I can read into people's own dispositions and characters," Burney offers the following revealing remarks:

> On my word, thinks I, if I had been aware of being watched thus, and with such a view, I should less have liked my *vis-à-vis* situation. I confessed myself, however, to have just the same propensity to drawing my conclusions, and honestly regretted that I had not the same ability, from the shortness of my sight.
>
> We then ran over almost the whole, both of the play and the farce, comparing notes, and re-diverting ourselves with all we had seen.
>
> The re-performance of our dramas was interrupted by the appearance of his Majesty, who, however, also talked them over, and commented upon them very judiciously. The King's judgement upon these subjects seems to me almost always good, because constantly his own, natural and unbiassed, and resulting from common sense, unadulterated by rules. (40–41)

It is a fascinating passage because it so vividly portrays Burney's situation as a marriageable woman in the theatre. Her discomfort at being watched while watching is due in part to Wellbred's glib objectification, but it is also due to the differences in their capacity to see. After confessing that she too likes to watch others watch in order to evaluate their characters, she emphasizes that her shortness of sight prevents her from entering into the characters of as many people. It is a striking allegory for the limitations of femininity because her shortness of sight figures for her restricted public circulation.[4]

Burney's discussion of shortsightedness partakes of the same visual economy as the satires on Burke's spectacles, and again it is hard to know how to handle her remarks. There is a subtle satire of Mr. Wellbred's farsightedness that resonates with the frequent jokes on Burke's shortsightedness throughout the proceedings. Wellbred's ability to see and evaluate characters across the expanses of the theatre is contrasted with Burney's own inability to focus on distant objects. If Burney and Burke share a similar visual impairment, then their vision of distant characters is equally compromised. Burke's reliance on some kind of optical mechanism to bring both Indian affairs and the scene of impeachment into focus allows for a whole series of jabs regarding the truth of appearances. The fact that Burney does not wear glasses to the trial can be understood as an acceptance of her limited purview that contrasts with the distorting qualities of Burke's spectacles.

But the passage takes on further significance in relation to her account of the trial. Once inside Westminster Hall, Burney's shortsightedness is never directly mentioned. There are times, when for decorum's sake, she insists on her lack of education and inexperience in public matters, but these apologies are always staged as preliminary remarks for direct analyses of the trial's operation. Sitting in the box of the great chamberlain, Burney gives her reader clear and detailed descriptions of the reactions of various personages to the reading of the charges against Hastings. With the Wellbred conversation in mind, it is clear that the *Diary* is engaged in a focalizing exercise whose ultimate aim is to render the characters of those who watch the drama between the managers and Mr. Hastings. It is for this reason that she is so uncomfortable with her own visibility in Westminster Hall, for her very presence in the space renders her subject to the same gaze. Because she is affiliated with the royal family, her fraternization with the managers is politically discomfiting; more important, her visibility unveils the narrative apparatus in a fashion that requires some consideration.

One of the strangest dynamics in the *Diary* is that the oratorical performances on the floor of Westminster Hall are represented through conversation between Burney and Wyndham, one of the lesser managers charged with prosecuting the impeachment. William Wyndham was an up-and-coming star in the Whig Party and a protégé of Burke.[5] As such, he operates in Burney's *Diary* not only as a voice for the managers and for Burke in particular, but also as a figure for the political future of the country. Yet despite the public notoriety of Burney and Wyndham, everything about their recorded conversations is always framed by gendered notions of propriety and by Burney's sexualized role in public space. This private mediation of the public events is highlighted again and again throughout the *Diary*, but nowhere more evocatively than when Wyndham states that "we are only prosecutors there—(pointing to the Committee-Box), we are at play up here" (83). This distinction between the work of prosecution, which is itself a form of play, and the erotic play between the managers and the ladies in the gallery, which Burney skillfully turns into a form of prosecutorial work, effectively divides Westminster Hall into a space of homosocial conflict and heterosexual repartee. But Burney consistently deflects Wyndham's desire to speak to her by engaging in a critique of the homosocial violence of Burke and Fox. As a narrative technique, this embedding of unfeminine political commentary in a frame of proper conversation not only insulates Burney from charges of gender insubordination but also emphasizes that everything she says and does in the space of the impeachment is framed by codes of gender decorum.

Significantly, Burke's difficulties during the impeachment process also impinge upon the question of narration. As noted in the previous chapter, Suleri emphasizes that Burke's decision to affix the historical and ongoing crimes of a nation onto one man

> left the charges dangerously vulnerable to being forgotten even at the moment of their utterance. . . . Whichever way the verdict fell, Burke was destined to failure, in that he continued to stand in too inchoate a relation to the enormity of his claims. The exercise of "arbitrary power" for which he sought to impeach Hastings could not be so easily expunged from the history of colonization; much of Burke's rhetorical extravagance suggests a subterranean admission that it was indeed too facile to assume that Hastings alone could be held responsible for the exigencies of what it means to colonize. (51)

Burke's inchoate relation to the charges is in many respects a problem of narration, for, in recounting the tale, Burke partakes in it. For observers of the proceedings, the question of Burke's reliability as a narrator is crucial. One of the most important elements of the impeachment, as Suleri emphasizes, is that Burke's rhetoric was so excessive that it cast doubt on its veracity:

> [T]he charges were both excessively long and excessively interested in breaking down the constraints of their own legalism, continually spilling over into dialogue and narrative that muddies rather than clarifies the specificity of each accusation. For the overwhelming detail with which Burke narrates the enactment of Hastings's violations is designed to obliterate a belief in the graspability of its narrative: facticity thus ironically becomes a casualty of an overabundance of facts. (51)

Burney was extremely cognizant of this problem in Burke's presentation of the case and of the implications for her own narration. As her account of the trial unfolds, she uses her limited point of view—specifically ascribed to her femininity and to her position in the royal family—to maintain Hastings's nonculpability. Furthermore, she uses the distinction between being the object of the gaze as part of the spectacle itself and her role as narrating spectator of the trial to highlight the degree to which judgment requires a temporary cessation of complicity. In moments of judgment, Burney takes herself out of the spectacle of Westminster Hall either through masquerading as another or through shifts of address. However, as an agent of judgment she repeatedly allows her complicity in the scene to compromise her status as judge. This playing at, and subsequent unraveling of, judgment is arguably the *Diary*'s most profound intervention in the trial for it insists upon a commutability between the managers and the indicted governor-general of Bengal, between Burke and Hastings, that emphasizes their and her complicity in the process of colonization. If Burney's remarks on *The Humorist* are about the discomforting simultaneity of watching and being watched, then her description of the impeachment proceedings focuses on the similarly disorienting simultaneity of judging and being judged.

Burney's account of the first day of the impeachment is marked by two moments of trembling, moments where her body is literally overcome by emotion. The first occurs after a long and detailed account of the seating arrangement when Burke enters Westminster Hall:

> The business did not begin till near twelve o'clock. The opening to the whole then took place, by the entrance of the *Managers of the Prosecution;* all the company were already long in their boxes or galleries.
>
> I shuddered, and drew involuntarily back, when, as the doors were flung open, I saw Mr. Burke, as Head of the Committee, make his solemn entry. He held a scroll in his hand, and walked alone, his brow knit with corroding care and deep labouring thought,—a brow how different to that which had proved so alluring to my warmest admiration when first I met him! so highly as he had been my favourite, so captivating as I had found his manners and conversation in our first acquaintance, and so much as I had owed to his zeal and kindness to me and my affairs in its progress! How did I grieve to behold him now the cruel Prosecutor (such to me he appeared) of an injured and innocent man! (47)

The second occurs when Warren Hastings is called to the bar, and it bears comparison to the entrance of the managers:

Then some other officer, in a loud voice, called out, as well as I can recollect, words to this purpose:—"Warren Hastings, Esquire, come forth! Answer to the charges brought against you; save your bail, or forfeit your recognizance!"

Indeed I trembled at these words, and hardly could keep my place when I found Mr. Hastings was being brought to the bar. He came forth from some place immediately under the Great Chamberlain's Box. . . .

The moment he came in sight, which was not for a full ten minutes after his awful summons, he made a low bow to the Chancellor and Court facing him. I saw not his face, as he was directly under me. He moved on slowly, and, I think, supported between his two Bails, to the opening of his own Box; there, lower still, he bowed again; and then, advancing to the bar, he leant his hands upon it, dropped on his knees; but a voice in the same moment proclaiming he had leave to rise, he stood up almost instantaneously, and a third time profoundly bowed to the Court.

What an awful moment this for such a man!—a man fallen from such height of power to a situation so humiliating—from the almost unlimited command of so large a part of the Eastern World to be cast at the feet of his enemies, of the Tribunal of his Country, and of the Nation at large, assembled thus in a body to try to judge him! Could even his Prosecutors at that moment look on—and not shudder at least, if they did not blush? (48–49)

The scenes are remarkable for their similarity, for their theatricality, but above all for the shared affect they generate in Burney the viewer. The entrances of Burke and Hastings both elicit fear and a certain level of projection. The question that closes this passage is essentially the same as that posed by Burke in the *Reflections on the Revolution in France* with regard to Mrs. Siddons's performance of suffering: what kind of person could witness such a scene and not be stirred by compassion and sympathy for the actor. It is a subtle move, but one that cuts to the core of Burke's own aestheticization of the political throughout his career. In light of our discussion in the previous chapter, the fact that Burney shudders and the managers, to her observation, do not, is evidence of a perversion of human nature that she attributes specifically to the rage for party. As we have seen, this kind of political analysis of normative emotional response is thoroughly grounded in Burkean aesthetics. Burke's campaign is being judged according to his own principles.

And that judgment extends to both Burke's public and private inter-actions in Westminster Hall. Her difficulties with Burke, whether they be with his public oration or his personal courtesies, are marked by the same bodily response. As she states, "I trembled as he approached me, with con-scious change of sentiments, and with a dread of his pressing from me a disapprobation he might resent, but which I knew not how to disguise" (93). Burke poses a social problem for Burney because it is improper for her to disapprove of Burke's courteous applications to her on strictly po-litical grounds. Her coldness and disapprobation are not only difficult to contain but are also contrary to her gendered relation to the political. For Burney to exhibit disapprobation either through word or gesture— and I think that it is the latter that is of utmost concern for her—is to claim a place in the political outside the bounds of normative femininity.[6] Conversing with Burke in the space of Westminster Hall is hazardous be-cause Burney may exhibit signs of unfeminine political engagement.

This problematic gets beautifully expressed in Burney's only sustained conversation with Burke in the *Diary:*

> I turned to speak to Mr. Burke . . . but [he] was in so profound a reverie he did not hear me.
> I wished Mr. Wyndham had not either, for he called upon him aloud, "Mr. Burke, Miss Burney speaks to you!"
> He gave me his immediate attention with an air so full of respect that it quite shamed me.
> "Indeed," I cried, "I had never meant to speak to Mr. Burke again after hearing him in Westminster Hall. I had meant to keep at least that *geographical timidity.*"
> I alluded to an expression in his great speech of "geographical morality" which had struck me very much. He laughed heartily, in-stantly comprehending me, and assured me it was an idea that had occurred to him on the moment he had uttered it, wholly without study. (94)

Unlike her direct criticism of Burke's oratory later in the *Diary,* Burney embeds her disapprobation in a protective layer of wit. Her turn on Burke's widely discussed notion of "geographical morality" takes on the critical edge of mimicry, for the rewriting of Burke's phrase means that she operates, like Hastings, according to rules suitable to particular lo-cations. Burke scorned this kind of moral variability, but here Burney is basically arguing that her decision not to speak or socialize with Burke is based on her place in the scene of impeachment. In a highly subtle manner, Burney is pointing out that the gendered separation of spheres, of which Burke is complicit, establishes different modes of moral and social conduct appropriate to different locations. In other words, Burney suggests that "geographical morality" is a structuring principle of metropolitan life that incorporates Burney, Hastings, and Burke himself.

But this kind of raillery is the exception, not the norm, in the *Diary*. The following passage is more typical of her reaction when faced with the possibility of conversing with Burke:

> In a minute, however, Mr. Burke himself saw me, and he bowed with the most marked civility of manner; my courtesy was the most ungrateful, distant, and cold; I could not do otherwise; so hurt I felt to see him the head of such a cause, so impossible I found it to utter one word of admiration for a performance whose nobleness was so disgraced by its tenour, and so conscious was I the whole time that at such a moment to say nothing must seem almost an affront, that I hardly knew which way to look, or what to do with myself. How happy and how proud would any distinction from such a man have made me, had he been engaged in a pursuit of which I could have thought as highly as I think of the abilities with which he has conducted it! (87)

For Burney, the tenor of Burke's prosecution makes him an unfit social interlocutor. And it is notable that her sudden perplexity at where to look or what to do when he approaches is much the same as her inability to look at Hastings when, under the influence of Burke's oratory, she is momentarily persuaded of his guilt. The implication is that Burke's charges against Hastings rebound on his own character, making him a kind of social pariah. This suggested substitutability between Burke and Hastings is consistently maintained throughout the *Diary*. The glance of both men causes Burney to tremble, though for different reasons. She accords both of them the utmost respect based on her prior familiarity with them in society, but Burke's public performance causes her to reappraise his character.

The reappraisal of character is a troubling problem for Burney because it is necessitated by the inconstancy of the affect exhibited by participants and viewers of the impeachment. How could Burke, who excited nothing but reverence in an earlier meeting, be so alienated from her own feelings in this theatrical moment? And with evidence of this kind of shift in character before her, how can her defense of Hastings, which is based on the assumption that an earlier demonstration of rectitude is extendable to all of a man's actions, be sustained? Her appraisal of the managers' characters threatens to undermine the theory of the subject—a theory based on how an individual takes up its position in society—which subtends her faith in Hastings's innocence. What I hope to demonstrate here is that the oratorical strategies of the managers themselves precipitate a crisis in the definition of the political that could arguably be used to distinguish between Enlightenment and Romantic understandings of the social.

Fox's Countenance

Burney's anxiety is illuminated by Peter de Bolla's discussion of the legislation of the body in oratory. Casting over a series of texts from the elocutionary movement, de Bolla isolates a set of strategies through which the orator contains the languages of the body. Because the effect of oratory lies not in the words of a speech but rather in the conjunction of words and bodily performance, the relationship between gesture and text is crucial. In an effort to prevent the language of the body from communicating errantly, many elocutionary texts recommend a careful regulation of decorum and in particular an avoidance of direct visual contact between orator and listener. As de Bolla states, "This avoidance [of any intimate or indecorous eye contact] amounts to the erasure or covering up of the subject to and within itself; a negation of those inner thoughts and desires which we take to be the very representatives of subjectivity, personality and individuality, in favour of the complete or total legibility of the social subject, the public self. The trajectory of the legislation is clear: public sociability should erase private subjectivity."[7] De Bolla's distinction between public sociability and private subjectivity is helpful for comprehending Burney's critique of the managers' performances, for she is extremely cognizant not only of moments when the private subject displaces the public man but also of inappropriate moments of visual contact. For Burney, problems emerge when the body does not transparently reflect the sentiments contained within the text.

The most straightforward statement of this problematic comes during Burney's critique of Fox's speech on the Benares charge. Her remarks on Fox are divided into a brief summary of the effect his speech had on her and a retrospective analysis of its failings. The former is careful to differentiate between Fox and Burke:

Mr. Fox spoke for five hours, and with a violence that did not make me forget what I had heard of his being in such a fury; but I shall never give any account of these speeches, as they will all be printed. I shall only say a word of the speakers as far as relates to my own feelings about them, and that briefly will be to say that I adhere to Mr. Burke, whose oratorical powers appeared to me far more gentleman-like, scholar-like, and fraught with true genius than those of Mr. Fox. It may be I am prejudiced by old kindnesses of Mr. Burke, and it may be that the countenance of Mr. Fox may have turned me against him, for it struck me to have a boldness in it quite hard and callous. (92)

Burney is disturbed by the fact that Fox's anger over the Peers' decision on how to hear evidence bleeds over into his attack on Hastings.[8] The suggestion is that he lacks the control necessary to prevent his personal fury from infiltrating and contaminating his speech. And it is Fox's face, or his countenance (with all that implies about performance), that testifies to his lack of control. In this light, Fox's face interrupts his claim to public sociability, and thus the entire speech becomes an expression of mere private emotion.

Burney offers a more sustained discussion of the disjunction between Fox's body and his words a bit later in the *Diary;* however, it is important first to consider how Burney stages her intervention. Her most extensive discussion of the trial's oratory is framed by a remarkable reorientation of the trial's theatricality. As part of her back and forth with Wyndham, she casts herself in a role adjacent to theatrical production:

"Molière, you know, in order to obtain a natural opinion of his plays, applied to an old woman; you, upon the same principle, to obtain a natural opinion of political matters, should apply to an ignorant one;—for you will never, I am sure, gain it *down there.*"

He smiled, whether he would or not, but protested this was the severest stricture upon his Committee that had ever yet been uttered.

I told him as it was the last time he was likely to hear unbiassed sentiments upon this subject, it was right they should be spoken very intelligibly. (97)

This complex and conscious accession to a position of "natural" ignorance has significant ramifications for all that follows. First, by playing this role, Burney both takes up the place ascribed to her by masculinist definitions of the political and emphasizes that it is her very privation that renders her an "unbiassed" critic of the trial's theatricality. Yet, by invoking Molière, she is also implying that the same qualities that make the old woman a good judge of comedy, make her a good judge of political matters. So if the role playing both protects and enables her critique, it also undercuts the managers' pretensions to tragic seriousness. Burney attributes seriousness to the events in Westminster Hall, but they are better understood through the lens of comedy.

Burney's hazardous entry into the realm of political critique is facilitated by Burney's and Wyndham's mutual respect and affection for Samuel Johnson. The shared affective bonds of their prior intimacy with Johnson are thus put forward as the ground on which Burney can negotiate with Wyndham. Burney will eventually use the shared respect for Johnson as a wedge to separate Wyndham from Burke and Fox. This is a crucial gesture because Wyndham plays two roles in Burney's discourse. He is an interlocutor who gives her occasion to enter the realm of political commentary, and he potentially figures as Burney's prosecutorial ideal. Much of Burney's intervention is explicitly staged as an attempt to re-form or educate Wyndham so that he does not become like Burke or Fox. The critical commentary of Molière's old woman is explicitly staged as part of the education of one who has been accepted into the same social circle. And the terms of that educational contract are explicitly stated midway through the account: "[S]hould he prove as violent and as personal as the rest, I had no objection to his previously understanding I could have no future pleasure in discoursing with him" (97). As we will see, excessive violence and an overly personal enmity toward the accused are precisely what alienate Burney from the more famous managers.

Having cast herself as Molière's old woman, Burney goes on to analyze the performances of Burke and Fox. I look at the analyses in reverse order, for her remarks on Fox's primary speech bring out issues in harsh relief that are more subtly rendered in her discussion of Burke. The *Times* account of Fox's speech on the Benares charge emphasizes both the severity of his language and the impact of his words on Hastings: "At times he was so particularly severe on Mr. Hastings and bore down on him with such a torrent of eloquence and argument, that Mr. Hastings was frequently obliged to turn his face from him."[9] But Burney is less interested in the aversion of Hastings's glance than in how Fox uses his own eyes during his speech: "[A]mongst the things most striking to an unbiassed spectator was that action of the Orator that led him to look full at the prisoner upon every hard part of the charge. There was no courage in it, since the accused is so situated he must make no answer; and, *not* being courage, to *Molière's old woman* it could only seem *cruelty!*" (101). As we have already noted, regulating the movements of the eyes and face is of key importance for an elocutionist's attempt to negate the private self from the public performance of a text. Burney reads Fox's eye contact with Hastings as immediately excessive and proceeds to interpret its significance. Because Hastings is already arraigned, Burney argues that there is no necessity to single out Hastings. In her eyes, Fox's excessive glance amounts to a repetitive digression: it has no public purpose. The only reason she can determine for Fox to stare at Hastings in this way is his own personal cruelty, which springs from a private animosity toward the defendant. And this is sufficient in and of itself to undercut Fox's charge, for it suddenly takes on the character of a disagreement between two men and not that of an affair of state. As we will see, there is a breakdown between text and performance, here signaled by signs of Fox's "cruelty," that is symptomatic of a certain breakdown in national consolidation. However, understanding the nationalist aspects of Burney's critique requires more sustained engagement not only with the substance of Fox's speech but also with the place of oratory in the protonationalist gestures of the elocutionary movement.

Again, casting herself as Molière's old woman, Burney draws attention to discontinuities between text and performance in her discussion of Fox's speech on the Benares charge:

> I next, therefore, began upon Mr. Fox; and I ran through the general matter of his speech, with such observations as had occurred to me in hearing it. "His violence," I said, "had that sort of monotony that seemed to result from its being factitious, and I felt less pardon for that than for extravagance in Mr. Burke, whose excesses seemed at least to be unaffected, and, if they spoke against his judgment, spared his probity. Mr. Fox appeared to have no such excuse; he looked all good humour and negligent ease the instant before he began a speech of uninterrupted passion and vehemence, and he wore the same careless and disengaged air the very instant he had finished. A display of talents in which the inward man took so little share could have no powers of persuasion to those who saw them in that light; and therefore, however their brilliancy might be admired, they were useless to their cause, for they left the mind of the hearer in the same state that they found it." (99–100)

Burney's specificity regarding the disjunction between Fox's performance during the speech and that immediately prior to and following it is revealing on two counts: she isolates the violence of Fox's speech for disapprobation and then attributes the monotony of that violence to a split in Fox's subjectivity. Fox's monotony has a quasi-pathological quality that needs to be thoroughly considered because she reads the discontinuity as more than a mere indication of Fox's lack of private investment in the matter at hand. A brief digression on the substance of Fox's speech is helpful to comprehend the full ramifications of Burney's critique.

Burney is suggesting that Fox has performed precisely the split that the managers are trying to overcome, for the image of a man by turns languorously disengaged and vehemently impassioned maps onto a spatial split that Burke had earlier described as "geographical morality." Prior to and following his speech, Fox performs according to the commonplace descriptions of his character in metropolitan society; during his speech Fox becomes the public man angrily concerned with abuses of power in the colony. Burney seems to be suggesting that the disjunction between the styles of bodily performance reveals a discontinuity within the managers' case, which is otherwise hidden behind their brilliant textual refutation of Hastings's primary defense—namely, that he acted according to principles of governance ostensibly endemic to India. As noted in the previous chapter, Burke's famous critique of Hastings's claim to be merely rehearsing the Eastern pattern of governing by arbitrary power was focused through the trope of "geographical morality":

On speaking of the appointment and character of Mr. Hastings, the conduct of this gentleman . . . had been distinguished for an adherence, not to the general principles which actuate mankind, but to a kind of GEOGRAPHICAL MORALITY—a set of principles suited only to a particular climate, so that what was peculation and tyranny in Europe, lost both its essence and its name in India. The nature of things changed, in the opinion of Mr. Hastings; and as the seamen have a custom of dipping persons crossing the EQUINOCTIAL, so by that operation every one who went to INDIA was to be un-BAPTIZED, and lose every idea of religion and morality which had been impressed on him in Europe. But this doctrine . . . would now no longer be advanced. It was the duty of a British Governor to enforce British laws; to correct the opinions and practices of the people, not to conform his opinion to their practice; and their Lordships would undoubtedly try Mr. Hastings by the laws with which they were acquainted, not by those which they did not know.[10]

Aside from the remarkably blunt assertion that the British should be correcting the practices of Indian peoples, Burke's contrast between the Lords' mode of governance during the impeachment with that practiced by Hastings as governor-general is a fundamental element of the managers' case. As Burke continues, it becomes clear that Hastings's claim to "arbitrary power" not only operates outside the models of British governance but also verges on treason:

> Mr. Hastings had pleaded the local customs of Hindostan, as requiring the coercion of arbitrary power. He claimed ARBITRARY POWER. From whom, in the name of all that was strange, could he derive, or how had he the audacity to claim such a power? He could not have derived it from the East India Company, for they had none to confer. He could not have received it from his Sovereign, for the Sovereign had it not to bestow. It could not have been given by either House of Parliament—for it was unknown to the British Constitution![11]

By stating that Hastings's defense of his actions was contrary to the British Constitution, Burke effectively argued that Hastings's excesses were dangerous not only to those he directly coerced in Bengal but also to the very body that sat in judgment of him. However, this gesture, at once so rhetorically powerful, carried with it certain responsibilities that would cause problems for the managers because they themselves were often figured as threats to the balance of power between the sovereign and Parliament. And it was Fox more than anyone else who embodied this Whig threat to the will of the king and the ministry.

After Burke carefully constructed Hastings's actions not only as a usurpation of the power conferred by the British Constitution but also as a form of blasphemy in the opening speeches, it rather ironically fell to Fox to detail Hastings's accession to arbitrary power in his speech on the Benares charge. From the early 1780s Fox's political career was widely understood to be devoted to the progressive restraint of the sovereign's will over Parliament. During and after the fractious election of 1784, he was recognized by both friends and enemies alike as bitterly opposed to the interventions of George III in the affairs of the nation. In this light, it is interesting to consider what was going through the managers' minds when Fox was chosen to lead the Benares charge, because his speech is so thoroughly entwined with the definition of sovereignty. Fox's sarcasm in passages such as the following targets more than just Hastings:

> Neither did the *European* ideas of sovereignty accord with the defini-tion contained in his *Indian* dictionary.—By *sovereignty,* says Mr. Hastings in his defence delivered to the Commons—I mean *arbi-trary power!* And lest his meaning should be misunderstood—lest he should be thought to have spoken of *absolute* power, he adds, "What I mean by arbitrary power is that state where the will of the sover-eign is *every thing,* and the rights of the subject—*nothing!*[12]

Fox uses the closing quotation to great effect throughout the speech by staging complaints from various Rajahs and then responding in Hast-ings voice: "My will, as a sovereign, is EVERYTHING; and your rights, as a subject, are NOTHING."[13] But Fox's discussion of the definition of sover-eignty provides him with more than a rhetorical device. It also allows him to insinuate two things about Hastings that are of some consequence in relation to his own oratorical practice. First, the careful distinction be-tween absolute and arbitrary sovereignty suggests that Hastings's mode of governance exceeds that of the king. In light of the frequent allegations that George III was in Hastings's pocket, Fox's remarks sarcastically sug-gest that the king's partiality to Hastings may be a form of identification. Furthermore, his remarks carry a subtle reminder that the struggle against absolute power, which in some senses defines Parliament, should be equally applied to the far more threatening specter of arbitrary power. And this rhetoric of threat is bound up with a complex form of linguistic na-tionalism.

By focusing on how Hastings defines words, Fox suggests that Hastings is not using his natural language, that he has traded in his English diction-ary for an Indian one. The gesture is telling because it resonates with the frequent British concern, from the midcentury onward, with the question of a national language. At the heart of Johnson's dictionary and much of the elocutionary movement is a desire to cultivate and codify a unified na-tional tongue.[14]

> Language and empire go hand in hand. . . . Correct language use was a sign of English political authority; moreover, it marked one as a gentleman. In several installments of the *Rambler,* Johnson features the importance of proper language use and pure pronunciation as

an indication of acceptable manliness. To Johnson and his contemporaries, "Language was an index of intelligence and reflected human mentality, knowledge, memory, imagination, sensibility."[15]

Fox's suggestion, therefore, is that such an incursion on the definition of sovereignty is a threat not only to principles of national governance but also to the practice of linguistic exchange, which defines a nation-state.

We can focus our remarks here by looking briefly at Thomas Sheridan's popular lectures on the question of a national language. Sheridan was arguably the most influential theorist of elocution in the period, and he strongly advocated the dissemination of a uniform English grammar and dictionary for the unification of the nation-state:

> [I]f such a Grammar and Dictionary were published, they must soon be adopted into use by all schools professing to teach English. The consequence of teaching children by one method, and one uniform system of rules, would be an uniformity of pronunciation in all so instructed. Thus might be the rising generation, born and bred in different Countries and Counties, no longer have a variety of dialects, but as subjects of one King, like sons of one father, have one common tongue.[16]

As Peter de Bolla argues in relation to this strain in Sheridan's thought, the argument that the unified state is the political reflection of the public production of the unified subject means that the relationship between public and private, between the subject as an authentic place of speech and the nation as an authentic place of representation for the individual are all put on stage in the act of oratory.[17]

> [U]nhealthy habits in speech, and lack of skill in oration both reflect and produce an unhealthy state. . . . The role of education . . . is to help fix and codify the language, so that each individual can both speak and be moved by a common tongue: all of this, of course, in the interests of fixing and stabilizing a national identity, of placing the representation of the self within the context of the greater whole, the nation. From here it is but a mere short step to the welding of the image of self to national self-image.[18]

In this light, Sheridan's discussion of the propriety of speech in *British Education* and in his *A Course of Lectures on Elocution* takes on remarkable significance because it suggests that the infiltration of foreign languages into English and the failure to meld word and gesture are symptomatic of a degeneration not only in the speaker, but also in the language and hence the strength of the nation. The latter problem is the site of intense concern because the language of the body may run counter to the language of the spoken text and thus destabilize the oratory. As de Bolla summarizes, the "exterior speech, the speech of the orator, should to all intents and purposes represent the interior: public and private voice should be made identical."[19]

Fox's remarks on Hastings's definitions of sovereignty partake in this kind of protonationalist concern with language, but I would argue that Burney's remarks pick up on this aspect of Fox's critique and turn it on his own oration. The key distinction is that her concern is less with linguistic definition than with linguistic performance. If Fox is to act according to the moral standard set out by Burke in the "Speech on Opening of Impeachment of Warren Hastings" and by his own sarcastic remarks on Hastings's unrestrained governance, then it is crucial that no split between private subject and public orator be revealed to the audience, for as soon as one starts to question the continuity between these two actors, the unified theory of the moral Christian governing subject is destabilized. And, most important, Fox himself may be characterized, like Hastings, as a degenerate linguistic subject.

Much of the elocutionary thought of the period was explicitly concerned with preventing revelations of this kind of disjunction and often recommended that orators speak only from their natural feelings. As de Bolla remarks with regard to Sheridan's recommendation that orators "deliver those words, as proceeding from the immediate sentiments of his own mind":

> The text must become internalized, thereby turning the dead text into living speech; more than this, however, the voice itself becomes a text for the audience, for it is emphasis that communicates the correct or proper meaning. The textualization is a kind of healing process, in which the exterior textual matter is assimilated within the interior sentiments of the mind of the orator, who then expresses the combined text/internal sentiment in a soothing manner. The result of this is for Sheridan to recognize the need for an absolute identity between the public and the private in order to forestall the possibility of a split subject.[20]

In this context the splitting of the subject into public and private entities signifies a weakening form of hybridity akin to the linguistic hybridity ascribed to Hastings. What is so complex and compelling about this countergesture is the implication that the intermixture of Indian and English in Hastings's usage—clearly marked as an inappropriate form of ethnic intermixture—is similarly suspect as the intermixture of the private and public man. It is significant that Burney's description of the radical distinction between Fox the speaker and Fox the lounging manager is presented as an elaboration of his "monotony." Monotony in elocution is largely a matter of variation, technically an inability to vary one's tone and expression. So the lack of modulation in Fox's utterances is marked as a sign of weakness that is then specified by the remarks on Fox's body language. What is needed therefore is a type of elocution and a type of national subject that does not devolve into these pathological conditions. And that is to be found according to someone like Sheridan in a careful internal regulation that adequates sentiment and passion—and their attendant bodily expression—with the text.

Burney makes precisely this suggestion when, at an earlier point in the *Diary*, she offers what amounts to a theory of acting for Wyndham's edification. The context is interesting because Wyndham confesses that "in his little essays in the House of Commons, the very sound of his own voice almost stopped and confounded him; and the first moment he heard nothing else, he felt quite lost, quite gone!" and that he wishes he was more fully prepared for his speech (84–85). Burney responds that the lack of time and study will make a more effective speech precisely because it will be free of artifice. Wyndham's response to this and Burney's rejoinder clearly reveal the stakes in the supposed identity between the natural feelings of the private man and the public performance of the social subject. Wyndham states that "something of previous thought is absolutely necessary: mere facts will not do, where an audience is so mixed and miscellaneous; some other ingredients are indispensably requisite, in order to seize and secure attention" (85). In her response, Burney locates the persuasiveness of the public subject in his ability to convey his immediate natural feelings on the facts presented:

> "They will all come! and the more, perhaps, for a little agitation, and surely with greater power and effect: for where there is sufficient study for all the rules to be strictly observed, I should think there must be an air of something so practised, so artificial, as rather to

harden than affect the hearts of the hearers. When the facts are once stated, I cannot but suppose they must have much more force where followed only by unstudied arguments, and by comments rising at the moment, than by any laboured preparations; and have far more chance of making a deep impression, because more natural and more original. (85)

What Fox's factitious performance indicates to Burney is a certain distance between the "facts" and his interpretation of them. At one level, she could be arguing that Fox, as Burke's mouthpiece, has insufficiently learned his part—a charge we have seen elsewhere (see fig. 4.6)—but she could equally well be insinuating that his interpretations of the facts in the Hastings impeachment are not natural because they are not his own. It is here that the ironic tone of much of Fox's speech is so important because the multiple registers of his sarcasm make the adequation of inner and outer by definition that much more elusive. What is important for us to remember is that for Sheridan, and, I would argue, Burney, this inability of the audience to hear Fox's speech as the expression of his inner beliefs amounts to a failure to properly own and practice one's national language that is no less dangerous than Hastings's supposed contamination of English with Indian meanings.

Bodily Legislation

Throughout the trial, the managers frequently allude to Hastings's prevarications and subtleties of usage, and the thematic makes its way into Burney's *Diary* in an important exchange between Burney and Wyndham. After Wyndham animadverts on Burke's eloquence, Burney asks if Hastings will speak in his own defense:

> "No," he answered, "he will only speak by counsel. But do not regret that, for his own sake, as he is not used to public speaking, and has some impediment in his speech besides. He writes wonderfully—there he shines—and with a facility quite astonishing. Have you ever happened to see any of his writings?"
> "No: only one short account, which he calls Memoirs relative to some India transactions, and that struck me to be extremely unequal—in some places strong and finely expressed, in others obscure and scarce intelligible."

"That is just the case—that ambiguity runs through him in every-thing. Burke has found an admirable word for it in the Persian tongue, for which we have no translation, but it means an intricacy involved so deep as to be nearly unfathomable—an artificial entanglement."

Then he spoke the original word, but I do not presume to write Persian.

I took this occasion to mention to him that his friend Dr. Johnson, in observing how little lenity he ever had to more words than matter. He looked at me with a respectful attention when I named that honoured name, that gratified my own respect for it. He then said he must be gone, and show himself again in the committee.[21] (73–74)

The invocation of Johnson at the close of passage is intriguing because Burney consistently mobilizes Johnson as the arbiter of moral judgment in this section of the *Diary*. Johnson becomes a crucial sign here not only of the correct relationship between words and subject matter, but also a key point of negotiation between Burney and Wyndham. Assured of Wyndham's respect for Johnson, she pulls out Johnson to critique not only Burke's prolixity but also Burke's reliance on a Persian word to describe the unevenness of Hastings's writings and character. Are we to interpret the invocation of Johnson here as a protectionist gesture? If so, then Burney is in effect accusing Burke and the other managers with the same inappropriate usage that they attribute to Hastings. Does the unnamed Persian word capture Hastings's guilt or does it signal a kind of characterization that cannot be assimilated into the scene of English judgment? Burney's analysis of Fox certainly opens the door for such an interpretation especially when one factors in Johnson's place in the codification of the national language.

Furthermore, Burney's invocation does something important in her relation to Wyndham, and in the relationship between Wyndham and Burke. Wyndham's respect for Burke borders on enthusiasm, and Burney mobilizes Johnson to counteract the following outburst:

"Come," cried [Wyndham] with energy, "and hear Burke!—Come but and hear him!—'tis an eloquence irresistible!—a torrent that sweeps all before it with the force of a whirlwind! It will cure you, indeed, of your prepossession, but it will give you truth and right in its place. What discoveries has he not made!—what gulfs has he not dived into! Come and hear him, and your conflict will end!"

I could hardly stand this, and, to turn it off, asked him if Mr. Hastings was to make his own defense? (73)

It is difficult to determine whether Burney is more offended by the suggestion that Burke's oratory is an unstoppable force that will evacuate the listener's subjectivity or by the implication that her "prepossession" for Hastings is contrary to "truth and right." Regardless, Burney responds with a withering reference to Johnson aimed at undercutting Wyndham's enthusiasm by reminding him of his prior personal attachment to Johnson. And that attachment is one that he shares with Burney. The implication is that Wyndham's admiration of Burke's irresistible eloquence is somehow disrespectful not only to Wyndham's deceased friend but also to Burney's mentor. Burney subtly highlights the degree to which the whirlwind effect of Burke's oratory interferes with the ties of private society. In other words, she emphasizes the degree to which oratory disjoins the audience from its private beliefs and thus points to another form of splitting that needs to be taken into account in an assessment of character.

Burney's reactions to Burke can be divided into public and private interactions. As we have already noted, the latter are dominated by moments of trembling unsociability and her private difficulties are clarified by her explicit discussion of the second day of Burke's "Speech on Opening of Impeachment of Warren Hastings."[22] This is the section of the opening speech in which Burke inveighs against "geographical morality." But that famous declamation comes after the extended narration, first, of Company intervention in the transference of sovereignty from Siraj-ud Daula to Mir Jafar to Mir Kasim and, second, of the oppression of Muhammad Reza Khan.[23] Burney's initial description of the speech is highly cognizant of these two separate modes of presentation and of how they interact. But more important is the careful rendering of her response to the shifts and turns in Burke's discourse:

> All I had heard of his eloquence, and all I had conceived of his great abilities, was more than answered by his performance. Nervous, clear, and striking was almost all that he uttered: the main business, indeed, of his coming forth was frequently neglected, and not seldom wholly lost; but his excursions were so fanciful, so entertaining, and so ingenious, that no miscellaneous hearer, like myself, could blame them. It is true he was unequal, but his inequality produced the effect which, in so long a speech, was perhaps preferable to

greater consistency, since, though it lost attention in its falling off, it recovered it with additional energy by some ascent unexpected and wonderful. When he narrated, he was easy, flowing, and natural; when he declaimed, energetic, warm, and brilliant. The sentiments he interspersed were as nobly conceived as they were highly coloured; his satire had a poignancy of wit that make it as entertaining as it was penetrating; his allusions and quotations, as far as they were English and within my reach, were apt and ingenious; and the wild and sudden flights of his fancy, bursting forth from his creative imagination in language fluent, forcible, and varied, had a charm for my ear and my attention wholly new and perfectly irresistible. . . . But though frequently he made me tremble by his strong and horrible representations, his own violence recovered me, by stigmatizing his assertions with personal ill-will and designing illiberality. Yet, at times I confess, with all that I felt, wished, and thought concerning Mr. Hastings, the whirlwind of his eloquence nearly drew me into its vortex. (78–79)

The contrast with her description of Fox's speech is palpable. Nowhere do we find Burney dwelling on Burke's physicality—his body does not figure in the description except through the range and timbre of his voice. Unlike Fox, Burke's body does not interfere with the reception of the text but rather seems to highlight it, and there is no suggestion that Burke's performance ever becomes monotonous. Since there appears to be a harmonization of gesture and text, Burney intimates, in terms very similar to Wyndham's, that she is nearly drawn into the vortex of rhetoric in spite of her predisposition in favor of Hastings. With the body of the orator operating properly, Burney's concern becomes with the body of the auditor, with her own bodily legislation. As we will see, this particular vortex disassembles the auditor and reassembles her according to the principles of the text and does so in a fashion that works directly on the body of the audience.

This incursion on the body of the listener is the chief focus of Burney's analysis of Burke's rhetoric. Again casting herself as Molière's old woman and thus retheatricalizing the scene, Burney focuses not on Burke's body but on her own:

I told him [Wyndham] that his [Burke's] opening had struck me with the highest admiration of his powers, from the eloquence, the imagination, the fire, the diversity of expression, and the ready flow of language, with which he seemed gifted, in a most superior man-ner, for any and every purpose to which rhetoric could lead. "And when he came to his two narratives," I continued, "when he related the particulars of those dreadful murders, he interested, he engaged, he at last overpowered me; I felt my cause lost. I could hardly keep on my seat. My eyes dreaded a single glance towards a man so ac-cused as Mr. Hastings; I wanted to sink on the floor, that they might be saved so painful a sight. I had no hope he could clear himself; not another wish in his favour remained. (98–99)

This passage becomes resonant in light of her commentary on Fox's eyes, for Burke's speech makes it painful for her to look at Hastings. The aver-sion of the eyes from Hastings that she deemed appropriate to the man-agers' cause is now—if only transiently—her own. Burke's performance not only convinces her of Hastings's guilt, but it also forces an adequation of inner private conviction and outer bodily performance that he alone among the managers seems to exhibit.

However, Burney also emphasizes that this resubjectification is con-fined to the narrative part of Burke's speech. When he moves into the declamation, which includes his trope of geographical morality, Burney regains possession of her eyes and her judgment:

But when from this narration Mr. Burke proceeded to his own com-ments and declamation—when the charges of rapacity, cruelty, tyranny were general, and made with all the violence of personal de-testation, and continued and aggravated without any further fact or illustration; then there appeared more of study than of truth, more of invective than of justice; and, in short, so little of proof to so much of passion, that in a very short time I began to lift up my head, my seat was no longer uneasy, my eyes were indifferent which way they looked, or what object caught them; and before I was my-self aware of the declension of Mr. Burke's powers over my feelings, I found myself a mere spectator in a public place, and looking all around it, with my opera-glass in my hand. (99)

As in the previous description, it is the violence of Burke's tone and its dis-tantiation from narrative proof that breaks the identification between au-dience and orator. If Fox's body betrays him, then here it is clearly Burke's excessive discourse that indicates "all the violence of personal detesta-tion."[24] This incursion of the merely private into the public performance effects a series of returns: a return of her body to her own possession, a return of her own judgment regarding Hastings, and most importantly a return to the theatrical space of Westminster Hall. This latter return is particularly significant because it indicates that the torrent of Burke's oratory in the narration figuratively takes Burney not only out of herself but also out of Westminster Hall. Her careful description of her return as a spectator with an opera glass in her hand suggests that the "departure" is essentially a departure from the theatre. When Burke's oratory is working properly, the very theatricality that makes it possible evaporates, and the auditor is suddenly set in what Wyndham previously described as a space of truth and right. In this light, Burney contains her momentary re-subjectification as a theatrical effect, an illusion whose claim to truth can only be transient.

Significantly, Burney records Wyndham's response to her discourse in a similar fashion by focusing on the bodily signs of his concession to her position: "His eyes sought the ground on hearing this, and with no other comment than a rather uncomfortable shrug of the shoulders, he expressively and concisely said—'I comprehend you perfectly!'" (99). But unlike Burke, she does not move into a triumphant declamation but rather shifts directly to her critique of Fox. The very economy of her critique avoids precisely what she sees as Burke's failure—his willingness to move away from narration toward elaborately prepared rhetorical flourishes. And this failure amounts to a dramaturgical error, for it allows the audience to disidentify with the performance and retroactively contain their conviction in Hastings's guilt. Suddenly Burney's self-characterization as Molière's old woman becomes resonant, because her critique of each individual act of oratory is consistent with her overall dramaturgical analysis of the scene of impeachment:

> "And another thing," I cried, "which strikes those ignorant of senatorial licence, is this, —that those perpetual repetitions, from all the speakers, of inveighing against the power, the rapacity, the tyranny, the despotism of the *Gentleman at the Bar,* being uttered now, when we see him without any power, without even liberty—confined to that spot, and the only person in this large assembly who may not leave it when he will;—when we *see* such a contrast to all we *hear,* we think the simplest relation would be sufficient for all purposes of justice, as all that goes beyond plain narrative, instead of sharpening indignation, only calls to mind the greatness of the fall, and raises involuntary commiseration!" (101)

Burney's critique straightforwardly declares not only that the managers are not paying enough attention to the disjunction between what the audience sees and what it hears, but also that they fail to recognize that dramatizing the "plain narrative" of Hastings's actions should be their primary concern. Furthermore, she is also making a generic critique because her invocation of the "involuntary commiseration" with the accused is perfectly in keeping with Burke's analysis of tragedy. It is as though Burney is stating that no amount of speechifying from the prosecution will counteract the sympathy generated by the embodiment on stage of fallen greatness. In this analysis, the very constitution of the theatre of impeachment works against the managers. And it is interesting how Hastings's impassive body, referred to frequently not only in Burney but also in the accounts of the trial, only heightens the distinction between the Hastings the audience hears about and the Hastings the audience sees.[25] These accounts of Hastings's public impassivity were supplemented in the newspapers by accounts of the propriety of his private actions:

> [Mr. Hastings's] time . . . is said to be laid out with singular propriety—he neither visits nor receives any company in his present situation—most of his evenings being spent in consultation with his lawyers, or arranging by himself the business of the next day—his only relaxation being a game of backgammon in his own family.[26]

As we will see, questions of propriety and the family become a vital part of Burney's critique of the impeachment.

From this perspective Burney's affective response to Hastings's impassivity begins to signify, for it is in her interest, as an advocate for Hastings, that he remain a subject seen in bonds. But this also requires that he be seen as an object not seeing. From her first description of trembling at Hastings's approach to the bar on the opening day of impeachment, Burney emphasizes that she cannot see his face. As we have noted already in relation to Fox, the face or countenance is a signifying medium that needs to be carefully controlled so that it does not counter the language of the orator's text. Hastings's bodily performance is of no less importance, but because the Lords decided that he did not have to respond to the charges until after they were all fully presented and because he chose to speak through his counsel, it operates according to different rules. Of crucial importance to the maintenance of the scene of "involuntary commiseration" is the performance of isolation. To this end it is important that Hastings not have eye contact with specific audience members, not only because it would allow the audience to construe relations of alliance between the accused and specific public figures, but also because it covers up the subject to and within itself in a fashion that negates inner thoughts and desires in favor of total legibility of the public self. This concealment of private thoughts is key because, as Burney explicitly recognizes, the imprecations against Hastings's rapacity that fill out Burke's declamation tend to focus on his moral criminality, not on his specific public actions. Hence, Burney carefully distinguishes between the persuasiveness of narrative and the failure of repeated character assassination—and, hence, Burney's extreme discomfort when Hastings looks at her:

> A little after, while we were observing Mr. Hastings, Mr. Wyndham exclaimed, "He's looking up; I believe he is looking for you."
> I turned hastily away, fairly saying, "I hope not."
> "Yes, he is; he seems as if he wanted to bow to you."
> I shrank back.
> "No, he looks off; he thinks you in too bad company!" (120)

Eye contact between Burney—a member of the royal household—and Hastings would be open to construal both as a sign of alliance to the king and queen, and as a sign of private character itself. Burney's bodily response therefore is protective. One of Burney's highest marks of approbation comes when Wyndham states that "he did not think it right to look at [Hastings] during the speech, nor from the Committee-Box; and, therefore, I constantly kept my eyes another way" (83). As we will see, a shared reluctance to look is an important component of the relationship between Burney and Wyndham, but its significance remains obscured until we more fully appreciate the performative predicament of Hastings himself.

What emerges are two possibilities for Hastings: either he keeps his private character a cipher and allows the audience to lose faith in the managers' characterization of him, or he can undertake the far more difficult task of performing in a fashion consistent with his public defense, and yet divergent from the image being formed by Burke. The difficulty here is that Hastings's primary defense is that he acted out of necessity and therefore would have to develop a mode of bodily performance that simultaneously testified to his rectitude and allowed for acts understood to be immoral. In short, Burke's notion of geographical morality put stringent limits on Hastings performance of private character, but it was precisely these constraints that served Hastings so well because they saved him from signifying errantly. Burney herself takes on the defense of Hastings's private character to Wyndham, owning that her predisposition for him is based on her favorable sense of his character from previous social interactions. But nowhere does she suggest that this would be an effective public defense. I would argue that this is because Burney is extremely conscious of the way in which limits on the public defense of one's private reputation effectively allow for the external projection of interiorities onto those constrained. In such an economy of character one's silence is itself significant. Burney is cognizant of this predicament because it is precisely the one that constrains feminine performance in society and which she wrote about so eloquently not only in *Evelina* but throughout her career as a novelist.

Burney's *Diary* deploys *Evelina* in a fashion that opens up the ground for a consideration of her identification with Hastings and of her education of Wyndham. As we have seen, much of Burney's *Diary* focuses on how she defends herself in private conversation from Wyndham's disapproval of her support for Hastings, but here Burney records a conversation in which Wyndham engages with her public authorial self:

> You may remember his coming straight from the managers, in their first procession to their box, and beginning at once a most animated attack . . . before he exclaimed "I have a great quarrel with you! . . . you have done me mischief irreparable—you have ruined me!" . . . I begged him to let me understand how.
>
> "I will," he cried. "When the Trial broke up for the recess I went into the country, purposing to give my whole time to study and business; but, most unfortunately, I had just sent for a new set of 'Evelina;' and intending only to look at it, I was so cruelly caught that I could not let it out of my hands, and have been living with nothing but the Branghtons ever since!"
>
> . . . He ran on to this purpose much longer, with great rapidity, and then, suddenly stopping, again said, "But I have yet another quarrel with you, and one you must answer. How comes it that the moment you have attached us to the hero and the heroine—the instant you have made us cling to them so that there is no getting disengaged—twined, twisted, twirled around them round our very heart-strings—how is it that then you make them undergo such persecutions? There is really no enduring their distresses, their suspenses, their perplexities. Why are you so cruel to all around—to them and their readers?"

> I longed to say—Do *you* object to a persecution?—but I know he spells it prosecution. (115–16)

The passage works on a number levels, not least of which is as a further quasi-erotic exchange in which Wyndham shows himself subject to, at least, the public Miss Burney. But the terms in which Burney records that subjection are extremely evocative, for throughout the *Diary* she not only upbraids Wyndham for the cruelty of Burke and the managers against Hastings, but also indicates that the managers—despite themselves—have singled out Hastings for the audience's "involuntary commiseration." Wyndham's aesthetic response to the distresses of Evelina is remarkably similar to Burney's aesthetic response to Hastings's predicament, but his charge of cruelty is distinguished from that of the managers on quite specific grounds. First, Burney is cruel to her readers in order to demonstrate more fully the rapacity of Willoughby and the structural alignments of the sex-gender system that are complicit with it; she quite consciously allows the narrative events to argue her point. In contrast, Burney suggests that the attribution of cruelty to the managers by the audience is a result of their failure to mobilize their narrative effectively. Second, in the case of *Evelina,* the private act of reading—of being subjected to narrative cruelty—opens onto a scene of public edification. In contrast, at the trial of Warren Hastings, the public consumption of oratory—of being subjected to Burke and Fox's excesses—devolves into a merely private conflict. Oddly enough we are witness here to two forms of cruelty whose distinction overrides the apparent frivolity of the comparison between *Evelina*'s "persecution" of Wyndham and Burney's sense of the managers' part in the prosecution of Hastings.

Wyndham argues that he is ruined—again an important word choice in light of the managers' repeated invocation of the violation of Indian women—because the demands of *Evelina* interfere with the preparation of his speech before the trial. One could argue that such an easy distraction indicates precisely how uninteresting the process is to a man such as Wyndham. It would certainly not be beyond Burney's anti-Whig sentiment to make such an insinuation. But perhaps there is something further at stake that requires some knowledge of the argument of *Evelina.* As Gina Campbell has ably demonstrated, Burney's first novel can be read as a primer on how to be a gentleman.[27] Crucial to that lesson is the recognition that women must be accorded some space in public to express themselves without by definition undoing their reputation. Just as Evelina must speak for herself to correct the representation of her reputation, so too must the woman novelist be able to operate to ensure that society does not devolve into or rather remain a scene of exchange where women are circulated according to male fantasies of who and what they are. By extension one could argue that Burney's *Diary* demonstrates that the women viewing the actions of the state in Westminster Hall must become political participants in order to prevent the unrestrained mobilization of feminine tropes for the advantage of party. That Wyndham has to ask why Burney makes Lord Orville, Evelina, and her readers undergo her "persecution" indicates that he does not understand the novel's critique of its male readers and of the homosociality of their desires. This is important because it is essentially what Burney argues about the managers' prosecution of Hastings. Burke's deployment of the feminized and violated Indian subcontinent as a rhetorical weapon against Hastings carries with it the silencing of this very constituency. What emerges instead are two competing fantasies of subjection whose conflict is driven by party difference rather than any real concern for colonial atrocity.

But more to the point, the deployment of *Evelina* shows us something about how Burney reads Hastings's performative predicament. Like Evelina, his ability to defend his reputation publicly is constrained to such an extent that any public performance, any utterance, will only confirm his guilt. This would suggest that Burney is reading Hastings's vulnerability as parallel to that of women in society. If we use *Evelina* as a guide, then the only exculpatory utterance is one that is not intended for public consumption. As in Evelina's overheard self-defense, what Hastings needs is an indirect communication of his private rectitude. Perhaps a private document like Burney's *Diary* that attests to his moral probity but does not demand that he speak publicly. After all this is one of the most important discursive aspects of *Evelina*'s epistolary discourse. It establishes a fictional space where Evelina can privately exonerate herself to the reader and to her guardian for acts that, on the exterior, appear highly improper. With this in mind I wish to conclude this chapter by considering Burney's private encounters with Wyndham as a complex form of indirect exculpation that nevertheless points toward a critique of Hastings's actions in Bengal.

Winding Up Wyndham, or Burney's Prosecutor

As noted earlier, the discourse between Burney and Wyndham is socially hazardous to her but viable because of the shared affection for Dr. Johnson. Her performance in the role of Molière's old woman is explicitly undertaken because Burney reads Wyndham's loyalty to Johnson as an indication that he will be a suitable audience for her critique. That suitability is based not only on what she calls his liberality, but also on his prior actions with regard to Hastings. Burney's knowledge of these actions is withheld until quite late in her account, but they indicate not only the depth of her knowledge of Indian affairs but also the precise terms of her hope for Wyndham. The chief narrative enigma that drives much of the reported conversation relates to how and when Wyndham will perform when he is called to orate. As the reader tracks Wyndham's nervousness and Burney's advice to him, it becomes clear that Wyndham exists in the narrative as the exemplar of a kind of oratory distinct from that of Burke and Fox. Indeed, the training of Wyndham amounts to a restoration or heightening of those qualities that Burney suggests met with Johnson's approval and have been temporarily occluded by his association with Burke. And her intervention here is remarkably specific:

> "I have been putting my expectations from your speech to a kind of test . . . I have been reading—running over, rather—a set of speeches, in which almost the whole House made a part, upon the India Bill; and in looking those over I saw not one that had not in it something positively and pointedly personal, except Mr. Wyndham's."
>
> "O, that was a mere accident!"
>
> "But it was just the accident I expected from Mr. Wyndham. I do not mean that there was invective in all the others, for in some there was panegyric—plenty! but that panegyric was always so directed as to convey more of severe censure to one party than of real praise to the other. Yours was all to the business, and thence I infer you will deal just so by Mr. Hastings." (117–18)

Burney's return to the speeches regarding Fox's East India Bill five years earlier should forestall any suggestion that she was not cognizant of the issues under discussion during the impeachment, but there is more to this passage than a mere revelation of her political acumen. By commending Wyndham for avoiding the personal in his earlier speeches, Burney is setting him up as a natural contrast to the debilitating disclosure of personal animosity in Fox's gestures and in Burke's voice.

But the key issue is that the strength of Wyndham's oratory is accidental. As we have seen, Burney repeatedly suggests that overpreparation leads the orator away from the facts and hence away from the "natural" expression of his moral feelings: "When the facts are once stated, I cannot but suppose they must have much more force where followed only by unstudied arguments, and by comments rising at the moment, than by any laboured preparations; and have far more chance of making a deep impression, because more natural and more original" (85). This fetishization of the natural, the momentary, and the accidental is built on the supposition that oratory is prone to distort facts artificially. But more to the point is the assumption that accidental and unprepared disclosures demonstrate the morality and justice of the speaker because they minimize the difference between inner private subject and public social performance. Burney's defense of Hastings is built on the continuity of these two modes of subjectivity. She knows Hastings to be a gentleman in his private capacities and therefore presumes that his public performances will also be honorable. It is not surprising therefore that she wishes for the same continuity of inner and outer in a prosecutor. And Burney figures this parallel between the accuser and the accused not only in oratorical terms, but also visually:

> "Ah, Mr. Wyndham," cried I, "you should not be so hard-hearted towards him, whoever else may; and I could tell you, and I will tell you if you please, a very forcible reason. . . . You must know, then, that people there are in this world who scruple not to assert that there is a very strong personal resemblance between Mr. Wyndham and Mr. Hastings; nay, in the profile, I see it myself at this moment; and therefore ought not you to be a little softer than the rest, if merely in sympathy?"
>   He laughed very heartily; and owned he heard of the resemblance before.
>   "I could take him extremely well," I cried, "for your uncle."
>   "No, no; if he looks like my elder brother, I aspire at no more."
>   "No, no; he is more like your uncle; he has just that air; he seems just of that time of life. Can you then be so unnatural as to prosecute him with this eagerness?" (120–21)

As in the earlier remarks on "geographical timidity," Burney's raillery carries with it a certain level of gravity, for she suggests not that Hastings shouldn't be prosecuted, but rather that he should be prosecuted in a manner that one would prosecute oneself. This refusal of Hastings's alterity, of his isolation, is figured first in terms of visual resemblance and then in terms of familial relations. The aptness of this figural extrapolation lies in its ability to capture the political scenario. In the scene of impeachment, Burney is asserting that a proper prosecution of Hastings would be a prosecution not of one man but of an entire system of governance. However, such a systemic prosecution would require the dissolution of party difference and of the difference between accuser and accused in order that the "facts" of the case could "naturally" unfold. It is as though Burney is asking for the disclosure of historical events without the distorting mediation of individual subjects or institutions. In short, a return to natural society.

It is here that the invocation of the familial relation between Hastings and Wyndham is so resonant because it is mobilized as a model of natural sociality. The implication is that to pursue Hastings as Burke and Fox have done is unnatural or perverse. This explains why Burney makes such a point of the breakdown in social relations between herself and Burke that is effected by his public discourse: it is symptomatic of a pervasive splitting of the bonds of society. Counter to this split, Burney proffers the circle of society around Johnson of which she and Wyndham are exemplary citizens. It is only a small step to recognize that this is a fantasy of national consolidation that may be obsolete upon its utterance, but which may also capture the specific parameters of a nationalist resistance to the impeachment that is ultimately reliant on a very tendentious assertion of natural familial association.

A Theatre of Perpetual War

ON 5 APRIL 1805, in the midst of a debate on the state of affairs in India, Charles James Fox stood up in the House and wearily observed that "We in fact, seemed in India, to be like Macbeth 'so steeped in blood' that we thought it vain to get back."[1] More than thirty years prior to the utterance of these words, observers had been witness to a series of wars against the Rohillas, the Marathas, and the sultans of Mysore that were initiated during Warren Hastings's term as governor-general of Bengal, but which raged on through the terms of Cornwallis and Wellesley. Along the way, the public sense that these wars were unnecessary and at times embarrassing was superseded by the feeling that their outcome was vital to both the national and imperial identity of Britain. This shift in public opinion corresponds to the changing fate of East India Company's military actions, for during the 1770s and 1780s many of the conflicts resulted either inconclusively, as in the Treaty of Mangalore, which resolved the Second Mysore War into a draw, or in outright defeat, as in the failed action at Pollilur. At moments during these setbacks, observers would look back on Clive's previous victories with a combination of nostalgia and anxiety, for it was his extraordinary success that forced fundamental modifications in Company rule as the diwani was incorporated into commercial and governmental strategy. It was not until Tipu Sultan was killed by Wellesley's forces at Seringapatam in 1799 and the Marathas were decisively defeated in 1803 and 1804, that the ambivalence regarding war in the Asian subcontinent was put to rest.

But Fox's uneasy interpretation of this history should give us pause. His statement is startling not only because it registers his complicity in what he recognizes is a state of perpetual war, but also because the Shakespearean analogue suggests that, despite Lord Wellesley's subjugation of the remaining pockets of military resistance, British domination was an aberration in the order of things that would be rectified at some future date. Fox is modifying the famous passage in *Macbeth,* where, after encountering Banquo's ghost and resolving to seek advice from the Witches, Macbeth sums up his historical predicament:

> I am in blood
> Stepped in so far that, should I wade no more,
> Returning were as tedious as go o'er.
> Strange things I have in head, that will to hand,
> Which must be acted ere they may be scanned.[2]

By invoking Macbeth's recognition that it is too late to go backward and that the cycle of murder cannot be undone, Fox is doing more than stating that British affairs in India are mired in violence. He is positing both a surrogate fantasy aimed at displacing political events in the 1790s and positing a tragic future for the empire that will reconstitute his own Whig understanding of governance. Here it is the hybrid of company, state and military, cast as Macbeth, that has strange things "in head, that will to hand,/Which must be acted ere they may be scanned." If the future is fearsome, the reconstruction of the past is no less disturbing for one is hard pressed to separate the wars in India from the battles staged in Parliament by Fox, Burke, and Sheridan during this period. The blood on the hands of the East India Company's soldiers is figuratively tied to the dismembered body of the Whigs and the oligarchical imperatives they once stood for. One has the sense that the blood in Fox's remark is not only that of Tipu or of the Marathas but also his own and that it will be avenged at some undisclosed point in the future.

Joseph Roach refers to this kind of historical performance as surrogation, and there is no doubt that Fox is attempting to refigure, however clumsily, one history with a version of the past aimed at keeping himself politically alive even after he is effectively dead.[3] Of course, the very act of surrogation here is imbued with spectrality for it is the murdered yet still lingering Banquo who instantiates this recognition of perpetual war. One way of parsing this surrogative performance is simply to ask, Who is Banquo? Is it India or is it a past version of the Whig establishment that interrupts the imperial feast in 1805? Fox, like Macbeth, seems unable to celebrate the new form of sovereignty consolidated by Wellesley's victories in the Asian subcontinent. That that new form of sovereignty involves a radically increased profile for the military should not go unnoticed for, as John Brewer has demonstrated, the infiltration of the state by the military in the eighteenth century is one of the most significant modulations in British governmentality.[4] Prior to the eighteenth century, the military played a very minor role in the formulation and practice of government in Britain. In many ways, Britain's much-vaunted liberty and its relative lack of absolutism was a result of its underdeveloped military class. The particular form of governance developed during the seventeenth century went through a remarkable transformation as the military slowly began to be integrated into the commercial interests of the state. By the beginning of the nineteenth century it would be impossible to think of Britain's imperial future without some reckoning of the incorporation of the military into the political and social life of the nation. And yet, for Fox's Whiggish interpretation of history, this relationship between the military and the state points toward the very absolutism he resisted throughout his career, but with one crucial difference. The absolutism he fears at this juncture is not that of the king but rather of a hybrid governmental form that incorporates the King-in-Parliament, the military, the East India Company, and a whole panoply of intermediate institutions who actually regulate social interaction and economic exchange.

Fox's remark may be a symptom of oligarchic nostalgia, but there is a vital countermemory inscribed in the very words he uses to shore up his own political subjectivity and mourn the passing of one interpretation of "natural liberty." The violent battles for control of colonial territory and the unending struggles that attended the recalibration of metropolitan politics were quite literally "steeped in blood" but not only in the senses that Fox's allusion to *Macbeth* would suggest. As Ann Laura Stoler emphasizes, Foucault's engagement with questions of race in *The History of Sexuality* and in *Society Must Be Defended* focuses "on the shift in the eighteenth and nineteenth centuries from a 'symbolics of blood' to an 'analytics of sexuality.' In societies in which systems of alliance, descent and death are dominant, blood was a 'reality with symbolic function.'"[5] When dealing with this issue, Foucault is careful to refer to the symbolics or the thematics of blood because, in the long history he is tracing, this symbolic assemblage is infiltrated and detached by a new form of power:

> Beginning in the second half of the nineteenth century, the thematics of blood was sometimes called on to lend its entire historical weight toward revitalizing the type of political power that was exercized through the devices of sexuality. Racism took shape at this point (racism in its modern, 'biologizing,' statist form): it was then that a whole politics of settlement . . . , family, marriage, social hierarchization, and property, accompanied by a long series of permanent interventions at the level of the body, conduct, health, and everyday life, received their color and their justification from the mythical concern with protecting the purity of the blood and ensuring the triumph of the race.[6]

But this deployment of the symbolics of blood took over from an earlier discourse that did not think about race in a singular fashion. In his more extended meditation on the genealogy of racism, Foucault tracks his analysis back to the moment in European history when wars ceased to be private affairs and were carried on by sovereign states. With the emergence of juridical sovereignty came a new discourse in which society itself was conceived as an entity saturated by relations of war. . . . In both its bourgeois and aristocratic form, it is an instrument of political opposition and struggle against sovereign rule. . . . It is a discourse that interrogates law and sees its formation as the consequence of massacres, conquests and domination, not as the embodiment of natural rights. It is not however, a discourse that detaches itself from the language of rights; on the contrary, its truth claims are made to specific rights and by specific holders of them; the rights of a family (to property), of a class (to privilege), of a race (to rule).[7]

This discourse was structured around the perpetual war of two competing races who invariably couched their rights and privileges in the language of blood. This unending conflict is described by Foucault as the war among the races.

This race war and its symbolics of blood has particular resonance for the English case because Foucault explicitly ties the emergence of this discourse to the bourgeois revolution of the seventeenth century and to the texts of Sir Edward Coke and John Lilburne. This is significant because this discourse of race war runs alongside of and impinges upon not only the development of the British Constitution's notion of King-in-Parliament but also of the various forms of resistance to this particular manifestation of sovereignty. It is not unusual to see widely divergent social groups staging resistance to juridical sovereignty in terms of blood and in opposition to some internal other. And nowhere is this more evident than in endless attribution of Jacobitism to various constituencies. That this tag should be so regularly attached to Fox in the 1780s and 1790s demonstrates the capriciousness not only of the discourse but also of the long history of the political manipulation of the symbolics of blood.

Foucault argues that these kinds of internal social dynamics undergo two transcriptions. The first, arising in the seventeenth century, was openly biological and attended the figuration of nations as races. This racialization of the nation is then articulated in European policies of colonization, but, as Stoler notes, Foucault does little to expand this aspect of the argument. Instead, Foucault's key recognition is that this already fluid discourse underwent a crucial transformation:

And then you find a second transcription based upon the great theme and theory of social war, which emerges in the very first years of the nineteenth century, and which tends to erase every trace of racial conflict in order to define itself as class struggle. We have, then, a sort of major parting of the ways, which I will try to reconstruct. It corresponds . . . to a recasting of the theme of racial confrontations in terms of the theory of evolutionism and the struggle for existence. . . . By this, I mean the idea—which is absolutely new and which will make the discourse function very differently—that the other race is basically not the race that came from elsewhere or that was, for a time triumphant or dominant, but that is a race that is permanently, ceaselessly infiltrating the social body, or which is, rather, constantly being re-created in and by the social fabric. In other words, what we see as a polarity, as a binary rift in society, is not a clash between two distinct races. It is the splitting of a single race into a superrace and a subrace. To put it a different way, it is the reappearance, within a single race, of the past of that race. In a word, the obverse and the underside of the race reappears within it.[8]

This reduction from the binary war among the races to the defense of a now normative social category amounts to an important genealogy of whiteness as well as an inversion of the politics of race discourse. In the era of the sanguinary politics of aristocratic alliance, the discourse of race war was a critical tool against the juridical power of the state. In the shift from the symbolics of blood to the deployment of sexuality, "the racist thematic is no longer a moment in the struggle between one social group and another; it will promote the global strategy of social conservatisms. At this point, and this is the paradox, given the goals and the first form of the discourse . . . we see the appearance of State racism: a racism that society will direct against itself, against its own elements and its own products. This is the internal racism of permanent purification, and it will become one of the basic dimensions of social normalization."[9] It is this genealogy of normativity that is so important to our discussion at this juncture.

For Fox to argue that Indian policy was steeped in blood recognizes the history of bloodshed in the region, but it also allows us to suggest that the metropolitan reaction to Indian affairs shifted from one in which the various social strata laid claim to the thematics of blood in a struggle for real and symbolic power to one in which the middle classes began to develop a politics of normativity whose chief focus was sexuality and whose initial application was on itself. Burke's and Fox's reactions to the political problems posed by the East India Company were always analyzed in a combative field that located political legitimacy in the opposition to absolute sovereignty. What we begin to see in the later years of the eighteenth century and the beginning of the nineteenth century is a shift toward an analysis of the relationship between Britain and its colonial holdings that worries less about conflict in the metropole than about contamination of the metropolitan subjects in the colonies. As Sen, Stoler, Collingham, Teltscher, Dalrymple, and others have argued, the constitutional—that is, political—questions of imperial governance give way to the governance of bodily constitutions in the colonies. The legitimation of political privilege through the symbolics of blood that was so crucial to the history of British politics slowly found itself taking on altogether new meanings as the sexual deployments that defined a largely racialized class body began to take hold until, eventually, to speak of blood in a colonial context was to speak of miscegenation.[10]

Stoler has persuasively argued that the deployment of sexuality and the regulation of classed bodies was the result of a deeply intertwined project that took place between the metropole and the colony. We can see two aspects of the metropolitan side of this project in part 3, and both are intertwined with new understandings of the place of war in imperial policy. As Pocock and Wahrman have argued, war in the American colonies posed extremely difficult problems for British subjectification. Whether considered as a social war or as a civil war, the American conflict played a key role in the transformation of the war among the races that lay beneath much of British constitutional and social tension. As the largely Whiggish colonists took on a revolutionary relation to the king and Parliament, an internal bifurcation in British society that demanded that Britons in the British Isles define themselves in contrast to "foreign Britons" suddenly emerged. This demand for self-definition involved the progressive establishment of norms that derived from ancient claims of nationhood as well as current social practices. One can argue that the consolidation of the middle class in post-American Britain is integrally tied to the early phases of the second transcription of racial discourse outlined by Foucault. The evidence for this second transcription lies in the subtle racialization of class relations that slowly works its way through the culture at the end of the eighteenth century.

As I have argued elsewhere, George Colman's *Inkle and Yarico* provides the most vivid examples of this process in part because it can be read against the myriad versions of the tale that derive from a much earlier understanding of the British polity, and in part because it obliquely addresses the relationship between the decline of mercantilism and the emergent normativity of military masculinity.[11] As an indicator of colonial transformation, its mobilization of the category of whiteness is something very new, which nonetheless relied on tropes and narratives that were very old. In that sense, it is a useful example of how one discourse on empire is reoriented to serve the purposes of a very different social movement and a very different understanding of the state. *Inkle and Yarico*'s complex containment and redeployment of interracial sexuality promotes a form of normative whiteness whose parameters are both unstable and in need of constant surveillance. In Colman's comic opera, the ultimate act of racial surveillance is accorded to a military officer, and I contend that he follows two mutually supporting sets of orders. On the one hand, his explicit orders are to defend British West Indian interests against hostile threats from both American and French vessels, but, on the other, he also conducts a kind of surreptitious warfare against himself and against his wife. As the embodiment of an almost transparent whiteness, Captain Campley wages wars at the borders of the white body.

A similar war against the self can be found in Mariana Starke's *The Sword of Peace,* but this time it is staged in India. As we will see in chapter 6, Starke's comedy explicitly engages with Colman's comic opera, and its careful parsing of colonial Indian society allows us to affirm Stoler's conviction that "Colonialism was not a secure bourgeois project. It was not only about the importation of middle-class sensibilities to the colonies, but about the *making* of them"; in addition, it allows us to specify the fine gradation of transcolonial subjects into competent or inappropriate manifestations of white Britishness.[12] That competency has a great deal to do with the relationship between British functionaries and their racialized servants. In *Inkle and Yarico,* the interracial sexuality between master and slave is a locus of intense anxiety, and the opera mobilizes a series of substitutions to bring it under control. In *The Sword of Peace,* which also engages with the question of slavery, the focus shifts from the interracial sexual practices between male masters and fetished female slaves, to the interracial desire of questionable women of British origin and their Indian servants. I make the suggestion that Starke's strategies are not at all distant from those employed by Lord Cornwallis to reform the military forces of the East India Company in the late 1780s and early 1790s. The army plays a vital role in securing sexual, racial, and class normativity both in Cornwallis's regime and in Starke's play, but Starke's consideration of interracial desire is supplemented by an analysis of violent conflict that bridges the gap between colony and metropole by engaging quite explicitly with the homosocial violence both uncovered and enacted in the Hastings impeachment. In this regard, Starke's play, like Cornwallis's institutional reforms, attempts to erase Hastings's legacy through strategies of self-reform aimed at bodily practices.[13]

Starke's play poses fundamental questions regarding the consolidation of masculinity that cannot be separated from the project of self-regulation that would become so important to British policy in India, and she does so in a fashion that mobilizes the theatre as a place where the audience can stage a war against itself that purifies rather than sheds blood. However, the limits of this kind of regulatory strategy can be charted in the reception and containment of Starke's next play, *The Widow of Malabar*. Again, I draw a relation between Starke's metropolitan dramaturgy and Cornwallis's colonial policy, except this time the emphasis is less on the military than on the array of fantasies attending the Permanent Settlement. I argue not that the play directly engages with the policy—the Permanent Settlement was proposed two years after the brief run of Starke's play—but rather that the play and its reception are inflected by the same nostalgia for the natural liberty of landed property that swept through metropolitan society at the time of the French Revolution, and which found itself enacted in the Permanent Settlement. What I hope to demonstrate is that the deliberate misreading of Starke's play in the press is evidence of the ideological quality of that nostalgic construction.

If Colman and Starke bring the question of war, blood, and sovereignty into crisis in order to offer a model of governmentality based on the regulation of bodies, then the theatrical experiments staged at Astley's Royal Amphitheatre to mark the victory of British forces over Tipu Sultan in the Mysore Wars offer a remarkable opportunity for examining the relationship between imperial war and the management of national subjectivity. The final chapter argues that military logistics became a technique for subjectification in the theatre, and that the political effects of these techniques far exceed those formerly contained under the category of manners. The ameliorative qualities of manners, civility, and virtue played a crucial role in stabilizing the volatile public of eighteenth-century Britain, but the new tactics employed by Astley and others were less interested in ideological amelioration than with the production of a new kind of citizen suited to a new state form whose effectivity no longer derives solely from the long juridical history of the British Constitution. As we have already noted, Phillipson, Pocock, and Foucault argue the early modern state form is irreversibly altered after the 1790s. Under the veil of a mystified constitution, the state was increasingly militarized, and disciplinary power suffused the social fabric through a range of institutions such that the polity was subjected to fundamentally different forms of control. The autoethnographic imperative that focused so insistently on manners and virtue is supplemented by more productive forms of subject maintenance. The emergent entertainment industry borne out of the illegitimate theatre is not simply a mirror of the times but an active producer of subject-citizens who can best be described as subagential—disempowered and incorporated by the very fantasies of supremacy accorded to them. In this sense, the audiences at Astley's no longer adjudicate over British imperial policy as ethical spectators; rather, they accede to positions of normativity and take on the project of self-purification outlined but not specified by Foucault. That this should happen via the incorporation of military spectacle is resonant because it suggests that the integration of a military cadre into the workings of the state, which Brewer has shown to be so important for British political life, was supplemented by the consolidation of a class that zealously guarded itself with the same martial tactics used to fend off the "subrace," whether it be defined as a classed other or as a racially distinct and subjugated people. The standing army so feared by theorists of British liberty in the eighteenth century was now manifest, in the field, in the state, in the body, and in the soul of the citizenry.

Starke Reforms

Martial Masculinity and the

Perils of Indianization

DURING THE LAST thirty years of the eighteenth century, one can discern a fundamental reorientation of both public and official opinion on the status of the British Empire. As Bruce P. Lenman states, popular sentiment between 1770 and 1785 was marked by intense anxiety if not pessimism:

> Robert Clive had died in 1774, convinced that he lived in a disintegrating Empire. There was much to be said for this opinion by 1783. Britain had been forced to recognize the independence of the thirteen colonies. . . . Moreover, the Irish volunteer movement of some 60,000 at its peak had given Irish public opinion a focus through which to demand redress of grievances with the implication that force would be used were redress refused. With America largely lost; British India wasted by war, famine and corruption; Ireland restive; and the British West Indies in economic difficulties, it looked in 1783 as if the British Empire faced an uncertain future.[1]

In the 1770s Hastings's costly and ineffective conflicts with the Maratha confederacy, the Nizam of Hyderabad, and the sultans of Mysore drained the East India Company of resources and failed to stabilize the region. These three principalities were the source of intermittent, if not continual, resistance until the end of the century. Of these, Mysore was the most serious threat to British imperial interests following the loss of the American war. It was not until after Hastings was recalled that Lord Cornwallis, now the governor-general of Bengal, managed to temporarily defeat Tipu Sultan in 1792. Much of British reaction to Indian affairs at this time focused on the sultans of Mysore's resistance to the East India Company, and it was not until the end of the decade when Tipu was killed that the Mysorean threat to British territorial domination was ended.

The conflicts between the East India Company armies and Haider Ali and Tipu Sultan of Mysore are instructive because they chart a course from humiliating defeat to triumphant proclamations of global supremacy that are inextricably tied to the complex British reaction to the American Revolution. As Linda Colley has recently reminded us, news of Haider Ali's victory over the British at Pollilur in 1780 arrived in London in 1781 and provoked "universal consternation" in part because the news came at roughly the same time as the fall of Yorktown.[2] To observers in the American colonies and in metropolitan London, Britain's Indian empire seemed in equal jeopardy. Like the first war with Mysore in 1767–69, the Second Mysore War ended inconclusively in 1784, after costing the East India Company a great deal both in resources and confidence. The close affiliation between Tipu Sultan and French forces not only raised the question of renewed French intervention in India, but also replicated the trajectory of the American campaign. Metropolitan anxiety about these defeats was at its height throughout the 1780s, so when the Third Mysore War commenced in 1790, both the newspapers and the print satirists predicted further humiliation of the British forces. This opinion was founded not only on past defeat but also on the very real recognition of Tipu Sultan's remarkable military power. It is against this backdrop of past and potential failure that the ideological effect of Cornwallis's temporary victory over Tipu in 1792 and the final defeat and death of Tipu in 1799 need to be reckoned. What we see in the theatrical representation and public reception of this period of imperial activity in India is a transformation of national humiliation into a fearsome form of national election. I consider this transformation in two parts. The current chapter focuses on the transitional period shortly after Cornwallis took up his post in Bengal and argues that Mariana Starke's *The Sword of Peace* and *The Widow of Malabar* displace past military humiliation while also offering social correctives that complement Cornwallis's own attempts to reform both the East India Company army and administration of the colony. Chapter 7 focuses on the triumphal phantasms resulting from the spectacular celebrations of British victory in the Third and Fourth Mysore Wars. As we will see in both chapters, colonial military activity is intimately tied to scenes of bodily regulation on the metropolitan stage. This chapter, however, demonstrates the complex regulatory relation between these plays and their audiences. I move beyond the plays themselves to the paratextual materials—the prologues, epilogues, and newspaper coverage—that extend or contain Starke's satirical critique of metropolitan culture. In spite of the fact that both plays use colonial social relations as a heuristic site for proposing social reforms in the metropole, Starke's negative critique of aristocratic masculinity in *The Sword of Peace* is allowed to unfold in ways that her attempts to positively reform aristocratic femininity in *The Widow of Malabar* are not. Although both gestures are integrally related, one could argue that the resurgence of ideological investment in landed property, following the French Revolution and immediately prior to implementation of the Permanent Settlement in 1793, played a key role in the reception of Starke's reforms.

Cornwallis, Starke, and Military Reform

Mariana Starke's *The Sword of Peace* reveals a great deal about the theatrical displacement of colonial violence in metropolitan London during this transitional period of imperial governance.[3] It is thoroughly engaged with the problematics of the Hastings impeachment, but it supplements Burke's critique of Hastings's accession to arbitrary power with a prescient critique of the East India Company's former military regime. This critique works on two fronts. Much of the comedy focuses on the navigation of two marriageable women, Eliza and Louisa Moreton, through the sexual and social dangers of colonial Indian society. Under the rule of a sexually suspect Resident who figures for Hastings, the British social milieu in India has devolved into a state of corrupted civility where interracial desire, class insubordination, gambling, and overt sexual commodification permeate all social relations. All of these vices are explicitly tied to the Indianization of British men and women working for the East India Company.[4] As the play unfolds, the blurring of the lines separating European and Indian cultures, which had been the norm during this period of Company rule, is subject to a kind of reverse prophylaxis that seeks to limit European fraternization with native populations within specific codes of behavior.

Over and against this putative zone of corrupt intercultural relations, Starke introduces as a second front a group of current and former military officers whose honor and civility make them worthy replacements for the dissolute Resident and rightful rulers of the East India Company's holdings. At the head of this cadre of normative masculinity, Starke offers Mr. David Northcote. His accession to proper rule coincides with the resolution of the play's heterosexual love plots, the ejection of suspect forms of sociability, and the declaration of British hegemony. Northcote's replacement of the Resident clearly mimics Lord Cornwallis's replacement of Hastings, and Starke posits fundamental shifts not only in the social relations of British subjects under the new ruler but also in the constitution and function of the military.

These two shifts are tied together by the play's central prop: the sword from the title. Louisa Moreton is charged with the task of recovering a sword that belonged to the recently deceased Clairville and returning it to his uncle, Sir Thomas Clairville. The current protector of the sword is "a poor Lieutenant of Seapoys" named Dormer who, while an honorable soldier in his own right, is also the object of Louisa's desire. As the play unfolds, the exchange of the sword is directly tied to the marriage not only of Louisa and Dormer but also of Eliza and Dormer's friend, Edwards. Like Captain Campley and Narcissa in *Inkle and Yarico,* these newly married military couples become the repository of normative racial, sexual, and class identity. By the end of the play, such normativity rigorously distinguishes both deviant forms of colonial interracial desire and suspect forms of aristocratic honor in the metropole. Louisa's task is consistently intertwined with notions of aristocratic honor and the recovery of a failed masculinity:

ELIZA: [Y]ou know, the generous Clairville, deserted by a father, through Sir Thomas Clairville's generous assistance, sought a fortune here, denied him by a parent. Death put a stop to the noble youth's career, and has occasioned your commission of the sword, for which I honour Sir Thomas with enthusiasm.

LOUISA: And he deserves it.—His nobly offering the legacy of Clairville's gratitude has left him, to purchase the sword of the deceas'd youth, that he may preserve it as a trophy of honor to his memory—

ELIZA: An exertion of delicate, generous sensibility towards deceased merit, that characterizes Sir Thomas in that glorious singularity of an Englishmen, who repays with munificent gratitude everlasting remembrance to the noble actions of their deceas'd heroes.—Who would not sacrifice life to be thus gloriously remembered? (7)

As Starke is at pains to emphasize, Clairville's eastern career is necessitated by an act of paternal neglect that Louisa's embassy is designed to set right. Clairville's father's error is telling, for he interrupts his son's rightful claim to his landed property and is therefore destabilizing that which was commonly understood to secure the liberty of not only the landed gentry but the nation. This is why the praise accorded to Sir Thomas Clairville is for his desire to commemorate a past but not a present glory. Clairville's death marks a shift from failed aristocratic paternalism to a new form of social security: one figured by Dormer's care for the sword. As the sword moves from Clairville to Dormer to Louisa, one can track the emergence of a new form of social regulation in which the sign of aristocratic exemplarity—the sword—is permeated by middle-class forms of sociability to such an extent that the military couples take on its cultural authority.

Significantly, the play's exemplary male character, Mr. David Northcote, performs none of the intricate codes of aristocratic masculinity. In this detail, his character erases Cornwallis's aristocratic heritage and advances a new kind imperial hero. Northcote's honor is a function of his "generosity" and "benevolence":

NORTH: Yes, Mr. Resident, I feel for human nature, of whatever coulour or description; I feel for the name and character of an Englishman. I feel neither the power of gold, prejudice, nor partiality: and where the lives and properties, or even happiness, of others are concerned, I have ever regarded the impulse of *humanity*. (51)

Northcote ends the play as the new resident, but Starke is careful to distance his humane commitment to the rule of law from the practice of warfare. The accession of Northcote is represented as a necessary step toward hegemonic control of all sectors of the population but it is an event in which arms have a solely ceremonial purpose:

JEF.:   Mr. Northcote made Resident—the whole place is run wild for joy, Sir—blacks and whites, masters and slaves, half casts and blue casts, Gentoos and Mussulmen, Hindoos and Bramins, officers and soldiers, sailors and captains—and if his honor the Resident don't stop them, they won't have an ounce of gunpowder in the whole garrison. (57)

The fact that Northcote sees no reason for stopping the depletion of the garrison's gunpowder is a sign of his confidence in the effectiveness of British justice practiced without the corruption of his predecessors. Here Starke's indictment of Hastings's past bellicosity is at its most biting, for it implies that proper sovereignty would make warfare largely unnecessary. This subtle shift from gunpowder's role in military domination to its expenditure as celebratory spectacle suggests a confident—and self-congratulatory—shift away from violent governance toward a kind of inculcation of acquiescence among the colonial population that is modeled on the audience's consumption of theatrical effects. In this play, military spectacle obscures and ultimately obviates military action.

However, this obfuscation is also a historical mystification. Despite Pitt's India Act of 1784, which attempted to curtail warfare in the region by limiting inflammatory treaties between the East India Company and native powers, Cornwallis recognized that conflict with Mysore was inevitable. The shift from Hastings's rule to that of Cornwallis was matched by an enhancement of the military battalions under the East India Company's control, and the following fifteen years would be far from peaceful.[5] At the same time that Starke was constructing this fantasy of native acquiescence to liberal management, Cornwallis was thoroughly engaged in reforming British troops in India.[6] Crucial to that reformation was his conviction that the colonial military needed to be composed of vigorous white British subjects: "I think it must be universally admitted that without a large and well-regulated body of Europeans, our hold of these valuable dominions must be very insecure. . . . It would be painful for me to enlarge much on the present state of the European troops in the Company's service, but . . . I have every reason to believe that in quality of men, as well as in discipline, they are at all three Presidencies extremely inferior to those in the service of his Majesty."[7] In spite of the demonstrable loyalty and courage of the Sepoy battalions, Cornwallis had "no favourable idea of their discipline," so the "inferiority" of the European infantry was a matter of grave concern.[8] The officer class was in his eyes corrupted by financial interest in the Company's exploits and weakened by the climate.[9]

Cornwallis was especially concerned about the lack of health and the moral decrepitude that seemed to characterize the European component of the East India Company troops. Referring to recruits as "contemptible trash," it is clear that Cornwallis was disturbed by soldiers' social hybridity:

> I found a disorderly mass of debauched invalids living in Fort William almost without officers and without regulation of any kind corrupting, of course, all the recruits and all the other Europeans in garrison. Compassion for many who have brown families and for a number of Frenchmen with whom the caprice and infatuation of Sir Eyre Coote had filled his army, prevented my sending them all home, which in justice to the Company and the service I ought to have done.[10]

There is a tacit recognition here that the intermarriage of European soldiers and Indian women is part and parcel of a dangerous blending of interests.[11] Throughout Cornwallis's correspondence, one finds him insistently linking various forms of vice that threaten the integrity of his forces to the assimilation of British and Indian subjects. The specter of "brown families" suggests a propensity for degeneration among the colonial British population, and one can track the beginnings of a policy of segregation in Cornwallis's early military reforms that would eventually dominate Indian policy.[12] Cornwallis's reconfiguration of British forces was an essential precursor to his first campaign against Tipu Sultan in the Third Mysore War and was the beginning of an exponential increase in the militarization of British rule in India. And it is important that we recognize the degree to which this process of reform focused its attention on maintaining the health of the East India Company forces. Cornwallis's reforms were aimed at stabilizing British subjectivity within an ethnically diverse military cadre through the rigorous segmentation and surveillance of personnel.

Cornwallis's regulation of the East India Company forces had its metropolitan counterpart in Starke's comedy, for she argues, in quite explicit terms, that the customary leaders of the nation have devolved into a debauched and effete nobility, obsessed with symbolic battles over obsolete notions of honor. Into this power vacuum, she deploys the regulatory imperatives of the middle classes to restore vigor to the empire. If it sounds strange to be equating Cornwallis's military reforms and Starke's theatrical intervention, then it is the task of this chapter to demonstrate that both practices perform social diagnostics by examining symptoms of health and vice in the bodies of British colonials. For both observers, because the proliferation of "brown families" poses a threat to the stability of Britain's distant sovereignty, it must be regulated in the micrological processes of military and social discipline. As we will see in the next chapter, this catalog of vice lays the groundwork for the future figuration of Cornwallis as the embodiment of paternal virtue. But the knowledge practices mobilized by Cornwallis and Starke in this diagnostic phase of Anglo-Indian relations are connected on more fundamental grounds. The relationship between colony and metropole at this time is such that Cornwallis's military actions operate ancillary to Starke's game of love: they do not directly affect but rather secure the ground for Starke's metropolitan critique of interracial desire and class insubordination. It is thus that colonial warfare is mystified and replaced by metropolitan satire. And, in so doing, the metropole becomes the locus of war, not against native

resistance in India, but rather against threatening instabilities in normative white middle-class subjectivities. In order to demonstrate the convergence between Cornwallis's military reforms and Starke's satire, we
need to show, first, how the comedy engages with the sexual connotations
of anti-Company discourse circulating prior to and during the Hastings
impeachment and, second, how she mobilizes the discourse of Indianization to represent the danger of intercultural relations in India to the
familial relations at the core of middle-class notions of British imperial
ascendancy.

The Specters of Indianization: The Sword of Peace

The Sword of Peace was first performed after the first season of the Hastings trial and was printed in an expanded edition three years into the proceedings. The play features a corrupt Resident who with the assistance
of his servile minion Supple abuses the power of his office to achieve personal ends. The Resident's avarice is specifically attached to suspect forms
of private trade, but the economic critique of his actions is subsumed into
figures of gender transgression and sexual depravity that are reminiscent
of *The Nabob* and of much anti-Company discourse in the 1770s and
1780s.[13] Starke's Resident is repeatedly presented as overdressed and the
very name of his primary attendant, Supple, indicates that he is as slippery as he is effete. As Teltscher argues, the feminization of British functionaries in contemporary accounts of colonial life amounts to an Indianization that betrays a palpable anxiety about the public and private
integration of British and Indian populations.[14] When the Resident, like
Hastings, is recalled from his post and replaced by "one generous, exalted
character . . . Mr. David Northcote"—a more morally sound official modeled on Lord Cornwallis—Starke clearly indicates that the empire is entering a new phase of more just and less sanguine rule.[15]

But the swift relegation of injustice, violence, and social corruption
to the past is not only wishful thinking but also an act of self-defense on
Starke's part. Anti-Company discourse in the 1780s was a much more tame
version of the materials printed in the early 1770s aimed at publicly shaming Clive. Representations of Clive from this period incorporate every sexual excess imaginable. According to the most vitriolic of these documents,
Life of Lord Clive by Charles Carracioli and the anonymous *The Intrigues
of a Nabob; or, Bengall the Fittest Soil for the Growth of Lust, Injustice, and
Dishonesty,* Clive's sexual appetites were insatiable and he was represented

in turns as the King of Sodom, as the lover of any number of actresses and prostitutes, as a pederast, and as an compulsive onanist.[16] Anti-Company discourse has its roots in the deeply factionalized political world of the 1770s where pornographic excess was an active component of political pamphleteering. One could argue that these strategies lurk behind almost all anti-Company discourse and that if they don't actively emerge as they did in Burke's famous catalog of sexual violence perpetrated under Hastings's rule, they are always present *in potentia*.[17] This helps to explain why the opening-night review is at pains to argue that the play is

> devoid of all false attempts at wit, and of what is more unpardonable, though we are sorry to say not unfrequent from the pens of female authors, of allusions that partake of *double-entendre;* or are liable to a gross construction. The play was received, generally speaking with applause. Some few of the auditors hissed during the performance, but they must have been either peculiarly ill-natured, or fuddled or foolish, because no one incident in the piece deserved reprobation.[18]

As the reviewer indicates, anti-Company discourse is a dangerous realm for female authors because it historically partakes in sexual innuendo, even in direct scurrility. *The Sword of Peace* shares a great deal with *The Nabob* but tends to work more subtly. As with Sir Matthew Mite, the Resident is figured as a foppish despot, but the question of sexual predation is only slightly less overt. Audience members hissing at the play may be reacting to the further sexual connotations of this representation, or their response could be attached to party politics. If it is both, then Starke is infringing on the bounds of feminine propriety in more ways than one.

While the battle in the press during the 1770s and 1780s deployed sexual tropes to establish a pathology concomitant with charges of economic and political wrongdoing, the Resident's corruption in *The Sword of Peace* has primarily sexual ends. He abuses his power to eliminate his chief sexual rival in the pursuit of Eliza. This translation of political scandal into the realm of private affairs capitalizes on the sexualization of the discursive formation at hand, while also opening the way for an allegorization of colonial governance in terms of heterosexual relations. Because the construction of gender and the deployment of sexuality are themselves in a state of flux at this historical moment, Starke's rhetorical strategy is extraordinarily volatile, but it allows her to play out significant anxieties about colonial activity within the generic confines of late eighteenth-century comedy. This has important ramifications for how Starke represents British women in India and her own practice in the metropole.

Beyond its indirect engagement with the Hastings affair, the play also thematizes abolitionist concerns that were coming into focus at this time. *The Sword of Peace* features an abolitionist subplot in which the servant Jeffreys buys one of Mrs. Tartar's slaves in order to grant him his freedom.[19] The scenes between Jeffreys and Caesar are intriguing for two reasons. First, they demonstrate that English notions of liberty were so firmly ensconced that they could be the subject of light satire. Jeffreys argues that English liberty consists primarily of the right to assault a fellow Englishman. This passage may be an indirect reference to the Hastings impeachment because Caesar's question is one that was very much on the mind of Persian chroniclers as they "watched Warren Hastings and his councillor Phillip Francis proceed from bad words to dueling with pistols in 1780 over matters of state."[20] As Rajat Kanta Ray argues, Indian observers took the duel as a sign of political weakness. For metropolitan viewers, the conflict between Hastings and Francis was well known, but it is hard to imagine precisely how Jeffrey's words would play. He is the play's only enlisted soldier, and his advocacy of violent conflict as the sine qua non of English national character can be seen as a corruption of the ideal of civil governance. Making the link between Jeffrey's remarks and Hastings seems to imply that East India agents are nothing more than a bunch of louts with pretensions to higher social standing. This, of course, was a prominent feature of antinabob discourse and one that proved to be quite discursively useful for Burke and Sheridan.

This reading is admittedly oblique but is supported by George Colman's remarkable epilogue to the play. For our purposes here it is enough to recognize the way in which it refers to the intense factionalism that characterized both the fall of Clive and the impeachment of Warren Hastings:

> How prone is man to quarrel with plain sense!
> Suspecting harmless words of foul offense.
> Too soon, alas! our minds to frailty leaning,
> Accuse the simple phrase of double meaning.
> . . . .
> Nay, in these days, there's scarce a City Prig
> Who dares confess his fondness for a wig;
> Lest he shou'd find in this same touchy town,
> Some angry tory who wou'd knock him down.
>   (58)

The poem goes on to applaud partially the cessation of the vice of dueling and its replacement by the current fashion for boxing over matters of honor. However, the pun on "wig" is one among many clues that Colman is invoking the satirical prints published in the months prior to Starke's play that render the impeachment of Hastings as a battle or a boxing match. Of particular resonance is William Dent's *The Grand Pitch Battle* of 13 February 1788, which portrays Hastings and Burke duking it out complete with seconds and umpires (see fig. 6.1). The metaphor of the prize fight allows Dent to specify not only the teams—Burke's second is, of course, Fox, and Sheridan is his bottle holder, whereas Hastings is seconded by Mr. Law—but also the corrupt adjudication of Lord Chancellor Thurlow and the speaker of the house, who are graphically placed in Hastings's corner. But unlike Dent, Colman and Starke are interested less in the formal structures of the fight than in the dynamics of boxing as such.

The second verse paragraph becomes quite intriguing in light of Jeffrey's remarks on the intimate relation between love and fisticuffs, for it directly condemns dueling, ridicules boxing, and then offers the satirical gibes of *The Sword of Peace* as a civil form of critique:

Speak not, ye beaux! we cannot move your passions;
The Sword with you has long been out of fashion.
For now each sparring beau in flannel stands;
To muffled gauntlets trusts his chicken hands;
Learns, generously, how to bruise,—not slay men!
And justifies his honour—on the dray-mue!
Soon shall we see, thank Heaven! the extirpation
Of barbarous duelling, throughout the nation;
Soon shall we read, instead of running through,
That, in Hyde-Park, two nobles have set to;
That Lord met Lord—that each, no Cesar bolder,
Brought a Right Honourable *bottle-holder!*
No carte and tierce—but bruise on bruise shall rise,
Till blows, not death, have clos'd the hero's eyes!—

(59)

Extrapolating from the scene between Jeffreys and Caesar, Colman's fighting beaux are men of fashion not unlike those in the audience. In this play, the sword is one of reconciliation, and masculine conflict is bathetically downgraded into a fashionable pursuit. If we read the epilogue as a commentary on the conflict between Hastings and Francis, or Hastings and Burke, the implication is that the duel and the ensuing impeachment are reducible to deviant homosocial relations that threaten the foundation of British imperial power.[21] Taking up Dent's declaration that Sheridan is "the Right Honourable bottle-holder," Colman extends the critique to the managers' dissipation. But equally as important as these topical resonances, the epilogue draws a comparison between aristocratic men fighting in Hyde-Park and the bonds of friendship between Jeffreys and Caesar. That the equation features signs of effeminacy and dissipation on one side and interracial relations on the other should give us pause, for these same terms surface in the discursive construction of both Hastings and the managers in the popular press. Representations of Hastings at this time swerve between signs of excessive gentility and Indianization (figs. 4.4, 4.9, and 5.1). And as we have already seen in chapter 4, Burke, Fox, and Sheridan are all satirized as Indianized subjects at different stages of the trial, especially during the presentation of the charge pertaining to the Begams of Oudh (see figs. 4.14 and 4.15).

The scenes between Jeffreys and Caesar are also important for a second reason—namely, because the conjunction of abolitionist and anti–East India Company rhetoric specifically locates the play's political investment.

As Kate Teltscher and P. J. Marshall remind us, "at the start of the [Hastings] impeachment India and the slave trade were linked, both in parliament and outside, as issues which raised questions about the morality of British policy overseas."[22] During the late 1780s, as the amount of public knowledge about colonial affairs was expanding, it began going through political convulsions. It is not uncommon to see abolitionist texts deploy figures of Eastern despotism, or anti–East India Company texts mobilizing figures more traditionally associated with the campaign against the slave trade, to argue for reform in imperial governance. As I have argued elsewhere with regard to Colman's *Inkle and Yarico,* protoabolitionist discourse attacked the violence and dehumanization required for the maintenance of the slave trade along with the centrality of interracial sexuality to the plantation economy.[23] As discourses of sexual regulation began to play a more central role in the aspirations and self-configuration of the middle classes, the interracial sexual practices endemic to the slave economy and the widely reported integration of British functionaries and their "brown families" under Hastings's rule became the object of intense anxiety. Starke's response to this anxiety counters both interracial relations in the colony and errant metropolitan practices with a fantasy of civil military rule. Colman's prologue and epilogue to Starke's comedy—and their collaboration here is I think conspicuous—merely highlight that, while aristocrats, public officials, and the lower orders play at fighting with each other in the name of the nation, a real war is being waged against the devolution of British subjectivity in the colonies by the middle classes. In short, the scenes of boxing and dueling through which the two playwrights ridicule the conventional repositories of landed and state power are set in contrast to the struggle being enacted in the theatre by plays such as *Inkle and Yarico* and *The Sword of Peace.*

Character and the Long Minuet as Danced at Coromandel

Starke's war on racial and class contamination is managed primarily through a careful regulation of the line between character and caricature. During this period, protoabolitionist and anti–East India Company discourse often blend into one another such that the careful reduction of the nabob and the Creole or of the Moslem and the African to a handful of discursive or visual tags enables them to be made equivalent. In *The Sword of Peace,* Louisa and Eliza Moreton, Edwards, Dormer, and Northcote can be described as characters, whereas the Resident, Supple, Caesar, Mazinghi Dowza, and the other British women in India are active in an economy of caricature. In the reviews, the former are all discussed in terms of particular actors' and actresses' ability to bring them "to life"— that is, there is a close relationship between the performance and the verisimilitude of the embodied character—whereas the latter are consistently figured as "exhibitions of character":

> The performers deserved great commendation for the powerful support they lent this Comedy, Miss Farren, Mr. Bannister, and Mrs. Kemble especially. Miss Farren [as Eliza] never displayed the gaiety of a well-bred woman, whose chief characteristick was natural vivacity, with a better grace; Mrs. Kemble spoke interestingly, and Bannister . . . made an excellent part of Jeffries. Baddeley also played well [as Northcote], and Robert Palmer was extremely happy in his manner of exhibiting the character of Supple; nor should Palmer himself be forgotten; his governed style, both of delivery and deportment, gave the characteristick modesty of Dormer a fulness and force of effect, that it could not have received from a less skilful comedian.[24]

The difference being established here between the fullness of effect generated by the governed style of delivery and deportment and the excessive performance required to exhibit Supple's "character" is fundamentally tied to the social distinctions that structure the play. With the distinctions of rank and respectability lying in the balance, the performance of the subtle difference between "fullness" of character and characteristic excess carries immense significance.

In contrast to the normative English characters, what the latter group of caricatures all share is a certain alterity or hybridity: they are either Indian, African, or "Indianized" English men and women. The play merely continues the representational economy of anti-Company discourse that we find from Dow through Burke. However, Deidre Lynch's discussion of the centrality of this distinction between character and caricature in mid- to late eighteenth-century cultural production clarifies some of the play's more audacious strategies:

> Eighteenth-century culture, we should remember, made *person* both a word for someone's physical appearance and a word for someone. It made *trait* cognate with words such as *stroke* or *line*—words for the graphic elements from which both pictorial and written representation are composed and through which they are identified. . . .

Indeed, the particular Englishness of the continuing national enthusiasm for character owes much to the fact that the English . . . conceptualize the characters they read about not as the French do, as "personnages" (that is, not as so many theatrical masks), but semiologically (as so many marks in a book).[25]

In almost novelistic fashion, the print version of *The Sword of Peace* exhibits precisely this semiological conceptualization of character that makes the surface of the body—whether it be complexion or costume—synonymous with personhood. As Roxann Wheeler states, clothing "was key to the constitution of religious, class, national and personal identity during the eighteenth-century" and many of its connotations were eventually transferred to skin surfaces.[26] Act 3, scene 2 contains two stage directions, which, more than anything else in the printed text of the play, allow one to recognize Starke's precise interventions in contemporary discussions of race, sexuality, and class in colonial representation. If nothing else the opening direction for the scene is notable for its sheer volume of information:

> SCENE *A Card Room discovered.*
> *Three Tables on a Side, ranged with Gentlemen and Ladies at Cards. At the upper End of the Stage a Door opens into a Ball-room, where you see Couples standing cross the Door as dancing; Music playing as at a distance, not too loud. At the first Table, next the audience, on one side,* Mrs. Garnish, *with her natural brown complexion, her dark hair dressed out with a number of Jewels, and her whole Dress as fine, and overloaded with Finery as possible in the Indian Style, lolling in her Chair, holding her Cards, and a black Slave standing by her, playing them for her as she speaks them, or points to them; taking up her Tricks, shuffling and taking up the Cards, and dealing for her. Another Slave by the side of the other Lady does the same for her. This other Lady to be a contrast to* Mrs. Garnish *in every Degree, looking pale and sick, peevish, ill natured and unhappy; dressed fine and awkward.* Mrs. Garnish *all Spirits, Pride, Vulgarity, and Self-consequence. The other Table in front of the opposite side. A great fat woman, very brown, sitting full front to the Audience, as fine as can be, but dressed as ridiculously as possible; this is* Mrs. Gobble. *The other Lady the Colour of Yarico.* Miss Bronze *dressed with elegance, in a silver or gold Gauze, Flowers, Jewels, &c. a good Figure, and smart, with black slaves playing their Cards, as before. Some of the men elegant and genteel;*

others brown, sickly Skeletons; and the elderly men very Fat; as these two extremes prevail most in India; and in general an awkward, square Manner of holding their Shoulders very high, and stooping their Heads. Some tables with no Blacks attending, to show it is the Distinction of Consequence and Grandeur; and the Blacks who thus attend must be dressed finer and with more Attention than the others, who are seen coming about with Refreshments. The two Tables next to the Ball-room Door purposely neglected, to show they are People to be known Nobodies; where such Folks are generally placed to keep the Wind off from their Betters. The whole Group as much in the Bunbury Stile as possible. (31–32)

The scenario is as much a visual tableau of colonial excess as it is of metropolitan class anxiety. The various tropes and figures that animate anti-nabob discourse are conveniently enacted and embodied for the audience. The scene of gaming itself figures an anxiety regarding speculation, which, since at least time of the Clive trial and Foote's *The Nabob,* runs through anti–East India Company writings. The fact that the card players are too indolent to even lift their cards to the table replays the kind of overattendance that so fascinated observers of colonial life.[27] The description of extreme body types is also a common gesture, as is the insinuation that India eats away at one's bodily and moral constitution. The stage direction is also remarkably precise about complexion, although clothing operates as an equally significant political surface—the former speaks to emergent understandings of race and nationality, whereas the latter is the locus of anxieties about rank. When Starke emphasizes the "brownness" of Mrs. Garnish and Mrs. Gobble, it is as much a sign of the women's Indianization as it is of their failed pretension to gentility, and therefore should be understood as the mark of suspect hybridity.

The flowers and gauze that adorn Miss Bronze, as much as the suggestion that she is the color of Yarico, mark her as a "country born" woman.[28] The comparison to Yarico is interesting for Colman's *Inkle and Yarico* is on the stage almost constantly in the season prior to *The Sword of Peace.* On first glance, it would appear that Starke is establishing a link between British imperial domination in two spaces in much the same fashion as Raynal's *Histoire des deux Indes.* However, Starke refrains from employing the sentimental strategies used by Colman to gain sympathy for Yarico's predicament and opts instead for a kind of racist containment more akin to his treatment of Wowski, which suggests that all the suspect qualities of the nouveaux riches Mrs. Garnish and Mrs. Gobble are being inculcated in the impressionable Hindu woman. That this strategy can be employed with so little effort indicates precisely how prevalent the figure of innocent and wronged Yarico is in the mind of the theatre-going public at this historical moment. The careful emphasis placed on her elegance and her good figure implies that, like Yarico in Colman's play, her innocence and her desirable femininity are in the process of being contaminated by contact with the avarice of British subjects abroad. The Indianization that Starke so readily invokes is complemented by a kind of reverse contamination that threatens the integrity of Hindu society. This twofold romanticization of Hindu feminine propriety and demonization of British governance is, of course, one of the most famous elements of both Burke and Sheridan's rhetorical assault on Warren Hastings.

But we can be much more specific about the play's semiological gestures and its relation to the bristling market for satirical prints. The final sentence of the stage direction is itself a direction for reading because the reference to "the Bunbury Stile" firmly establishes the economy of caricature as one composed of visual marks and lines. Henry William Bunbury was one of the most highly regarded caricaturists of his generation, and his career was at its height in 1787 and 1788 when Starke's play was initially composed and performed. Bunbury was a social caricaturist whose most famous work was a seven-foot-long strip entitled *A Long Minuet as Danced at Bath,* which was exhibited and reproduced in the months immediately preceding the play's first performance (fig. 6.2). Bunbury's strip depicts a range of figures all engaged in various aspects of the minuet, and the satire emerges out of a certain anxiety regarding the embodiment of class, for the strip implies that the minuet will act as a filter for class identity. As David Kunzle states, "The minuet was the most intricate and difficult of dances; Bath was the most fashionable of all resorts, to which there flocked the nouveaux-riches and social climbers. . . . Bunbury seized with lightning brilliance various attitudes expressing degrees of awkwardness, naive enthusiasm, and even . . . a sly grace. Male and female dancers are by no means uniformly ugly, but run the gamut of peculiarity in expression and physiognomic type."[29] Bunbury's strip therefore targets with varying degrees of severity those who are challenging the rigid boundaries of class propriety. If one assumes that the gentry has the grace and physical facility to perform the dance, the strip focuses attention on the failure of the bodies of the nouveaux riches to accede to gentility. The volatility of such an assumption is registered by the ambiguity of some of the caricatures, for the flip side of the satire is that all it takes to accede to gentility is the right combination of dress and accomplishments.

FIG. 6.2. Henry William Bunbury, detail from *A Long Minuet as Danced at Bath*, 25 June 1787 *(courtesy of the Department of Prints and Drawings, The British Museum, London; BM 7229)*

Instead of replicating Bunbury's minuet, Starke stages her dance off-stage such that the card game becomes the locus of satire. The card game is in a sense surrounded both materially and culturally by a scene of dancing that nevertheless remains unenacted on the stage. This is an interesting shift because it resolves the key problem of the representation of classed bodies highlighted by Bunbury's strip. When Eliza enters midway through the scene, Supple's effusions on her dancing simultaneously invoke and ignore the Bunburian scene:

ELIZA: I am glad we have left the ball-room; I declare, Resident, there's no dancing a minuet here with any satisfaction; one is as much crowded as at the ball at St. James on a birth night.

MISS BRONZE: (*in a loud whisper to Mrs. Gobble*) Do you think she was ever there!

RESIDENT: That was owing to your fine dancing Eliza, and not to the smallness of the room.

SUP: Oh! such a minuet! (*turns to Mrs. Garnish in a lower voice*) You never, Mrs. Garnish, saw such dancing in your life.

MRS GARN: (loud) What, so monstrous *bad,* hey?

ELIZA: (*looking down at Mrs. Garnish with a smile of triumph*) La! Mrs. Garnish, have you forgot me—I'm sure I shall never forget you—with your nice plumb cakes, so frosted and decorated; and your pies and your puffs, and ices and creams, all so nice:—I used to buy of you in Oxford road. (33–34)

The minuet becomes a scene of interpretation and Starke's play performs a startling reversal of the Bunburian glance. The audience of Bunbury's strip is assumed to be capable of discerning the signs of gentility and therefore able to judge the shortcomings of the nouveaux riches. In *The Sword of Peace* the audience watches the social climbers attempting to interpret the accomplishments of the Miss Moretons. The reversal instantiates a twofold satire, for not only does Starke ridicule Supple's, Garnish's, and Bronze's excessive concern with Eliza's dancing skills, but she also subtly introduces enough ambiguity into the scene of interpretation to force the audience to consider the class identity of Eliza and Louisa. Eliza and Louisa are themselves extremely concerned that they not be lumped into the same category as the other women in the play who have come to India in search of monetary gain and class ascendancy through marriage. Eliza explicitly states that hers is a sentimental, not a financial, journey: "Hail! hail! thou land of mercenary interest, where love of gold destroys its thousands; where woman, lovely woman, for wealth and grandeur comes from far to sacrifice beauty, health, happiness! receive one votary to all-powerful love" (6). However, the fact of the matter is that Eliza and Louisa are also on the marriage market, but their search for husbands is, as the play's subtitle suggests, "A Voyage of Love." The problem is that the interpretation of their motivation, like their class identity, is not subject to clear determination. In a space where class boundaries are fluid and money supersedes all matters of sentiment, the representational economy promulgates confusion about the fullness and veracity of character, reputation, and, ultimately, value in the sexual marketplace.

This problematic is given ample consideration in the play's opening scene. Act 1, scene 1 commences with Eliza trying to rally Louisa's spirits for the difficult mission that awaits them. The opening-night review establishes the situation as follows:

> By the will of Mr. Morton, (who had obtained his fortune in the East Indies) Eliza, his only daughter, is obliged to take a voyage to the coast of Coromandel to receive her inheritance, and she is accompanied by her cousin Louisa, who is commissioned by Sir Thomas Clairville to endeavour to obtain from Lieutenant Dormer the sword of young Clairville, . . . the intention of Sir Thomas being to preserve it in the Clairville family, as a monumental trophy in honour of the deceased. In order to induce the lieutenant to part with it, Louisa is authorized to tender 5000 L . . . in exchange for the sword.[30]

The only thing that stands in the way of Eliza's marriage to her beloved Edwards is that his family thinks she is of insufficient fortune. Her voyage, therefore, amounts to a double acquisition, for her inheritance will gain her the hand of Edwards. There is no doubt from her attempts to alleviate Louisa's mortification over the fact that they have been placed in the house of the termagant Mrs. Tartar that Eliza not only understands that voyages of love are financial affairs but also recognizes that such travels are a threat to female reputations. Starke doesn't flinch from aligning Mrs. Tartar's immorality with her complexion and the insinuation that she is of mixed race:

ELIZA: Why, for our well-beloved lady hostess, dear Madam Tartar, I think we shall find her *blue*-cast, or half-cast complexion, the fairest part of her composition. But not withstanding her *hauteur*, I shall teach her the difference between women who come here to make their fortunes, and those who come to receive them. (5–6)

The phrase "blue-cast" condenses class and racial hybridity into one figure. The racialization of the line between making and receiving a fortune is crucial to the moral economy of Starke's play, for Mrs. Tartar is clearly below the line of respectability. The distinction is one of agency—that a woman must appear to be the passive recipient of her fortune to be truly modest and, by extension, truly white—but such an argument would downplay the degree to which Eliza and Louisa regulate not only their circulation as sexual commodities but also their accession to bourgeois normativity. In a sense, it is their palpable activity in the marketplace that makes them such a site of interpretive anxiety for Starke.

The ambiguities that trouble the interpretation of Eliza's and Louisa's mission at the play's outset are transferred to the interpretation of Eliza's dancing in act 3. These ambiguities are tempered by the fact that Starke's caricature has already undercut the reliability of witnesses such as Supple or Mrs. Garnish. But the play is also subtle enough to realize that the performance of the minuet on stage might create more problems than it would solve. The minuet may constitute too much of a test to be allowed into theatrical representation. Instead Eliza's class identity is secured in part by her testimony of prior knowledge of Mrs. Garnish and in part by her dress. The following is Starke's stage direction for Eliza and Louisa's entry into the scene immediately prior to the preceding interchange:

Enter ELIZA *and* LOUISA *from the Ball Room dress'd with the utmost Simplicity and Elegance of Taste and Fashion; but their hair without powder, in Curls and Ringlets, flowing in Abundance down their backs to the Bottom of their Waists. Several Gentlemen with them; among the rest,* MR. SUPPLE *and the* RESIDENT, *over dressed, and very hot. As* ELIZA *and* LOUISA *advance, the Ladies all eye them, wink and make all sorts of rude Signs to one another about them. As* ELIZA *advances towards* MRS. GARNISH, *she stares rudely and vulgarly in her Face and apparently examining her whole Dress and Figure.* ELIZA, *with the utmost ease and Elegance, sees it, but looks at her with such Nonchalance, and seems in high Spirits.* LOUISA, *all elegant softness on the other Side, seems disconcerted at their behaviour. During this time Music.* (33)

The stage direction explicitly contrasts the excessive qualities of Garnish, Gobble, and Bronze with the simplicity and lack of artifice in the appearance of the Moreton cousins. In this representational economy, "elegance" and "ease" are not only separated from luxury but also attached to veracity of character. In other words, the elegance of the Moreton cousins signifies that they are who they seem to be.

This is no small matter, for as I have argued with regard to Narcissa and Captain Campley in *Inkle and Yarico*, normativity comes with the privilege of representational lack.[31] When one compares the description of Eliza and Louisa with that of Mrs. Garnish, Mrs. Gobble, and Miss Bronze, it becomes clear that the critique of luxury that runs through the play extends to the economy of representation itself. Even at the level of naming, the distinction between character and caricature is manifest. Mrs. Garnish's name in contemporary usage means "tip" and carries with it the double connotation of corruption or bribery and implies that she is a gratuity or a trophy bride. Mrs. Gobble clearly connotes vulgar avarice and together they constitute a perfect complement not only to the figure of the dissipated company man discussed earlier but also to Foote's nabob Matthew Mite. Foote makes much of Mite's former career as a cheese monger, and Starke plays out a similar gesture in her description of Mrs. Garnish's baked goods. The degree to which the frostings and creams represent Mrs. Garnish's body is perhaps debatable, but such a figuration is in keeping with Starke's overall rhetorical strategies, for the caricature of Mrs. Garnish partakes in the general discourse of prostitution. At one level, Starke provides her audience with the perverse counterpart to the unmanly company servant, for Mrs. Garnish and Mrs. Gobble are at once hypersexualized and yet the epitome of indolence. The former process is explicit in their critique of Eliza's and Louisa's unwillingness to receive all the men of the factory:

MRS GOB: (*bawling*) Lord, Mrs. Garnish, why I hear they have receiv'd no company! There is not a man in the rooms can tell me one word what they're like.

MRS BRONZE: O Ma'am! Te, he, he, he! Mrs. Tartar was just now telling me the ladies were so squeamish, truly! they wou'd not admit the gentlemen to pay their compliments, for fear it should be thought they came to get husbands. Te, he, he!
[*The ladies at the tables laugh with affected airs.*] (33)

The *Morning Chronicle* review takes special notice of this scene and sin-gles out the laugh of Mrs. Edwin, who played Mrs. Gobble, "in the scene of the Rout as well as her tone of conversation [as] highly comic and [a] strong exemplification of character."[32]

Eliza's defense of her refusal to receive the men of the factory in the play's first scene also raises the question of female laughter, but only af-ter clarifying that she and Louisa will only be commodified in very spe-cific ways:

ELIZA: . . . Mrs. Tartar's very angry with me, because I don't like to be—to be kiss'd by all the five hundred gentlemen belonging to your presidency here; and—she says, *you* will make me.

RES: Ha, ha, ha! Why to be sure it's the usual form to receive visits of the factory at Ladies first arrival; and who would not wish to salute a pretty Lady, if he cou'd contrive it, you know? adod, it makes me long for a kiss myself.

ELIZA: Very likely, but as it is your sex's privilege to *ask,* so it is *our's* to *refuse;* and to be oblig'd to be dress'd up in grand gula, stuck on a Sopha, at the upper end of a room, for three nights running, to be view'd at will—as who should say—*what d'ye please to buy, gentle-men?* Monstrous, and then submitting to the salute of every man that approaches one, is such an indelicate custom.——(10–11)

In this defense of her sexual character, Eliza explicitly marks her resistance to both Indianization and overt commodification. What is more, the two processes are understood to be indistinguishable—to be stuck on the sofa is to be brought to market. This speech makes a link between the play's

FIG. 6.3. James Gillray, *A Sale of English Beauties in the East Indies*, 16 May 1786 (*courtesy of the Department of Prints and Drawings, The British Museum, London; BM 7014*)

abolitionist rhetoric and its protofeminist critique of the marriage market. As Eliza states, "I look upon [the practice of receiving all the men of the factory] with the most *sovereign contempt;* 'and I sincerely hope the traffic will be abolished, as still *more disgraceful* to our sex than that of poor slaves to a nation'" (9). This gains some resonance in light of Gillray's infamous print *A Sale of English Beauties in the East Indies*, which portrays a series of Indian men fondling buxom English women at a slave auction presided over by the Supreme Council of the East India Company (fig. 6.3). Like the Resident in *The Sword of Peace*, the auctioneer is rendered as an effeminate fop. Interracial sexual relations between Indian men and young English women are here hysterically rendered as a symptom of the evacuation of British masculinity. This attribution of perversion is figured by a package in the foreground labeled "For the Amusement of Military Gentlemen," which contains copies of *Female Flagellants, Fanny Hill, Elements of Nature,* and notably Crebillion fils's Orientalist novel of libertine desire, *The Sopha.* Gillray implies that military officers working for the company are too distracted by pornographic desire to protect the national interest in sexual normativity. The projected marketplace for English beauties among Indian gentlemen, therefore, is contingent on an already corrupt colonial military that fails to act properly in the realm of sexual exchange.

Interestingly, the direct invocation of the slave trade is relegated solely to the closet and may have been perceived as too inflammatory for the stage. But Eliza is also careful to emphasize that her critique here is not an absolute refusal to circulate in the sexual marketplace:

ELIZA: Nay, now, good Mrs. Tartar, don't hurry yourself—you and I shall never agree on this subject: "for though I despise prudery, I cannot bear any thing which *degrades* my sex,"—No one has a greater flow of spirits, or more laughing chearfulness than myself, by some ill-naturedly term'd coquetty [*sic*]. . . . (11)

Eliza recognizes that limited circulation is crucial for the maintenance of her value in the only marketplace she cares about—namely, the metropolitan marriage market. In terms of performance, it is the quality of Eliza's laugh that simultaneously separates her from the likes of Mrs. Gobble and Mrs. Garnish, yet still renders her susceptible to the charge of coquetry. Like the minuet, the subtle gradations of bodily performance that establish class distinction also require equally subtle skills of interpretation from the viewer. The ascription of the latter judgment to the "ill-natured" suggests that Starke not only advocates for a certain amount of sexual agency for women but also suggests that those viewers who are unable to distinguish between degrees of performance are themselves suspect. One could argue that Eliza and the *Morning Chronicle* are performing the same discursive containment of masculine critique, for the reviewer also uses the phrase "ill-natured" to describe the hissing auditors on opening night.

If the vulgar laughter of Mrs. Gobble, Mrs. Garnish, and Miss Bronze is a sign of too much sexual experience, then their actions at cards signify in a similarly complex fashion. The fact that they are playing cards at all weaves them into a discursive fabric that clothes much of the writing on English India in the 1770s and 1780s. The extraordinary financial gains that could be gained through a successful eastern career were frequently connected to the overall rhetoric surrounding gaming in the period. Late in the century, gaming and dueling are perhaps the only libertine vices that can be brought into representation, and therefore they become emblematic for excesses beyond those associated with luxury. In other words, there is a sexual connotation active beneath the surface of the discourse on gambling that emerges quite palpably in Starke's stage direction. The details of the card games are quite interesting in this light. Mrs. Garnish states that she "plays alone, in diamonds," thereby simultaneously linking her greed for jewels to a certain autoeroticism (32). Similarly, when Mrs. Gobble discovers that hearts are trump, she states "Ah, hearts! I like that—I have always so many of 'em.—My lead—play a club, Pompey" (32). The joke cuts in two directions at once, for although she boasts of many loves or hearts, she has only clubs or black cards to lead with. It is difficult to say if the audience would have received this as a racial joke or simply an expression of Mrs. Gobble's palpable undesirability. The specter of interracial sexuality haunts the entire scene because the relationship between Mrs. Garnish, Mrs. Gobble, and their slaves clearly translates the excessive bodily intimacy and laziness of earlier representations of male nabobs, and with that translation comes the implied charge of sexual impropriety of a quite specific kind. If prior anti-Company discourse feminized company employees, then Starke's women are doubly perverse, for they imitate a flawed masculinity. The caricature is of women behaving as feminized men.[33]

Precisely this economy of caricature, however, threatens the characterization of Eliza and Louisa. Both the mission and the actions of the Moreton cousins are susceptible to charges of gender impropriety. The excessive caricature of Mrs. Garnish and company establishes the relative normativity of Eliza's and Louisa's characters. The important qualification here is the word "relative" for I would argue that Starke preserves a certain amount of agency for her characters through this comparative excess. The question of female agency is explicitly addressed by Colman's epilogue, and it marks precisely what must be contained in Eliza's and Louisa's characters for *The Sword of Peace* to avoid charges of impropriety. When Miss Farren comes on stage for the epilogue, she is still dressed as Eliza and hence speaks with that character's mildly coquettish demeanor. With this in mind, it is important to imagine the effect of a woman speaking Colman's lines, for the first verse paragraph ridicules excessive factionalism in the realm of politics, and the second ridicules male homosocial violence in the realm of fashionable society. Recognizing that Starke's play attacked the dissolution of colonial British women through the vice of gambling, Colman's epilogue attacks corrupt metropolitan masculinity via the vice of dueling and offers a critique of specific forms of public masculinity.[34]

Colman brings the critique of factionalism into the theatre by addressing the male audience directly:

Are there not some among you, then, who cease
To smile, when hearing of a Sword of Peace?
Speak, ye *Militia Captains! Train Bands,* speak!
Think ye, 'gainst you our Author wrote in pique?—
Dumb! like your swords, unus'd to face the light!
Speak, then, Sir Matthew Plumb, the addressing Knight!
You who have seen the sword—ah, great beholder!
Have seen it, *flaming,* peaceful o'er your shoulder. (58)

As a critique of those committed to conflict for the sake of conflict—a group that may include not only the various factions of the East India Company, which scapegoated Clive, but also those who wish to isolate imperial mismanagement in the person of Warren Hastings—the lines suggest that those who make a career of conflict like politicians and noncombatant "Militia Captains" do so in backrooms safe from the light of scrutiny. The image of the sword behind the back implies that backstabbing remains an active and shameful part of metropolitan political life.

In contrast *The Sword of Peace,* by nature of its publicity, operates differently because it is in the hands of a woman:

But that our Sword of Peace may frighten no man,
Know, brave gallants! 'tis wielded by a woman.
Let it not, then, with others, be abolish'd,
'Tis harmless, and, she hopes, not quite unpolish'd
Such as it is, we can't be apprehensive
That this, our Sword of Peace, will prove a sword offensive. (59)

Emphasizing the fact of female authorship aimed to soften the rhetoric of the play's critics, but the epilogue's antidueling rhetoric participates in a larger cultural turn away from the intricate codes of honor that were integral to aristocratic self-stylization in the eighteenth century. At the time of Starke's play, dueling was in disrepute, and, as Donna Andrew persuasively argues, "an outcome of the long struggle against dueling was the emergence of a body of thinking, which, while at first identifying itself merely negatively, that is, as against dueling, came to a new vision of society based on reasonableness, Christianity and commerce, in which dueling ceased to be practiced simply because it appeared incongruous and foolish."[35] This new vision of society suited the ascendancy of the commercial class:

This new class . . . could and did reject the established norms of gentlemanliness, which the code of honour represented, and substituted its own redefinition of the term. Duelling ceased being described by its opponents as a practice indulged in by the man of honour or fashion; duelling became represented instead as a preoccupation of vicious indulgence of a *class*. Duelling was identified as a failing of the upper classes and, as such, roundly condemned.[36]

Importantly, because the disapprobation of dueling partook of the discourse of degeneracy and monstrosity, the discourses of antidueling and of antinabobry shared rhetorical strategies.

The epilogue's second verse paragraph not only ridicules the downgrading of dueling to fisticuffs but also offers satirical comedy and specifically Starke's play as a more socially appropriate mode of conflict resolution. Rather than retiring to the field of honor, the audience is encouraged to attend the theatre. What interests me here is that Colman's critique of boxing works primarily through the feminization of his fighting lords. For these men "The sword . . . has long been out of fashion," thereby leaving the sword to be taken up by the female knight. This implies that Starke wields the sword and figuratively enters the masculinized realm of publicity because men have failed to accede to their phallic responsibilities. And this masculinization is continuous not only with how the sword functions in the play but also with the limited masculinization of Eliza and Louisa, which relegates their characters to the near margin of feminine normativity.

As in the epilogue, it would appear that the female figure, whether it be Louisa or Starke herself, plays a mediating role between an outmoded aristocratic code of masculine behavior and an emergent form of commercial civility exemplified by the space of the theatre itself. In other words, Louisa is able to handle the sword but only to discharge its phallic qualities in the present so that it can take its place in the invention of tradition so crucial to Britain's self-fashioning at this historical moment. Could it be that a sword in any other hands than a woman's threatens to weaken the very claims to civility that are increasingly bearing the moral burden of the metropolitan nation's just governance of colonial affairs? An affirmative answer to this question underscores the importance of the kind of femininity enacted by Eliza and Louisa and by Starke herself—a femininity that partakes of a limited amount of masculinized public agency to dramatize the necessity of restraining male homosocial desires in the realm of politics, of commerce, and of love.[37]

But as we will see in the next chapter, this representation of restraint in the metropole is shadowed by an escalation in military activity in Mysore.

The campaigns of Cornwallis and Wellesley against Tipu Sultan in the 1790s were the topic of intense public interest. But at the heart of reports of Cornwallis's victories over Tipu lies an entire assemblage of tropes that depict the military defeat of Tipu as an instantiation of sentimental paternal care for subject peoples. In the proliferation of celebratory texts and performances, Cornwallis, the icon of paternal restraint, accedes to precisely the position of normativity promoted by Starke and Colman and, in doing so, becomes in Roach's terms, the surrogate for Clairville, the now deceased model of defective aristocratic paternality. However, that accession is only part of the story. When colonial warfare eventually made its way into the theatre of metropolitan life via the illegitimate dramaturgy practiced at venues such as Astley's Royal Amphitheatre, audiences' attempts to police their own volatile racial identities were supplemented by self-confirming assaults on their own phantasmatic projections of alterity.

Starke, Cornwallis, and the Reform of Landed Society

Starke's attempt to intervene in the dramatic practice and political life of London was not received with unanimous approbation. Speaking of her next play, the *St. James Chronicle* directly castigated Starke for entering the public sphere: "[W]e cannot help repeating a wish, often expressed by us, that the ladies would not quit domestick duties, and the various provinces of early education, for the rugged paths of masculine fame either in the drama or in politicks."[38] The discomfort generated by Starke's adoption of ostensibly masculine roles was part of a larger anxiety regarding social hybridity. The Rout scene in *The Sword of Peace* must have been a strange spectacle for London audiences because its critique of colonial hybridity had a certain applicability to unsettling forms of social hybridity in the metropole, of which the theatre was perhaps exemplary. The audience at Starke's play was composed of members of various ranks whose extratheatrical sociability was quite limited. However, within the confines of the playhouse, persons of all ranks were in close contact. And the relations among these people were exceedingly complex because class itself was in such a state of flux and negotiation at this historical juncture. As I have already suggested, Colman's prologue and epilogue to Starke's comedy link the threat posed by degenerate colonials such as the Resident and Mrs. Tartar to that posed by obsolete styles of aristocratic masculinity. The critique of aristocratic dueling in Colman's epilogue is linked to Starke's attacks both on the interracial sexuality of social climbers in the colonies, and on the vicious desires—both sexual and economic—of Company officials during the period of Hastings's rule. However, all of these attacks operate via the economy of caricature—Mrs. Garnish, the effete Resident, and the effeminate gentry of Colman's epilogue represent disturbing but ultimately receding threats. The attacks on Indianization, on Hastings's corruption, and on the dissolute aristocracy are possible and effective because they constitute the soon-to-be-obsolete models of social and imperial governance against which emergent norms are being defined.

This relationship between obsolescence and emergent norms was also a feature of colonial governmentality at this historical juncture. As Nicholas B. Dirks emphasizes in his discussion of the impact of the Hastings impeachment on colonial policy,

> In Burke's obsessional litany of Hastings's excess, what was embarrassing was neither Hastings's greed nor his methods so much as his manifest success in making the horrors and pleasures of empire realizable. In the wake of Burke's attack, a colonial bureaucracy was established to monitor the greed with which all Britons went to India from the late eighteenth century on. Burke shifted the balance of power to the state rather than the mercantile elite, and it was under his scrutiny that the colonial state was born. Colonial rapacity could not be curtailed either by Hastings's recall or the India Act of 1784, however: it could only be bureaucratized through the high minded rhetoric of the [Permanent Settlement]. British rule represented its interest in securing steady revenue through a language of improvement predicated on the rule of property and the benevolent intent of a new "postdespotic" state.[39]

The initial phases of "postdespotic" rule fell to Cornwallis and we have already outlined his impact on the reform of the military. These reforms, which resulted in a shift in military supremacy in India, were later accompanied by the Permanent Settlement, which resulted in a shift in sovereignty.

> [T]he Permanent Settlement was an attempt to erase Hastings's legacy in more ways than one. As formulated initially by [Philip] Francis and implemented by Cornwallis, it was meant to regularize Company revenues through a steady tax rather than by extortion, to normalize administration by setting high public standards for the service of the Company officers, and to create a loyal elite based on

landed property rather than military alliance, by restoring putatively traditional landholders to their rightful position. . . . Cornwallis . . . was intent on reproducing the landed gentry of England, in a dramatic enunciation of imperial policy that seemed a denial of the entrepreneurial origins of Indian empire even as it sought to stabilize a new kind of Indian elite.[40]

This act of reproduction has been extensively documented, but for our purposes we need to recognize that it involved multiple crises of legitimation. Aside from the tortuous problems of reconfiguring property relations in India according to British notions of the sanctity of private property and of inventing an Indian landed class, the ideological investment in the Permanent Settlement also required an erasure of the preceding thirty years of British economic history, which had demonstrated that landed property could no longer be understood as unrelated to mercantile commerce. To pretend that the problems of sovereignty would be rectified by establishing a landed elite was to indulge in a misrecognition of the stability of the landed classes and of the "natural" accommodation of liberty and property that would act as foundation for governmentality.[41] C.A. Bayly aptly captures this misrecognition as "a massive effort of wishful thinking."[42]

Guha, Sen, Thompson, and others have written extensively on the impact of the Permanent Settlement's displaced fantasy of landed property. As one might expect, the new estates were less a source of stability, than a site of high turnover and, eventually, of absenteeism. These problems were also a part of the metropolitan economy in the 1760s and 1770s, and the early 1790s saw both a radical threat to, and an ideological reinvestment in, the values of the landed gentry: ownership, inheritance, and succession.[43] The vociferousness of Burke's defense of the sanctity of landed property in *Reflections on the Revolution in France* is itself evidence of the purchase of radical political arguments that dissociated political liberty from property. The following passage exhibits a "massive effort of wishful thinking" that nevertheless had palpable effects on British national fantasy: "The power of perpetuating our property in our families is one of the most valuable and interesting circumstances belonging to it, and that which tends the most to the perpetuation of society itself. It makes our weakness subservient to our virtue; it grafts benevolence even upon avarice. The possessors of family wealth, and of the distinction which attends the hereditary possession . . . are the natural securities for this transmission."[44] Everything about this passage begs to be read against previous accounts of metropolitan corruption, for it implies that weakness and avarice would be everywhere rampant but for the hygienic effects of hereditary possession. If we take Burke's words as the statement of a problematic, rather than an expression of historical truth, then it is possible to see the export of British models of landed property to India as a bulwark against metropolitan social anxieties. The violent suppression of radical critiques of British polity in the early 1790s partook of a similar invention of "tradition" that play a fundamental role in patriotic discourse throughout the romantic period. That ideological project was not at all distant from the fantasies that drove the Permanent Settlement. The maintenance of "tradition" through its forced implementation elsewhere had significant implications not only for those on whom it was foisted but also for those in whose name it was perpetrated.

Mariana Starke's second play does not broach the issues raised by the Permanent Settlement directly—it precedes that development by two years. But *The Widow of Malabar* is deeply concerned with the problems of tradition, and of aristocratic succession and inheritance that would ultimately impinge on both Cornwallis's reforms and on Burke's polemics.[45] If we can understand the Permanent Settlement as an allegorical policy—one that utilizes one form of social and economic relations to figure forth another—then it is illuminating to look at the instability of Starke's own allegorical gestures in her adaptation of Le Mierre's tragedy *La veuve du Malabar*. The Permanent Settlement attempted to regulate Indian society by rendering it as a shadow of an England that no longer existed except in the nationalist fantasies that consolidated British identity after the state's active suppression of Jacobinism. As such, its reforms did not produce an elite constituency that would govern the land, but rather a bureaucracy that would generate knowledge about the people.[46] The disciplinary effects of that knowledge practice defined the managerial practice of nineteenth-century colonial India. In a similar allegorical gesture, *The Widow of Malabar* attempted to regulate its London audience by rendering troubling aspects of its class formation in terms derived from Indian culture. However, the play's attempt to regulate the metropolitan elite, to return it to its past glory—or at least to the fantasy of security exemplified by Burke—did not reform the aristocracy but rather occasioned even more rigid notions of class stratification than those articulated in *The Sword of Peace*. As we will see, this particular project of elite reform was contained and reoriented not only by the play's epilogue, but also by the newspapers in a fashion that further consolidated the many strains of normative national identity following the French Revolution and prior to the imposition of the Permanent Settlement.

The Mirror and the Dart: The Widow of Malabar

The Widow of Malabar is a play about suttee, and, as in *The Sword of Peace,* the British military in India plays a crucial role in containing and regulating social deviance. Indamora, the potential sati in Starke's play, is saved both from death and ignominy by what the newspapers identified as "British humanity" embodied in the character of Raymond, general of the English Forces.[47] Indamora was played by the highly respectable Miss Brunton, but her performance of rectitude was complicated by the sexualization of the sati figure in the press. Before exploring this issue, however, it is helpful to consider Starke's source text and how her adaptation makes its way to the London stage. As Dorothy M. Figueira has argued, Le Mierre's tragedy *La veuve du Malabar,* like much of the continental representation of suttee, diverges significantly from the British accounts discussed by Courtwright, Mani, and others.[48] Most important, the sexual economy of the representation is markedly different from the eyewitness accounts that played such an important role in the legislative discussion of the practice in the early nineteenth century. Le Mierre's popular tragedy of 1770 represents the sati figures as the victim of religious superstition and social custom. The struggle between reason and superstition is staged as an intracaste conflict between a Young and an Old Bramin. However, the resolution of this conflict is effected by the intervention of the handsome General Montalban who, upon saving the potential sati, discovers that she is none other than the long lost Lanassa whom he loved in his youth. As Figueira notes, this effectively casts the sati figure as "an exemplar of bourgeois conjugal virtues and as a courageous rebel against social rigidity."[49] But the sudden suturing of the heterosexual love plot to the Enlightenment victory over superstition raises a number of problems that were immediately capitalized on by various theatrical parodists, for it doesn't take much to transform the tragedy into a sexual farce.[50] After all, the entire history of libertine fiction happily conflates Enlightenment rebellion against religious doxa with men's and women's sexual license. These parodies highlight the volatility of the sati figure's exemplarity, for the retroactive establishment of a relationship between Lanassa and Montalban raises the question of desire and thereby puts women's sexual agency under intense scrutiny. What this means is that the ideological success of the play turns on the performance of virtue in the part of Lanassa.

Virtue's performativity became a crucial issue for Starke's adaptation because so much depended on the context of its initial production. Starke prepared the play for private performance under the auspices of Mrs. Crespigny at Camberwell. This fact alone opened the play to heterodox interpretations for three reasons. First, private theatricals tended to obviate the contestatory possibilities of public performance. The audience and the performers were consolidated by social ties.[51] Second, this consolidation was built on a relationship that would otherwise encapsulate much of the bourgeois suspicion about aristocratic vice. By the 1760s private theatricals employed professional actors and designers from the London theatres and hence brought together two groups of people routinely associated with sexual dissipation. This is why so much is made of Mrs. Crespigny's respectability in Starke's advertisement to the play. Third, the play is the product of a collaboration of sorts between two public women. Starke's *The Sword of Peace* carefully legitimated Eliza's and Louisa's—and by extension Starke's own—public and private reputations at the expense of social upstarts in the colonies. As I have argued, that legitimation not only promoted an emergent kind of normative commercial civility, but also attempted to bury codes of masculine behavior that were perceived to be destabilizing the political and social elites of metropolitan society. In *The Widow of Malabar,* a similar kind of critique is engaged, but the press used the play as an occasion for scrutinizing upperclass women and the threat their sexual agency posed to the maintenance of "tradition." As we will see, the fate of that regulatory effort is integrally tied to the social function of the sati figure at this juncture in metropolitan culture.

The Widow of Malabar was chosen by Miss Brunton for her benefit night in May 1790.[52] It is clear from the Larpent text of the play that it was submitted as a vehicle for the popular actress, and this enlarges the collaboration to one between three very public figures.[53] What Miss Brunton brings to the mix is the question of her reputation. Despite repeated assertions of her spotless reputation in the reviews, Anne Brunton was a known associate of Robert "Revolution" Merry, whom she would marry shortly after the play's run.[54] Merry was one of the most active radical journalists in the period immediately following the French Revolution.[55] Brunton's reputation, therefore, can be described as troubled: regardless of her sexual respectability, her social and political connections render her subject to calumny. Performing on her benefit night, Miss Brunton appears before the audience at least as much as herself as Indamora. This is not insignificant because, as we have already noted, the performance of virtue in the part of Indamora prevents the love plot from devolving into low sexual comedy or transforming into libertine critique. The opening-night reviews were unanimous in their praise of her performance, but one review in the *New Lady's Magazine,* notorious for its scrutiny of women's public conduct, sets the stage for a rather different interpretation not only of Miss Brunton, Mrs. Crespigny, and Mariana Starke, but also of the sati figure: "On this lady's night a new tragedy, in three acts, was brought forward called 'The Widow of Malabar,' which we must own afforded us great entertainment—throughout the whole we laughed very heartily—but that is no wonder, as it is said to be the production of a [house/lady] of fashion and originally written for a *private theatrical.*"[56] The play here is understood as a folly of fashion and entertaining inasmuch as it demonstrates the ridiculousness of those associated with it. This amounts to a key shift from the positive exemplarity of a particular actress to the shaming of fashionable society. My suspicion is that the laughter afforded here is not one based on the play's ineptitude—both the reviews and the receipts indicate that it is a proficient play—but rather in its capacity to exemplify the very opposite of virtue.

Something of this instability is captured in the *English Review*'s commentary on the first printed version of the play:

> The best quality in the Widow of Malabar is, its being comprised of three acts. There are indeed a few failings in it. Among others we might mention that the plot discovers itself in the first act; that it is unnatural, in many respects, and contrary to the customs it pretends to describe in that the widow, instead of *requesting* to be burnt, is *forced* to comply; and that the bramins are supposed to have no object in view but her jewels. This makes the thing new and pretty, but neither interesting nor instructive. On the whole, the piece is well calculated to please a modern audience since comedy is become pantomime, and tragedy a kind of sentimental comedy.[57]

It is important to remember that Burke in the *Reflections* had characterized the social devolution of France as a dangerous mixing of genres, as a "monstrous tragi-comic scene."[58] The reviewer's invocation of generic devolution is telling because Raymond's rescue of his beloved Indamora contravenes the expectations of tragedy and thus downgrades the threat of suttee from a scene of potential tragic catharsis to a comic obstacle to be overcome by heroic masculinity. This is why the reviewer, whose confident knowledge of suttee is most likely derived from accounts in Holwell and Dow, raises questions about the accuracy of the customs presented.[59] The combined suggestion that the play diverges from the "customs" it pretends to describe and that it is in fact a sentimental comedy subtly indicates that the widow presented in the play is quite literally calculated "to please a modern audience" because her predicament is really that of an English widow. Indamora has been married to an older man not of her choosing in part to foil an interracial attachment with Raymond and in part to secure an alliance with the family of her husband. In this context, her loveless marriage of alliance is set in contrast to a sentimental relationship that crosses racial, cultural, and class barriers. The threat of suttee in the play has always been vestigial not only because Indamora's situation is contrived to speak to the plight of aristocratic women caught in the tangled web of marriages built on alliance, not love, but also because the staging of the act is impossible. This carries with it the implication that the sati could in fact be understood as a tragic heroine, but it would require a strict adherence to "custom." In the terms set forward by the reviewer, she would have to request to die, and the play would have allow for her immolation.

The impossibility of actually staging the suttee causes key dramaturgical problems because as many of the reviews indicate it means that there is never any doubt about Indamora's fate. There is never any question of representing suttee, but the play is obsessed with bringing the potential sati onto the stage and into representation. Of course, it is possible to imagine a way of indirectly presenting a suttee by having the pyre offstage, but the Covent Garden production cancels such a possibility when it diverges from Le Mierre's play and makes the funeral pyre the center of its set design in the third act. (33) Not only is the Funeral Pile center stage and framed by rocks; it is also connected by a bridge to the other key architectural feature of the stage—the Pagod of Eswara. This arrangement ensures that Indamora's magnificent procession, noted in all the reviews, has to swirl around the Pile and eventually rise above the stage for maximum visual effect. The ethnographic specificity of the scene is evident from the details regarding costume and props in the stage directions for Indamora's ascent of the pyre: "Indamora advances towards the Pile—the Mirror and dart are thrown into it—Slaves throw in oil and incense—Bramins kneel to Indamora, who waves her hand as if to bless them. Indamora stops when she reaches the middle of the Platform, stands ready to cast herself on the Pile" (43). Ironically, once the Funeral Pile is set alight, the very centrality of the fiery spectacle guarantees Indamora's rescue and union with Raymond. But the very surplus of detail—the mirror, the dart, the oil and incense—and the specificity of the architecture and costume raise important questions regarding the relationship between metropolitan viewers and represented colonial subjects.[60]

If the potential sati is being understood as an English widow as the *English Review* suggests, then what is the function of this quasi-ethnographic material that on the face of it does play a role in the production of knowledge about Hindu social practices? Many of the reviews suggest that this is not an incidental concern of the play. The *Gazetteer and Daily Advertiser* is typical in its claims for the play's authenticity: "The Widow of Malabar . . . is the production of Miss Starke, whose father was formerly the governor of the country where the scene of the tragedy lies, of course the *costume* of the piece is preserved with great truth. The procession is extremely magnificent, and affords a very striking picture of oriental manners."[61] Establishing Starke as one or two steps removed from a native informant has a curious effect on how one reads the play for it sets two interpretive modes at odds with one another. The first reads the play as a sentimental comedy about aristocratic love veiled behind a surface of distorted Oriental detail. The second tenuously clings to the play as a representation of Hindu social practice whose divergence from tragedy is compensated for by a self-consolidating celebration of masculine British humanity. Importantly, the latter interpretation also accepts the idealized interracial and interclass sexual union between Raymond and Indamora as a necessary step in the Enlightened suppression of superstition. However, as these two competing interpretations of the play make their way through the press, the latter position finds itself occluded by the former, and the terms on which the interracial desire between Raymond and Indamora are put in abeyance are symptomatic not only of the racialization of class relations in the early 1790s but also of the ideological importance of the supposed security of landed property following the French Revolution.

When the *The Widow of Malabar* is given a more thorough run in the winter of 1791, the daily newspapers, no longer concerned with paying compliments to Miss Brunton, turn their attention to the satirical possibilities opened by the play's generic instability. After the wave of opening-night reviews, pointed jokes on the sexual proclivities of aristocratic wives begin to emerge. The *Gazetteer and Daily Advertiser* leads the way with an opinion attributed to Lady Wallace who had come to public notice for a particularly messy divorce proceeding: "Lady W.[allace] is charmed by the *Widow of Malabar*. Her Ladyship, with her usual vivacity, declares, that she has more than once *burned* for a husband; but that, *salamander* like, she can live in the midst of *flames*."[62] The insinuation here is quite complex in light of the damnation of Lady Wallace's *The Ton; or, The Follies of Fashion* three years earlier. That play ridiculed the vices of the aristocracy, but occasioned near riots in the theatre because its diagnosis of aristocratic vice seemed to indict the very audience it courted. Like Starke, Lady Wallace's protofeminist arguments aimed to stabilize and reinvigorate aristocratic identity by ridding it of the suspect gender performances and sexual transgressions associated with fashionable society.[63] At the time of the damnation of *The Ton*, the press argued that there was a disjunction between the playwright's decency and the decency of her aesthetic practice. The invocation of Lady Wallace here continues in the same vein by casting aspersion on her sexual desires. But it also attempts to undercut Starke's—and by extension Crespigny's—renegotiation of traditional gender roles in aristocratic marriage by suggesting that the play's moral suits one such as Lady Wallace. In other words, the play provides an opportunity for ridiculing female sexual agency by raising the specter of adultery. After all, Lady Wallace not only ostensibly declares her desire for someone else's husband but also ostensibly resolves to happily burn in hell for its fulfillment. What is so disturbing is that a certain level of commutability is asserted between Lady Wallace's sexual desires and Indamora's love for Raymond that ultimately reinterprets Indamora's reluctance to become a sati as a sign of adulterous proclivities.

The specificity of the *Gazetteer and Daily Advertiser*'s attack was not widespread, but the assertion of commutability and the implied metaphorization of suttee surface in almost all the papers. The Whig organ, the *Morning Chronicle*, was the most insistent, offering nuggets such as the following: "The Widows by no means find the fiery ordeal in the new Tragedy so formidable as they had imagined. Having *warm* constitutions, they find the *flame*, which succeeds the death of a first Husband, a *kindred element*."[64] The puns on burning and on flames proliferate over the next weeks, and the jokes, however feeble, operate in two directions. First, they emphasize the ubiquity and intensity of an English widow's desire and, second, they insinuate that Indamora shares this passion. The first gesture contains female desire in a familiar stereotype, and the second implies that female desire operates in this way irrespective of cultural and racial difference. This double act of containment and then forced equivalence is manifest in perhaps the most telling contribution from the *Morning Chronicle*:

In *India's* climes when ancient husbands die,
Their youthful Widows to a *bonfire* fly,
Ascend the pile—and 'midst surrounding fire,
In honour of their *dear good man*—expire.

In *Britain's* Isle the case is much the same,
An old man's wife retains a *secret* flame;
And when he dies—a few short days past over,
The flame burst forth, and *fires—a youthful* LOVER.[65]

What is so strange about this poem's assertion of similitude is that it ultimately resolves into a fundamental distinction. In the first verse, the Indian
widow burns with her dead husband. In the second verse, the English
widow figuratively burns on the occasion of her husband's death but not
with him. By the slippage inherent to the metaphorization of suttee, the
English widow burns with desire for a youthful lover. However, the second verse also describes Indamora's situation on the London stage to the
letter, for she not only retains a secret flame for Raymond throughout
her marriage but also unites with him a few short days after her husband's
death. What I hope is clear is the degree to which the papers capture the
contradiction generated when the play's struggle between reason and superstition is resolved by a retroactive assertion of heterosexual desire. As
the *Morning Chronicle* aptly and carefully summarizes, "The new Tragedy
conveys a most excellent moral, which is sanctioned by the authority of
scripture, and will, we dare say, meet the approbation of all widows, that
it is better to marry than to burn. Every body will agree that if, after the
death of a first husband, a widow should be destined to the flame, her best
security is in the arms of a second."[66] Significantly, both the play and the
satirical reception of it de-realize the colonial practice of suttee by retroactively sexualizing the widow. In the case of Starke, this happens at the level
of plot, but in the case of the papers this is achieved by less than subtle figural substitutions of British widows for potential satis.

This widespread tendency toward the figural cancellation of the potential sati responds to a series of anxieties activated by Starke's play. Most
obviously, it cancels the very notion of cultural difference by simply rel-
egating the potential sati to figural oblivion. But perhaps more important,
it obviates the play's threatening suggestion that interracial desire is not
only admirable but also necessary for resolving the social conflict between
rational British imperialists and ostensibly superstitious Hindu subjects.
And nestled within the relationship between Indamora and Raymond is

a further complication: their union appears to be between an aristocratic woman and a bourgeois soldier. With caste understood as translatable to class, the sexual resolution of the play's social and cultural conflict turns on the mixing not only of ethnically distinct characters but also of town and city. The papers quickly contain this gesture and direct readers' attention to specifically intraclass sexual relations by focusing on both aristocratic marriage and on specific women of fashion in the audience. A number of papers list notable ladies in the boxes and discuss their approbation of the play.[67] The *St. James Chronicle* produces an extensive list and suggests that the play will "become a favourite of the town."[68] However, the *New London Magazine* subtly damns the play with the same observation when it suggests that considering "the Present State of Covent Garden Theatre, . . . [*The Widow of Malabar*] may probably draw a few fashionable houses to it."[69] A subsequent letter to the editor of the *Public Advertiser* recognizes the implied criticism—that such a production could only interest the dissipated upper orders—and attributes the critique to malice toward the theatre.[70]

But it is clear that the play has also activated malice toward its fashionable patrons that opens onto an allegorical reading of Indamora's desire for Raymond that conforms to the widespread critique of aristocratic vice in the period. However, that critique is itself undergoing a certain refinement. In accordance with the reactivation of the notion of landed liberty and of the sanctity of property in the antiradical rhetoric of Burke and others in 1790 and 1791, the landed classes accede to a condition of national normativity, whereas more "fashionable" aristocrats become scrutinized for their perceived threat to this ideological formation. Wahrman's discussion of Burke's demonization of the middle ranks in the early phases of reaction to the French Revolution indicates that one of the objectives of the *Reflections* was to consolidate British society according to arguments formerly advocated by country ideologues and thus warn the largely Whig readership not to align itself too closely with the "malignant monied interest."[71] Aside from the erasure of his own former investment in the shared objectives of the Whig elite and the moneyed interest, Burke's move exerted intense pressure not only on emerging middle-class formations but also on forms of social interaction that imagined some kind of social accommodation between City and Town. Wahrman has written extensively on the former pressure, but the latter speaks directly to Starke's practice, for it is clear that her reformist gestures are attempting to reconfigure elite femininity according to notions of bourgeois conjugal virtue.[72] That reform is allegorized in the Young Bramin's arguments for a break from tradition and in Indamora's desire to marry Raymond. In the terms set forward by that allegory, to argue for "tradition" is to find oneself aligned with the Chief Bramin. In this light, one could tendentiously suggest that the struggle between the Young Bramin and the Chief Bramin is a very biting allegory for the struggle between New and Old Whigs signaled by Burke's publication of *An Appeal from the New to the Old Whigs* in 1791. Casting Burke as the exemplar of superstition, tradition, and class rigidity would not be an unusual gesture for those involved in or sympathetic to radical reform. In short, *The Widow of Malabar* seems to precipitate the audience into distinct groups according to ideological affiliation, and this gesture is a significant incursion on the hybridity of theatrical sociability that speaks to the precarious ideological situation of middle-class reform at this moment.

In this scenario, it is important to recognize that the insinuation that the play is only suitable to the vicious tastes of the aristocracy carries with it two key implications: first, that women of fashion are desiring subjects and, second, that interracial sexuality does not constitute a contravention of fashionable identity but rather is a symptom of the aristocracy's social decay. What I see here are two perfectly adequated substitutions. Just as the papers substitute fantasies of metropolitan sexuality for equally phantasmatic constructions of Hindu subjectivity, so the antiradical component of the audience indulges in fantasies about the dissolution of the very class it is in the process of occluding. And yet this occlusion requires a phantasmatic investment in a now iconic landed elite whose political and economic power have long since passed their prime. It is thus that the derogation of "fashionable" identities participates in the complex ideological maneuver wherein the increasingly economically dominant middle classes eventually find themselves operating behind a national fantasy of benevolent country landlords. In the former substitution, the body of the sati disappears from view in favor of a negative example of metropolitan female desire. In the latter substitution, the bodies of the fashionable women cataloged in the audience of Starke's play become signifiers of a negative example of class and gender identity. The adequation of these two substitutions is possible because Indamora and the women of fashion are linked by more than rank in the eyes of the bourgeois audience. They are being understood as racially distinct from normative national identity.

This assertion is confirmed by the remarkable epilogue to *The Widow of Malabar,* which not only assumes precisely this racialization but also attempts to counter it. In the epilogue, the great comic actress Mrs. Mattocks enters as if pushed onto the stage by the prompter, and she carries the mirror and the dart previously carried by Indamora and thrown into the funeral pile. The two props—now separated from their specifically Hindu significations—figure for the play's allegorical presentation and critical evaluation of metropolitan life, respectively. Allegorical reflection and satirical critique are the primary methodological axes of theatrical autoethnography in the period. The entrance of Mrs. Mattocks and the figuration of the autoethnographic project initiates, or rather confirms, not only the comic interpretation of the play but also the metaphorization of suttee. Throughout the epilogue, Mrs. Mattocks, who did not play a role in the play, satirically casts herself as a woman forced against her will to save the play and by extension its author from burning in the fiery rancor of theatrical criticism. She wittily argues that the audience can take one of two positions in relation to *The Widow of Malabar* that are derived from the play itself. They can take the role of the Chief Bramin in relation to the now feminized play and threaten "our little Realm" with "dread rage," or they can allow their applause to imitate the thunder of the British guns that overthrow the town just prior to Indamora's rescue in the third act.[73] It is a cunning trope because it figuratively associates the critics of the play with heathen cruelty and aligns the play's advocates with heroic British masculinity. In other words, a positive reaction to the play not only consolidates "British humanity" but also makes the audience complicit with the play's martial resolution of the struggle between superstition and reason in the colonies. This kind of gesture is not unusual for an epilogue whose primary function is to mold audience opinion such that the play lives on for another production.

But the metaphorical linkage between play and potential sati becomes quite pointed when Mrs. Mattocks starts to break down the house into its class and gender components. Her first satirical attack is aimed at those of the lower ranks seated in the "Gods" or the balcony:

> We've just been taught—nor was it deem'd a wonder
> That JOVE's decrees are usher'd in by thunder.
> Come then, one clap, ye mighty Powers on High!
> I love the pealing thunders of your sky,
> They augur well—yet hold!—it may be odds
> But there's some lurking Fiend among you Gods,
> Whose baleful wrath a hissing bolt may aim,

To burn poor me, and blast our POET's fame;
And I'm not like our Heroine, in such haste
For fiery trials—they don't hit my taste.[74]

Throughout the play the enlightened Young Bramin refers to the Chief Bramin as a fiend— therefore Mattocks's remarks here effectively racialize the play's nonaristocratic critics in what amounts to a preemptive first strike. A similar gesture follows but this time aimed at fashionable women in the boxes who are unwilling to embrace the radical possibilities lying beneath the union between Indamora and Raymond:

Hark! In yon box I hear some Fair One say,
"We really shou'd not like to die that way,
"'Tis a bad precedent—let's damn the Play."
Hold, gentle creatures, in these happy times,
Mercy extends her sway o'er distant climes,
And makes the Human Race her fondest care,
Whether the hue be tawny, black or fair:
Then, since the age is thus to mercy prone,
In *this Tribunal* let us fix her throne;
Break Criticism's shaft, quench Rancour's fire,
Nor light our trembling Author's funeral Pyre.[75]

Suddenly the class separation that distinguishes the balcony from the boxes is figuratively transformed into a racial distinction. Both the dark fiendish critics in the upper seats and the fair women of the boxes wish to damn the play, but Mrs. Mattocks responds in such a way that both groups are found to be in error precisely because they identify too rigidly with their racialized and classed location in the theatre. As an antidote, she invokes Mercy who rules over all the colors subsumed under the universal category of "the Human Race" and squelches the fire threatening to consume the author and the play.

Aside from the surplus of wit, what is interesting here is the degree to which Mrs. Mattocks's words counter attempts to naturalize whiteness as a property of any class. Although more complex than the attack on the critics in the balconies, the aim is similarly prophylactic: the objective is to protect the racial and class hybridity nascent in the play's heterosexual love plot from precisely the kind of antiaristocratic criticism that attempts to mobilize racial purity as a sign of national strength. That the newspapers nevertheless go on to enact precisely this containment strategy is a sign not only that this racialization has been a site of contestation in the period but also that the ascendancy of antiradical sentiment is by this point so well assured that the contest has devolved into feeble guffaws in the London dailies. And this assertion of national ascendancy unfolds despite the specious figural substitution of Indian and British elites. So we are left with a curious parallel.

Despite Starke's and Cornwallis's shared misrecognition of both the stability and the portability of British models of landed liberty, their interventions, although in many ways incomparable, precipitated discourses and performances that would confirm the obsolescence of their social vision. In the case of Starke's obfuscations, that declaration of obsolescence took a matter of weeks in part because negotiation between invented "tradition" and emergent social forces was happening apace in the consolidation of national identity following the French Revolution. In the case of Cornwallis's phantasmatic investments, the process of obsolescence would be much slower, for the attempt to promote a landed elite would be supplemented and ultimately taken over by the institutional and bureaucratic functions of British rule and the increasingly utilitarian practices of the state. The idea of the Permanent Settlement, like many allegories, was compelling in its simplicity, but it only achieved partial application in very select regions of Madras and Bengal. Through the work of administrators such as Thomas Munro, who is credited with the invention of the *ryotwari* system of revenue collection, the Permanent Settlement was displaced by micrological processes of social control that relied on and called forth the extraordinary proliferation of knowledge practices regarding Indian social life that would eventually be the hallmark of British governmentality during the Raj.[76]

War and Precinema

Tipu Sultan and the Allure

of Mechanical Display

IN THE 1790S new forms of popular entertainment began to compete with and eventually infiltrated the domain of the legitimate theatre. As nonpatent houses sprung up around London, technological innovations and transformations in scale altered the way narratives and scenes were presented to audiences.[1] The problem of technologically visualizing colonial space already explored in relation to Loutherbourg's museological strategies in *Omai* and in my discussion of the figural deployment of the magic lantern show, the raree show, the camera obscura, and other visual machines in the discourse surrounding the Hastings trial takes a new turn at this historical juncture. The spectacles staged at Astley's Royal Amphitheatre, Sadler's Wells, and the Royal Circus fused dramaturgical elements derived from pantomime and opera, with forms of action and display whose origins were largely nontheatrical.[2] Military spectacles involving trained animals and soldier-actors, musical entertainment, acrobatics, and mechanical entertainments that had formerly been staged in outdoor spaces or in exhibition halls were mobilized in new dramaturgical tactics. These hybrid performances were in dialogue not only with conventional comedy, comic opera, and pantomime, but also with forms of entertainment that relied heavily either on bodily regimen, or mechanical ingenuity. In addition, new technologies of display, including the panorama, the phantasmagoria, and other visual machines that have usefully been described as precinematic, expanded the means through which an audience could be addressed and subjectified.[3]

In the interplay between bodies, animals, and machines in these performances, one can discern a complex negotiation between disciplinary and regulatory power. The new dramaturgical strategies first tested in the illegitimate theatre directly incorporated the body such that regulatory and disciplinary power permeated one another. Foucault argues that discipline and regulation operate as two series that are both distinct and constantly infiltrating one another.[4] This notion of two series operating on the same set of signs offers a way of understanding what is otherwise a chaotic transformation. In the permeation of disciplinary by regulatory technology, we have a model for the resignification of the body itself that downplays the visibility of individual traits in favor of the mobilization of mass qualities.

This chapter charts shifts not only in theatrical presentation but also in imperial subjectification by attending to the relationship between these two regulatory modes. This double genealogy follows a recognizable trajectory whose broad contours are directly related to increasing British militarization in India. Unlike the 1770s and 1780s, the 1790s were a period of consolidation in the empire. Military victories over Tipu and the establishment of the Permanent Settlement not only confirmed actual British domination in the Asian subcontinent but also provided an occasion for phantasmatic constructions of supremacy.[5] It is not surprising that as the decade unfolds we begin to see signs of triumphalism in metropolitan accounts of Anglo-Indian affairs, but this confidence was fueled by prior anxieties. Earlier losses both in Mysore and in America had a lingering effect on future actions in India because the British could not afford further defeat and also because the primary British actor in the Mysore Wars and the Permanent Settlement, Lord Cornwallis, carried his experience of defeat at Yorktown and other American campaigns to India when he was appointed governor-general of Bengal in 1786. As an icon of both imperial humiliation and domination, Cornwallis plays an oddly double role in the plays celebrating victory in Mysore. Because commemoration of Cornwallis's actions in India always carries with it the threat of reactivating traumatic memories of the American war, the plays I discuss in this chapter explicitly engage in what Joseph Roach has described as surrogation: the process whereby a community attempts to fill a hole rent in the social fabric by death or loss with a substitute fantasy.[6] The theatrical effects mobilized in these performances are always already tied to defensive tactics of obfuscation and displacement and thus need to be understood as compensatory tropes. One of the most disturbing elements of the readings that follow is the degree to which these defensive tactics congeal or solidify into regulatory fantasies whose locus was very real indeed—the bodies of imperial and colonial subjects.

In addition, this chapter supplements the previous chapter's discussion of the reforms generated in response to both the corruption of Hastings's governance and the East India Company's poor showing in the First and Second Mysore Wars with a genealogy of fantasies of British imperial supremacy that swept through the metropole in the 1790s. This genealogy tracks the staging of the Third and Fourth Mysore Wars in both the non-patent and the patent houses. Spectacular productions such as *Tippoo Saib; or, British Valour in India* (1791), *Tippoo Sultan; or, The Siege of Bangalore* (1792), *Tippoo Saib; or, East India Campaigning* (1792), and *Tippoo Saib's Two Sons* (1792) literally dramatized the incoming news from each of Cornwallis's campaigns against Tipu Sultan in the Third Mysore War. All of these productions attempted to obviate lingering accounts of atrocity, both British and Mysorean, by building fantasies of British valor and paternalism following Cornwallis's victory over Tipu in 1792. The degree to which this modeling of metropolitan opinion was successful can be gauged from a reading of James Cobb's *Ramah Droog* (1798). *Ramah Droog* is the only theatrical production in the patent houses to directly address the Mysore Wars, and it crystallizes much of my argument about the deployment of sexuality in this book. But what I wish to demonstrate is that the comic opera deploys images associated with Cornwallis's victory over Tipu Sultan in order to play out and endorse Cornwallis's suppression of the Irish rebellion. In so doing, we can discern a moment where distinct strategies of imperial consolidation are brought together to generate a fantasy of global supremacy. That fantasy is brought into focus late in this chapter through a consideration of Astley's *The Siege and Storming of Seringapatam* (1800). Astley's play theatricalized an important panorama of the fall of Tipu's stronghold at Seringapatam that closed the Fourth Mysore War, and thus provides an example of how precinematic display and embodied performance merge to generate new forms of audience subjectification.

Many of the performances in the series of Tipu plays are related to prior nontheatrical visualizations of the Mysorean conflict, and I explore the subtle alterations in imperial self-fashioning that emerge when a visual representation, whether it be pictorial or precinematic, is reconfigured for public performance. Ancillary moments of sexualization and racialization play a key part in these representations, but these spectacles not only support but also partake in the military techniques employed in breaking down colonial resistance.[7] The ultimate objective of this chapter is to track the emergence of mass effects in the theatre and to demonstrate the way they reconfigure the question of racialization as British imperial domination in India became manifest.

This cascade of performances pertaining to the Mysore Wars not only put former imperial anxieties to rest but also advanced a new form of theatrical imperialism. It is possible to discern two tactical strands in the theatricalization of the Third Mysore War. The first is a technology of sex, whose basic structure we have been tracking in the preceding chapter, but which now takes the project of racially consolidating the middle ranks one step further by turning its attention to questions of ethnic difference in metropolitan British society. The second is a technology of the self whose primary aim is to draw the body of the viewing subject into increasingly regulated dispositions, and whose target is less the individual audience member than the collectivity of the audience itself. These two tactics can be distinguished by their relation to the body of the viewer, for the largely sexual deployments focus attention on the fantasies that surround and undergird bodily identity, whereas the dramaturgy of war targets the sensorium of the viewer in a fashion that reconfigures the subject as a nonspecific element in a larger political mass. These tactics have their roots in the very disciplinary regimes that Foucault analyzed so conclusively in *Discipline and Punish:* military drill and the generation of disciplinary effects through the spatial deployment of bodies. Astley's specialized in staged military spectacles, but rather than subjecting the audience to drill and regimen, these productions presented drill for consideration. This distancing from the spectacle of disciplinary power rendered the audience members not docile viewers but rather active agents in the process of racial consolidation.

What I wish to demonstrate here is the way the performance of sexual deviance endures as an avenue of critique even as it is superseded by representational tactics more closely akin to the exhibition hall than to the conventional theatre. Because visuality plays such a key role in the massification of the audience, forms of precinematic display, such as the panorama, provide a useful heuristic for understanding the emergence of these regulatory fantasies. As we will see, the fluid boundaries between painting, projection, set design, and spectacle play a key role in the presentation of British victory in Mysore throughout this period.

Anxious Symptoms and Tactical Bifurcations:
The Third Mysore War

The period prior to Cornwallis's tenure as governor-general was marked by serious reservations about the East India Company's military strategy and the effectiveness of British forces in the Asian subcontinent. These reservations ranged from outright declarations of wrongdoing to less visible, but nevertheless persistent, signs of a lack of confidence in the company's military capacities. These reservations are most evident in the widely published accounts of British prisoners published in the late 1780s and 1790s. In the early 1780s British forces suffered as many reverses as successes in the campaigns against the sultans of Mysore. Significant battles were lost and numerous prisoners were taken. Kate Teltscher's exhaustive account of the British representations of the wars in Mysore underlines two key issues in the early accounts of the conflicts that are largely erased after Seringapatam falls and Tipu is killed in 1799. In the early phases of the conflict, both Haider Ali and Tipu Sultan were predictably demonized in the various military accounts. But in the mid-1780s there is a significant strain of dissent from representations of the sultans as the embodiment of despotic cruelty. None other than Edmund Burke, in articles in the *Annual Register* and in his speeches during the Hastings trial, argued that much of the cruelty attributed to the sultans of Mysore was a reaction to the tyrannical policies of the East India Company.[8] At roughly the same time that Burke was representing Haider Ali as a reasonable statesman pushed into barbarism by the unwarranted depredations of the East India Company, other less politically motivated observers were alarmed at the degree to which Haider Ali had successfully incorporated European tactics into his resistance to the Company. Teltscher's crucial observation here is that Haider Ali and Tipu Sultan were threatening not only because they had proved to be able despotic adversaries, but also because they blurred the line separating Christian British and Muslim Indian subjects.

> The Mysore army, actively supported by France from 1780 to 1784, derived its strength from contemporary European military principles: both Haider and his son were quick to adopt the strategies and technology of their British enemies. The construct of oriental tyranny, with all its traditional overtones, to some extent obscured the westernized efficiency of the Mysore army. . . . By erecting a wall of difference between East and West, the rhetoric of oriental despotism helped to conceal the similarities between the two powers' policies: the British were freed from the recognition of disturbing correspondences with their enemy.[9]

The extraordinary controversy regarding John Charles Sheen's account of the atrocities perpetrated by British forces at Anantpaur published in

Henry Oakes's *Authentic Narrative of the Treatment of the English, Who Were Taken Prisoner on the Reduction of Bednore by Tippoo Saib* (1785) is indicative of precisely how disturbing these correspondences were to the British public. Sheen accused East India Company soldiers of raping and massacring the women of the zenana and, in so doing, argued that Tipu's ferocious response was in effect a retaliation for British inhumanity. Despite recantations from Sheen himself and a host of rebuttals, the scene continued to exist as a kernel of doubt that implicitly troubled subsequent accounts of Tipu's barbarity. Like similar moments in Burke's speeches in the Hastings impeachment, these scenes of British depravity were historically resilient not only because they are attached to fantasies of the violence of the lower orders of the military, but also because subsequent representations of British triumph so thoroughly repressed the very real violence of colonial warfare.

Unlike the arguments that raged about whether his father Hyder Ali's actions were justified by the depredations of the East India Company or whether they were simply a symptom of Eastern despotism, Tipu Sultan, now mythologized as the "Tiger of Mysore," became an icon of native resistance to British imperial interests. In spite of the fact that Cornwallis won decisive battles against Tipu at Bangalore in 1791 and Seringapatam in 1792, earlier losses inflicted significant psychic damage to the imperial imaginary. Like earlier campaigns against Hyder and Tipu, the Third Mysore War did not start well for the British forces. The initial campaigns were conducted under the leadership of General William Medows, the governor of Madras. Medows served under Cornwallis in the American war and, despite his prior experience, made a number of tactical errors that reminded Cornwallis of his own miscalculations in Pennsylvania and South Carolina.[10] Tipu took almost immediate strategic advantage in the early phases of the conflict and forced Cornwallis to take over Medows's command in mid-December of 1791. Cornwallis undertook one of the most massive deployments of men, animals, and artillery in British military history and eventually conquered the strategic fortress of Bangalore. Insufficient supply lines and uncooperative weather, however, prevented him from successfully taking Tipu's capital Seringapatam. The monsoon and other logistical problems forced Cornwallis to retreat. In November and December, he moved again with a larger force, overwhelmed the supposedly impregnable hill forts of Nundydroog and Severndroog, and moved on to besiege Seringapatam in early February of 1792.

Some sense of the resilience of metropolitan anxiety regarding military actions in India can be gleaned from James Gillray's *The Coming on of the Monsoons,* which shows Tipu pissing on the British forces (fig. 7.1).[11] Gillray's print comes in response to the temporary reversal in the British pursuit of Tipu following successful siege of Bangalore in March 1791. Gillray's caricature of Cornwallis as Falstaff satirizes hyperbolic accounts of the war, but it is also haunted by a decade of far more tangible losses to the sultan. That even a temporary setback in the campaign to entrap Tipu is understood as a form of physical and arguably sexual degradation is significant because many of the British captives' narratives from the 1780s revolve around scenes of bodily degradation and mutilation whose connotations are similarly sexual. Many of Tipu's prisoners were enslaved and forced to fight against the British forces. These cheyla battalions were the site of intense anxiety because most of the cheylas, or slaves, were forced to convert to Islam and were circumcised.[12] As Teltscher states, "The British cheylas, marked with the stigma of Muslim difference but otherwise unconverted to Islam, were stranded in a doctrinal no man's land, and the texts reveal their sense of marginalization."[13] However, she is also quick to point out, following Pratt, that the very fact of the existence of the survival narratives performs a kind of inoculation of their dangerous contents.[14] Presented within the frame of a survivor's tale, the mutilation of the penis—and, by extension, of the religious and national subject—can be presented and contained. However, the line separating circumcision and castration is at times hard to discern in these texts because the mutilation, whether partial or complete, seems to instantiate a form of subjectivity that for all attempts at containment continues to inhere in the narratives and haunts even the most triumphant accounts.

Teltscher's reading of the case of James Scurry is instructive, for she demonstrates how his narrative, in spite of itself, denies the possibility of patriotism. *The Captivity, Sufferings, and Escape of James Scurry* was not published until 1824, but its account of forced Indianization and the subsequent meltdown in national and racial identity required careful mediation. Highly sensitive to the defensiveness of Scurry's text, Teltscher emphasizes how the account is framed by an editor's description of the returned prisoner's life in England:

> After ten years captivity, Scurry has almost forgotten English customs and "the delicate refinements of his native land." When he first returns, he dislikes wearing European clothes, finds it hard to sit in a chair or handle a knife or a fork; his English is "broken and confused, having lost nearly all its vernacular idiom" and his skin colour "nearly resembled the swarthy complexion of the negroes." . . . Po-

FIG. 7.1. James Gillray, *The Coming on of the Monsoons; or, The Retreat from Seringapatam*, 6 December 1791 *(courtesy of the Department of Prints and Drawings, The British Museum, London; BM 7929)*

tentially a disturbing symbol of alienation, Scurry is rehabilitated through humour: he becomes an object of ridicule.[15]

The description of Scurry and the subsequent jokes made about his table manners are extremely reminiscent of the accounts of Mai's circulation in London society in the 1770s. However, here the racialization of Scurry and the feminization implied by the insinuation that he wears Indian clothes constitute a falling away from soldierly masculinity that requires further discursive regulation. We have seen this economy of ridicule in Starke's satirical attack on the passive Indianization of British women in *The Sword of Peace*, but here it is deployed to allay the threat of forced degeneration, which ostensibly characterizes captivity and conversion. The rendering of Scurry as a joke needs to be read symptomatically, and as we will see in our discussion of *Ramah Droog*, which also features a feminized British prisoner in Indian clothes, the joke can be easily turned around to perform an extremely disturbing critique of colonial rebellion in Ireland.

With some sense of the threat—both to actual territorial domination and to imagined forms of imperial identification—posed by Tipu Sultan, it should come as no surprise that the imperial theatre produced in the patent houses in the 1780s and early 1790s assiduously avoids anything like a historical account of military campaigns in the colonies. In *Omai, The Sword of Peace, The Widow of Malabar,* and *Inkle and Yarico,* soldierly characters not only accede to states of relative representational lack but also perform amatory rather than martial roles. As subjects and objects of desire, officers such as Captain Campley, Captain Cook, and Lieutenant Dormer become icons of sexual, racial, national, and class normativity, rather than heroic soldiers. This is due in part to the disturbing legacy of the American war and in part to the complex treatment of war on the stage following the declaration of war on France. Direct patriotic expression was primarily reserved for afterpieces and for venues that were not under the direct supervision of the examiner of plays. As Russell and Moody have argued, the tight regulation of political content on the patent stages ceded direct enactment of patriotism to the illegitimate theatre. These unregulated venues were free to pursue a dramaturgy of war whose technical innovations and ideological functions would exceed the immediate context of war with France.[16]

Between 1791 and 1793, Astley's Royal Amphitheatre and Sadler's Wells offered spectacular versions of Cornwallis's campaigns against Tipu Sultan as quickly as news came back from India. The resulting productions galvanized a new kind of imperial spectatorship that explicitly addressed both the anxious scenes of humiliation associated with previous defeat in America and Mysore and the recurrent scenes of blockage that seemed to characterize Burke's attempts to render events in India during the Hastings trial. The British assault on Bangalore in February and March of 1791 was in many ways the watershed of the Third Mysore War, and it signaled the maturation of Cornwallis's forces despite the fact that Tipu escaped capture.[17] *Tippoo Sultan; or, The Siege of Bangalore* was staged on 9 April 1792 at Astley's Amphitheatre roughly one year after the events it represented and, like all such productions, was an amalgamation of action, animal husbandry, and complex scenic effects. Advertisements refer to it as "A Compiled, Whimsical, Oriental, Tragic, Comic, Pantomimical Sketch, in Three Parts."[18] Cornwallis's military operation involved a double siege, first of the pettah and then of the citadel, and there is no doubt that all the vaunted energies of Astley's production team were employed to restage the battles. Tellingly, one reviewer describes the theatrical enterprise at Astley's as a military operation: "Mr. Astley, jun. commenced the present Campaign last Monday evening, in presence of a crouded and brilliant Audience, who seemed as highly delighted with the improvements of the Theatre, as with the excellence of the Performances."[19] At the close of the run another reviewer makes a similar metaphorical gesture and, in so doing, aligns the production with the trajectory of the Mysore campaign: "On Saturday the Siege of Bangalore takes its leave of the Royal Saloon and the public, Tippoo Saib being compelled to fly. It is reported that he has bled freely, as young Astley can testify."[20]

In general the papers are far more interested in the sheer size and variety of the audience attending the play than in its particulars, but there are interesting reports regarding the representation's authenticity.[21] The *Oracle* reports that "Mr. Astley, junior, obtained Patterns of the Uniforms worn by Tippoo Saib's Army at the siege of Bangalore, from the Prince's Ambassadors at Paris. The incidents, dances, and other matters, are certainly very ingeniously displayed, and does the young Manager the highest credit."[22] We have seen these claims to ethnographic specificity before, but this remark should give us pause and not simply because it so unlikely. Why does Astley's information regarding the uniforms need to come from Tipu's ambassador via France when there is no shortage of British reports? Throughout the Mysorean campaigns, Britain was extremely concerned by the tactical, political, and economic alliances between Tipu and the French. For Astley to be ostensibly communicating with Tipu's representative in Paris puts the manager in a rather nebulous zone between the British and the Mysorean-French forces. The notion that Astley is himself involved in some sort of negotiation with Tipu's representatives implies that by staging—or restaging—war with Tipu, Astley is in some sense waging war on Tipu. As Moody has argued, "Astley's, the Royal Circus and Sadler's Wells Theatre began to pioneer their own physical dramaturgy of war. In these shows military knowledge, technical innovation and topographical illusion went hand in hand: managers like the gruff, blunt Philip Astley . . . shrewdly exploited his first-hand knowledge of military strategy and organization."[23] It is this latter term that we need to pay attention to because the singular advancement both in the practice of warfare in the colonies and in the illegitimate theatre of war is logistical.

Manuel De Landa's analysis of the relationship between bodies and machines in warfare marks a fundamental distinction between the clockwork army of the eighteenth century and the motorized armies first developed by Napoleon. Motorized here is understood as a conceptual quality. To paraphrase De Landa, the idea of the motorization of the European armies should call to mind a form of "internal" motorization, not simply the motorization of their means of transportation. Napoleon, for instance, rejected the use of the physical motor, but assembled his armies in the form of an "abstract motor." While a clockwork mechanism simply transmits an initial motion along a predetermined path, a motor produces new motion.[24] These types of fighting units were defined by their internal organization. In the face of limited communication technologies, the clockwork army maximized the sheer volume of projectile force by drilling soldiers until they operated as a single organism. Because the unit was held together by intense discipline and the range of communicative strategies up and down the ranks was limited to the bugle and simple visual signs, these type of armies were slow moving and thus unable to give pursuit when a situation changed suddenly. Armies operating for the East India Company were among the last solely clockwork armies in operation prior to the change in tactical command structure required when the French army suddenly adopted unit organization based on citizen loyalty rather than forced drill and discipline.[25] In fact, the British forces, despite repeated assertions to the contrary, possessed neither superior military technology nor larger numbers than their Mysorean enemies; what military superiority the British had was largely administrative. Discipline and logistical skill enabled them to deploy their forces more effectively than Tipu.

In the case of the siege of Bangalore, we see both the strengths and weaknesses of a clockwork army: it was highly effective in a siege format, but Tipu escaped before Cornwallis could give chase. Two points about the clockwork army are significant for us here. First, Kate Teltscher has ably shown that one of the primary fears of British commanders in the Mysorean Wars was that Haider Ali and Tipu Sultan would learn European clockwork tactics. There are frequent references to both sultans' acquisition of military texts. James Bristow, a captured British officer, reports being forced "to instruct these *Chaylahs* in the manual exercise," but he indicates that he passed on faulty commands.[26] Aside from the disturbing questions of the loyalty of cheyla battalions, Bristow's anxiety is rooted in the widely disseminated, but partly inaccurate, distinction between the highly organized and disciplined European troops and the antiquated chaotic forces of the sultans. The following passage from Wilks is typical:

> It is probable that no national or private collection of ancient armour in Europe contains any weapon or article of personal equipment which might not be traced in this motley crowd. . . . The osten-

tatious display of these antique novelties was equally curious in their kind. The free and equal use of two sword arms, the precise and perfect command of a balanced spear 18 feet long, of the club which was to shiver an iron helmet, of the arrow discharged in flight, but above all the total absence of order, or obedience, or command, excepting groups collected around their respective flags; every individual was an independent warrior, self-impelled, affecting to be the champion whose single arm was to achieve victory; scampering among each other in wild confusion.[27]

Here the distinction between European and Indian forces is precisely that between modernity and antiquity, between clockwork drill and chaotic disorder, between an overwhelming integration of ranks arising from the rational mechanization of bodies and a force perpetually disintegrating into individualized animalized subjects. In short, clockwork here signifies not only military but also national and racial superiority.

And this is the second key recognition: the clockwork qualities of drill take on national and racial significance in and of themselves, because they are attached to a fantasy of European modernity. As De Landa states, fascination with the clockwork paradigm had cultural manifestations beyond the army:

> These rigid squares of men and weapons, incapable of exercising any individual initiative on the battlefield, resembled a well-oiled clockwork mechanism. The time when the phalanx reached its peak, during the late eighteenth century, was also a time when technology had extended the clockwork paradigm to its ultimate consequences, as can be seen in the elaborate mechanical gardens and toy automata of the period.[28]

Like the automata offered for public viewing at Cox's Museum that are described by Frances Burney in *Evelina,* the extraordinary synchronization of faux armies and animals for which Astley was famous are part of a celebration of the very processes that, in distinguishing British troops from their colonial adversaries, also claimed their manifest superiority.[29] In this light, the procession of Indian arms that always makes up a part of Astley's Tipu plays exhibits precisely the combination of antiquity and disorder that establishes the superiority of British order, which is itself enacted for the audience in Astley's practice.

As the following description of the performance indicates, however, a significant portion of the action in *The Siege of Bangalore* was explicitly nonmilitaristic:

> Had Astley resided all his life in Mysore and its neighbouring countries . . . he could not be better informed than he is respecting the manners, customs, etc. of Tippoo Saib, his court and subjects.
>
> Tippoo in the first act, is discovered seated at a table, surrounded by his nobility dressed in the Turkish manner, but instead of turbans they all appear in *Armenian caps* enriched with plumes and feathers. His guards, who are seen at a distance, are clothed in Tyger's skins and armed with halberds, resembling very much the Beef Eaters in the Tower.
>
> In the second Act the manners and customs of the people are introduced. The High Priest of the Sun, who comes forward attended by numbers of priests of various orders, having made his invocation, he retires to commence the sacrifices of the day, the victims for which are seen bound, with wreathes of flowers round their necks, and consist of Hares, Rams and Hogs.
>
> In the back part of the stage there are a number of people *wrestling* and others running races, a party of *beautiful virgins* urging them to victory and to the prize. Others are dancing, leaping, *skating* etc. etc.[30]

The parade of animal sacrifices, priests, and scantily clothed virgins in the second act seems staged to obviate the explicit comparison between Tipu's guards and the Beefeaters that ends the description of the first act. In other words, a sexualized spectacle of cultural difference immediately supersedes a moment where such differences appear to dissolve. That the play opens in ambivalence is important, because it is this visual equation between iconic guards of the British state and Tipu's soldiers, as much as Tipu himself, that must be overcome. Astley's production both elicits and quells anxieties regarding not only past military failures but also ongoing concerns about the "dangerous" potential for British subjects to be assimilated into Indian society that we saw both in Cornwallis's correspondence and in Starke's *The Sword of Peace*.

Tippoo Sultan; or, The Siege of Bangalore stages the primary anxiety elicited by the First and Second Mysore Wars—that difference dissolves into similitude—in its opening scene and then stages two intertwined forms of tactical resistance. The exhibition of military drill as a figure for

European modernity supplements ethnographic fantasies of racial superiority that are grounded in sexual normativity. The balance between the sexual and the martial is tipped toward the latter in this play, and it is the obvious precursor to much more violent theatrical experiences staged to commemorate the final victory over Tipu in 1799. In 1791, however, the mechanical exhibition of supremacy remains not an end in itself but rather an explicit compensation for previous humiliation. And the specter of humiliation ensures the resilience of sexual normativity as a tactical weapon in the cascade of Tipu plays that followed *The Siege of Bangalore.*

Sadler's Wells was quick to pick up on Astley's success and staged *Tippoo Saib; or, East-India Campaigning* less than a month later, but the production's focus was less on the thrill of militarized discipline than on the spectacle of captivity.[31] Rather than enact the logistical superiority of British warfare, the play opens with "The manner in which several English families concealed themselves from the ravage and Plunder of the enemy."[32] As the play unfolds each spectacle of Tippoo's strength, magnificence, and cruelty is superseded by a scene of native loyalty to British rule. This reaches its culmination with a performance of "The signal bravery of a detachment of Sepoys, who released the English Prisoners, defeated a part of Tippoo's army, and brought off an Elephant."[33] Narratives of "sepoys' faithfulness act as a kind of emblem for the continuance of British authority," and the Sadler's Wells production extends this fantasy of voluntary subordination to the Brahminic caste.[34] Reviews of the performance indicate that "The interesting situation of several English Officers when confined in the Prisons of Seringapatam, with the extraordinary fidelity of a Black Servant, in forming and executing a plan of escape"[35] was the play's highlight largely because it depicted British mastery as the ardent desire of an Indian subject: "The most flattering applause attended every scene of Tippoo Saib last night at Sadler's Wells, but most particularly in that of the prison, where the faithful black discovers himself to his master."[36] If Astley's spectacle could be described as a phantasmatic enactment of the tactical superiority of modernity, then the production at Sadler's Wells could best be described as a fantasy of native capitulation that exorcizes the horrors of imprisonment but does not fully allay Tipu's threat. After all, the loyal sepoys only destroy part of Tipu's army and make off with an elephant. Scenes of voluntary subordination now emerge as temporary compensations for an unresolved will to domination. Taken together, the two productions capture the ambivalent combination of hyperbolic triumphalism and residual fear of Tipu that characterizes British response to the reports of Cornwallis's actions in the winter and spring of 1792.

Significantly, the release of the prisoners in the final scene of *Tippoo Saib; or, East-India Campaigning* was itself an anticipatory fantasy, for while it was widely believed that Cornwallis would overrun Seringapatam, news of the victory did not reach London until 23 June 1792.[37] When that news came, Astley immediately sought to capitalize on the extraordinary terms of Cornwallis's victory, for the defeat of Tipu at Seringapatam involved not a decisive military annihilation, but rather an extraordinary diplomatic transferal of money, lands, and two of Tipu's sons as hostages to British rule. That transferal had already generated important moments of performance in Mysore and Calcutta. Cornwallis himself engineered the first of these some months earlier. On 23 February 1792, Cornwallis carefully staged a spectacle involving elephants, artillery, and soldiers in full ceremonial costume, in which he publicly received Tipu's two sons, "dressed for the melancholy occasion in muslin adorned with pearls and assorted jewellry," with a gesture of paternal care.[38]

This spectacle of military paternalism outside of Seringapatam was followed by elaborate celebratory performances in Calcutta on 23 April 1792. A gala concert was performed using amateur musicians and singers from the ranks of the company, and an extraordinary number of illuminations or projected transparencies were displayed throughout the town.[39] As the *Calcutta Gazette* reported,

> Company servants . . . brightened the Calcutta night with illuminations, each vying with the other for splendor and ingenuity in design. Government house strung up lights of different colors. A large transparent painting depicted Fame with her trumpet over a bust of Cornwallis. Beneath it Britannia received the treaty from Tippoo's sons. Hercules stood behind Britannia, and a large panoramic view of Seringapatam filled the background. The accountant general's office displayed a large transparency showing the captured forts. Lights flooded the Post Office.[40]

Precinematic transparencies had been used to powerful effect in other colonial locales, but in this case it is the screens themselves that are most important.[41] By illuminating the key offices of the East India Company, the celebrations in Calcutta took icons of the governmental care and bureaucratic regulation of subject peoples and made them contiguous with Cornwallis's paternal care of Tipu's sons. As P. J. Marshall argues, "the effusions provoked by the Third Mysore War suggest that the British were coming to see themselves not only as a great military power in India but as people of justice and moderation. Victory was a triumph for British humanity as well as for British arms."[42]

But there was more at stake than the expression of this particular form of patriotic paternalism. The colonial newspaper accounts devote extensive coverage to the technical achievements of the illuminations that I would argue amounts to a subtle declaration of the cultural superiority of technological modernity. The following example is typical of the descriptions of the "external illuminations":

> The Accountant General's house formed a grand and characteristic display of lights, transparent paintings and apposite device [sic] and inscriptions, in the center of the main front, on the top of a large frame of transparent silk, was painted his Lordship's arms proper, with the British colours superior over those of the Sultaun Tippoo, and on the sides the names of the hostages "Prince *Abdul Kalifh*" "Prince *Murrad Dien*" and in the center lower down in large character—"*Definitive treaty of peace* signed under the walls of Sieringapatam on the 17th of March, between Earl *Cornwallis,* the Mahrattas, Nizam, and Tippoo Sultaun." And covering a considerable share of the rest of the painting in small circular spaces were exactly enumerated the *names* and *dates* of the capture of all the fortresses . . . during the war. At the bottom the following lines:
>
> True fortitude is seen in great exploits
> That justice warrants, and that wisdom guides
>
> On the east end of the house was an elegant transparency of Justice and Fame supporting a medallion of his Lordship, and bearing the emblems of plenty and glory—with the following inscription:
>
> In this triumphant, this long wish'd for hour,
> Say what could our festive joys encrease?
> That HERO's presence who the Tyrants power
> O'er-threw, and gave to our fond wishes Peace.[43]

Throughout the newspaper coverage there is a fascination with how the illuminations transform the quotidian spaces of Calcutta into "one continuous blaze" of allegorical splendor in which the very loci of formerly precarious rule emerge as classical emblems of virtue.[44] As the *Madras Courier* declared, "suffice it to say, that where so general a display of beauty, splendor, and magnificence were combined to render Calcutta, and its vicinity, one of the most superb Coup d'oeil's it has ever exhibited."[45]

This collocation of might, moderation, and precinematic visual wonder was similarly enacted in the gala concert held in the Calcutta theatre:

> Entering at the west door, the first object that rivetted the attention was a beautiful semicircular temple, of the Ionic order, dedicated to Victory, placed at the east end, whose dome reached within a foot of the ceiling. In this was placed a transparency, representing a bust of Lord Cornwallis on a pedestal, with the Goddess of Victory flying over it, with a wreath of Laurel in her hand, which she was in the act of placing on his Lordship's brows:— on the plinth of the pedestal was his Lordship's motto,

> *Virtus Vincit Invidiam.*

> And over the bust

> *Regna Assignata.*

> And on each side of this was a nich, —in one of which a figure of Fortitude, and in the other, of Clemency, was placed. Over these, and extending the whole breadth of the temple, was a transparent painting of the action of the 6th of Feb. 1792, and beneath, the following four lines:

> *Still pressing forward to the fight, they broke*
> *Through flames of sulpher, and a night of smoke,*
> *Till slaughter's legions fill'd the trench below,*
> *And bore their fierce avengers to the foe.*[46]

The contiguity of the emblem of Clemency and the images of slaughter encapsulate a specific patriotic style that unites the illuminations and the musical entertainment. The accounts of the concert indicate that transparencies were illuminated and extinguished in order to direct audience attention to various patriotic emblems before the actual performance of excerpts from Handel's *Judas Maccabeus*. Handel's famous patriotic oratorio was originally, and continued to be, understood as an allegory for George II's victory over the Jacobite rebellion of 1745. Staging the oratorio in Calcutta at this moment carried double significance, for it not only celebrated the temporary termination of Tipu's rebellion but also promoted a fantasy of British unity, which would not have been lost on the large number of Scottish employees of the East India Company attending the spectacle.

When the news of Cornwallis's victory reached Britain, London was flooded by quickly published books and a profusion of celebratory verse.[47] In addition, the English public was inundated with visual images of both the "hill forts" (*drugs*) that were the focus of British military pressure and the transfer of Tipu's two sons to Cornwallis as hostages. This latter event was the subject of everything from paintings and prints to illustrated tea trays and large-scale illuminated transparencies.[48] The *Gentleman's Magazine*'s account of the event is symptomatic:

> Lord Cornwallis received [Tipu's sons] in his tent; which was guarded by a battalion of Sepoys, and they were then formally delivered to his Lordship Gullam Ally Beg, the Sultan's Vackeel, as hostages for the due performance of the treaty. . . . At length Gullum Ally, approaching Lord Cornwallis, much agitated, thus emphatically addressed his Lordship: "These children," pointing to the young princes, whom he then presented, "were this morning the sons of the Sultan, my master: their situation is changed, and they must now look up to your Lordship as their father." The tender and affectionate manner in which his Lordship received them, seemed to confirm the truth of the expression. The attendants of the young princes appeared astonished, and their countenances were highly expressive of the satisfaction they felt in the benevolence of his Lordship.[49]

Teltscher argues that the representation of Cornwallis's acceptance of Tipu's sons as a scene of paternal benevolence contrasts with the popular accounts of Tipu's alleged mistreatment of British captives. War between the East India Company and Mysore was now refigured as a tropological struggle between normative and errant models of paternal care. The wide circulation of this image achieved the twofold effect of downplaying the atrocities revealed during the Warren Hastings trial and of reinforcing Whig fantasies of colonial rule as a form of affectionate paternalism.

The relationship between arms and paternal care was brought into palpable tension when Astley's *Tippoo Saib's Two Sons* opened on 20 August 1792. The play is divided into three parts: the first, aside from offering a spectacular view of Seringapatam, introduces "the affecting, pleasing, and interesting Departure of TIPPOO'S TWO SONS from their FATHER, at the Gates of Seringapatam, previous to their being delivered up as hostages to His

Majesties Forces"; the second offers a view of the Hill Fort and stages "the noble reception experienced by the INDIAN PRINCES on their Delivery to the Commander in Chief"; and the third offers "an ORIENTAL MILITARY FESTI-VAL, which took place on the occasion."[50] Again the play was extremely successful and generated an imitation at Sadler's Wells.[51] Reviews of the Astley's show stress the way the two first parts play off of one another: "The departure of the Royal Hostages from the Capital of their Father, is as affecting as their delivery to the British Troops is glorious."[52] In this scenario, Cornwallis becomes both the triumphant commander in chief and the father that Tipu's sons never had. The generation of affective sympathy for the hostage sons is managed such that it emphasizes Tipu's defective paternal care and downplays systematic British aggression in the region. Within the structure of Astley's entertainments, the emblematic construction of British benevolence is enacted in two registers in front of similarly contrasting views. The affecting departure of the sons is staged in front of a painting of the civil space of Tipu's capital, whereas the triumphant transference of the hostages takes place in front of the defeated hill fortress. The very transition in scene ties British paternalism to a scene of Mysorean military defeat.

Rather than conclude with this emblematic scene, however, *Tippoo Saib's Two Sons* revs up into an "Oriental Military Festival," which, despite its title, refers to a British victory celebration. After all, large-scale display was Astley's forte, and while the transfer of the hostages could be managed with infinite pomp and circumstance, it does not leave much room for the musical interludes that characterize these types of productions. It would be a mistake to downplay the generic hybridity of these plays because they often shift from scenes of sympathetic affect to tightly executed military drills to moments of quasi-ethnographic observation to patriotic or racist musical acts. Judging from the emphasis placed on this variety, this was a fundamental component of this form of display, and we are fortunate in that the *Oracle* preserved one of the featured songs in the closing festival. The opening verses of "Patrick O'Conner's Description of the India Campaign, with his Friend TIPPOO" tells us a great deal about the ideological imperatives of Astley's entertainments because it is performed in "the exact brogue of a Paddy" by Mr. Johanot to the tune of "Corporal Casey":

> I.
> From sweet Tipperary, to pick up some honour;
> I'm here, to be sure, little Patrick O'Connor;

With Dennis O'Neal, Teddy Blane, and O'Carty,
By my soul we have routed the Black-a-moor Party.
Och! rub a dub, row de dow, faith, Mr. Tippoo,
We have bothered your head, and we've made you skip O!
Devil burn me, you're quiet, so good-bye, Mr. Tippoo.

II.
Now, d'ye see, the queer Chief would have fain made us bellow,
But for gallant CORNWALLIS, that fine British fellow,
While Tippoo made sure now, to kill us and eat us,
With half of his Kingdom we made him to treat us.
Och! rub a dob, row de dow, so, Mr. Tippoo,
You fain wou'd have give us, my jewel, the slip O!
Arrah, honey, be easy, now do, Mr. Tippoo.[53]

After alluding to the financial settlement exacted by Cornwallis, the song goes on the describe the other terms of the peace including the hostage sons. The image of the cannibal Tipu is not surprising, but what is notable is the complex effect of mobilizing an Irish character in this celebration of Cornwallis.[54] If the opening verse is any indication, the British army is composed of loyal Irish subjects fighting on behalf of the crown, and thus this victory also testifies to the voluntary subordination of another colonized population to British rule. Like the loyal sepoys, Patrick O'Connor and his associates consolidate an imperial fantasy that is not only not yet operative but also in a state of permanent contestation. London audiences are incited both to laugh at the Irishman and to identify with his literal investment in a unified Britain. As the song unfolds, metaphors of monetary gain and expense suddenly take over; Tipu's loss is both military and economic, and the Irish fighters stand to gain both power and "Lacks of Rupees" by joining in the English cause:

O England and Ireland, my jewel, for ever,
Their hearts are so great, and their Soldiers so clever;
Now Tippoo wou'd fain send us back with pretences,
But d'ye mind, it won't do till he's paid all expences.[55]

This deployment of the loyal Irish soldier in a scene of Tipu's subjugation plays out the desires of many an imperial viewer at this moment in the history of British colonial rule. But it is important to remember that, despite the claims to victory in Mysore and unity in the British Isles in this play, both Tipu Sultan and the United Irishmen will seek French assistance in almost simultaneous rebellions before the decade is out.

Strategic Substitutions: Ramah Droog*'s* Indianization of Ireland

As the 1790s unfolded, the spectacular qualities of illegitimate dramaturgy infiltrated productions in the patent houses to such an extent that legitimate theatre was hollowed out from within.[56] Productions such as Colman's *Blue-Beard* thrilled audiences at Covent Garden, but theatrical commentators mourned the loss of legitimate comedy as a sign of cultural devolution. James Cobb's *Ramah Droog; or, Wine Does Wonders* plays a significant role in this history because it exhibits many of the qualities of illegitimate production and also engages with the sequence of Tipu plays, which were so important to the development of Astley's craft.[57] As I have argued thus far, the performative, textual, and visual archive surrounding the Third Mysore War built a fantasy of benevolent paternalism that displaced the representation of military violence. This refiguring of colonial conquest as familial care was tied to emergent sexual norms that have important ramifications for *Ramah Droog.* However, the more violent desires that ground these fantasies of benevolent British governance are encoded into the comic opera's sets and its spectacular procession. One could argue that here the line between a patent production and Astley's entertainments can be drawn, for what has to be coded in the patent houses can be enacted in the illegitimate venues. The *Morning Herald*'s opening-night review declared that "the first objects that attract our attention in the representation of this piece, are the Scenery and the Dresses. The ingenuity, beauty, and magnificence of these surpass every thing of a similar description that we have for many years witnessed."[58] Aside from their aesthetic qualities, the scenery is the occasion for a monetary thrill not unrelated to that of the Orient itself. The sets materialize the potential for surplus value in the colonial enterprise: "[T]he Expence attending their construction and decoration must have been immense . . . the Piece bids fair to become so attractive, that we have no doubt of the liberality of the Manager meeting proper return from the attention of the Public."[59] The excitement generated here deserves careful consideration for the sets themselves resolve a series of political anxieties that impinge upon the economic stability of colonial activity in India.

As if to underline the importance of the stage effects, the *Morning Herald* provided a complete catalog of every set in order of appearance. The play opens in the fortress of Ramah Droog with "British captives on one side, the walls of the palace garden on the other," and quickly shifts to "a distant view of the hill of the fort of Ramah Droog."[60] By opening in a prison, the play gestures toward the widely reported cruelties suffered by British prisoners of Tipu Sultan. Like the cascade of Tipu plays in the early 1790s, Cobb activates all of the anxieties of captivity right at the play's outset, thereby establishing specific forms of vulnerability—sexual and military—that are to be overcome during the course of the entertainment. In this sense, much of the opera's ideological effect relies on the assumption that victory over Tipu five years earlier has generated enough security for the audience to revisit and play at colonial anxiety. This playing at anxiety allows Cobb to explore sites of real and current instability. Put simply, an earlier scene of anxiety is being reactivated to gain access to an altogether different instance of imperial concern: India is deployed as a safe field in which to explore Irish problematics.

Close attention to the list of sets reveals that the opera shuttles the audience in and out of the phantasmatic space of the prison in spite of the fact that almost all of the onstage action and dialogue happen within the walls of the fortress. The moments when the opera provides either distance from the fortress or a respite from the narrative problematic of imprisonment are therefore extremely important. Of these I focus on two: the extraordinary procession with its mechanical elephant, and the long-range view of the fortress that accompanies the second scene. Midway through the play a "splendid procession" interrupts the action:

> The Rajah . . . on an Elephant, returning from hunting the Tiger hunt, preceded by his Harcarrahs, or Military Messengers, and his State Palanquin. The Vizier on another Elephant—the Princess in a gaurie, drawn by Buffaloes. The Rajah is attended by his Fakeer or Soothsayer—his Officers of State, and by an Ambassador from Tippoo Sultun in a Palanquin; also by Nairs or Soldiers, from the South of India—Poligars, or Inhabitants of the hilly districts, with their hunting dogs—other Indians carrying a dead tiger, and young tigers in a cage, a number of sepoys—musicians on camels on foot— Dancing Girls, &c.[61]

Unlike similar processions in earlier plays, a great deal of attention is placed on the mechanical elephant as a figure not only for military might but also for technological rationality. A great deal of ink was spilled on how Cornwallis's assault on Bangalore was the first British campaign in

India to use elephants on a large scale. But in keeping with the display of military technology pioneered at Astley's, the handbills and advertisements emphasized the ingenuity of the elephant's mechanism, and some reviewers suggested that witnessing its movements was sufficient incentive to go to the theatre. Plans for the elephant were reportedly published during the first run of the opera. What is important for us to recognize is that the technological display afforded by the elephant and the ethnographic accounting of various attendants are not divergent practices. The former implicitly declares the superiority of British technological innovation and the latter gestures toward the supposed combination of Hindu servility and Moslem bellicosity that undercuts Indian attempts to become a similarly modern and legitimate society capable of such technological sophistication.

But one detail in the procession above all others raises fundamental political and dramaturgical questions. Cobb's procession features a dead tiger and young tigers in a cage. Widely known to the English public as the "Tiger of Mysore," Tipu is here figured a year before his death as a dead tiger and his already-hostage sons as captive tiger cubs. *Ramah Droog*'s procession acts as an allegory for acts of domination already achieved and yet to come. In this light, the procession draws the audience into a very particular historical juncture, one that not only analeptically stages Tipu's political and military defeat but also proleptically instantiates the desire for his actual death. The opera's less-than-subtle revisions of the history of British intervention in India opens the way for the self-congratulatory combination of humanitarianism and military strength that dominates the third act of *Ramah Droog*.

What is so remarkable about this opera is that this instantiation of the desire for the death of colonial resistance is geographically transferable. The temporal problematic established in the theatricalized space of India is transferred to a more proximate space in order to deal with a similar historical juncture in Britain's imperial subjugation of Ireland. This commutability turns on the widespread public acceptance of Cornwallis's exemplary moderation, for he is a lurking presence in this play as much for his Indian career as for his role in putting down the Irish rebellion of 1798. Perhaps the most complex aspect of Cobb's opera is the way in which it invokes Britain's ostensibly parental relation to India as a model for hegemonic accounts of the Irish rebellion. *Ramah Droog* opened one day after the death of Wolfe Tone, and its audience members would have been suffused with accounts of violent uprising in Wexford. In short, the national fantasy of just moderation that allowed the English to justify colonial policy in spite of the revelation of abuses of power by the East India Company is deployed by Cobb to consolidate ideological support for government policy in Ireland.

Within the political plot of the opera, English, Irish, and Indian prisoners enable other British troops to overthrow the usurper Mahah Rajah Surooj Seing and restore the rightful princess Zelma and her lover Zemaun to the throne. The finale, which is sung by Zemaun and a chorus of British soldiers, should give ample sense of the opera's nationalist gestures:

> Joy shall swell the choral strain,
>> Loyalty and truth to prove;
> Gratitude in Freedom's fane
>> Shall hail the monarch of a people's love.
> Sacred to Freedom's glorious cause,
>> Britain the sword of justice draws;
> A lesson to the admiring world:
>> Oppression from his seat is hurl'd.
>
> (191)

This song's involution of loyalty and gratitude is the culmination of a series of speeches extolling not only the virtues of British law and governance but also the benevolence of British military intervention in Indian politics. Chief among these comes when Barney Liffey—the opera's principal Irish character[62]—is threatened with death by the Princess Alminah:

> What the devil! Condemned without a trial?. . . . in my country the monarch and the meanest subject are bound and protected by the same laws. . . . It seems very odd that we should find the value of the blessings of home, by looking for them abroad, where they are not to be found. But it is very true; and well may they say in our little kingdoms, that a man should travel to know the worth of his country and its constitution. (179)

Liffey's expression of the worth of his country and its constitution rehearses an earlier speech in which he teaches the Rajah that "An Irishman is an Englishman with another name . . . and we are like two arms, when one needs defence, the other naturally comes to his assistance" (172). The naturalness of this coembodiment is perhaps the play's most violent rewriting of contemporary colonial conflict. However, to gain a full sense of *Ramah Droog*'s manipulation of Anglo-Irish affairs requires further spatial analysis.

The assault on the Rajah's fort that brings the opera to its conclusion is reminiscent of a series of sieges conducted by Cornwallis against Tipu's *drug* fortresses in the region of *Barramah'l*—hence the title "Ramah Droog." After conquering Bangalore in 1791, Cornwallis methodically secured his supply lines by laying siege to a number of strategic fortresses, including the supposedly impregnable forts at Nundydroog and Sevendroog. When they fell, most of the other hill forts in the region surrendered. Cobb fuses these historical moments when Zelma's servant Agra describes a military action that is reminiscent of Clive's use of a diversionary attack at Arcot to conceal the surreptitious ascent of the *drug* (190). This ties the resolution of the opera's conflict to similar moments of violent conflict resolution in the history of British colonization. These two campaigns, more than any other military actions in the subcontinent, aroused intense interest among the British reading and viewing public. As Mildred Archer argues "The South Indian word 'droog' for a great fortified hill early became absorbed into the English language."[63]

It was precisely this public interest that incited illustrators like Thomas and William Daniell to follow British forces into the region. The two artists painted a series of *drug* fortresses and a number of famous views of the fort at the rock of Tritchinopoly that were subsequently engraved and in circulation less than three months before the opening of *Ramah Droog*.[64] The *Morning Chronicle*'s opening-night review emphasizes the role of Daniell in the design of the opera's scenography:

> We are prevented by want of room from going . . . into a more regular animadventure on work upon which infinite expence of decoration has been bestowed, and that with perfect taste; for the scenes and dresses we understand have been prepared under the skilful direction of Mr. Daniels, who, as an artist that enriched the world with exquisite specimens of the picturesque scenery of India. In point of spectacle, therefore, it is superb, and the procession will please upon repetition.[65]

The reviewer, perhaps inadvertently, recognizes that the elephant-laden procession at the end of the second act seems to exist separate from the primary field of action. If the pageant is excised, then a rather different spectacle captures the audience's attention—that of the *drug* itself. John Inigo Richards's sketch for the staging of the opera's second scene, in

FIG. 7.2. John Inigo Richards, Set design drawing for James Cobb's *Ramah Droog* (*courtesy of the Department of Prints and Drawings, Enthoven Collection, Victoria and Albert Museum, London*)

which the audience is given a spectacular view of the *drug* fortress, is explicitly derived from Daniell's engravings (fig. 7.2). The set change, therefore, shifts the audience from the phantasmatic space of colonial catastrophe to a famous scene of British victory in India. However, this visual resolution of one form of colonial anxiety is complicated by the appearance of a second phantasmatic assemblage, whose operation is primarily sexual and which speaks directly to scenes of colonial violence much closer—both spatially and temporally—to the opera's audience.

The Daniells' frequently painted groups of Indian subjects or each other in the foreground to give the viewing public a sense of scale of the buildings or fortresses they portrayed. But the figures in the foreground do more than help to clarify the physical size of the object viewed; they also insert an English subject within the visual field, thereby mediating between that which is recognizable and that which is entirely other. Richards's sketch replicates this gesture, but the two figures in the foreground destabilize this mediation because they are anything but normative English subjects. The first is Barney Liffey, whose "Irish pleasantries" according to the *Morning Herald* "frequently enliven the scene, and convulse the audience with laughter."[66] The second is Eliza, Captain Sidney's wife, who enters "in male attire." These examples of ethnic difference and gender transgression standing between the audience and the distant fort are telling, for normative English men rarely appear on stage. With the exception of Captain Sidney, the British are represented by an Irishman and two women in breeches. Sidney's and Liffey's wives, Elizabeth and Margaret, have joined their husbands as soldiers in the colonial project.[67] That the "female knight" gratuitously reemerges first in front of the *drug* and later inside the fortress walls indicates precisely where emergent forms of sexual and colonial governance intersect on the London stage.

Ramah Droog presents two kinds of women—the heavily eroticized Princess Alminah, who is in love with Captain Sidney, and the British female knights. In terms of the erotics of stage presentation, Cobb is mobilizing two forms of exoticism, one based on interracial heterosexual desire and another that plays on tropes of sapphic desire. As the play unfolds, the threat of miscegenation on the one hand and gender insubordination on the other are obviated when Elizabeth interrupts Alminah's pursuit of Sidney by revealing her femininity. At one level it is not surprising to see both forms of nonnormative sexuality simultaneously ejected, but Elizabeth harmonizes her sex and her gender at precisely the moment in the final act when the British soldiers take over Ramah Droog. As the British regain colonial dominance, English cross-dressing is cast off in favor of normative gender relations. What this suggests is that the play rectifies related "perversions" in the sexual and the political world.

This conjunction of sexual and colonial regulation gains some depth when we look closely at the representation of the Irish in *Ramah Droog*. The relationship between Liffey and his English "master," Captain Sidney, allegorizes an act of union that would have warmed the hearts of English audience members. However, Liffey is also placed in a subordinate relation to the Indian Rajah. In a complex plan to help liberate the British prisoners, Liffey impersonates a European doctor and cures the ailing Rajah with a potato. The potato becomes a crucial prop in the play, not only because it figures for Liffey's Irishness but also because it occasions an intriguing cultural exchange between the Irish character and the Indian Rajah. To compensate Liffey for curing his hangover, the Rajah makes Liffey a vizier and grants him a zenana of his own.[68] The gesture draws Liffey into broadly held cultural assumptions that the sexual excess implied by access to the seraglio devolves into compromised masculinity. For the remainder of the play Liffey wears a ceremonial "khelaut," and he is included in the tiger hunting party described earlier. Nestled, therefore, in the elaborate spectacle of Oriental splendor, we find an Irish vizier dressed in what London audience members would have considered effeminate clothing. Cobb reorients the containment strategy discussed earlier with regard to James Scurry in which the emasculated and Orientalized cheyla is ridiculed for his incivility in order to effect a critique of Irish disaffection. Like the stereotypical cheyla, Barney collaborates with the Rajah but all anxiety is contained under the rubric of ridicule. This is significant because the primary anxiety associated with Irish rebellion was that the rebels, like the sultans of Mysore, were allied with the French. In short, the stakes are high and Cobb figuratively circumcises/castrates Barney in an entirely symptomatic fashion. The feminization of Liffey is a significant departure from the hypermasculinization of male Irish characters earlier in the century, but it is consistent not only with the ideological disarmament of the Irish and Indian rebels in the English press, but also with the representation of Barney's wife Margaret as a pistol-toting duelist who terrifies her Indian captors.

Liffey's inclusion in the procession has the potential to unsettle the play's overt endorsement of union between Ireland and England. But the threat posed by this collocation of two fractious colonial spaces is contained in advance by the opera's pastiche of British military victory in the subcontinent, both at the level of set design and narrative. It is not only Elizabeth who reassumes her normative gender identity as the threat posed by the Rajah is erased. When the British storm Ramah Droog, Liffey casts off his Indian garb, reassumes his soldierly masculinity, and resumes his subservient relation to his English "master." The consolidation of gender roles in the emergent heterosexuality of the late eighteenth century is matched by a parallel consolidation of ethnic difference within the emergent political entity of Great Britain. And that difference is regulated by the subtle deployment of nonnormative sexualities that ultimately connects Ireland and India as "unhealthy" sites in the colonial imaginary.

Margaret's masculinization, unlike Eliza's, remains intact at the close of *Ramah Droog*. What this means is that the relation between Barney and Margaret diverges from the normative heterosexuality exemplified by Eliza and Captain Sidney. Margaret and Barney's closing duet allows us to recognize the political importance of this sexual distinction. As the British troops scale the *drug*, the opera's principal Irish characters narrate in song the extraordinary restraint of British victory in a fashion that is reminiscent of what the *Gentleman's Magazine* called "the humane yet spirited conduct of the Marquis Cornwallis" not only in Mysore but also in Ireland.[69] For two Irish characters to be cheering "our Country and our King" and identifying with *British* "sons of freedom" (189) on the London stage in early November 1798—less than six months after the bloody extermination of the United Irishmen—is not only wishful thinking but also an indication of the importance and the longevity of the image of "moderate Cornwallis" to English fantasies of "humanitarian" imperial domination. These fantasies rely on figures of benevolent paternal governance in the family that are consolidated by the attribution of nonnormative masculinities to colonized others. In this light, the opera's subtle destabilization of Irish masculinity through the continuing presence of the Irish female knight helps pave the way for subsequent imperial policy. Significantly, the Indian characters who benefit from the British displacement of the "despotic" rajah embody a similarly nonnormative heterosexuality. Zemaun, the heroic Indian figure in the opera, is always understood to be subordinate to Princess Zelma. This similarity between Indian and Irish heterosexuality is, I believe, crucial to the opera's image of coloniality, for the continuing presence of masculinized colonial women and subordinate colonial men is the defining distinction between colonized ethnicities and imperial British identity following the ejection of more threatening colonial others, such as Tipu Sultan and Wolfe Tone. In this light, the buoyant celebration of normative middle-class sexuality in this comic opera is intimately tied to the careful concealment—from metropolitan subjects—of violent dominance without hegemony in the colonial realm.[70]

Exhibiting Supremacy: The Siege and Storming of Seringapatam

The relationship between *Ramah Droog*'s sets and the prior circulation of images of *drug* fortresses by the Daniell brothers raises a series of questions regarding the place of visual spectacle in the reception and interpretation of war in the cultural memory. The previous section has argued that, in spite of the fleeting moments when actual conflict is staged in *Ramah Droog,* the real engagement with the question of colonial war takes place somewhat surreptitiously at the level of visual memory, and that it is the recent uprising in Ireland that is being indirectly presented through analogies with the earlier victories at Tritchnopoly, Nundydroog, Severndroog, and Seringapatam. This containment of colonial anxiety and its redeployment to a separate colonial space implies an extraordinary level of commutability that ultimately rests on the metropolitan audience's ability to strip colonial subjects of their specificity and deal with them as similarly subjugated beings. This ability rests on a particular form of sanctioned ignorance that misrecognizes triumphant rule in one colonial locale for enduring political instability in another.

The sentimental paintings and prints of the hostage sons of Tipu lurk behind Cobb's opera, and their conjunction of triumphalism and paternal care lives on in *Ramah Droog*'s careful suturing of British ascendancy and sexual normativity. The hostage scene in all its manifestations becomes a kind of screen memory for the reconstitution of British military control after the earlier humiliations rendered by Gillray and others.[71] But despite the displacement of military domination in the paintings and prints, a kind of countermemory of violence was enacted all through this period in the military performances at Astley's Royal Amphitheatre. As the decade came to a close, British forces would once again capture Seringapatam, but this time victory was sealed by the death of Tipu Sultan. Like the profusion of images of Cornwallis's reception of the hostages that closed the Third Mysore War, the Fourth Mysore War was visually commemorated by a series of paintings and prints, but artists focused on two very different scenes, both of which were based on Lieutenant Colonel Alexander Beatson's firsthand account of the fall of the fortress.[72] Beatson's text offers detailed accounts of the siege of the fortress and of the discovery of Tipu's body. These two sections of Beatson's text occasion two sets of paintings that are as distinct in their representational tactics as they are in their subject matter.[73]

With its references to *Hamlet* and its transcriptions of Tipu's dream premonitions, Beatson's text provides more than enough material for the composition of a tragedy.[74] But the emotional response in the viewer that lies at the heart of tragedy may exceed the ideological work necessary at this historical moment immediately following the news of Tipu's defeat. What was necessary in 1800 was the combined effect of forgetting past defeats and of promoting heroic British martyrs. And what better to occlude the threatening bodies not only of Tipu but also of the cheylas than the distinct, but related, mechanical entertainments offered at the Lyceum and at Astley's Amphitheatre. In Gillian Russell's words, what appears to have been necessary was a paradoxical "de-theatricalization of the representation of war" in forms of theatre that emerged beyond the purview of the patent houses.[75] This process of detheatricalization shifted the emphasis from identification with particular actants to the visual experience of mechanized war, and thus what emerges is "war without the mediation of actors."[76] Despite the opportunities presented by Tipu's defeat for the sentimental performance of triumphant national identity or the staging of tragic reversal, the most important performative commemoration of British victory over Tipu opted instead to stage a "Grand Military Spectacle," titled *The Siege and Storming of Seringapatam,* which was itself based on a panoramic view of the battle.[77]

In the spring of 1800, two representations of the fall of Seringapatam were competing for public attention. On 17 April 1800, Robert Ker Porter's immense panoramic view of the event, *The Storming of Seringapatam,* was opened for public viewing at the Lyceum. The panorama was longer than two hundred feet, covered more than "2,550 square feet of canvas, and contain[ed] several hundred figures as large as life, with near twenty Portraits of British Officers."[78] As one can imagine, the semicircular panorama overwhelmed its viewers (fig. 7.3). Thomas Dibdin recalled the panorama's effect:

> The learned were amazed, and the unlearned were enraptured. I can never forget its first impression upon my own mind. It was as a thing dropped down from the clouds—all fire, energy, intelligence, and animation. You looked a second time, the figures moved, and were commingled in hot and bloody fight. You saw the flash of the cannon, the glitter of the bayonet, the gleam of the falchion. You longed to be leaping from crag to crag with Sir David Baird, who is hallooing his men on to victory! Then, again, you seemed to be listening to the groans of the wounded and the dying—and more than one female was carried out swooning.[79]

The illusion of motion and immediacy is typical of panoramic display, but it is important to recognize that the painting is both an optical and a narrative machine. The fact that Dibdin's account pulls the viewer first into the place of General Baird is not incidental because he occupies the very center of the central panel. In other words, the panorama's convex shape, much like a convex mirror, forces the viewer into the center of the semicircle. Once there, Baird's line of sight and other compositional factors, such as the placement of the ramparts of the fort, move the viewer's attention back along the curved wings to incorporate other elements of the battle. This places the viewer in the place of the commander of the forces, but then enables the viewer to see more than Baird could ever see. In short, the viewer accedes to a position that both incorporates and exceeds that of command. As Gillian Russell argues, "part of the politics of making war possible has involved the privileging of the vision of the civilian audience: the viewer . . . must 'see' more than even the ordinary soldier in the field,

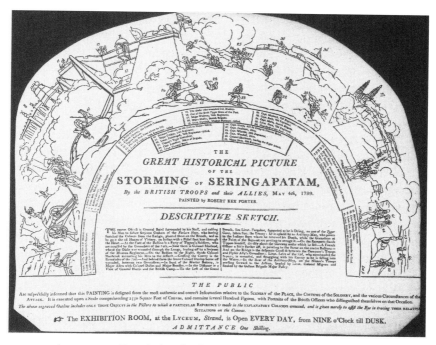

FIG. 7.3. Anonymous, *Descriptive Sketch of Robert Ker Porter's "The Storming of Seringapatam," A Key to the Panorama (courtesy of the Department of Prints and Drawings, Victoria and Albert Museum, London)*

assuming the position of a Wellington or a Napoleon," or, in this case, a Baird or a Harris.[80]

This regulation of the lines of sight is crucial to the panorama's message and it is reinforced by the paratext that viewers could buy to decode the image. *Narrative Sketches of the Conquest of Mysore* was available in the lobby of the Lyceum for two shillings, or twice the price of admission to the panorama. This guidebook not only identifies the various officers portrayed in the painting, but also establishes a viewing order. As one might expect, the guide starts with the "Principal Group on the Breach" at the center of the painting and immediately identifies General Baird. It then directs the viewer to observe various martyrs to the cause and only late in the order of presentation does it recognize "On the Rampart, to the left of the breach, is TIPPOO SULTAUN, attended by his Chiefs and Standard Bearers. He stands near an open veranda, directly above the gate-way in which he afterwards fell, and appears reconnoitering the attack, in concert with a French Officer, General Chapuy, who is stationed on the battlement, a little further to the left."[81] This relegation of Tipu to the left side of the panorama and to the last phase of the proposed order of observation literally decenters the sultan and thus accords him far less narrative significance than the various British soldiers shown dying for their country. Hence, the troubling corpse of Tipu is not only not presented but the structure of the optical mechanism focuses viewer attention on the dead bodies of both named and unnamed soldiers.

Dibdin makes precisely this point when he sums up the aftereffects of viewing the panorama: "[T]he accompaniments about the sally-port, half choked up with the bodies of the dead, made you look on with a shuddering awe, and retreat as you shuddered. The public poured in by hundreds and thousands for even a transient gaze—for such a sight was altogether as marvellous as it was novel. You carried it home, and did nothing but think of it, talk of it, and dream of it."[82] As a mechanism for inculcating the sublime, the panorama was perhaps unmatched, but the key observation here is that, unlike the transient effects of the sublime, Porter's painting was able to instill a sense of dread and wonder in its viewer well past the viewing moment. As such, the painting needs to be understood primarily as a historical machine: a machine that narrativizes events and generates phantasmatic identifications with historical personages. In this sense, the panorama is similar to the staging of topical historical events in the illegitimate theatre, and it is perhaps this common objective that prompted Astley to not only stage his own production of these events a few weeks later, but also to incorporate a scaled-down version of Porter's panorama into a pantomimical pastiche of London life called *The Pirate; or, Harlequin Victor* in the fall.[83]

Astley was Porter's chief competitor for the attention of the viewing public and was involved in a similarly complex narrative game. However, the relationship between machinelike performance and phantasmatic investment was quite distinct and hailed its viewers in an altogether different fashion. On 5 May 1800, ostensibly to fulfill the "particular desire of several Military Officers," Astley opened *The Siege and Storming of Seringapatam* to universal acclaim. The following excerpt from the advertisement gives a sense of the overall trajectory of the performance:

> In the course of this interesting Spectacle the following most striking Scenery will be displayed, viz. 1st, A view of an Indian Sea Port; 2d, A view near the River Cavery; 3d, The Banqueting Garden of Tippoo Sultaun; 4th, The Commander in Chief General Harris's Marquee; 5th, A correct view of the City of Seringapatam, the whole of Tip-

poo's Army, elephants, camels, &c. in motion, together with the Mysore Army, consisting of Peadars, Bungaries, Sirdars, &c. forming the Camp near Fort Periapatam; 6th, A British Battery opening brisk fire on Tippoo's Advanced Guard, particularly the blowing up of a Powder Mill; 7th, The Fortifications and City of Seringapatam, with the Springing of a Mine; 8th, External view of Tippoo's Palace, and his two Sons firing from the windows; and 9th, The Zenana and City on Fire. With a variety of circumstances which attended this important conquest.[84]

Because Astley's military action unfolds in time, its narrative effects are more conventionally recognizable. The first four scenes visually transport the viewer to the scene of the conflict, but they do so by constructing a series of spaces each geographically more proximate to the campaign. The buffering effect here is important because it establishes the distance of the events from the metropole, but the increasing enlargement of scale—each successive scene corresponds to a smaller geographical space—has a telescopic effect. Although the size of the performing space remains constant, the spatial parameters of the spectacle become increasingly magnified. As in Porter's panorama, the viewer is given the illusion of proximity, but here the succession of scenes effectively generates the fantasy of hurtling into the space. This phantasmatic motion stops momentarily in General Harris's camp in order to secure audience identification before the onset of clockwork motion and mechanical spectacle turns the space into one of simulated war.

As soon as *The Siege and Storming of Seringapatam* puts the armies in motion in the fifth scene, the visual experience of the audience undergoes a crucial transformation. The scene opens with a view of the city, but the static pictorial spectacle is immediately subordinated to the choreographed motion of Orientalized soldiers and animals—some of which may have been mechanical. If the effect of the first four scenes was figuratively to move viewers through space toward the scene of conflict, then the effect of the fifth scene is simultaneously to render the viewer static and to put the performing space into motion. From his or her newly secured position, the viewer can now marvel at the moving array of Tipu's forces. The display of Tipu's armies was likely one of choreographed chaos. As the preceding description indicates, there would be no standard uniform but rather an amalgamation of types of warriors, and it is important to consider the effect this would have had in the enclosed space of Astley's Royal Amphitheatre.[85] The excitement generated by the sheer number of moving bodies and machines would enact the threat of Tipu's forces and would also open the door for the demonstration of the superiority of the clockwork action that defined British military operations. It is entirely predictable that the scene of martial chaos would be superseded by the efficient performance of "A British Battery opening a brisk fire on Tippoo's Advanced Guard . . . [and] the blowing up of a Powder Mill." As Mark Seltzer has discussed in *Bodies and Machines,* the artillery battery involves a mechanization of the soldier's body. Each artillery soldier performs a single task, and the order and duration of tasks are defined by the firing mechanism. Seltzer uses the phrase "body-machine complex" to indicate how these interactions create an expanded notion of the subject that can best be understood as prosthetic, and it is in this light that we have to consider the fifth and sixth scenes.[86] If the fifth scene constitutes the clockwork regulation of human motion, then the sixth scene stages the superiority of integrated human-machine interaction. This development is significant because, as we saw earlier, the very staging of clockwork motion in Astley's was a sign of British martial superiority. Here Astley deploys many of the same techniques to establish the threat of Tipu's forces and then renders them subordinate to another technological innovation—the "blow up."

The spectacular explosion that destroys the tyrant's castle was a prominent feature of illegitimate dramaturgy and "the blow-up actually marks a radical departure in the dramatization of nation and empire. It makes representable in an entirely new way that irreducible confrontation between freedom and despotism, good and evil. In so doing, the dramaturgy of illegitimate theatre implicitly reveals the failure of rationality, the inadequacy of rhetoric and the impossibility of benevolence."[87] *The Siege and Storming of Seringapatam* seems to conform to the first part of Moody's argument, but I would argue that what is demonstrated for the viewers in Astley's is not a failure of rationality but rather its resilience. By using these same logistical techniques to move Tipu's forces around the Royal Amphitheatre, Astley is engaging with precisely this historical problematic: namely, that the Sultan effectively mimicked European tactics of row and column warfare. Astley's answer to this is to counter the clockwork movement of bodies with an even more radical incorporation of the soldier/actor into the body-machine complex of the battery. Not only has the performance shifted attention away from actors, it has also drawn attention to the articulation of particular bodily motions and machine processes. The explosion that rocks the powder mill at the end of scene 6 and the mine that explodes in scene 7 are themselves the product of a technological rationality engineered both on the battlefield and in the amphitheatre, and, as such, they literally punctuate the viewing experience with evidence of supremacy.

This redeployment of the performer as part of well-oiled action activates specific fantasies of national consolidation both in the scene of performance and in the audience. After the dissolution of the individual performers as discrete entities and the ensuing blowups of scenes 6 and 7, the viewer is suddenly confronted with two specific individuals. Tippoo's two sons fire from the windows, and then the audience is treated to a spectacle of mass death with the zenana and the city on fire. After the fearsome display of the power of group cohesion in the body-machine complex of the British battery, the two sons would appear as soldiers pathetically working with insufficient arms and caught in an antiquated tactical mode. It is the same distinction between modernity and antiquity deployed in earlier accounts of the Mysore Wars, but here there is an ancillary implication: namely, that the British force is powerful because the soldier/actor gives up his subjective specificity in order to play a role in the larger national/theatrical machine. The zenana and the city burn not only because the British are technically superior, but also because Tippoo's sons are fighting as mere individuals. Much could be made of this correlation between the shedding of specific subjectivity in favor of fantasies of national consolidation, especially at a moment when the pressures of the war with France accelerated the emergence of an abstract British subjectivity from the host of distinct ethnic and political groups that inhabited the British Isles.[88]

Preliminary advertisements for the Astley's performance state that it will present "the Death of Tippoo Saib."[89] However, accounts of *The Siege and Storming of Seringapatam* after opening night indicate that the show does not conclude with Tipu's death but rather with the burning of the zenana. In terms of arguments put forward elsewhere in this book, this substitution is crucial because the sexual deviance implied by the zenana is the primary figure for Tipu's despotic governance, and thus the theatregoers watch the entire figurative assemblage of despotism ablaze before them. As a metaphorical transaction, this has the distinct ideological advantage of staging the death of Tipu without actually rendering his corpse. This has the double effect not only of canceling any sympathetic or tragic identification with Tipu's body but also of configuring the audience as a realm of sexual and political normativity. If we imagine Astley's show as a careful management of incendiary devices and tropes, then we can suggest that the same heat that consumes Tipu, his wives, and his city melts the audience into a patriotic amalgam. As Astley's dramaturgical strategies deindividuate the audience members, the audience can no longer be considered a disparate collective, for it now aspires to a kind of mass identity assimilable to the species being of the nation. And hence we gain some sense of the importance of the performance's initial distancing effects. Just as the audience must be sufficiently distant from the stage to allow for the blowups and fires to occur, so too must the metropolitan subject be brought close enough, but not too close, to the colonial fire to ensure the proper cohesion of disparate elements. Astley's success at maintaining effective proximity needs to be understood not only as one of the singular innovations in the representation of colonial space—one that Burke and the managers in the Hastings case were unable to achieve—but also as a metropolitan enactment of the segregationist policies that characterized British governance in India following Cornwallis's interventions.[90]

AFTERWORD | *Recreational Alterity*

THE HISTORICAL PROBLEMS confronted by scholars working on late eighteenth-century materials are perennially those of how to theorize change. Indeed, the careers of Romantic scholars are built on the accepted notion that something changes in the last two decades of the century. That something can be narrowly or broadly defined, but this book has argued that we can isolate fundamental changes in almost every element of social, economic, and cultural production in the late eighteenth century. If we imagine all of the forces of eighteenth-century life as vectors ebbing and flowing, then something happens in the 1780s that alters the flow of life. I use the word *life* advisedly, because I want to think through the historical turbulence of the period as the transformation in styles of living. This implies that there is a correspondence between the events and processes that we conventionally recognize as political and the practices that shape and define embodied selves in everyday life. Following rudimentary chaos theory, I want to suggest that a series of bifurcations initiated changes in the flow of life that became perceptible somewhere in the 1780s, and that the period commonly referred to as Romanticism constitutes a turbulence that found its proper margins and flow characteristics sometime in the nineteenth century. The metaphorics of turbulence, flow, and the like are a useful heuristic here because they allow not only for infinite complication but also for reductively drawing attention to a field of action for research.[1]

One way of thinking of Romantic studies since its inception is that it has attempted to understand these changes in flow immanently. Hence, attention has been focused on the turbulence. We likely have no other choice, but the focus on nation is one of the fundamentally constraining limits on how we think through this problem. This limit above all others obscures the bifurcations, those strange events—often minor or perhaps so major that their full import is impossible to register—that generate change. Finding the triggers for the emergence of bourgeois sexuality, of the middle and working classes, of new forms of political organization and action, and, above all, of metropolitan identity, requires that we reevaluate the flows, exchanges, and movements of all kinds of economies not simply in a national frame but in an imperial and transnational field.

It is obviously impossible for one person to follow these broad changes in their totality. It may not be possible for a generation of scholars. But we can follow particular rivulets and watch carefully how they shift from one set of attractors to another. This book has focused on the surge of discourse pertaining to the East India Company from the economic collapse in private credit in 1772 to the initial wave of interest in the trial of Warren Hastings in the late 1780s to the British fascination with Tipu Sultan in the 1790s. However, I have taken as my archive the theatrical culture of this turbulent period, in part because the theatre operates explicitly as a form of autoethnography, and in part because the fact of performance brings many of the key problematics regarding self-stylization and subjectification into crisis.

If the concept of nationhood deforms our historical sense of imperialism in this period, then we also have to acknowledge that the wealth of scholarship on the 1790s exerts undue influence on our understanding of the flow of life in this period. It is not surprising that the real advances of Romantic New Historicism have their roots in this decade, but what is often seen as an originary or disjunctive period is perhaps best understood as a midpoint in a much longer temporal arc. In terms of my earlier metaphors, the flow of eighteenth-century life sets off triggers in the seventies that initiate changes in flow in the eighties, which are in turn channeled into fairly rigid canals of identity by the nineties. What strikes me as interesting about this reductive account of eighteenth-century life is the degree to which it is an almost perfect photographic negative of the scholarship of the early decades of Romanticism.[2] The 1790s dominate much of our understanding of the late eighteenth-century sex and gender system, of apostasy and nationalism, and of the emergence of specifically Romantic literary production. Rather than attributing that dominance to the inherent significance of the decade, could we not argue that the task of understanding, that historical comprehension, is easier because the object of inquiry is becoming more recognizable as the subject of Romanticism. Following a series of connected bifurcations, the attractors that organize the social body have modulated and stabilized into a recognizable social system of which we are a part. In other words, our own Romanticism makes the 1790s not only accessible but also vital. To pick up the vague invocation of the sublime here, I would suggest that the 1790s offer a stabilizing compensation that acts as an as-if presentation of something altogether less threatening than the incoherence that immediately precedes it.

In this light, the incessant creation and disintegration of the Romantic subject—I am thinking especially of Wordsworth here—begins to look like the metropolitan symptom of a series of traumatic events in the colonies that remain unresolved to this day. It also suggests something about the importance of performance to a full understanding of Romantic subjectivity. The relative lack of scholarship on oratory, theatre, and other forms of performance may be a function of a kind of self-protective reluctance to go to the very scene of instability, to the place where the hole rent in British subjectivity is least effectively patched over—least, because performance is so transitory and what the imperial imaginary is striving for at this time is some kind of permanent solution to the injury inflicted by the American war and by other setbacks in the colonies. Perhaps this is why the latter decades of Romanticism turn to the East in a far more genocidal fashion. The biological state racism that eventually dominates the imagination of empire in the nineteenth century is subtended not by the defensive performances outlined here, but rather by the kind of rigid phantasmatic projections indulged in by Thomas De Quincey and others.[3] The turbulent flow and flux of the 1770s and 1780s finds itself channeled into discursive pathways whose very violence depends on the sharp management of the flow of life between the nation and its colonial holdings.

FROM SUCH A RECOGNITION, this book has focused attention on the hole rent in British political subjectivity by the perceived breakdown in imperial sovereignty in the 1770s and 1780s. I have argued that, like many traumatic events, the crises in imperial governance are everywhere evident but yet in many ways insusceptible to direct analysis because the strategies used to reconsolidate national and imperial subjectivity appear unconnected to the constitutional and economic questions posed by Britain's accession to global dominance. Transformations in the sex and gender system, in class relations, in the performance of embodied sociability each in their own way and sometimes in concert build temporary tissues to cover the traumatic wound. But it is my sense that this healing process was both interminably delayed and deformed by events in France. P. J. Marshall has argued that interest in India declined in the 1790s, and if one consults the Parliamentary Register or the newspapers, there is clear evidence of such an abatement in direct public concern. But this need not be read as a sign of apathy regarding colonial affairs.[4]

One can argue that the ideological and military engagement with France is a kind of anodynal moment: one that suspends certain global problematics but never fully solves key ruptures in British identity. This is not to downplay the role played by the French Revolution and the Napoleonic Wars in the consolidation of British national identity, but rather to ask whether the national subject that emerges so forcefully during this conflict is at all equipped to deal with the earlier anxieties that remain active at a subterranean level until they explode in times of later crisis. This would help to explain, however tentatively, the overdetermined responses to events such as the Indian mutiny. And this would imply that two economies of alterity remain incommensurable right through the dissolution of the British Empire. On the one hand, a form of national fantasy congeals in response to the self-consolidating alterity of France, and on the other, a myriad of disjunctive imperial fantasies not only fails to demonstrate any internal coherence but also eventually attempts to contain scenes of colonial alterity through the mechanisms of segregation and blunt assertions of racial supremacy. In this scenario, the national subjectification developed during the conflict with France becomes an impediment to further engaging with colonial alterity because it so successfully obfuscates the proliferation of British domination in the empire and of the increasing incursion of the state into everyday life in the metropole.

This would suggest that the 1780s and the period immediately following the Napoleonic Wars constitute zones of instructive instability. If Burke exemplifies the strange adjacency of India and France in the phantasmatic legislation of British identity for the 1780s, then Hazlitt's essay "The Indian Jugglers" may sketch in one instance how these competing forms of alterity are temporarily reconciled in fearsome, yet symptomatic ways. As we have seen, many of Burke's difficulties are directly related to the geographical and cultural distance between Britain and India. That distance requires a rhetoric that ultimately undermines Burke's political objectives. For Hazlitt, it is the close proximity of four Indian men that instantiates a related resituation not only of the French but of his self.

As a concluding gesture for this book, I want to consider the remarkable feats of dexterity and bodily regimen put on display for London audiences by a group of Indian jugglers from Seringapatam in the fall of 1815 and the winter of 1816[5]—the same jugglers who came to Hazlitt's attention. I believe that Hazlitt's aesthetics of power coalesces not only with a series of raciological fantasies regarding the distinction between the machinic and the human, but also with a historically specific fantasy of vulnerability that accompanied Britain's accession to global supremacy in the early years of the nineteenth century. To make that argument, however, requires that we attend both to transformations in the practice of warfare and to the consolidation of national subjectivity in the illegitimate theatre during and immediately following the Mysore Wars. These topoi are linked by a fascination with bodily discipline, whether it be on the battlefield or in London's various entertainment venues. As we have already seen in our discussion of precinematic technique in the representation of the Mysore Wars, the mobilization of the body itself at this time of imperial supremacy becomes a matter of xenophobic concern. This earlier discussion allows us to gain some purchase on how the bodies of the jugglers' audience are hailed into a complex economy of recreational alterity.

At one level, the audience at the rooms in New Bond Street was deeply involved in calibrating the limits of human capacity. The jugglers' feats of balancing, sword swallowing, and prestidigitation all rely on precise training of the body, but these skills, as remarkable as they are, are overshadowed according to Hazlitt by the near miraculous circulation of balls:

> Coming forward and seating himself on the ground in his white dress and tightened turban, the chief of the Indian Jugglers begins with tossing up two brass balls, which is what any of us could do, and concludes with keeping up four at the same time, which is what none of us could do to save our lives, nor if we were to take our whole lives to do it in. . . . It is the utmost stretch of human ingenuity, which nothing but the bending the faculties of body and mind to it from the tenderest infancy with incessant, ever-anxious application up to manhood can accomplish or make even a slight approach to.[6]

The opening sentence of Hazlitt's essay establishes a comparative mode that takes on structural implications when he turns the comparison on his own practice:

I ask what there is that I can do as well as this? Nothing. What have I been doing all my life? Have I been idle, or have I nothing to shew for all by labour and pains? Or have I passed my time in pouring words like water into empty sieves, rolling a stone up a hill and then down again, trying to prove an argument in the teeth of facts, and looking for causes in the dark, and not finding them? Is there no one thing in which I can challenge competition, that I can bring as an instance of exact perfection, in which others cannot find a flaw? The utmost I can pretend to is to write a description of what this fellow can do.[7]

This expression of self-doubt and vulnerability is superseded later in the essay when Hazlitt argues that it is precisely the nonmechanical quality of working with language rather than with objects that elevates writing to the status of art and derogates juggling as a triviality. However, there is a key conundrum put on stage in these seemingly trivial actions: the distinction between the body of the juggler and the body of the audience member, which characterizes the chief effect of the performance, relies on the continual assertion of similitude. As John Whale argues, "juggling effaces the recognition of difference. At the same time as triumphing over the limits of the body, it triumphs over an overdetermined awareness of ethnic difference."[8] In the process of ignoring ethnic difference in the essay, David Bromwich nevertheless captures this paradox in his reading of Hazlitt's panegyric on Cavanagh, the fives player:

> "The Indian Jugglers" offers Cavanagh as a test case for distinguishing the artist from the mechanic. The truth is that only Hazlitt's ability to see depth of art in the surface of mechanical skill . . . has made the question an interesting one. The practiced eye more than finds, it invents the glory of the things that concern it. In this sense one might say that Hazlitt does for Cavanagh what the essayist does for his own experience all the time. His gift of immortality to one player marks his ascendancy over a limited contest, only as much as it marks his kinship with the contestant.[9]

Similitude is necessary to make comparison possible, but difference is crucial for the essay's act of sublation. The jugglers now come forward as a surface from which the essayist not only projects his own depth of character but also subtly proclaims his genius. Unlike a number of newspaper articles that contested the "Superiority" of the Indian jugglers by offering European counterexamples, Hazlitt recognizes their superiority and then turns that recognition into the epitome of his overcoming of mere physical perfection.[10]

This is why the essay both stresses the everydayness of particular actions and emphasizes that "the precision of the movements must be like a mathematical truth."[11] At one level, Hazlitt is merely picking up on the geometric discourse that characterizes the advertisement's attempts to identify the physical manipulation of balls as something otherworldly:

> The next feat of the Juggler is, to perform a series of evolutions with four hollow brass balls, about the bigness of oranges. His power over these is almost miraculous. He causes them to describe every possible circle horizontally, perpendicularly, obliquely, transversely, round his legs, under his arms, about his head, in small and in large circumferences, with wondrous rapidity, and keeping the whole number in motion at the same time.[12]

The Euclidean discourse employed to describe the juggler's actions insinuates a degree of ideality to the performance that effectively makes it a figure for mathematical rationality. Hazlitt emphasizes the mathematical precision of the juggler's motions and thus paradoxically argues that their corporeal skill has attained the status of abstraction. They are other to the audience in the same way that a geometric abstraction is an idealization of the physical world.

And yet we have to speak here of a racialized abstraction or an abstract racial alterity because in the years preceding the performance in New Bond Street mathematical rationality as exhibited in precise bodily regimen has carried the connotation of racial and national superiority in the theatre of imperial warfare. The very presence of these jugglers from Seringapatam poses the question of alterity in an entirely different register: one now focused less on cultural difference than on xenophobic notions of national and racial distinction. As I have argued in the previous chapter, the military spectacles at Astley's Royal Amphitheatre redeployed the performer as part of well-oiled action in order to activate specific fantasies of national consolidation both in the scene of performance and in the audience. As the audience was hailed into the scene of conflict, it too became militarized. Defeating Tipu Sultan at Astley's involved the shedding of individuality in order to become part of the spectacle of imperial supremacy.

This performative manipulation of the viewing subject serves as a backdrop to Hazlitt's response to the Indian jugglers, but the scene in New Bond Street is also traversed by the more proximate national enthusiasm of post-Waterloo London. As the Napoleonic Wars unfolded, the extraordinary technological leap from the clockwork army to the motorized qualities of the Grand Armée meant that supremacy could no longer be figured by the body-machine complex but, according to De Landa, had to mobilize the subject itself in new ways.

> The basis for the new tactics was the creation of versatile, responsive soldiers. But this implied that the lower ranks of the war machine had to be given more responsibility, and this ran counter to all the tendencies of the mercenary-based armies of the eighteenth century. In order to break away from this impasse, a reservoir of loyalty had to be tapped: the external mechanical connection between ruler and ruled . . . was replaced by an internal link, one tying up the population as whole with the nation of which they were sovereign citizens. Besides using nationalism as a source of loyalty, the difference between friend and enemy had to be taken out of the context of a duel between Christian armies and transformed into a more radical form of difference: a kind of xenophobia capable of transforming a war from a contest between rulers into a clash between nations.[13]

The instigation of this xenophobic imperative at the heart of the new warfare not only supplemented rank and column discipline but also accelerated the importance of writing to the practice of war. Rank and column organization, although ubiquitous, was no longer sufficient to deal with tactical innovations. The new tactical flexibility of the French army required an intensification of data flow, and in this transitional period, written orders become a crucial part of military communications. These two developments are crucial because the widely disseminated proclamation of Wellington's ostensible "genius" and Hazlitt's own reverence for Napoleon were based not only on their ability to instill unit consolidation through patriotic individuation but also in their recognition of the importance of communicative prowess.[14]

In this light, Hazlitt's engagement with the Indian jugglers takes on a new aspect, for he sees the jugglers shortly after Waterloo, and the essay is published at roughly the time of Napoleon's death.[15] Just as the shows at Astley's projected obsolescence onto the armies of Mysore by emphasizing their lack of clockwork organization, so too does Hazlitt construct the juggler's cultural obsolescence by negatively comparing their mechanical art, first, with Reynolds's mimetic art and, second, with the linguistic art of the essay writing subject. What is so startling here is that the excessive individuation that was formerly understood as a symptom of antiquated weakness in the soldier of Mysore is revalued as a sign of both national and aesthetic preeminence in the British observer. Like the clockwork army, the jugglers simply redirect motion along a predetermined path, but the Napoleonic essayist generates energy from even the most banal materials by mobilizing his own subjectivity. Hazlitt's performance of conflicted subjectivity in writing is a sign of his and, by extension, Britain's capacity for tactical versatility in the struggle between imperial nations. However, it is a versatility or a singularity learned from the Napoleonic example, and thus it implies both an identification with and a sublation of the very qualities Hazlitt valorizes in Napoleon.

In the winter of 1816, British imperial and national fantasy began to coalesce into a global and hence universalist phantasm. This emergent global unconscious in Hazlitt's essay is at variance with the patriotic cult of Wellington and hence with establishment forms of nationalism in that it locates genius in "defeat."[16] That both the logistics of warfare and the practice of writing should turn on a desire to overcome the limitations of subjectivity is chilling, especially when one recalls that Hazlitt's theorization of genius and power is figured in purely combative terms in the essay. It is as though the modulations of imperial conflict up to this historical moment have brought the desire for supremacy not only into the very definition of the political and aesthetic subject, but also into the fabric of everyday life such that an evening's entertainment at New Bond Street is intimately tied to xenophobic fantasies of ascendancy. If the shows at Astley's were all about maintaining effective distance to enable audience consolidation, then Hazlitt's close proximity to the Indian jugglers instantiates what amounts to an imposition of superior distance from within the subject itself. The now-regulated flow of metropolitan life would appear to be carving increasingly deep channels not only in the social but also in the phantasms of one of its exemplary radical constituents.

But Hazlitt's essay is also notable for what it does not write about. As the performance unfolds, the bodily exercises extend far beyond the dexterous movement of objects and begin to test the boundaries between the exterior and the interior of the body:

The next performance is that of passing a steel hook (representing a large fish hook) through one of the nostrils into the mouth, a piece of string is then threaded through the hook, there being a small hole at the end of it like the eye of a needle, the hook is then drawn out with one end of the string through the nostril and the other in the mouth, a large stone of twenty pound weight is then made fast to the string, and suspended in the air by the upper jaw, and afterwards, what is most surprising, the stone is swung to and fro, and is thrown off at some distance without the string being either cut or broken.[17]

It is tempting read this scene allegorically and muse upon the spectacle of the burden of colonial identity. This temptation becomes even more insistent during the performance's final scene of sword swallowing, for it brings the specter of death into representation. Hazlitt offers no commentary on these aspects of the show except to say that sword swallowing should not be allowed. One could argue that his silence reveals a profound unease with the jugglers' ability to put pain and death fully in abeyance. In these feats, the jugglers seem to overcome the physicality of the flesh. Hazlitt's exclusive focus on the action of circulating balls draws attention away from the body of the juggler by emphasizing the mathematical perfection of his performance. But what are we to make of this other side of the evening's entertainment, which lies beyond Hazlitt's discourse? Does the flesh, especially the flesh of the subjugated colonial other, itself constitute that which will ultimately call phantasmatic projection to account? Or to put the question more polemically, does Hazlitt's care of the self in this essay, like the other moments of self-consolidation in this book, rely not only on the displacement of the pain of the colonized but also on the suppression of the potential for similar pain in the body of the colonizer. Hazlitt's abhorrence of the scene of an Indian man swallowing a sword may well derive from the recognition that the performance literalized a world-historical situation, in which, as one magazine reported some months later, the conquered are blamed for the very pleasures they afford the conquerors when things go horribly wrong:

> The Indian Juggler, who astonished the town a year or two back by his dangerous feat of passing a drawn sword down his stomach, has unfortunately fallen a sacrifice to his presumption, at an exhibition in Scotland; the sword, taking a wrong direction, wounded the ventricle of the stomach, and he died almost instantaneously.[18]

Introduction

1. As Kathleen Wilson argues in *The Island Race: Englishness, Empire and Gender in the Eighteenth Century* (New York: Routledge, 2003), this lack of accommodation is evident in the compensatory proliferation of texts that depict Britain as an island: "Indeed, at the precise moment when England was *less* an island than ever before—when the reach of British trade, arms, colonies and claims transected several seas in an increasingly global grasp; when an explosion of travel literature disseminated images of tropical island paradises to force a re-thinking of Britain's own pasts; when voyaging and exploration took on new psychological significance as mental and moral as well as political and commercial activities; and when the labor, movement, commodities and cultures of foreign and colonial peoples were underwriting English prosperity and 'character'—English people were most eager to stress the ways in which their nation was unique, culturally as well as topographically" (5). These arguments for cultural exceptionalism were most often mounted on the figure of British liberty and the Constitution that sprung from it. Both were frequently affiliated with Britain's topographical status as an island.

2. Michel Foucault, "Governmentality," in *Power: Essential Works of Foucault, 1954–1984,* vol. 3, ed. James D. Faubion (New York: New Press, 1994), 219–20.

3. This is largely because Foucault himself left much of this work undone. Ann Laura Stoler, *Race and the Education of Desire: Foucault's History of Sexuality and the Colonial Order of Things* (Durham: Duke Univ. Press, 1995), is the most extensive argument for the importance of Foucault's limited work on race and the necessity of its integration with postcolonial inquiries into the metropole-colony relationship. See also David Scott, "Colonial Governmentality," *Social Text* 43 (Fall 1995): 191–220, and Anupama Rao and Steven Pierce, "Discipline and the Other Body," *interventions* 3.2 (2001): 159–68.

4. J. G. A. Pocock, "Political Thought in the English-Speaking Atlantic, 1760–1790, Part 1: The Imperial Crisis," in *The Varieties of British Political Thought, 1500–1800*, ed. J. G. A Pocock, Gordon J. Schochet, and Lois Schwoeror (Cambridge: Cambridge Univ. Press, 1993), 257.

5. Pocock, "Political Thought," 260.

6. This partiality extends to much recent work on eighteenth-century imperialism except those explicitly focused on Indian problematics. Roxann Wheeler's *The Complexion of Race: Categories of Difference in Eighteenth-Century British Culture* (Philadelphia: Univ. of Pennsylvania Press, 2000), Laura Brown's *The Ends of Empire: Women and Ideology in Early Eighteenth-Century English Literature* (Ithaca: Cornell Univ. Press, 1993), Felicity Nussbaum's *Torrid Zones: Maternity, Sexuality, and Empire in Eighteenth-Century English Narratives* (Baltimore: Johns Hopkins Univ. Press, 1995), and Srinivas Aravamudan's *Tropicopolitans: Colonialism and Agency, 1688–1804* (Durham: Duke Univ. Press, 1999) are notable exceptions in that they discuss the interrelationships between various colonial locales.

7. See J. G. A. Pocock, "1776, The Revolution against Parliament," in *Virtue, Commerce, and History: Essays on Political Thought and History, Chiefly in the Eighteenth Century* (Cambridge: Cambridge Univ. Press, 1985), 73–88.

8. The notion of the state as company has a significant history in Whig discourse. As Nicholas Phillipson argues, *Cato's Letters* demonstrates the effect commerce was having on Whig analyses of the relationship between property and the figure of the constitution when it models the relationship between a ministry and parliament on that of a board and its shareholders. See "Politeness and Politics in the Reigns of Anne and the Early Hanoverians," in *The Varieties of British Political Thought, 1500–1800*, ed. J. G. A. Pocock (Cambridge: Cambridge Univ. Press, 1993), 230, and *Cato's Letters*, no. 60, 6 January 1721.

9. Edmund Burke, 18 December 1772, *Parliamentary History*, 17:672–73. Quoted in Nancy F. Koehn, *The Power of Commerce: Economy and Governance in the First British Empire* (Ithaca: Cornell Univ. Press, 1994), 213.

10. Pocock, *Virtue, Commerce, and History*, 48.

11. I concur with Graham Burchell's sense of the complementarity of Foucault and Pocock's thinking on political subjectivity and governmental practices. See "Peculiar Interests: Civil Society and Governing 'the System of Natural Liberty,'" in *The Foucault Effect: Studies in Governmentality*, ed. Graham Burchell, Colin Gordon, and Peter Miller (Chicago: Univ. of Chicago Press, 1991), 119–50.

12. See Dror Wahrman, *Imagining the Middle Class: The Political Representation of Class in Britain, c. 1780–1840* (Cambridge: Cambridge Univ. Press, 1995). As Wahrman notes, the emergence of the social middle has been the topic of intense historical revision; see Wahrman, 1–18, for an overview of the scholarly debate.

13. See E. P. Thompson, "The Patricians and the Plebs," in *Customs in Common: Studies in Traditional Popular Culture* (New York: New Press, 1993), 16–96.

14. For an exhaustive account of the complex consolidation of middle-class

life, see Leonore Davidoff and Catherine Hall, *Family Fortunes: Men and Women of the English Middle Class, 1780–1850* (New York: Routledge, 2002).

15. See Étienne Balibar, "Foucault and Marx: The Question of Nominalism," in *Michel Foucault Philosopher,* ed. and trans. Timothy J. Armstrong (New York: Routledge, 1992), 54–56.

16. Michel Foucault, *The History of Sexuality,* vol. 1, trans. Robert Hurley (New York: Vintage, 1980).

17. I am echoing Foucault's closing remarks from "What Is Enlightenment?" in *The Foucault Reader,* ed. Paul Rabinow (New York: Pantheon, 1984): "The critical ontology of ourselves has to be considered not, certainly, as a theory, a doctrine, nor even as a permanent body of knowledge that is accumulating; it has to be conceived as an attitude, an ethos, a philosophical life in which the critique of what we are is at one and the same time the historical analysis of the limits that are imposed upon us and an experiment with the possibility of going beyond them. . . . I continue to think that this task requires work on our limits, that is, a patient labor giving form to our impatience for liberty" (50).

18. Wilson, 23.

19. *London Magazine,* February 1772, 70.

20. See Wheeler, 15, for a sense of the ubiquity of theories of degeneration that accompanied monogenetic models of human variety.

21. Ronald Meek, *Social Science and the Ignoble Savage* (Cambridge: Cambridge Univ. Press, 1976), offers the most thorough account of four-stage theory. See Wheeler, 177–92, for a convincing discussion of how four-stage theory became the dominant racial discourse in Britain in the 1780s and 1790s.

22. See Greg Dening, *Mr. Bligh's Bad Language: Passion, Power and Theatre on the Bounty* (Cambridge: Cambridge Univ. Press, 1992), 269–76.

23. For a thorough discussion of this issue, see Jane Moody, *Illegitimate Theatre in London, 1770–1840* (Cambridge: Cambridge Univ. Press, 2000), 10–33.

24. Ellen Donkin, *Getting into the Act: Women Playwrights in London, 1776–1829* (New York: Routledge, 1995), 110–19.

25. See Susan Staves, *Players' Sceptres: Fictions of Authority in the Restoration* (Lincoln: Univ. of Nebraska Press, 1979), 113. This issue has recently been reengaged by Paula Backscheider in "Endless Aversion Rooted in the Soul: Divorce in the 1690–1730 Theater," *Eighteenth Century* 37.2 (1996): 99–135. For an earlier discussion of the analogy between state and family, see Gordon Schochet, "Patriarchalism, Politics, and Mass Attitudes in Stuart England," *Historical Journal* 12 (1969): 413–31.

26. See Foucault, *The History of Sexuality,* 1:106.

27. Foucault, "Governmentality," 216.

28. See my "Scissors and Needles: Inchbald's *Wives as They Were, Maids as They Are* and the Governance of Sexual Exchange," *Theatre Journal* 51 (Summer 1999): 105–25, for a detailed discussion of this issues in relation to one of Inchbald's later plays.

29. See Judith Butler, "Imitation and Gender Insubordination," in *inside/out: Lesbian Theories, Gay Theories,* ed. Diana Fuss (New York: Routledge, 1991), 20.

30. Elizabeth Inchbald, *The Mogul Tale; or, The Descent of the Balloon,* in *The Plays of Elizabeth Inchbald,* ed. Paula Backscheider (New York: Garland Publishing, 1980), 7. All subsequent page references will be included in the text. Backscheider's edition is a collection of facsimile reprints, so the citations are also applicable to the 1788 London edition.

31. See Mita Choudhury, "Gazing at His Seraglio: Late Eighteenth-Century Women Playwrights as Orientalists," *Theatre Journal* 47 (1995): 481–502, and Betsy Bolton, *Women, Nationalism and the Romantic Stage: Theatre and Politics in Britain, 1780–1800* (Cambridge: Cambridge Univ. Press, 2001), 204–6, for contrasting views on the politics of this ballooning incident. For a helpful survey of the aesthetics of Orientalist representations of the despot, see Aravamudan, 190–229.

32. See Peter A. Tasch, *The Dramatic Cobbler: The Life and Works of Isaac Bickerstaff* (Lewisburg: Bucknell Univ. Press, 1971), 246.

33. Kristina Straub, *Sexual Suspects: Eighteenth-Players and Sexual Ideology* (Princeton: Princeton Univ. Press, 1992), 258.

34. The poems included "Love in the Suds" by Kenrick, "Sodom and Onan" by the Reverend William Jackson—otherwise known as "Doctor Viper"—and the anonymous "Leap Frog." For a full account of the scandal and the paper war that ensued from it, see Tasch, 221–42.

35. Tasch, 241.

36. For an extended discussion of Inchbald's struggle to get *The Mogul Tale* staged and the play's importance in Inchbald's transition from actress to playwright, see Donkin, 115–22.

37. Quoted in Roger Manvell, *Elizabeth Inchbald: A Biographical Study* (Lanham: Univ. Press of America, 1987), 30.

38. See Donkin, 209 n. 15, for a discussion of the Selima/Irena confusion in the printed editions.

39. See Tasch, 206. The published text of *The Mogul Tale* retains the single "b" spelling of "cobler" used by Gentleman in his review of Bickerstaff.

40. I would also contend that the translation of setting from Arabia to India is bound up in the same transition.

41. See Bolton, 204, for a discussion of the play's political resonances. The prints, all in the Department of Prints and Drawings, The British Museum, include the anonymous work, *The Political Balloon; or, The Fall of East India Stock,* of 4 December 1783 (BM 6275); the anonymous work, *The Aerostatick Stage Balloon* of 23 December 1783 (BM 6284; fig. I.1); the seventh panel of Rowlandson's *Two New Sliders for the State Magic Lanthern* of 29 December 1783 (BM 6287); *Original Air Balloon* of 29 December 1783 (BM 6288); Dent's *The East India Air Balloon* of 30 December 1783 (BM 6289); and *The Times or the Downfall of Magna Far—ta* by Carlo Cromwell Esq. (BM 6290).

42. Mary Dorothy George, *Catalogue of Political and Personal Satires*, vol. 5 (London: British Museum Press, 1935), 744.

43. See Bolton, 204, for an explication of this topical reference.

44. Benedict Anderson, *Imagined Communities: Reflections on the Origins and Spread of Nationalism* (London: Verso, 1991), 35–36. In *The Politics of Aesthetics: Nationalism, Gender, Romanticism* (Stanford: Stanford Univ. Press, 2003), Marc Redfield gives some sense of this volatility when he emphasizes that "imagination and nation [are] figures inextricable from aesthetic discourse, which is another way of saying that they are fictions possessed of great referential force and chronic referential instability" (49).

45. See Koehn, 22–23, 183–84.

46. See Koehn, 105–47.

47. For a sense of the extremity of Burke's racist rhetoric during the debate on the Quebec Bill, see his fulminations regarding race war in the West Indies as recorded in the *Morning Chronicle*, 7 May 1791.

48. See John Barrell, "An Entire Change of Performances," *Lumen* 17 (1998): 11–50, for an illuminating discussion of the theatricalization of politics and politicization of theatre in the 1790s.

49. P. J. Marshall, *The Impeachment of Warren Hastings* (London: Oxford Univ. Press, 1965), 68.

50. Anonymous, *The History of the Trial of Warren Hastings, Esq. Late Governor-General of Bengal, before the High Court of Parliament in Westminster-Hall, on an Impeachment by the Commons of Great-Britain for High Crimes and Misdemeanours* (London: Debrett, Vernor and Hood, 1796), 11.

51. The dissenting opinion of the lords who did not concur with this decision is even more blunt, for it argues that it will not only "tend to the degradation of both Houses of Parliament" but also "to subvert the fundamental principles of the constitution." *History*, 11.

52. See *History*, 8 and 91 respectively.

53. *History*, 12.

54. See Jean François Lyotard, *The Differend: Phrases in Dispute* (Minneapolis: Univ. of Minnesota Press, 1988), 164–65, for a discussion of Kant's notion of a "sign of history."

55. Michel Foucault, *"Society Must Be Defended": Lectures at the Collège de France, 1975– 76*, trans. David Macey (New York: Picador, 2003), 239–63, and Paul Gilroy, *Against Race: Imagining Political Culture beyond the Color Line* (Cambridge: Belknap Press of Harvard Univ. Press, 2000).

56. Both Catherine Hall and Charlotte Sussman have argued that "scientific racism" does not cohere until after 1838. See Hall, "William Knibb and the Constitution of the New Black Subject," in *Empire and Others: British Encounters with Indigenous Peoples*, ed. Martin Daunton and Rick Halpern (Philadelphia: Univ. of Pennsylvania Press, 1999), 303–24, and Sussman, *Consuming Anxieties: Consumer*

Protest, Gender and British Slavery, 1713–1833 (Stanford: Stanford Univ. Press, 2000), 188–205.

57. See Wheeler, 38–45, for a stimulating discussion of the methodological implication of this multiplicity of coexistent racial significations.

58. See Wilson, 11. As she states, "The idea of 'nation' once referred to a breed, stock or race; and, although the idea of nation as a political entity was gaining ascendancy, the more restrictive racial sense remained embedded in its use" (7).

59. Foucault, *Society*, 242.

60. See Karl Marx, *Capital*, vol. 1, trans. Ben Fowkes (London: Penguin, 1976), 439–54, and Michel Foucault, *Discipline and Punish* (New York: Vintage, 1979), 156.

61. Marx, 447.

62. Foucault, *Society*, 242.

63. Foucault, *Society*, 251–52.

Part I. Ethnographic Acts

1. The notion of "audience-oriented privacy" is discussed in relation to letters, diaries, and the epistolary novel in Jürgen Habermas, *The Structural Transformation of the Public Sphere: An Inquiry into a Category of Bourgeois Society*, trans. Thomas Burger and Frederick Lawrence (Cambridge: MIT Press, 1989), 48–51. The "codification of intimacy" defines Niklas Luhmann's approach to similar issues in *Love as Passion: The Codification of Intimacy*, trans. Jeremy Gaines and Doris L. Jones (Stanford: Stanford Univ. Press, 1986), 17. For significant interventions in these arguments for the late eighteenth and early nineteenth centuries, see Mary Favret, *Romantic Correspondence: Women, Politics, and the Fiction of Letters* (Cambridge: Cambridge Univ. Press, 1993); Jon P. Klancher, *The Making of English Reading Audiences, 1790–1832* (Madison: Univ. of Wisconsin Press, 1987); Paul Magnuson, *Reading Public Romanticism* (Princeton: Princeton Univ. Press, 1998); Michael Warner, *The Letters of the Republic: Publication and the Public Sphere in Eighteenth-Century America* (Cambridge: Harvard Univ. Press, 1990); Clifford Siskin, *The Work of Writing: Literature and Social Change in Britain* (Baltimore: Johns Hopkins Univ. Press, 1998); Nancy Armstrong, *Desire and Domestic Fiction: A Political History of the Novel* (New York: Oxford Univ. Press, 1987); and "Romanticism and Its Publics: A Forum Organized and Introduced by Jon Klaneher," *Studies in Romanticism* 33 (1994): 523–88.

2. Gillian Russell and Clara Tuite, "Introducing Romantic Sociability," in *Romantic Sociability: Social Networks and Literary Culture in Britain, 1770–1840* (Cambridge: Cambridge Univ. Press, 2002), 10.

3. This is most influentially articulated in Georg Simmel, "Sociability," in *The Sociology of Georg Simmel*, trans. Kurt H. Wolff (Glencoe, IL: Free Press, 1950), 40–57. See Russell and Tuite's discussion (10) of this argument. For an example of a more historically sound analysis of social interaction in the late eighteenth

century, see David S. Shields, *Civil Tongues and Polite Letters in British America* (Chapel Hill: Univ. of North Carolina Press, 1997).

4. Judith Butler, *Bodies That Matter: On the Discursive Limits of "Sex"* (New York: Routledge, 1993), 95.

5. Joseph Roach, *Cities of the Dead: Circum-Atlantic Performance* (New York: Columbia Univ. Press, 1996).

6. See Roxann Wheeler, *The Complexion of Race: Categories of Difference in Eighteenth-Century British Culture* (Philadelphia: Univ. of Pennsylvania Press, 2000). Wheeler's analysis of how certain forms of racialization achieved social purchase and how others did not is the most sustained attempt for the eighteenth century to follow Stuart Hall's crucial suggestion that racisms and racial discourses have different historical specificities in "Gramsci's Relevance for the Study of Race and Ethnicity," in *Stuart Hall: Critical Dialogues in Cultural Studies,* ed. David Morley, Kuan-Hsing Chen, and Stuart Hall (London: Routledge, 1996), 411–40.

7. Peter Clark, *British Clubs and Societies, 1580–1800: The Origins of an Associational World* (New York: Oxford Univ. Press, 2000), 192, 39, 451. My adumbration of Clark's complex argument is indebted to Russell and Tuite, 5.

8. Russell and Tuite, 5.

9. See John Dwyer, "Enlightened Spectators and Classical Moralists: Sympathetic Relations in Eighteenth-Century Scotland," in *Sociability and Society in Eighteenth-Century Scotland,* ed. John Dwyer and Richard B. Sher (Edinburgh: Mercat Press, 1993), 96–118, and "The Imperative of Sociability: Moral Culture in the Late Scottish Enlightenment," *British Journal for Eighteenth-Century Studies* 13 (1990): 169–84.

10. See Adam Smith, *The Theory of Moral Sentiments,* ed. D. D. Raphael and A. L. Macfie (Indianapolis: Liberty Press, 1982), 147. See section III.3 for a full discussion of this model of spectatorship. For the importance of this ethics for colonial legislation, see C. A. Bayly, *Imperial Meridian: The British Empire and the World, 1780–1830* (London: Longman, 1989), 151–52.

11. Kathleen Wilson, *The Island Race: Englishness, Empire and Gender in the Eighteenth Century* (New York: Routledge, 2003), 7.

12. See Wilson, 70–80, for a discussion of the deformation and adequation of Cook's voyages to existing theories of the progress of nations.

13. For strikingly different examples of how to engage with this issue, see Johannes Fabian, *Time and the Other: How Anthropology Makes It Object* (New York: Columbia Univ. Press, 1983); P. J. Marshall and Glyndwr Williams, *The Great Map of Mankind: British Perceptions of the World in the Age of Enlightenment* (London: J. M. Dent, 1982).

14. For a succinct account of these theories, see Sudipta Sen, *Distant Sovereignty: National Imperialism and the Origins of British India* (New York: Routledge, 2002), 120–21. Wheeler, 177–92, has argued for the centrality of Scottish Enlightenment thinking on human variety. See Ronald Meek, *Social Science and the Ignoble Savage* (Cambridge: Cambridge Univ. Press, 1976) not only for the most

exhaustive discussion of Scottish four-stages theory, but also for his persuasive argument that four-stages theory became the orthodox view of human variety in the 1780s and 1790s (195). Among the most influential attempts to categorize human societies and beings in the eighteenth century were George Louis Leclerc, comte de Buffon, *Natural History: General and Particular* (1749), trans. William Smellie, vol. 3 (London: T. Cadell and W. Davies, 1812); Oliver Goldsmith, "A Comparative View of the Races and Nations" (1760), in *Collected Works of Oliver Goldsmith*, ed. Arthur Friedman (Oxford: Oxford Univ. Press, 1966), 3:66–71; David Hume, "Of National Characters," in *Essays Moral, Political and Literary*, ed. Eugene F. Miller (Indianapolis: Liberty Classics, 1985), 197–215; Henry Home, Lord Kames, *Sketches of the History of Man* (London: W. Strahan and T. Cadell, 1778); Johann Friedrich Blumenbach, *On the Natural Variety of Mankind* (1775), in *The Anthropological Treatises of Johann Friedrich Blumenbach*, trans. and ed. Thomas Bendyshe (Boston: Milford House, 1973), 145–276. In addition to these canonical texts, there are myriad travel accounts, natural histories, and treatises that attempt to rationalize national and racial distinction.

15. See Arthur O. Lovejoy, *The Great Chain of Being* (Cambridge: Harvard Univ. Press, 1966), 244, and Richard H. Popkin, "The Philosophical Bases of Modern Racism," in *Philosophy and the Civilizing Arts: Essays Presented to Herbert W. Schneider,* ed. Craig Walton and John P. Anton (Athens: Ohio Univ. Press, 1974), 132.

16. Sen, 13–14.

17. Thomas Pownall, *The Right, Interest, and Duty of the State as Concerned in the Affairs of the East Indies* (London: S. Bladdon, 1773), 44–45. Quoted in Sen, 25.

18. See Sen's account of the veiling of British power behind the nominal power of the Moghul emperor and the subsequent unraveling of this relationship, xi–xiii.

19. Sen, 101.

20. Sen, 104.

21. Uday Singh Mehta, *Liberalism and Empire: A Study in Nineteenth Century British Liberal Thought* (Chicago: Univ. of Chicago Press, 1999), 159.

22. Sen, 13.

23. See, for example, William Dalrymple, *White Mughals: Love and Betrayal in Eighteenth-Century India* (London: Harper Collins, 2003); Sen, 85–149; L. M. Collingham, *Imperial Bodies: The Physical Experience of the Raj, 1800–1947* (Cambridge: Polity, 2001), 13–49; Beth Fowkes Tobin, *Picturing Imperial Power: Colonial Subjects in Eighteenth-Century British Painting* (Durham: Duke Univ. Press, 1999), 110–38; Kenneth Ballhatchet, *Race, Sex and Class under the Raj: Imperial Attitudes and Policies and Their Critics, 1793–1905* (New York: St. Martin's Press, 1980).

24. The Permanent Settlement describes a series of experiments in revenue acquisition that effectively attempted to reform rents according to standardized notions of land tenure endemic to Britain. As Sen summarizes, "Ushered in during the period of Lord Cornwallis as governor-general, this was an effort to improve the collection of land revenue by creating a society of landed estates in the Ben-

gal countryside. Historians have seen this decision, which included an appeal to physiocracy, as instrumental in severing the feudal ties of Indian society in order to inculcate a new sense of enterprise in landed property" (94). Ranajit Guha's analysis of this incursion on Indian society emphasizes the way in which the English regard for the "sanctity of private property" was literally and phantasmatically exported to Bengal with catastrophic effects. See Guha, *A Rule of Property for Bengal: An Essay on the Idea of Permanent Settlement* (Durham: Duke Univ. Press, 1996).

25. John Brewer, *Sinews of Power* (New York: Alfred A. Knopf, 1989), 199.

26. Kristina Straub, *Sexual Suspects: Eighteenth-Century Players and Sexual Ideology* (Princeton: Princeton Univ. Press, 1992).

27. Foucault, "Governmentality," in *Power: Essential Works of Foucault, 1954–1984*, ed. James D. Faubion, vol. 3 (New York: New Press, 1994), 208.

Chapter 1. Empire's Vicious Expenses

1. See Nancy F. Koehn, *The Power of Commerce: Economy and Governance in the First British Empire* (Ithaca: Cornell Univ. Press, 1994), for an in-depth analysis of this problem.

2. Edmund Burke, Commons debate, 27 February 1769. Quoted in Koehn, 205.

3. As Koehn notes, 134–35, Chatham, Charles Townshend, and George III all subscribed to this ambitious solution to the American problem.

4. For an example of the former position, see Thomas Pownall, *The Right, Interest, and Duty, of the State, as Concerned in the Affairs of the East Indies* (London, 1773), 5–6. The latter concern was expressed frequently in the papers. Koehn's citation of Grenville's remarks before Parliament on 28 February 1769 are typical of this financial anxiety: "What condition will you be in, when a war [in India] breaks out! [Some] have seen East India stock fall before, but never from such a height to nothing. This [stock] is an object of 11 millions of money. If, in the commencement of that war, the whole 11 million should be blown into the air at once—if that misfortune should befall you—do you believe that the City of London would lose 11 million without threatening the [entire stock market] at once. This is, perhaps, the last stake of our finances" (203).

5. Koehn, 22–23, 182–83, makes precisely this point with regard to the popularity of Gibbon's *Decline and Fall of the Roman Empire.*

6. See Andrew Jackson O'Shaughnessy, *An Empire Divided: The American Revolution and the British Caribbean* (Philadelphia: Univ. of Pennsylvania Press, 2000), for a discussion of the rupture in the Atlantic empire.

7. Koehn, 111, uses the rhetoric of trauma.

8. See, for example, the *London Evening Post,* 20 and 25 August 1772; the stories literally flow into one another.

9. Koehn, 208–9.

10. For a brief account of this complex series of events and of the scholarly

debate surrounding them, see P. J. Marshall, "The British in Asia: Trade to Dominion, 1700–65," in *The Oxford History of the British Empire,* vol. 2, *The Eighteenth Century,* ed. P. J. Marshall (Oxford: Oxford Univ. Press, 1998), 487–507.

11. Marshall, 506.

12. For an exhaustive account of the place of the East India Company in eighteenth-century British politics, see Dame Lucy Sutherland, *East India Company in Eighteenth-Century Politics* (Oxford: Oxford Univ. Press, 1952).

13. See William Bolts, *Considerations on Indian Affairs, Particularly Respecting the Present State of Bengal and Its Dependencies,* and Alexander Dow, *The History of Hindostan,* 3 vols. (London: S. A. Bechert and P. A. De Hontd, 1768–72). Excerpts from Bolts's book appeared in the *London Magazine,* May 1772, under the title "The Nature and Defects of the Constitution of the East India Company" and in the *London Evening Post* for 2 April 1772.

14. Koehn, 110–11.

15. See Koehn, 212–14, for a succinct account of Burke and the Rockingham Whigs' constitutional objections to the act.

16. See H. V. Bowen, "British India, 1765–1813: The Metropolitan Context," in *The Oxford History of the British Empire,* vol. 2, *The Eighteenth Century,* ed. P. J. Marshall (Oxford: Oxford Univ. Press, 1998), 537–41, for a succinct account of the genesis and effect of the Regulating Act. See also Koehn, 200–17, for an illuminating discussion of the relationship between economic and constitutional issues in the Regulating Act.

17. The speech was widely excerpted in the popular press.

18. *Gazetteer and New Daily Advertiser,* 4 April 1772.

19. *Gazetteer and New Daily Advertiser,* 4 April 1772.

20. The Secret Committee was composed entirely of parliamentarians, and unlike the Select Committee none of its members had direct interests in the East India Company. For a precise discussion of the two committees' differing mandates, see H. V. Bowen, *Revenue and Reform: The Indian Problem in British Politics, 1757–1773* (Cambridge: Cambridge Univ. Press, 1991), 134–36 and143–47.

21. "To Mann, 9 April 1772," in *Horace Walpole's Correspondence with Sir Horace Mann,* ed. W. S. Lewis, Warren Hunting Smith, and George L. Lam, vol. 7 (New Haven: Yale Univ. Press, 1967), 400.

22. See Susan Staves, "A Few Kind Words for the Fop," *Studies in English Literature, 1500–1900* 22.3 (Summer 1982): 413–28.

23. This print was one a series, *Macaronies, Characters, Caricatures,* published by Darly in 1772; see also fig. 1.2. For an illuminating discussion of these prints, see Shearer West, "The Darly Macaroni Prints and the Politics of Private Man," *Eighteenth-Century Life* 25.2 (2001): 170–82.

24. *London Evening Post,* 27 August 1772.

25. For a discussion of the wide-ranging impact of Fordyce's activities and of the decisiveness of the ensuing financial collapse on colonial policy, see Bowen, *Revenue,* 122–30. The classical account of the collapse of the Ayr Bank is, of course,

provided by Adam Smith in book 2 of *The Wealth of Nations* (London: Penguin, 1986), 381–429.

26. See J. H. Clapham, *The Bank of England, A History* (Cambridge: Cambridge Univ. Press, 1945), 245. See Donna Andrew and Randall McGowen, *The Perreaus and Mrs. Rudd: Love and Betrayal in 18th Century London* (Berkeley: Univ. of California Press, 2001), 154–57, for a discussion of the anti-Jewish and anti-Scots sentiments precipitated by the crash.

27. See Koehn, 209, and Bowen, *Revenue,* 127–30.

28. *Gentleman's Magazine* 42 (June 1772): 293.

29. Andrew and McGowen, 138–39.

30. *Gentleman's Magazine* 42 (May 1772): 213.

31. *London Chronicle,* 9 July 1772.

32. Fordyce was speculating on British attempts to establish a base in the Falklands and hence on an entrance into commerce in the Pacific. These speculations came to naught when Britain was forced to concede the Falklands as one of the conditions for ending the Anglo-Spanish conflict over the islands in 1770–71. See Andrew and McGowan, 148, and Glyndwr Williams, "The Pacific: Exploration and Exploitation," in *The Oxford History of the British Empire,* vol. 2, *The Eighteenth Century,* ed. P. J. Marshall (Oxford: Oxford Univ. Press, 1998), 561.

33. "To Mann, 1 July 1772," in *Horace Walpole's Correspondence,* 7:418–19.

34. *Gentleman's Magazine* 42 (July 1772): 311.

35. W. K. Wimsatt, "Foote and a Friend of Boswell's: A Note on *The Nabob,*" *Modern Language Notes* 57.5 (May 1942): 326–27.

36. *Morning Chronicle,* 24 June 1772.

37. See, for example, Renu Juneja, "The Native and the Nabob: Representations of the Indian Experience in Eighteenth-Century English Literature," *Journal of Commonwealth Literature* 27.1 (1992): 183–98, and Jyotsna G. Singh, *Colonial Narratives/Cultural Dialogues* (New York: Routledge, 1996), 60–76.

38. Samuel Foote, *The Nabob* (London: T. Cadell, 1778), 7–9. All references are cited in the text hereafter.

39. See Mary Megie Belden, *The Dramatic Work of Samuel Foote* (New Haven: Yale Univ. Press, 1929), 148–50, for a discussion of this joke.

40. See E. J. Hobsbawm, *The Invention of Tradition* (Cambridge: Cambridge Univ. Press, 1992), for a discussion of this phrase.

41. Simon Trefman, *Sam. Foote, Comedian, 1720–1777* (New York: New York Univ. Press, 1971), recognizes this structural feature of the play, but argues that the story of the marriage proposal is effectively disconnected from "the various swindles, machinations, and social climbing efforts of Sir Matthew Mite, and it is in these scenes that we find the farcical humour and topical satire that were celebrated by Foote's audience" (204). I would argue that the play's satirical force lies precisely in how one reads the bracketing effect of act 1, scene 1 and act 3, scene 3.

42. *London Magazine,* July 1772, 309.

43. According to Koehn, 109, political elites were increasingly courting commercial or moneyed interest in the late 1760s and early 1770s.

44. See the *Gazetteer*, 1 July 1772; *London Evening Post*, 30 June 1772; and *London Chronicle*, 2 July 1772.

45. This latter group included Rockingham Whigs and most notably Edmund Burke. See Koehn, 212–13.

46. *London Magazine*, July 1772, 308.

47. See Kristina Straub, *Sexual Suspects: Eighteenth-Century Players and Sexual Ideology* (Princeton: Princeton Univ. Press, 1992), 47–68, for an extensive discussion of Cibber and Garrick's differing deployments of the fop.

48. See Bowen, *Revenue*, 122–23, and Koehn, 206.

49. See L. M. Collingham, *Imperial Bodies: The Physical Experience of the Raj, c. 1800– 1947* (Cambridge: Polity Press, 2001), 34–35, for a discussion of this fear of creolization.

50. This parallel has significant implications because it ties Mite's and Match'em's corruption of femininity to a similar corruption of Sir John's masculinity. In both cases, financial embarrassments are the precursors to gender impropriety. This helps to explain why Foote constructs the Oldham household as one that is dominated by the quasi-Amazonian Lady Oldham.

Chapter 2. "As Much as Science Can Approach Barbarity"

1. *Omai; or, A Trip round the World* was first performed on 20 December 1785 under Harris's management at Covent Garden. The pantomime was largely designed and planned by Philippe Jacques de Loutherbourg with songs written by John O'Keefe and music by William Shields. Because *Omai* was significantly altered in almost every subsequent production, it is necessary to consult John O'Keefe, *Songs for the New Pantomime of Omai*, Larpent Collection, MS 713, Huntington Library, San Marino, California; the descriptions of the pantomime in the newspapers; and the print version of airs entitled *A Short Account of the New Pantomime called Omai; or, A Trip round the World* of 1785 to get a full sense of the production. In general, the detailed descriptions of the pantomime are far more informative than the skeletal account offered in the print version or in the Larpent text. In general, I rely on the published text and on Larpent for spoken dialogue and libretto, and on the newspapers for both the mechanical and improvised action. Of the newspaper sources, I use the December 1785 edition of the *Town and Country* most frequently because it is the most detailed. An almost identical account is available in the *Universal Magazine* for December 1785.

2. Greg Dening, *Mr. Bligh's Bad Language* (Cambridge: Cambridge Univ. Press, 1992), 271.

3. Johannes Fabian, *Time and the Other: How Anthropology Makes Its Object* (New York: Columbia Univ. Press, 1983), 11–12.

4. Kathleen Wilson, *The Island Race: Englishness, Empire and Gender in the Eighteenth Century* (New York: Routledge, 2003), 72–73. See Wilson, 70–80, for a review of the variations in these accounts.

5. *London Chronicle,* 22 December 1785.

6. *European Magazine and London Review,* December 1785.

7. See Rudiger Joppien, "Philippe Jacques de Loutherbourg's Pantomime 'Omai, or, a Trip round the World' and the Artists of Captain Cook's Voyages," in *The British Museum Yearbook: Captain Cook and the South Pacific,* ed. T. C. Mitchell, vol. 3 (London: British Museum Publications, 1975), 81–137, and Ralph G. Allen, "De Loutherbourg and Captain Cook," *Theatre Research/Recherches Theatrales* 4.3 (1962): 195–213.

8. For recent analyses of the role played by narratives of Pacific exploration in metropolitan European culture, see Jonathan Lamb, *Preserving the Self in the South Seas* (Chicago: Univ. of Chicago Press, 2001); Alex Calder, Jonathan Lamb, and Bridget Orr, *Voyages and Beaches: Pacific Encounters, 1769–1840* (Honolulu: Univ. of Hawai'i Press, 1999); and Pamela Cheek, *Enlightenment Globalization and the Placing of Sex* (Stanford: Stanford Univ. Press, 2003), 123–63.

9. See Gananath Obeyesekere, *The Apotheosis of Captain Cook: European Mythmaking in the Pacific* (Princeton: Princeton Univ. Press, 1992), and Marshall Salins, *How "Natives" Think: About Captain Cook, for Example* (Chicago: Univ. of Chicago Press, 1996), for a debate on the European deification of Cook. The first edition of Hawkesworth's epic of British exploration was published under the title *An Account of the Voyages Undertaken by the Order of His Present Majesty for Making Discoveries in the Southern Hemisphere* (London, 1773).

10. See Greg Dening, *Performances* (Chicago: Univ. of Chicago Press, 1996), 147–67, for a detailed discussion of the European treatments of Pūrea. Throughout this chapter I use the European spelling of her name, Oberea, when I am referring to the character in European representations.

11. See Hawkesworth, *Account* 2:108 and 128 respectively, for the source scenes. For some sense of the complexity of interpreting these scenes, see Nicholas Thomas's discussion of public sex acts in *Cook: The Extraordinary Voyages of Captain James Cook* (Toronto: Penguin, 2003), 154–59.

12. Anonymous, "An Epistle from Mr. Banks, Voyager, Monster-Hunter, and Amoroso, to Oberea, Queen of Otaheite" (London, 1773), 12–13, lines 136–45.

13. For a discussion of this poem and the scene it is based on, see Dening, 154–55.

14. Anonymous, "An Epistle from Mr. Banks, 13, lines 146–57.

15. I use Omai when referring to European representations and Mai when referring to the historical person.

16. See E. H. McCormick, *Omai: Pacific Envoy* (Auckland: Auckland Univ. Press, 1977), for a detailed history of Mai's life, travels, and reception in England. McCormick's text, 73–93, also offers an insightful discussion on the critiques of Hawksworth's *Account* and of the cycle of satires on Joseph Banks and Pūrea.

17. Joppien, 82.

18. *London Chronicle,* 6 August 1774.

19. *London Chronicle,* 3 September 1774.

20. *London Chronicle,* 27 September 1774.

21. Hawkesworth, 206–9. For illuminating discussions of the Arioi, see Alfred Gell, *Wrapping in Images: Tattooing and Polynesia* (Oxford: Clarendon Press, 1993), 146–62, and Douglas Oliver, *Ancient Tahitian Society,* vol. 2 (Honolulu: Univ. of Hawai'i Press, 1974), 913–64.

22. Hawkesworth, 207.

23. *London Chronicle,* 27 September 1774.

24. This equation extends to other ethnically distinct populations as well. The satirical insinuations of sexual desire between the Begams of Oude and Edmund Burke during the trial of Warren Hastings are a notable case in point.

25. An advertisement in the *Public Advertiser,* 24 December 1785, for an abridged account of Cook's voyages for children argues that the product is a natural outgrowth of the pedagogical effect of Loutherbourg's pantomime.

26. See Joppien, 89–90, for a discussion of the complex problem of attribution surrounding this image. The *Morning Post,* 21 December 1785, indicates that the image was designed by Loutherbourg and "generously executed" by Mr. Peters.

27. "Account of the New Pantomime, Omai," *Town and Country Magazine,* December 1785, 614. This account of the pantomime is the most comprehensive; however, it was compiled prior to the excision of D'Elpini's airs in the second part and the introduction of Edwin's songs.

28. *Public Advertiser,* 24 December 1785.

29. *Public Advertiser,* 24 December 1785.

30. *Times,* 22 December 1785.

31. Larpent 713. The air is not presented in the printed text but is widely circulated in the press. See, for example, *Times,* 22 December 1785.

32. Cook records his own meetings with Pūrea in his journal and was witness to many of the sexual scenes described in Hawkesworth. See *The Journals of Captain Cook,* ed. Philip Edwards (New York: Penguin, 1999), 47–65, for Cook's account of Tahiti.

33. Larpent 713.

34. Wilson, 69.

35. Ann Laura Stoler, *Race and the Education of Desire: Foucault's History of Sexuality and the Colonial Order of Things* (Durham: Duke Univ. Press, 1995), 93.

36. See Michel Foucault, *"Society Must Be Defended": Lectures at the Collège de France, 1975–76,* trans. David Macey (New York: Picador, 2003), 253–63.

37. Sudipta Sen, *Distant Sovereignty: National Imperialism and Origins of British India* (New York: Routledge, 2002), 2.

38. Foucault, 252.

39. *Morning Post,* 26 December 1785.

40. When Richard Altick discusses *Omai* in *The Shows of London* (Cambridge:

Belknap Press of Harvard Univ. Press, 1978), 120–21, he focuses on the sheer visual excess of the production—one scene depicting the Kamchatkan coast presents moving ice floes with forty-two separate and simultaneously moving flats—and on the lighting technology for which Loutherbourg was famous.

41. Joppien gives an exhaustive account of the correlations.

42. *Morning Post,* 22 December 1785.

43. See Roxann Wheeler, *The Complexion of Race: Categories of Difference in Eighteenth-Century British Culture* (Philadelphia: Univ. of Pennsylvania Press, 2000), 17–21.

44. See Dening, 272, for an illuminating discussion regarding the fictionalization of historical Pacific islanders.

45. *Town and Country Magazine,* December 1785.

46. *Town and Country Magazine,* December 1785.

47. Adrienne L. Kaeppler, "Tracing the History of Hawaiian Cook Voyage Artefacts in the Museum of Mankind," in *Captain Cook and the South Pacific,* ed. T. C. Mitchell (London: British Museum Publications, 1979), 167–83, especially 167–76. See also Nicholas Thomas, "Licensed Curiosity: Cook's Pacific Voyages," in *The Cultures of Collecting,* ed. John Elsner and Roger Cardinal (Cambridge: Harvard Univ. Press, 1994), 116–36.

48. *Morning Chronicle,* 22 December 1785.

49. *Morning Chronicle,* 23 December 1785.

50. *Morning Chronicle,* 24 December 1785.

51. *A Short Account of the New Pantomime Called Omai; or, A Trip round the World,* i.

52. I am indebted to Jeffrey Cox, who in response to an oral version of this chapter generously offered these observations regarding the structure of the pantomime.

53. *Morning Chronicle,* 29 December 29 1785.

54. *Times,* 26 December 1785.

55. *Town and Country Magazine,* December 1785.

56. *Morning Post,* 21 December 1785.

57. See Robert Nicole's informative chapter on Bougainville in his *The Word, the Pen, and the Pistol: Literature and Power in Tahiti* (Albany: SUNY Press, 2001), 35–63, for discussions of the attribution of fantasies of sexual license and for a careful account of the function of clothing in the narrative.

58. See Marcel Hénaff's introduction to Diderot's *Supplement to Bougainville's Voyage* entitled "Supplement to Diderot's Dream," in *The Libertine Reader* (New York: Zone Books, 1997), 52–75, for a thorough account of the political and philosophical parameters of Diderot's libertinism.

59. In eighteenth-century harlequinade, Harlequin conventionally carries a device of leather and wood, which is used much like a magic wand to effect sudden transformations of costumes or props.

60. *London Chronicle,* 11 August 1774.

61. As Wilson notes, Johann Reinhold Forster's *Observations Made during a Voyage round the World* (London, 1778), 73, classified various "nations" in the South Pacific into two "races."

62. In *Harlequin Britain: Pantomime and Entertainment, 1690–1760* (Baltimore: Johns Hopkins Univ. Press, 2004), John O'Brien has recently argued that by the end of the eighteenth century "African identity was clearly available as a referent for Harlequin's black mask" (136). These remarks resonate with reports of Omai's ostensible "negritude."

63. This is in keeping with Lee Wallace's recent analysis in *Sexual Encounters: Pacific Texts, Modern Sexualities* (Ithaca: Cornell Univ. Press, 2003), which demonstrates that much of the European representation of Pacific encounters downplays the Pacific as a zone of homoerotic fantasy or refigures it as a space of heterosexual freedom.

64. See Kristina Straub, *Sexual Suspects: Eighteenth-Century Players and Sexual Ideology* (Princeton: Princeton Univ. Press, 1992), 47–68, for a detailed history of the vicissitudes of the fop figure during this period.

65. *Town and Country,* December 1785, 613.

66. *Town and Country,* December 1785, 614.

67. See Nicholas Thomas, *Entangled Objects: Exchange, Material Culture, and Colonialism in the Pacific* (Cambridge: Harvard Univ. Press, 1991), for a discussion of the complex interpretation of value in these exchanges.

68. *A Short Account of the New Pantomime Called Omai; or, A Trip round the World,* 12.

69. *Town and Country,* December 1785, 612.

70. Larpent 713.

71. See Straub, 61, for a discussion of Daffodil in Garrick's *The Male Coquette.*

72. Larpent 713.

73. Larpent 713.

74. *Times,* 29 December 1785.

75. *Morning Chronicle,* 23 December 1785. The text of the song is here published before its initial performance as a kind of a teaser. The song itself is incorporated into the final printed version of the pantomime (16).

76. *Times,* 9 January 1786.

Part II. Women and the Trials of Imperial Masculinity

1. Both the impeachment and Lady Wallace's visit are reported in the *Times,* 5 March 1788.

2. *Times,* 12 March 1788.

3. See my introduction to *The Ton* on the *British Women Playwrights around 1800* website: http://www.etang.umontreal.ca/bnp1800/essays/oquinn_ton_intro .html.

4. One could make a similar argument regarding the trial of the Duchess of Kingston for bigamy.

5. See Anne K. Mellor, *Mothers of the Nation: Women's Political Writing in England, 1780–1830* (Bloomington: Indiana Univ. Press, 2000).

6. Dror Wahrman, "The English Problem of Identity in the American Revolution," *American Historical Review* 106.4 (October 2001): 1236–62. See also James E. Bradley, *Popular Politics and the American Revolution in England: Petitions, the Crown, and Public Opinion* (Macon: Univ. of Georgia Press, 1986); Linda Colley, *Britons: Forging the Nation, 1707–1837* (New Haven: Yale Univ. Press, 1992); Jonathan C. D. Clark, *The Language of Liberty, 1660–1832: Political Discourse and Social Dynamics in the Anglo-American World* (Cambridge: Cambridge Univ. Press, 1994); Peter N. Miller, *Defining the Common Good: Empire, Religion and Philosophy in Eighteenth-Century Britain* (Cambridge: Cambridge Univ. Press, 1994); Kathleen Wilson, *The Sense of the People: Politics, Culture and Imperialism in England, 1715–1785* (Cambridge: Cambridge Univ. Press, 1995); Eliga H. Gould, *The Persistence of Empire: British Political Culture in the Age of the American Revolution* (Chapel Hill: Univ. of North Carolina Press, 2000); and J. G. A. Pocock, *Virtue, Commerce and History: Essays on Political Thought and History, Chiefly in the Eighteenth Century* (Cambridge: Cambridge Univ. Press, 1985), and "Political Thought in the English-Speaking Atlantic, 1760–1790: (i) The Imperial Crisis," in *The Varieties of British Political Thought, 1500–1800*, ed. J. G. A. Pocock, Gordon J. Schochet, and Lois Schwoeror (Cambridge: Cambridge Univ. Press, 1993), 246–82.

7. Nancy F. Koehn, *The Power of Commerce: Economy and Governance in the First British Empire* (Ithaca: Cornell Univ. Press, 1994), 107.

8. See, for example, James Sayers's *A Reverie of Prince Demetrius Cantemir, Ospidar of Moldavia* (BM 7307; fig. 4.14) or *The Princess's Bow Alias the Bow Begum* (BM 7309; fig. 4.15). For Wollstonecraft's attack on Burke's deployment of these tropes, see *The Vindications of the Rights of Men in a Letter to the Right Honourable Edmund Burke*, ed. David L. Macdonald and Kathleen Scherf (Peterborough: Broadview Press, 1997). Perhaps the most incisive attack on Burke's sexualization of foreign affairs can be found in Hannah Cowley's *A Day in Turkey* (London: G. G. J. and J. Robinson, 1792), 86. See my "Hannah Cowley's *A Day in Turkey* and the Political Efficacy of Charles James Fox," *European Romantic Review* 14 (2003): 18–20, for a discussion of this issue.

9. Fox makes precisely this insinuation in his famous response to Burke's attack during the debate on the Quebec Bill on 6 May 1791. See *Morning Chronicle*, 7 May 1791.

10. Saree Makdisi is trenchant on this point. See *Romantic Imperialism* (Cambridge: Cambridge Univ. Press, 1998), 9.

11. The key exception here is H. V. Bowen, *Revenue and Reform: The Indian Problem in British Politics, 1757–1773* (Cambridge: Cambridge Univ. Press, 1991). For an important discussion of the South Sea Bubble's impact on British literary culture, see Patrick Brantlinger, *Fictions of State* (Ithaca: Cornell Univ. Press, 1996).

12. See Linda Colley, *Captives* (New York: Pantheon, 2002), 269–95, and Kate Teltscher, *India Inscribed: European and British Writing on India, 1600–1800* (Delhi: Oxford Univ. Press, 1995), 229–46.

13. See Koehn, 105–47, 185–217, for illuminating discussions of the interrelationship between American and Indian political and economic policy in the 1760s and 1770s.

14. Colley makes a similar argument with regard to narratives of captivity in the eighteenth century in *Captives,* 15–17.

15. H. V. Bowen, "A Question of Sovereignty? The Bengal Land Revenue Issue, 1765–7," *Journal of Imperial and Commonwealth History* 16 (1988): 155–76, and Sudipta Sen, *Distant Sovereignty: National Imperialism and Origins of British India* (New York: Routledge, 2002), 20.

16. Koehn, 147.

17. Sen, 20.

18. Edmund Burke, 18 December 1772, *Parliamentary History,* 17:671. Quoted in Koehn, 213. For an illuminating discussion of the feminization of India in late eighteenth-century novelistic discourse, see Balachandra Rajan, *Under Western Eyes: India from Milton to Macaulay* (Durham: Duke Univ. Press, 1999), 118–38.

19. See Ranajit Guha, *A Rule of Property for Bengal: An Essay on the Idea of Permanent Settlement* (Durham: Duke Univ. Press, 1996), for an extended discussion of this issue, and Nicholas B. Dirks, *Colonialism and the Making of Modern India* (Princeton: Princeton Univ. Press, 2001), 109–16, for a succinct account of the Permanent Settlement.

Chapter 3. Inchbald's Indies

1. Major John Taylor, *Travels from England to India, in the Year 1789,* 2 vols. (London, 1799), 1:21–22. Taylor's text is quoted in Felicity Nussbaum's *Torrid Zones: Maternity, Sexuality, and Empire in Eighteenth-Century English Narratives* (Baltimore: Johns Hopkins Univ. Press, 1995), 17.

2. All of Inchbald's published plays are included in *The Plays of Elizabeth Inchbald,* ed. Paula R. Backscheider (New York: Garland Publishing, 1980), a collection of facsimile reprints of the 1797 London edition.

3. This was a significant reversal of Burke's earlier resistance to the Regulating Act's incursion on property. As with so many debates on imperial governance during this period, Burke found himself arguing against a position that he had formerly held.

4. Nicholas K. Robinson, *Edmund Burke: A Life in Caricature* (New Haven: Yale Univ. Press, 1996), 53.

5. See Susan Staves, "The Construction of the Public Interest in the Debates over Fox's India Bills," in *The Intersections of the Public and Private Spheres in Early*

Modern England, ed. Paula Backscheider and Timothy Dystal (London: Frank Cass, 1996), 175–98, for a detailed account of the bill's reception.

6. T. Orde to Lord Shelburne, 16 December 1783, Bowood MSS, Bodleian Library, Oxford. Quoted in Leslie G. Mitchell, *Charles James Fox* (London: Oxford Univ. Press, 1992), 65.

7. Orde was a Shelburnite who had a long-standing antipathy to Fox's leadership of the party.

8. Bridget Orr, *Empire on the English Stage, 1660–1714* (Cambridge: Cambridge Univ. Press, 2001), 195.

9. For a detailed discussion of the rumors in the print media about a relationship between Fox and the duchess, see Amanda Foreman, *Georgiana, Duchess of Devonshire* (New York: Harper Collins, 1999), 130.

10. As Robinson notes, Fox called this print the most effective blow at the India Bill (53).

11. See John Brewer, *Party Ideology and Popular Politics at the Accession of George III* (Cambridge: Cambridge Univ. Press, 1976), 129–34, for an analysis of the problem faced by political parties during the early part of George III's reign.

12. For an extended account of this influence, see F. T. H. Fletcher, *Montesquieu and English Politics, 1750–1800* (London: Edwin Arnold, 1939).

13. *The Parliamentary History of England, from the Earliest Period to the Year 1803,* vol. 23 (London: Hansard, 1814), 136. The text here is reproduced verbatim from the *Morning Chronicle,* 16 December 1783. The newspaper account would have been the primary source for political observers, but for reasons of convenience I henceforth provide page references to *The Parliamentary History* directly in the body of the text.

14. Montesquieu, *The Spirit of the Laws,* trans. Anne M. Cohler, Basia Carolyn Miller, and Harold Samuel Stone (Cambridge: Cambridge Univ. Press, 1989), 18. All subsequent references to this work are included parenthetically in the text.

15. Louis Althusser, *Montesquieu, Rousseau, Marx,* trans. Ben Brewster (London: Verso, 1982), 88. All subsequent references to this text are presented parenthetically in the text.

16. As Nancy F. Koehn argues, the Whig elite was actively cultivating relations with moneyed and commercial interests all through the decade immediately following the end of the Seven Years' War. See *The Power of Commerce: Economy and Government in the First British Empire* (Ithaca: Cornell Univ. Press, 1994), 109.

17. The Duke of Portland was the primary spokesperson for the coalition in the House of Lords.

18. Foreman, 138. The letter is from Lord Frederick Cavendish to LS and GD, December 1783, Althorp F121, British Library, London.

19. Alain Grosrichard, *The Sultan's Court: European Fantasies of the East,* trans. Liz Heron (London: Verso, 1998), 56.

20. Although the cited passage does not correspond verbatim to any known

newspaper publication, it is very similar to much of the coverage of the letter. This is most likely due to the way parliamentary debate was recorded at this time. The recorder would most likely have been working from memory.

21. *Morning Chronicle,* 18 December 1783.

22. *Morning Chronicle,* 18 December 1783.

23. Grosrichard, 73.

24. Althusser, 84–85.

25. Grosrichard, 73.

26. See Edmund Burke, "Appeal from the New to the Old Whigs," in *The Writings and Speeches of Edmund Burke,* vol. 4 (Toronto: George Morang, 1901), 211–12.

27. See Althusser, 96–106, for an elaboration of this insight.

28. See F. T. H. Fletcher, *Montesquieu and English Politics* (London: Edwin Arnold, 1939), 214–27, for a detailed account of how Burke's position on colonial governance in India is thoroughly imbued with Montesquieu's view of conquest, monarchy, and despotism.

29. Montesquieu, 119.

30. As Katherine Green has argued in "'You Should be My Master': Imperial Recognition Politics in Elizabeth Inchbald's *Such Things Are,*" *Clio* 27.3 (1998): 397–99, Inchbald's knowledge of Sumatra was most likely gleaned from William Marsden's *The History of Sumatra, Containing an Account of the Government, Laws, Customs, and Manner of the Native Inhabitants, with a Description of the Natural Productions, and a Relation of the Ancient Political State of that Island* (London, 1783; reprint, New York: Oxford Univ. Press, 1966) or from extracts published in the *Annual Register* 1783.

31. Elizabeth Inchbald, *Such Things Are* (London: Robinson, 1788), 2. All references to this play are included parenthetically in the text. The manuscript of *Such Things Are* and the submission text feature prominently in the following argument and are referred to accordingly.

32. Montesquieu, 28.

33. See Green, 407, and Betsy Bolton, *Women, Nationalism and the Romantic Stage: Theatre and Politics in Britain, 1780–1800* (Cambridge: Cambridge Univ. Press, 2001), 204–6.

34. Jane Moody, "Romantic Theatre, Contemporary Legacies (Unpublished essay), 7.

35. *Such Things Are* 1.1, manuscript, Add 27, 575, British Library, London.

36. Elizabeth Inchbald, *Such Things Are,* Larpent Collection, MS 761, Huntington Library, San Marino, California, and manuscript Add 27, 575, British Library.

37. See Bolton, 211–12. In the 1808 printing of the play, Inchbald asserts that Twineall is a caricature of Lord Chesterfield. Bolton recognizes that Twineall and Flint have a great deal in common, and I believe that both figures can also be associated with Lord Temple. The suppression of the Flint/Chesterfield connection in Inchbald's preface and the even more subterranean connection between

both figures and Temple may be a function of the political danger of such an insinuation, for Twineall is laughable whereas Flint is manifestly dangerous.

38. One could read this a prophetic account of the fate of the London Corresponding Society under Pitt's administration.

39. Italicized material appears in the manuscript and in the Larpent text.

40. Grosrichard, 73–74.

41. Elizabeth Inchbald, *Such Things Are,* in *The British Theatre; or, A Collection of Plays,* ed. Elizabeth Inchbald, vol. 23 (London: Longman, Hurst, Rees, and Orme, 1808), 2.

42. Inchbald's 1808 "Remarks" to the play explicitly make the connection to Howard: "When this play was written, in 1786, the hero of the piece, under the name of Haswell, was on his philanthropic travels through Europe and parts of Asia, to mitigate the sufferings of the prisoner. His fame, the anxiety of his countrymen for the success of his labours, and their pride in his beneficent character, suggested to the author a subject for the following pages" (4).

43. I am grateful to Mark Stephen for pointing out the architectural similarity of the prison and the typical British jail described by Howard.

44. See Green, 405–10, for a discussion of Howard's place in the play.

45. Inchbald's republican tendencies at this stage in her career can be corroborated by her social intercourse with various radicals, including Godwin, and by her own theatrical meditation on the French Revolution titled *The Massacre.* For a brief discussion of the political implications of this unperformed tragedy, see O'Quinn, "Elizabeth Inchbald's *The Massacre:* Tragedy, Violence, and the Networks of Political Fantasy," *British Women Playwrights around 1800* (June 1999), at http://www.etang.umontreal.ca/bnp1800/essays/oquinn_massacre.html.

46. See chapter 4 for a discussion of the early satirical prints from the impeachment for a sense of the longevity of this argument.

47. Edmund Burke, *On Empire, Liberty, and Reform: Speeches and Letters,* ed. David Bromwich (New Haven: Yale Univ. Press, 2000), 212. All references to the Guildhall speech are included parenthetically within the text.

48. See chapter 4 for a detailed discussion of this issue.

Chapter 4. The Raree Show of Impeachment

1. Rajat Kanta Ray, "Indian Society and British Supremacy," in *The Oxford History of the British Empire,* vol. 2, *The Eighteenth Century,* ed. P. J. Marshall (Oxford: Oxford Univ. Press, 1998), 513.

2. H. V. Bowen, "British India, 1765–1813: The Metropolitan Context," in *The Oxford History of the British Empire,* vol. 2, *The Eighteenth Century,* ed. P. J. Marshall (Oxford: Oxford Univ. Press, 1998), 541. Dundas's remarks are recorded in the *Parliamentary Register,* vol. 8 (1782), 32, and in *Reports from Committees of the House of Commons* (1783), 6:54–56.

3. Francis was Hastings's chief rival while in India and is widely believed to have been the author of influential letters of Junius. For a discussion of Francis's role in Burke's pursuit of Hastings, see P. J. Marshall, *The Impeachment of Warren Hastings* (London: Oxford Univ. Press, 1965), 14–17.

4. Bowen, 541.

5. P. J. Marshall, introduction to *The Writings and Speeches of Edmund Burke*, vol. 6, *India: The Launching of the Hastings Impeachment, 1786–1788*, ed. P. J. Marshall (Oxford: Clarendon Press, 1991), 6.

6. See Marshall, *The Impeachment*, for a detailed account of the specific charges and their consolidation.

7. Marshall, *The Impeachment*, 70–71.

8. When speaking of historical persons I have followed Marshall's spelling of Indian names as presented in *Writings and Speeches of Edmund Burke*, but have retained eighteenth-century spellings in the citations. For reasons of consistency, I have retained the word Oudh throughout when referring to the region of Awadh.

9. Sara Suleri, *The Rhetoric of English India* (Chicago: Univ. of Chicago Press, 1992), 53.

10. *Times*, 14 February 1788.

11. See, for example, *Times*, 8 May 1788, and *Morning Post*, 14 and 19 February 1788.

12. See Suleri, 57, for a reading of this image.

13. The prints figuring the king, queen, and Thurlow taking bribes are legion.

14. Mary Dorothy George, *Catalogue of Political and Personal Satires Preserved in the Department of Prints and Drawings in the British Museum*, vol. 6 (London: British Museum, 1938), 470–71.

15. George, 462.

16. Anonymous, *The History of the Trial of Warren Hastings, Esq. Late Governor-General of Bengal, before the High Court of Parliament in Westminster-Hall, on an Impeachment by the Commons of Great-Britain for High Crimes and Misdemeanours* (London: Debrett, Vernor and Hood, 1796), 16. During the summation of the Benares charge, Grey also makes a similar distinction between the two Alexanders. See *History*, 19.

17. Jane Moody, *Illegitimate Theatre in London, 1770–1840* (Cambridge: Cambridge Univ. Press, 2000), 16.

18. Moody, 17.

19. Moody, 18.

20. For a discussion of this passage, see Suleri, 29.

21. Edmund Burke, *A Philosophical Enquiry into the Origin of Our Ideas of the Sublime and the Beautiful*, ed. James T. Boulton (Notre Dame: Univ. of Notre Dame Press, 1968), 82.

22. The image of Burke, Sheridan, and Fox on the terrace bears a remarkable resemblance to a "turn-up" advertisement for a Punch show at Bartholomew Fair. Close scrutiny of *The Raree Show* can generate a fairly complete image of a Punch

show. With Fox as Punch, Thurlow is cast as the Devil, and the Prince of Wales can be construed as the Baby. Significantly, in the eighteenth century Punch almost always gets embroiled in a fight with the devil and frequently comes out the winner.

23. *History*, 17.

24. See *History*, 11.

25. *History*, 11.

26. Suleri, 28–29.

27. Burke, *Philosophical Enquiry*, 38.

28. Paul Hindson and Tim Gray, *Burke's Dramatic Theory of Politics* (Avebury: Aldershot, 1988).

29. Burke, *Philosophical Enquiry*, 40.

30. Burke, *Philosophical Enquiry*, 82.

31. Peter Linebaugh, *London's Hanged: Crime and Civil Society in the Eighteenth Century* (London: Penguin Books, 1993).

32. Burke, *Philosophical Enquiry*, 47.

33. Edmund Burke, "Speech on Fox's India Bill 1 December 1783," in Edmund Burke, *The Writings and Speeches of Edmund Burke*, vol. 5, ed. P. J. Marshall (Oxford: Clarendon Press, 1981), 389.

34. Speech, 18 February 1788, in *Writings and Speeches of Edmund Burke*, 6:420–21.

35. *Public Advertiser*, 27 February 1788. The same story appears verbatim in the *Times*, 26 February 1788. See also *Morning Chronicle*, 20 February 1788, for an account of Hastings's impassiveness.

36. For a forceful discussion of the relationship between Burke's deployment of sympathy in the impeachment speeches and in the *Reflections*, see Andrew McCann, *Cultural Politics in the 1790s: Literature, Radicalism and the Public Sphere* (Houndmills: Macmillan, 1999), 33–58.

37. Edmund Burke, *Reflections on the Revolution in France*, ed. Conor Cruise O'Brien (New York: Penguin, 1986), 175.

38. *Writings and Speeches of Edmund Burke*, 6:421.

39. Frances Ferguson, *Solitude and the Sublime: Romanticism and the Aesthetics of Individuation* (New York: Routledge, 1992), 50–53. The relevant passage in Burke's *A Philosophical Enquiry* makes the breast the prime example of the beautiful (115). For an extended discussion of Burke's complex deployment of maternal figures in his political writings, see Deidre Lynch, "Domesticating Fictions and Nationalizing Women: Edmund Burke, Property, and the Reproduction of Englishness," in *Romanticism, Race, and Imperial Culture, 1780–1834*, ed. Alan Richardson and Sonia Hofkosh (Bloomington: Indiana Univ. Press, 1996), 40–71.

40. Nicholas K. Robinson, *Edmund Burke: A Life in Caricature* (New Haven: Yale Univ. Press, 1996), 98.

41. Dent had used glasses as a device in an earlier satire on Burke, see *Impeachment* (BM 6926).

42. See Robinson, 111.

43. The citation is multilayered because the lines "Black spirits and white, red spirits and grey, / mingle, mingle, mingle, you that may" are from William Davenant's *The Witch* 5.2, but they also drifted into eighteenth-century versions of *Macbeth* via Davenant's preparation of the play for the King's Men in 1674. The song was usually introduced during Hecate's prophecy in *Macbeth* 3.5.

44. *History*, 4.

45. Anna Clark, *Scandal: The Sexual Politics of the British Constitution* (Princeton: Princeton Univ. Press, 2003), 98. Sheridan's remarks are from the *Public Advertiser*, 10 June 1788.

46. *Writings and Speeches of Edmund Burke*, 5:390.

47. For an illuminating reading of this print and its relation to the Burkean sublime, see Srinivas Aravamudan, *Tropicopolitans: Colonialism and Agency, 1688–1804* (Durham: Duke Univ. Press, 1999), 223–29.

48. George, 484–85.

49. George, 485.

50. William Shakespeare, *Hamlet*, in *The Complete Works*, ed. Alfred Harbage (New York: Viking Press, 1969), 3.2.359–69.

51. See Clark, 98. For a useful discussion of the convergence between Burke's rhetoric and the conventions of Gothic romance, see Frans De Bruyn, "Edmund Burke's Gothic Romance: The Portrayal of Warren Hastings in Burke's Writings and Speeches on India," *Criticism* 29.4 (1987): 415–38.

52. *Speeches of the Late Right Honourable Richard Brinsley Sheridan*, 2 vols. (London: Patrick Martin, 1816), 1:291. The record of Sheridan's great oration is quite incomplete even by late eighteenth-century standards. For a brief historical account of Bahu Begam's political power and her conflicts with the East India Company, see Clark, 89–92.

53. *Writings and Speeches of Edmund Burke*, 5:411.

54. The quotation is from Tacitus, *Agricola*, 45: "The flight and exile of most honorable women."

55. Writings and *Speeches of Edmund Burke*, 5:419.

56. *Writings and Speeches of Edmund Burke*, 5:402–3.

57. *Writings and Speeches of Edmund Burke*, 5:403.

58. *Speeches of Sheridan*, 1:272.

59. *Speeches of Sheridan*, 1:271.

60. See Julie Carlson, "Trying Sheridan's *Pizarro*," *Texas Studies in Literature and Language* 38.3–4 (Fall–Winter 1996): 366.

61. See Marshall, *The Impeachment*, 120–21, for a discussion of the collapse of Hastings's first defense against the Begams charge.

62. *Speeches* of Sheridan, 2:112–13. See *Speeches*, 1:291, for another reinscription of the birds-of-prey image.

63. Clark, 98.

64. *Speeches of Sheridan*, 2:116.

65. *Speeches of Sheridan,* 2:116.

66. Carlson, 368.

67. Marshall, *Impeachment,* 109.

68. *Speeches of Sheridan,* 2:117.

69. Laura Brown, *The Ends of Empire: Women and Ideology in Early Eighteenth-Century English Literature* (Ithaca: Cornell Univ. Press., 1993), 64–102, for a discussion of this dramatic mode.

70. *Speeches of Sheridan,* 2:65.

71. Carlson, 368.

72. As Clark notes, "the impeachment was the only political event extensively covered in the *Ladies Magazine* during the 1780s (96).

73. *Speeches of Sheridan,* 2:64.

74. Carlson, 368.

75. *History,* 40.

76. *Morning Post,* 23 April 1788.

77. *Morning Post,* 23 April 1788. The degree to which the crowd reaction to this reading is reported varies from paper to paper. For example, *Morning Chronicle* does not record Burke's remarks, but the *Times,* 23 April 1788, exhibits a certain level of censorship by not expatiating on the reaction of the women in the audience: "[T]he clerk read several extracts [from Cantemir's *History of the Turks*] to show the sacred manner with which their customs were observed. This was to point out the severity with which the mother of the Begums had been treated. Every mother among those of rank, is treated with the highest respect, and is consulted on all occasions, and among other customs, it is usual on every *Biram* for the mother to present a beautiful virgin for her son's use."

78. *Times,* 13 May 1788.

79. The story of Daniel and Susanna is one of the earliest detective stories, and various elements of the narrative resonate with elements of the Hastings trial. Divided into two sections, the story tells of the failed seduction of Joakim's wife Susanna by two elder judges and her successful and unconventional defense by the divinely inspired Daniel. In the seduction scene, the lusting elders watch Susanna preparing to bathe and immediately corner her when she is left alone in her garden. They demand that she yield to them or they will give evidence against her that she was committing adultery with an unidentified man and dismissed her maids in order to be with him. Although she is entrapped, Susanna refuses to yield; the judges bring false evidence against her, and she is condemned until Daniel questions the two men separately and demonstrates that their evidence is fundamentally contradictory. Daniel's successful defense of Susanna restores her innocence and leads to the execution of the judges.

80. *Times,* 13 May 1788.

81. For an illuminating account of the place of Mrs. Armstead in Fox's public and private life, see I. M. Davis, *The Harlot and the Statesman* (London: Kensall Press, 1986).

1. Sara Suleri, *The Rhetoric of English India* (Chicago: Univ. of Chicago Press, 1992), 62. All subsequent references are presented parenthetically in the text.

2. Frances Burney, *The Diary and Letters of Madame D'Arblay,* vol. 4 (London: Colburn, 1854), 39. All subsequent references to this work are made parenthetically within the text.

3. William Shakespeare, *Merchant of Venice,* in *The Complete Works,* ed. Alfred Harbage (New York: Viking Press, 1969), 4.1.182–90.

4. As we will see later in this chapter, *Evelina* is a helpful intertext because much of its attention is focused on the difficulties associated with Miss Mirvan's limited social purview.

5. William Windham would later become secretary of war. I have retained Burney's spelling of his name to avoid confusion.

6. For an extended analysis of the double bind faced by women writers in relation to the public sphere of politics, see Mary Poovey, *The Proper Lady and the Woman Writer: The Ideology of Style in Mary Wollstonecraft, Jane Austen and Mary Shelley* (Chicago: Univ. of Chicago Press, 1984).

7. Peter de Bolla, *The Discourse of the Sublime: History, Aesthetics and the Subject* (Oxford: Basil Blackwell, 1989), 151.

8. The Peers decided that evidence against Hastings relating to all the charges would be heard in their entirety before he would be called on to defend himself. This decision meant that the rules of evidence would follow those of civil rather than parliamentary procedure and all but guaranteed Hastings's acquittal.

9. *Times,* 23 February 1788.

10. Anonymous, *The History of the Trial of Warren Hastings, Esq. Late Governor-General of Bengal, before the High Court of Parliament in Westminster-Hall, on an Impeachment by the Commons of Great-Britain for High Crimes and Misdemeanours* (London: Debrett, Vernor and Hood, 1796), 4.

11. *History,* 4–5.

12. *History,* 13.

13. *History,* 13.

14. See John Barrell, *English Literature in History, 1730–1800: An Equal Wide Survey* (New York: St. Martin's Press, 1983), 111, and de Bolla, 164.

15. Roxann Wheeler, *The Complexion of Race: Categories of Difference in Eighteenth-Century British Culture* (Philadelphia: Univ. of Pennsylvania Press, 2000), 197–98. See also Nicholas Hudson, *Writing and European Thought, 1600–1830* (Cambridge: Cambridge Univ. Press, 1994), 102, and Michèle Cohen, *Fashioning Masculinity: National Identity and Language in the Eighteenth Century* (London: Routledge, 1996), 53, for further discussion of Johnson's views regarding the coterminality of national identity, language, and appropriate masculinity.

16. Thomas Sheridan, *A Dissertation on the causes of the difficulties which occur in learning the English tongue. With a scheme for publishing an English gram-*

mar and dictionary upon a plan entirely new (London, 1762), 36. Quoted in de Bolla,164.

17. De Bolla, 164.

18. De Bolla, 165.

19. De Bolla, 166.

20. De Bolla 167.

21. Wyndham was one of Johnson's closest associates in his later years.

22. Burney was not present for the third day of the opening speech in which Burke narrated the atrocities at Rangpur.

23. *History,* 4.

24. See Elizabeth D. Samet, "A Prosecutor and a Gentleman: Edmund Burke's Idiom of Impeachment," *ELH* 68 (2001): 397–418, for an illuminating discussion of the Ciceronian qualities of Burke's oratory. Burney's disapprobation of Burke's violence is a sign of her impatience with the "boldness" of Burke's idiom.

25. *Morning Chronicle,* 20 February 1788, for an account of Hastings's impassiveness.

26. *Public Advertiser,* 27 February 1788. The same story appears verbatim in the *Times,* 26 February 1788.

27. Gina Campbell, "How to Read Like a Gentleman: Burney's Instructions to Her Critics in *Evelina,*" *ELH* 57 (1990): 557–84.

Part III. A Theatre of Perpetual War

1. T. C. Hansard, ed., *The Parliamentary Debates, from the Year 1803 to the Present Time,* vol. 4 (London: Longman, Hurst, Rees, Orme, Brown, 1805), 251. Quoted in Sudipta Sen, *Distant Sovereignty: National Imperialism and the Origins of the British India* (New York: Routledge, 2002), 25.

2. William Shakespeare, *Macbeth,* in *The Complete Works,* ed. Alfred Harbage (New York: Viking Press, 1969), 3.4.136–40.

3. Joseph Roach, *Cities of the Dead: Circum-Atlantic Performance* (New York: Columbia Univ. Press, 1996), 2.

4. John Brewer, *Sinews of Power: War, Money and the English State, 1688–1783* (New York: Alfred A. Knopf, 1989).

5. Ann Laura Stoler, *Race and the Education of Desire: Foucault's History of Sexuality and the Colonial Order of Things* (Durham: Duke Univ. Press, 1995), 49.

6. Michel Foucault, *History of Sexuality,* vol. 1, trans. Robert Hurley (New York: Vintage, 1980), 149.

7. Stoler, 64–65.

8. Michel Foucault, *"Society Must Be Defended": Lectures at the Collège de France, 1975–76,* trans. David Macey (New York: Picador, 2003), 60–61.

9. Foucault, *Society,* 62.

10. As Joseph Lew argues in "The Necessary Orientalist? *The Giaour* and

Nineteenth-Century Imperialist Misogyny," in *Romanticism, Race, and Imperial Culture, 1780–1834,* ed. Alan Richardson and Sonia Hofkosh (Bloomington: Indiana Univ. Press, 1996), "Miscegenation became a problem when the British abandoned the rather clear-headed thinking of Warren Hastings and many of his contemporaries, who realized that the British had conquered and ruled parts of India because of temporary technological and organizational advantages" (196).

11. See my "Mercantile Deformities: George Colman's *Inkle and Yarico* and the Racialization of Class Relations," *Theatre Journal* 54.3 (October 2002): 389–410.

12. Stoler, 99.

13. See Nicholas B. Dirks, *Castes of Mind: Colonialism and the Making of Modern India* (Princeton: Princeton Univ. Press, 2001), 111, for a succinct statement of this policy of erasure.

Chapter 6. Starke Reforms

1. Bruce P. Lenman, "Colonial Wars and Imperial Instability, 1688–1793," in *The Oxford History of the British Empire,* vol. 2, *The Eighteenth Century,* ed. P. J. Marshall (Oxford: Oxford Univ. Press, 1998), 165–66.

2. Linda Colley, *Captives* (New York: Pantheon, 2002), 270.

3. The printed version most easily available if not easily read is a Dublin edition of 1790. The title page records that the play was "First Performed at The Theatre Royal, in the Hay-Market, On Saturday, August the 5th, 1788," and indicates that "The Lines in inverted Commas, are ommitted in Representation." The document therefore simultaneously records the public performance script and provides a longer version suited to the private act of reading. All references to the play are to this second edition.

4. See E. M. Collingham, *Imperial Bodies: The Physical Experience of the Raj, c. 1800– 1947* (Cambridge: Polity Press, 2001), 13–49, for an account of Indianization in the late eighteenth century, and William Dalrymple, *White Mughals: Love and Betrayal in Eighteenth-Century India* (London: Harper Collins, 2002), 3–54, for some sense of the high degree of integration between Company officials and Indian merchants and servants.

5. See Michael Duffy, "World-Wide War and British Expansion, 1793–1815," in *The Oxford History of the British Empire,* vol. 2, *The Eighteenth Century,* ed. P. J. Marshall (Oxford: Oxford Univ. Press, 1998), 202, for an account of the expansion of the East India Company army during this period.

6. See Franklin Wickwire and Mary Wickwire, *Cornwallis: The Imperial Years* (Chapel Hill: Univ. of North Carolina Press, 1980), 107–16, for an account of Cornwallis's military reforms in India.

7. *Correspondence of Charles, First Marquis Cornwallis,* vol. 1, ed. Charles Ross (London: John Murray, 1859), 523–24. This is part of a letter to the court of directors of the East India Company. One of the key problems was that soldiers

working for the Company were paid and promoted differently than soldiers working for the Crown; see *Correspondence, 229–31.*

8. *Correspondence,* 225.

9. As C. A. Bayly argues, there were similar "campaigns against the 'hydra of
dubashism' and the corruption of the banians. . . . Cornwallis moved heavily
against European revenue officers involved in Indian trade and tried to create a
wall of regulations to separate the Indian and European worlds" (149). See *Imperial Meridian: The British Empire and the World, 1780–1830* (London: Longman, 1989), 133–62, for a wide-ranging account of the consolidation of racial and
social hierarchies from the governor-generalship of Cornwallis.

10. Cited in Wickwire and Wickwire, 110.

11. As emphasized in Bayly, 149, and Beth Fowkes Tobin, *Picturing Imperial
Power: Colonial Subjects in Eighteenth-Century British Painting* (Durham: Duke
Univ. Press, 1999), 117– 18. Cornwallis's reforms were designed not only to minimize the amount of intermingling between British and Indian subjects in the
realms of commerce and civil administration, but also to avert miscegenation.

12. See Collingham, 51–89, for a detailed account the segregation policies that
infused nineteenth-century Anglo-Indian relations. See also Sudipta Sen, *Distant Sovereignty: National Imperialism and the Origins of British India* (New York:
Routledge, 2002), 119–49, for a discussion of "the decline of intimacy" promulgated during the Raj.

13. William Mackintosh's satirical portrait of the indolence and extravagance
of the British in Calcutta had wide circulation in the early 1780s. See William
Mackintosh, *Travels in Europe, Asia, and Africa,* 2 vols. (London, 1782), 2:214–16,
and Kate Teltscher's analysis of the scene in *India Inscribed: European and British
Writing on India, 1600–1800* (Delhi: Oxford Univ. Press, 1995), 160–61.

14. Teltscher, 160.

15. Cornwallis is I believe the most obvious alter ego, but Northcote's character also incorporates some of the qualities of Augustus Cleveland and his name-
sake Lord North. All three figures circulate as sober examples of civilized British governance. During the trial of Clive, Lord North was portrayed as the rat catcher who
was responsible for cleaning up the Company. See Percival Spear, *Master of Bengal:
Clive and His India* (London: Thames and Hudson, 1975), 187. As Teltscher argues
(121–24), Augustus Cleveland operated as the figure for the myth of benevolent British
rule throughout the 1780s and 1790s. During the trial of Warren Hastings, Hastings's defense frequently invoked the figure of Cleveland and the narrative of
civilizing rule in an exculpatory fashion through a series of Indian testimonials
(Teltscher,181). Cornwallis was frequently celebrated as a corrective to the excesses
of previous colonial administrators. For an explicit discussion of the parallels between Northcote and Cornwallis, see Jeanne Moskal, "English National Identity
in Mariana Starke's *The Sword of Peace:* India, Abolition and the Rights of Women,"
in *Women in British Romantic Theatre: Drama, Performance, and Society, 1790–1840,*
ed. Catherine Burroughs (Cambridge: Cambridge Univ. Press, 2000), 102–31.

16. For detailed accounts of these texts, see Allen Edwardes, *The Rape of India: A Biography of Lord Clive and a Sexual History of the Conquest of Hindustan* (New York: Julian Press, 1966). Edwardes's analysis should be treated with some skepticism, but unlike other biographers of Clive, he provides copious examples of the sexual discourse surrounding Clive.

17. For a detailed analysis of the place of sexual violence in Burke's opening charge, see Sara Suleri, *The Rhetoric of English India* (Chicago: Univ. of Chicago Press, 1992), 60–64.

18. *Morning Chronicle and London Advertiser,* 11 August 1788.

19. See Moskal, 102–32, for a sustained discussion of the play's abolitionist rhetoric. Jeffrey Cox also includes the play in his volume of abolitionist drama collected in Peter J. Kitson and Debbie Lee, eds., *Slavery, Abolition and Emancipation: Writings in the British Romantic Period,* vol. 5 (London: Pickering and Chatto, 1999).

20. Rajat Kanta Ray, "Indian Society and the Establishment of British Supremacy, 1765–1818," in *The Oxford History of the British Empire,* vol. 2, *The Eighteenth Century,* ed. P. J. Marshall (Oxford: Oxford Univ. Press, 1998), 512.

21. See Kathleen Wilson, *The Sense of the People: Politics, Culture and Imperialism in England, 1715–1785* (Cambridge: Cambridge Univ. Press, 1995), 185–205, for an illuminating discussion of the feminization of the body politic and imperial degeneracy.

22. Teltscher, 172. Marshall makes this point in *The Writings and Speeches of Edmund Burke,* vol. 6, ed. P. J. Marshall (Oxford: Oxford Univ. Press, 1991), 5.

23. See O'Quinn, "Mercantile Deformities: George Colman's *Inkle and Yarico* and the Racialization of Class Relations," *Theatre Journal* 54.3 (October 2002): 389–410.

24. *Morning Chronicle and London Advertiser,* 11 August 1788.

25. Deidre Lynch, *The Economy of Character: Novels, Market Culture, and the Business of Inner Meaning* (Chicago: Univ. of Chicago Press, 1999), 38.

26. See Roxann Wheeler, *The Complexion of Race: Categories of Difference in Eighteenth-Century British Culture* (Philadelphia: Univ. of Pennsylvania Press, 2000), 17–21, for the mutually supporting roles played by complexion and costume at this historical juncture.

27. See Mackintosh, 214–16.

28. For the use of the term *country born,* see Anonymous [Phoebe Gibbes], *Hartly House Calcutta* (London: Pluto Press, 1989), and Felicity Nussbaum's discussion of the novel in *Torrid Zones: Maternity, Sexuality, and Empire in Eighteenth-Century English Narratives* (Baltimore: Johns Hopkins Univ. Press, 1995), 167–91.

29. David Kunzle, *The Early Comic Strip: Narrative Strips and Picture Stories in the European Broadsheet from c. 1450–1825* (Berkeley: Univ. of California Press, 1973), 360–61.

30. *Morning Chronicle and London Advertiser,* 11 August 1788.

31. See O'Quinn, 398.

32. *Morning Chronicle and London Advertiser,* 11 August 1788.

33. This is nowhere more evident than in the repeated assertion of Mrs. Tartar's indolence.

34. In her response to an earlier version of this chapter, Marjean Purinton examines the masculinization of Eliza and Louisa at the level of the play's narrative specifically around their mission to acquire Clairville's sword. See "Response to Daniel J. O'Quinn's Essay: Dancing and Duelling in Mariana Starke's *Sword of Peace,*" *British Women Playwrights around 1800,* at http://www.etang.umontreal.ca/bwp1800/essays/purinton_sword.html. She argues that both women don the mask of masculinity in relation to an overtly feminized and idealized India. Her analysis resonates with Balachandra Rajan's discussion in "Feminizing the Feminine: Early Women Writers on India" of the feminization of Indian space in late eighteenth-century narrative representations of India and constitutes an important area of consideration that lies beyond the scope of this chapter. See Rajan, *Under Western Eyes: India from Milton to Macauley* (Durham: Duke Univ. Press, 1999), 118–38.

35. Donna Andrew, "The Code of Honour and Its Critics: The Opposition to Duelling in England, 1700–1850," *Social History* 5 (1980): 411.

36. Andrew, 429.

37. In *Reading the East India Company, 1720–1840: Colonial Currencies of Gender* (Chicago: Univ. of Chicago Press, 2004), Betty Joseph has recently demonstrated how gendered rhetoric and the cult of domesticity were incorporated not only into representations of colonial life but also into the articulation of colonial policy. See especially 61–122.

38. *St. James Chronicle,* 13 January 1791.

39. Nicholas B. Dirks, *Castes of Mind: Colonialism and the Making of Modern India* (Princeton: Princeton Univ. Press, 2001), 123.

40. Dirks, 111.

41. E. P. Thompson identifies this misrecognition as a form of nostalgia for Whig oligarchy in *Customs in Common: Studies in Traditional Popular Culture* (New York: New Press, 1993), 167–75.

42. Bayly, 186.

43. Sen, 93.

44. Quoted in Sen, 93.

45. *The Widow of Malabar* was performed for Miss Brunton's benefit on 6 May 1790 and revived for a successful run the following winter with performances on 12, 14, 19, and 26 January and 2, 9, 16, and 23 February 1791. Starke's play is an adaptation of Le Mierre's *La veuve du Malabar, ou L'empire des coutumes.* All references are to Mariana Starke, *The Widow of Malabar* (London: William Lane, 1791) and are included parenthetically in the text.

46. As Dirks states, "All the talk of improvement notwithstanding, no Indian public was recruited by (or to) the contradictory logic of colonial sovereignty. Colonial governmentality consisted of a bureaucracy without sovereignty, or

rather a form of sovereignty abstracted from even the most minimal conceits of political representation" (123).

47. *European Magazine and London Review,* May 1790, 388.

48. Dorothy M. Figueira, "Die Flambierte Frau: Sati in European Culture," in *Sati, the Blessing and the Curse,* ed. John Stratton Hawley (New York: Oxford Univ. Press, 1994), 61.

See Paul B. Courtwright, "The Iconographies of Sati," in *Sati, the Blessing and the Curse,* ed. John Stratton Hawley (New York: Oxford Univ. Press, 1994), 27–49; Lata Mani, *Contentious Traditions: The Debate on Sati in Colonial India* (Berkeley: Univ. of California Press, 1998); Nussbaum, *Torrid Zones,* 182–88; and Monika Fludernik, "Suttee Revisited: From the Iconography of Martyrdom to the Burkean Sublime," *New Literary History* 30 (1999): 411–37, for discussions of the representation of suttee in the late eighteenth century.

49. Figueira, 62.

50. For a discussion of these parodies, see Figueira, 62.

51. For a history of private theatricals in the period, see Sybil Marion Rosenfeld, *Temples of Thespis: Some Private Theatres and Theatricals in England and Wales, 1700–1820* (London: Society for Theatre Research, 1978).

52. The *St. James Chronicle,* 6 May 1790, states that "Miss Brunton last night produced for her benefit a new Tragedy under the title of *The Widow of Malabar.*"

53. Starke wrote an address for Miss Brunton which is included in the Larpent text. See Mariana Starke, *The Widow of Malabar,* Larpent Collection, MS 869, Huntington Library, San Marino, California.

54. See Jon Mee, "'Reciprocal Expressions of Kindness': Robert Merry, Della Cruscanism and the Limits of Sociability," in *Romantic Sociability: Social Networks and Literary Culture in Britain, 1770–1840,* ed. Gillian Russell and Clara Tuite (Cambridge: Cambridge Univ. Press, 2002), 104–22, for a discussion of Merry's radical activities. The *Morning Chronicle,* 5 February 1791, described her engagement at the end of the run as follows: "Miss Brunton, it is said, is soon to be married. Is it from her charming representation of a *Widow,* that she has recommended herself to appear in this new character."

55. Lucyle Werkmeister, *A Newspaper History of England, 1792–3* (Lincoln: Univ. of Nebraska Press, 1967), 39, identifies Merry as one of the preeminent opposition journalists practicing in 1792.

56. *New Lady's Magazine,* May 1790, 262.

57. *English Review,* May 1791, 387.

58. Edmund Burke, *Reflections on the Revolution in France,* ed. Conor Cruise O'Brien (New York: Penguin, 1986), 92–93.

59. See John Zephaniah Holwell, *Interesting Historical Events Relative to the Provinces of Bengal and the Empire of Indostan,* vol. 2 (London, 1767), and Alexander Dow, *The History of Hindostan,* vol. 1 (London, 1768). Both accounts of suttee are reprinted in P. J. Marshall, *The British Discovery of Hinduism in the Eighteenth Century* (Cambridge: Cambridge Univ. Press, 1970), 91–97 and 116, re-

spectively. Aside from these widely read sources, there are accounts of suttee published in the *Gentleman's Magazine* during the thirty years leading up to the production of the play. The most extensive version appears in a letter in volume 47 (1777) and, unlike some earlier accounts, adamantly argues that "it was intirely a voluntary act" (591).

60. The mirror and the dagger are ritual accessories of the sati that rarely appear in eighteenth-century accounts. The former object signifies her devotion to her husband because it is part of both female puberty rites and marriage ritual. The dagger signifies ritual sacrifice and is often accompanied by a lemon. For a discussion of the iconographic qualities of these objects, see Catherine Weinberger-Thomas, *Ashes of Immortality: Widow Burning in India,* trans. Jeffrey Mehlman and David Gordon White (Chicago: Univ. of Chicago Press, 1999), 52–84.

61. *Gazetteer and Daily Advertiser,* January 12, 1791.

62. *Gazetteer and Daily Advertiser,* January 14, 1791.

63. See my introduction to the edition of *The Ton* on *British Women Playwrights around 1800* website for a more detailed discussion of the politics of vice in this play: http://www.etang.umontreal.ca/bwp1800/essays/oquinn_ton_intro.html.

64. *Morning Chronicle,* 15 January 1791.

65. *Morning Chronicle,* 19 January 1791. The poem also appears in the *Public Advertiser,* 20 January 1791.

66. *Morning Chronicle,* 17 January 1791.

67. See the *World,* 13 January 1791, and *Star,* 13 January 1791.

68. *St. James Chronicle,* 20 January 1791.

69. *New London Magazine,* January 1791, 46.

70. *Public Advertiser,* 14 January 1791.

71. See Dror Wahrman, *Imagining the Middle Class: The Political Representation of Class in Britain, c. 1780–1840* (Cambridge: Cambridge Univ. Press, 1995), 24.

72. See Wahrman, 31–63.

73. I am working from the epilogue printed in the *World* and the *Whitehall Evening Post* on 6 May 1790 and the *Public Advertiser* on 8 May 1790 and not from the epilogue printed with the play. The latter version is missing a key passage where Mrs. Mattocks addresses the ladies in the audience that was in the epilogue submitted to Larpent. The short version of the epilogue makes its first appearance in the newspapers following the plays revival in January 1791. See the *Gazetteer and Daily Advertiser* for 19 January 1791, and the *General Evening Post, Public Advertiser,* and *Star* for 20 January 1791.

74. R. J. Starke, "Epilogue to *The Widow of Malabar*," *World,* 6 May 1790, lines 37–46.

75. "Epilogue," lines 47–57.

76. For a succinct account of the emergence of the *ryotwari* system and the displacement of Cornwallis rules, see Dirks, 111–16. For a more extended discussion

of this issue, see Burton Stein, *Thomas Munro: The Origins of the Colonial State and His Vision of Empire* (Delhi: Oxford Univ. Press, 1989).

Chapter 7. War and Precinema

1. Jane Moody's *Illegitimate Theatre in London, 1770–1840* (Cambridge: Cambridge Univ. Press, 2000) and Richard Altick's *The Shows of London* (Cambridge: Harvard Univ. Press, 1978) offer exhaustive accounts of this transformation.

2. For overviews of these developments at Astley's, see Marius Kwint, "The Legitimation of the Circus in Late Georgian England," *Past and Present* 174 (February 2002): 72–115.

3. Orrin Wang has recently suggested that romanticism is already a precinematic age in his extraordinary reading of "Lamia." See "Coming Attractions: *Lamia* and Cinematic Sensation," *Studies in Romanticism* 42.4 (Winter 2003): 461–500.

4. Michel Foucault, *"Society Must Be Defended": Lectures at the Collège de France, 1975–76*, trans. David Macey (New York: Picador, 2003), 249–51.

5. The canonical treatment of this misadventure remains Ranajit Guha, *A Rule of Property for Bengal: An Essay on the Idea of Permanent Settlement* (Durham: Duke Univ. Press, 1996).

6. Joseph Roach, *Cities of the Dead: Circum-Atlantic Performance* (New York: Columbia Univ. Press, 1996), 2.

7. After this highly topical array of productions, Tipu does not return to the stage until the 1820s. The most notable productions are J. H. Amherst's *Tippoo Saib; or, The Storming of Seringapatam*, which was produced at the Royal Coburg Theatre on 20 January 1823 and *The Storming of Seringapatam; or, The Death of Tippoo Saib*, which was produced at Astley's in the spring of 1829. See Denys Forrest, *Tiger of Mysore: The Life and Death of Tipu Sultan* (London: Chatto and Windus, 1970), 318–21, for descriptions of these plays.

8. See Kate Teltscher, *India Inscribed: European and British Writings on India, 1600–1800* (Oxford: Oxford Univ. Press, 1995), 230–31, for a discussion of Burke's often mercurial appraisal of Hyder Ali as an able statesman in the *Annual Register.*

9. Teltscher, 238. Teltscher's argument here is indebted to C. A. Bayly discussion of this issue in *Imperial Meridian: The British Empire and the World, 1780–1830* (London: Longman, 1989), 59–60, and resonates with much of Homi Bhabha's discussion of colonial ambivalence in "Of Mimicry and Man," and "Sly Civility," in *The Location of Culture* (New York: Routledge, 1994), 85–101.

10. See Franklin Wickwire and Mary Wickwire, *Cornwallis: The Imperial Years* (Chapel Hill: Univ. of North Carolina Press, 1980), for a detailed account of the place of prior American experience in Cornwallis's correspondence on Medows's failures in Mysore in 1790.

11. See also Dent's *Rare News from India; or, Things Going On Swimmingly in the East,* also in the Department of Prints and Drawings, The British Museum

(BM 7928), and Mary Dorothy George's discussion of these prints in *Catalogue of Political and Personal Satires Preserved in the Department of Prints and Drawings in the British Museum*, vol. 6 (London: British Museum, 1938), 819–20.

12. One of these narratives was printed concurrently with the reporting on Fox's speech on the Benares charge in the first season of the Hastings impeachment. See *Morning Chronicle*, 20 February 1788. The same extract from William Thomson's *Memoirs of the Late War in Asia. With a Narrative of the imprisonment and suffering of our officers and soldiers: By an Officer of Colonel Baillie's Detachment*, 2 vols. (London, 1788) appeared in the *Public Advertiser*, 23 February 1788.

13. Teltscher, 240.

14. Teltscher, 243.

15. Teltscher, 243.

16. For a thorough account of the theatricalization of the war with France, see Gillian Russell, *The Theatres of War: Performance, Politics, and Society, 1793–1815* (Oxford: Clarendon Press, 1995), and Moody, 27.

17. See Forrest, 152–56, and Wickwire and Wickwire, 119–78, for descriptions of the campaign. It is not difficult to imagine the attraction of a conflict involving elephants and extraordinary colonial armies for Astley's viewers.

18. *Morning Chronicle*, 14 April 1792.

19. *Oracle*, 11 April 1792.

20. *Star and Daily Advertiser*, 17 May 1792.

21. Astley's drew an extremely diverse crowd. On this issue, see Kwint, 109.

22. *Oracle*, 20 April 1792.

23. Moody, 27.

24. Manuel De Landa, *War in the Age of Intelligent Machines* (New York: Swerve Editions, 1994), 68.

25. For a discussion of this development, see De Landa, 65–67.

26. Quoted in Teltscher, 241.

27. Mark Wilks, *Historical Sketches of the South of India in an Attempt to Trace the History of Mysore*, vol. 3 (London, 1810–17), 135–36. Quoted in Forrest, 158.

28. De Landa, 65.

29. See Altick, 50–76, for a discussion of clockwork entertainments and exhibitions of mechanical ingenuity.

30. Quoted in Forrest, 317–18. Forrest also cites descriptions of "Tippoo's palace in the cypress garden" in the second act, which state that it was in "the first style of *Grecian architecture*, with this *happy difference* that the *chimneys* rise in the form of *minarets* . . . and give a magnificent effect to the whole" (318).

31. *Tippoo Saib; or, East-India Campaigning* opened on April 30, 1792. The play is likely based on *A Genuine Narrative of the Sufferings of the British Prisoners of War, Taken by His Son, Tippoo Saib*, which Francis Robson published as an appendix to his *Life of Hyder Ally* (London, 1786). This supposition is based on the order of events in the plot.

32. *Public Advertiser*, 14 May 1792.

33. *Public Advertiser,* 14 May 1792.

34. Teltscher, 245.

35. *Public Advertiser,* 14 May 1792.

36. *Gazetteer/New Daily Advertiser,* 2 May 1792. There is a distinct possibility that this part of the narrative is based on the much-celebrated sepoy Sayyad Ibrahim, who was imprisoned with the British officers at Seringapatam and who was celebrated for his loyalty in Thomson's *Memoirs of the Late War* and in Wilks's *Historical Sketches.* See Teltscher, 245, for a discussion of the Company's celebration of him as an exemplary figure.

37. This anticipation was also enacted in the realm of public affairs when Parliament opened in January 1792. Pitt, Dundas, and others reported that Seringapatam had fallen, East India Company stocks jumped, and all was proved to be inaccurate. As one might expect, the print satirists were quick to capitalize on what was perceived to be an attempt to falsely boost credit. For a discussion of the prints, see George, 886–87, 906–9.

38. See Wickwire and Wickwire, 170–71, and Forrest, for descriptions of this event.

39. Both the *World* and *Madras Courier* indicate that there were too many illuminations to describe within the confines of their extensive coverage of the event.

40. Wickwire and Wickwire, 173. This description is derived from the *Calcutta Gazette,* 26 April 1792.

41. See Jill H. Casid, "'His Master's Obi': Machine Magic, Colonial Violence, and Transculturation," in *Visual Culture Reader,* ed. Nicholas Mirzoeff (New York: Routledge, 2002), 533–45.

42. P. J. Marshall, "'Cornwallis Triumphant': War in India and the British Public in the Late Eighteenth Century," in *War, Strategy and International Politics,* ed. Lawrence Freedman, Paul Hayes, and Robert O'Neill (Oxford: Oxford Univ. Press, 1992), 71–72.

43. *World* (Calcutta), 28 April 1792. A similarly detailed account of the illuminations can be found in the *Madras Courier,* 17 May 1792.

44. *Madras Courier,* 17 May 1792.

45. *Madras Courier,* 17 May 1792.

46. *Madras Courier,* 17 May 1792.

47. See Marshall, 62–63, for a sampling of the verse.

48. See Marshall, 64. The transparencies were arranged for Cornwallis's arrival in London in early April 1794. According to the *General Evening Post,* 5–8 April 1794, the scene of Cornwallis accepting the hostages was projected onto Mansion House, whereas a more insidious transparency was projected outside Orme's print shop in Old Bond Street: "On the one side India presenting the bust of Lord Cornwallis to Britannia who receives him in full suit of armour, with sentiments of reverence and respect; at the top the figure of fame, with a crown of laurel, and a motto of the eastern conqueror. On the side of India, in the dis-

tance an elephant and an Indian pagoda, or place of worship; on the side of Britannia, a lion and St. Paul's Cathedral." See Teltscher, 248–52; Forrest, 347–50; and Marshall, 71–72, for discussions of the discursive and pictorial construction of Cornwallis's victory as an act of paternal benevolence.

49. This account was first published in the *Madras Courier* and reprinted in *Gentleman's Magazine* 72 (1792): 760. For thorough accounts of the discursive construction of this event and its significance for popular acceptance of British policy in India, see Marshall, "'Cornwallis Triumphant,'" and Teltscher, 248–51.

50. *Oracle,* 20 August 1792.

51. The *Public Advertiser,* 25 August 1792, reports that Sadler's Wells plans to present the deliverance of the hostage sons to Cornwallis as part of "an ornamental Picture of the Times" during an evening of various entertainments.

52. *Oracle,* 21 August 1792.

53. *Oracle,* 24 August 1792.

54. It is unlikely that Tipu's cannibalism refers to the remarkable automaton Tipu commissioned from French craftsmen in the 1780s popularly known as "Tippoo's Tiger." The automaton presents the viewer with an English red-coat being consumed by a tiger. For a detailed analysis of the automaton's provenance, see Mildred Archer, *Tippoo's Tiger* (London: Victoria and Albert Museum, 1959).

55. *Oracle,* 24 August 1792.

56. See Moody's exhaustive account of this process of disintegration.

57. All references to James Cobb's *Ramah Droog* embedded in the text are to the version reprinted in volume 6 of Elizabeth Inchbald's *The Modern Theatre: A Collection of Successful Modern Plays,* 10 vols. (London: Longman, Hurst, Rees, Orme and Brown, 1811), 138–91. The coincidence of *Bluebeard* and *Ramah Droog* on the same evening provides a particularly condensed entry point for a discussion of the supersession of "legitimate" theatre by various forms of spectacular entertainment. The following is John Genest's appraisal of Cobb's opera in *Some Account of the English Stage, from the Restoration in 1660 to 1830,* 10 vols. (Bath: H. E. Carrington, 1832): "[T]he comic scenes are farcical—the serious scenes are dull to the last degree—yet this piece was acted 35 times—Cumberland, in his Passive Husband, makes *Starling* say—I write professedly rank nonsense—*Runic.* Why do you so?—*Starling.* Because I write to live, and 'tis the readiest money at the market" (7:430). Genest's invocation of Cumberland resonates with the latter's assessment of the London stage at the turn of the century: "I have stood firm for the corps into which I enrolled myself, and never disgraced my colours by abandoning the cause of *legitimate* comedy, to whose service I am sworn, and in whose defence I have kept the field for nearly half a century, till at last I have survived all true national taste, and lived to see buffoonery, spectacle and puerility so effectually triumph, that now to be repulsed from the stage is to be recommended to the closet, and to be applauded by the theatre is little else than a passport to the puppet-show" (*Memoirs,* quoted in Barry Sutcliffe, *Plays by George Colman the Younger and Thomas Morton* [Cambridge: Cambridge Univ. Press,

1983], 3). For a useful discussion of the volatile critical climate for spectacles such as *Bluebeard* and *Ramah Droog,* see Sutcliffe, 1–13.

58. *Morning Herald,* 13 November 1798.

59. *Morning Herald,* 13 November 1798. As Mita Choudhury argues in "Gazing at His Seraglio: Late Eighteenth-Century Women Playwrights as Orientalists," *Theatre Journal* 47 (1995): 483, scenes like this "guarantee for the play a comfortable niche in a theatrical marketplace which was conducive for Oriental gazing and, in most cases, lucrative for those who staged the Oriental gaze."

60. *Morning Herald,* 13 November 1798.

61. *Morning Herald,* 13 November 1798.

62. Liffey was played by Mr. Johnstone and there is an interesting disjunction between the published version of his speeches and the reports of his performance. Despite the newspaper's approbation of his "Irish pleasantries," the printed text does not render Liffey's speeches in stage Irish. One could argue that this "rectification" of his speech is a further sign of his ideological incorporation into a model of British subjectivity based on normative Englishness. See *Morning Herald,* 13 November 1798.

63. As Captain Bellew, looking back in 1843 wrote, "Long before the period of my departure arrived—I may say almost from infancy—I had been inoculated by my mother, my great uncles, and sundry parchment-faced gentlemen who frequented our house, with a sort of Indomania. . . . What respect did the sonorous names Bangalore and Cuddalore, and Nundy Droog and Severn Droog and Hookahburdars and Soontaburdars, and a host of others, excite in our young minds." Quoted in Mildred Archer, *Early Views of India: The Picturesque Journeys of Thomas and William Daniell, 1786–1794* (London: Thames and Hudson, 1980), note for plate 105.

64. For an account of the publication of the Daniell engravings, see Archer, 234.

65. *Morning Chronicle,* 13 November 1798.

66. *Morning Herald,* 13 November 1798.

67. These cross-dressed characters pose an important problem for Dror Wahrman's argument regarding the shift from gender play to gender panic on the London stage throughout the 1790s—that the female knight effectively disappears from the stage in the last ten years of the eighteenth century. See Dror Wahrman, "*Percy's* Prologue: From Gender Play to Gender Panic in Eighteenth-Century England," *Past and Present* 159 (May 1998): 113–60.

68. Barney is also elevated to the rank of chief physician, the commander of the armies, grand judge in both civil and criminal courts, chief of elephants, purveyor of buffaloes, and principle hunter of tigers (171).

69. *Gentleman's Magazine* 84 (July 1798): 716.

70. For an account of the paucity of knowledge in the metropole of the Indian subcontinent and of the East India Company's activities, see H. V. Bowen, "British India, 1765–1813: The Metropolitan Context," in *The Oxford History of the British Empire* vol. 2, *The Eighteenth Century,* ed. P. J. Marshall (Oxford: Ox-

ford Univ. Press, 1999), 533–37. For an account of British rule that is signaled by the phrase "dominance without hegemony," see Ranajit Guha, *Dominance without Hegemony: History and Power in Colonial India* (Cambridge: Harvard Univ. Press, 1997).

71. Forrest, 347–50, lists eighteen paintings and engravings of the scene by more than nine artists including Mather Brown, George Carter, Arthur William Davis, Robert Home, James Northcote, Henry Singleton, John Smart, and John Zoffany. James Gillray's *The Coming on of the Monsoons* (BM 7929; fig. 7.1), shows Tipu pissing on the British forces.

72. Alexander Beatson, *A View of the Origin and Conduct of the War with Tippoo Sultan; comprising a Narrative of the Operations of the Army under the command of Lt. General George Harris; and of the Siege of Seringapatam* (London: W. Bulmer, 1800).

73. See Forrest, 350–52, for a catalog of these images.

74. Beatson, appendix XXXV, ciii–iv.

75. Russell, 77.

76. Russell, 78.

77. *Morning Post/Gazetteer,* 30 April 1800.

78. Anonymous, *Narrative Sketches of the Conquest of Mysore* (London: Justins, 1800), 2. This guidebook to the panorama was sold at the Lyceum and gives both a detailed description of the painting and identifies the portraits.

79. Thomas Frognall Dibdin, *Reminiscences of a Literary Life* (London, 1836), 1:146–48. Quoted in Altick, 135. For a discussion of the composition of Porter's panorama, see Altick, 134–35.

80. Russell, 78.

81. *Narrative Sketches of the Conquest of Mysore,* 2.

82. Dibdin, *Reminiscences of a Literary Life,* 1:146–48.

83. See *Morning Post/Gazetteer,* 1 September 1800, for a description of the pantomime and the place of Porter's panorama in it. According to the same paper for 10 November 1800, Porter's image was on display through at least November.

84. *Morning Post/Gazetteer,* 5 May 1800. *The Siege* was accompanied by the obligatory display of horsemanship, feats of strength by "The Flemish Hercules," and concluded with "A Serio-Comic Pantomime" titled *The Daemon's Tribunal, or Harlequin's Enterprizes.*

85. As Kwint suggests (104), there is a certain panoptic quality to the architectural design of Astley's theatre that would have maximized the disciplinary effects on the audience.

86. Mark Seltzer, *Bodies and Machines* (New York: Routledge, 1990), 162–64.

87. Moody, 28.

88. Linda Colley has offered a persuasive account of the shedding of ethnic specificity in the formation of an amalgamated British subjectivity in the early nineteenth century in *Britons: Forging the Nation, 1707–1837* (New Haven: Yale Univ. Press, 1992).

89. *Morning Post/Gazetteer,* 30 April 1800.

90. All accounts of the Astley's show indicate that it generated extraordinary receipts.

Afterword

1. I am following the example of Manuel De Landa's *War in the Age of Intelligent Machines* (New York: Zone Books, 1991), which lucidly follows the history of warfare as the emergence of an inorganic life-form. His brief account of bifurcations and attractors is both illuminating and careful to point out the limitations of applying these theories to human history. See especially 13–25, 234–37.

2. Marshall Brown's *Preromanticism* (Stanford: Stanford Univ. Press, 1991) is an instructive exception.

3. For an exhaustive discussion of these genocidal fantasies, see John Barrell, *The Infection of Thomas DeQuincey: A Psychopathology of Imperialism* (New Haven: Yale Univ. Press, 1991). For a discussion of De Quincey's cognizance of imperial complicity, see my "Murder, Hospitality, Philosophy: De Quincey and the Complicitous Grounds of National Identity, " *Studies in Romanticism* 38 (Summer 1999): 135–70.

4. See P. J. Marshall, *The Impeachment of Warren Hastings* (London: Oxford Univ. Press, 1965), 188–89.

5. The emergence of the illegitimate theatre is documented by Jane Moody, *Illegitimate Theatre in London, 1770–1840* (Cambridge: Cambridge Univ. Press, 2000).

6. William Hazlitt, "The Indian Jugglers," in *Table Talk* (London: John Warren, 1821), 181.

7. Hazlitt, 184.

8. John Whale, "Indian Jugglers: Hazlitt, Romantic Orientalism and the Difference of View," in *Romanticism and Colonialism: Writing and Empire, 1780–1830,* ed. Tim Fulford and Peter J. Kitson (Cambridge: Cambridge Univ. Press, 1998), 207–8.

9. David Bromwich, *William Hazlitt: The Mind of the Critic* (New York: Oxford Univ. Press, 1983), 354.

10. In an objection to the "superiority" of the Indian jugglers, a letter to the *Examiner,* 17 December 1815, argues that "who the parties to the comparison intended by the word *superior* may be, is a point by no means easy to determine" and goes on to state that "I could, Mr. Examiner, multiply examples of *jugglers* now in full exercise of their *art,* whose a*cquirements* are far beyond those on the '*superior'* gentlemen now in London" (813).

11. Hazlitt, 182.

12. *Description of the Performance of those Superior Indian Jugglers lately arrived from Seringapatam and Now Performing at the Public Room No. 23, New Bond Street*

(London, 1816), 6–7. This pamphlet is essentially an extended advertisement for the jugglers' performance.

13. De Landa, 69. For an in-depth discussion of these tactical issues, see Rory Muir's discussion of light infantry in *Tactics and the Experience of Battle in the Age of Napoleon* (New Haven: Yale Univ. Press, 1998), 51–67.

14. Battles during the Napoleonic Wars were not decided by moments of utter annihilation or the total number of casualties. As Muir argues, "What mattered in deciding a battle, as in the individual combatants of which it was composed, was not the body count, but the destruction of the enemy army's cohesion and will to fight" (239).

15. Hazlitt was devastated by the news of Waterloo, and it is important to recognize the spectral presence of the Napoleonic Wars in *Table Talk*. In "On the Pleasure in Painting"—the essay most thematically connected to "The Indian Jugglers"—Austerlitz plays a transformative role in how Hazlitt regards not only his artistic practice, but also his genealogy. See *Table Talk*, 21.

16. For an excellent discussion of the state-sanctioned hyperbole following Waterloo and various liberal responses to it, see Philip Shaw, "Leigh Hunt and the Aesthetics of Post-War Liberalism," in *Romantic Wars: Studies in Culture and Conflict, 1793–1822* (Aldershot: Ashgate, 1995), 185–200.

17. *Description*, 11.

18. *Gentleman's Magazine* 86 (March 1816): 272.

Bickerstaff, Isaac (*cont.*)
  *The Sultan; or, A Peep into the
    Seraglio,* 17-18, 126
biopower, 29, 88
Blumenbach, Johann Friedrich, 37
Boaden, James, 18
Bolla, Peter de, 234, 241-42
Bolton, Betsy, 153, 378n33
Bolts, William, 46, 368n13
bonds: Clive's manipulation of, 53; ma-
  nipulation of in *The Nabob,* 61-62
Bougainville, Louis-Antoine de, 103, 104
bourgeoisie, 134-35
Bowen, H. V., 122
breasts, as signifier of maternality,
  188-89, 210, 381n39
Brewer, John, 40, 261, 268
Bristow, James, 322
British Constitution: and Hastings's
  impeachment, 166, 239; incursion
  of the common law on, 25-26; as
  invoked in the debate over the East
  India Bill, 137-38; Montesquieu's
  view of, 132-35; in *The Nabob,* 63
British Empire: challenges to, 23; constitutional crises faced by, 23-24, 27;
  corruption in, 5; and the French
  Revolution, 119-20; impact of the
  American Revolution on, 2, 3, 23,
  118; as norm for judging other cul-
  tures and societies, 38; objectives of,
  87-88; paternalism of, 314, 326-27,
  329-30, 332; shift in public opinion
  regarding, 269; theatrical allusions to,
  65-66. *See also* East India Company
British identity: as affected by the
  American Revolution, 118
Bromwich, David, 162, 352
Brunton, Anne, 301-2
Buffon, Comte George-Louis Leclerc
  de, 37
Bunbury, Henry William, 285
Burgoyne, General John, 50

Burke, Edmund, 4, 9, 10, 46, 352; on
  the American Revolution, 117-18;
  *Appeal from the New to the Old
  Whigs,* 143; on the beautiful, 183;
  and the Begams of Oudh, 201-4,
  205-8, 214-18; on the British Empire, 43; as depicted by Dent, 179,
  190-99, 205-6, 279; as depicted by
  Gillray, 181, 195-99; as depicted by
  Sayers, 130-31, 179, 180, 194-95, 196,
  214-17; and the East India Company, 122-23, 127-28, 165-66, 182-83,
  193-94, 316; on execution, 184-85; on
  the French Revolution, 119-20, 188;
  and Hastings's impeachment, 25, 26,
  118, 119-20, 144, 159, 165-66, 167, 168,
  177, 182, 185-88, 189-94, 222, 229-33;
  on John Howard, 162-63; and the
  middle classes, 307; *A Philosophical
  Enquiry into the Origin of Our Ideas
  of the Sublime and the Beautiful,*
  183-86, 196, 381n39; *Reflections on
  the Revolution in France,* 119-20, 143,
  188-89, 231, 298-99; on sound, 184;
  spectacles as trope in satires of, 189-
  92, 214; "Speech at the Guildhall, in
  Bristol, Previous to the Election
  (1780)," 162; "Speech on Fox's India
  Bill (1783)," 185, 193-94, 201-4;
  "Speech on Opening of Impeachment of Warren Hastings (1787),"
  186-87, 189, 238-39; on the sublime,
  183-84; *Thoughts on the Cause of the
  Present Discontents,* 136, 139-40, 144,
  162
Burney, Frances, 24, 27, 117, 156; allusions to *Evelina* in *Diary* of, 252-54;
  on Burke's prosecution of Hastings,
  229-33, 245-49; on Fox's speech on
  the Benares charge, 234-41, 242-44;
  on Hastings's impeachment trial,
  222-57; as Molière's old woman,
  235-37, 247-49, 254-55; and William

Wyndham (Windham), 228-29, 235, 236, 243, 244-54
Butler, Judith, 34

Calcutta, India: celebratory performances in, 326-28
Campbell, Gina, 253
Cantemir, Prince Demetrius, 213-16
captivity narratives, 318-19, 333
Carlson, Julie, 205, 211, 212
Caroline, Queen, 196
Carracioli, Charles, 276
Cavendish, Lord Frederick, 137
characters: and caricature, 282-84, 292-93; recognizability of, 11-12, 148; in *The Nabob*, 13, 42, 44, 55-56, 65-66, 67, 68-69; in *Such Things Are*, 153, 157
Charter Act of 1813, 38
Chesterfield, Lord, 153, 157, 378n37
Choudhury, Mita, 362n31
Clark, Anna, 193
Clark, Peter, 35, 116
class identity: anxieties about, 72-73; in eighteenth-century Britain, 8-9; manifestations of, 288-89; and the minuet, 285-87; and private credit, 53, 73; racialization of, 13, 87, 114, 308-9, 310. *See also* middle classes
Cleveland, Augustus, 387n15
Clive, Lord Robert, 44, 45, 47-50, 165-66, 260, 269, 336; allusions to in Foote's *The Nabob*, 55, 58, 60; contemporary representations of, 276-77, 278; defense of Indian career in Parliament, 47-50
clockwork armies, 321-23
clothing: and the performance of civility, 103, 109; as synonymous with personhood, 91, 283-84
Cobb, James. See *The Humorist; Ramah Droog; or, Wine Does Wonders*
Coke, Sir Edward, 263

Colley, Linda, 120, 270
Collingham, 265
Colman, George (The Younger): as author of prologue and epilogue to Starke's *The Sword of Peace*, 31, 278-80, 281, 293-94, 295, 296-97; *Blue-Beard*, 332; *Inkle and Yarico*, 265-66, 272
colonialism, British, 88, 266; rationales for, 39, 40-41; as represented in *Omai*, 74, 103-4; as represented in *The Sword of* Peace, 271-72; resistance to, 117, 120
commedia dell'arte: and ethnography, 76; *Omai* as, 93-94, 100-108
Constitution. *See* American Constitution; British Constitution
Cook, James, 39; apotheosis of in *Omai*, 75, 82-86, 89, 101, 113-14; curiosities collected by, 96; voyages of as depicted in *Omai*, 74-76; Webber as illustrator for, 90-91
cooperation, Marx's concept of, 28-29
Cornwallis, Lord, 31; caricature of, 318; as embodiment of paternal virtue, 275, 326, 329-30; military actions in India, 260, 267, 269, 270, 313, 325-26, 336; and the Permanent Settlement, 297-298; theatrical allusions to, 272, 273, 273-76, 296, 339
costume: Loutherbourg's designs for *Omai*, 86, 90-92, 111; in *The Nabob*, 69; in *Ramah Droog*, 339-40; in *The Sword of Peace*, 284-85
Courtwright, Paul B., 390n48
Cowley, Hannah, 117
Cox, Jeffrey, 373n52, 388n19
Crespigny, Mrs., 301, 302
cross-dressing, 111, 116, 154, 338-40

Dalrymple, William, 40, 265
Dance, Nathaniel, 79
Daniell, Thomas, 336, 337, 340

Daniell, William, 336, 337, 340
al-Daula, Asaf, 200, 201, 209
al-Daula, Shuja, 200-201
Daula, Siraj-ud, 45, 246
Davenant, William, 129
De Landa, Manuel, 321-22, 323, 356, 398n1
Dening, Greg, 13, 74, 371n10
Dent, William, 22; *The Grand Pitch Battle*, 279; *The Long-Winded Speech*, 205, 206; *No Abatement*, 190-92, 214; *The Raree Show*, 172-82
De Quincey, Thomas, 351
despotism: in colonial India, 166; Charles James Fox accused of, 126, 136-37; of George III, 126, 130-31, 137, 140, 141-42; in Inchbald's *Such Things Are*, 126, 146, 148-49, 155, 160; as masculinity, 124; Montesquieu on, 27, 126-27, 130-33, 141; signs associated with, 41
Devonshire, Duchess of, 137
Dibdin, Charles, 18
Dibdin, Thomas, 342, 344
Diderot, Dénis, 104
difference, origins of, 37
Dirks, Nicholas B., 297
disciplinary power, 28
diwani, 43, 45
Donkin, Ellen, 14
Dow, Alexander, 46
Dryden, John, 129
dueling, 294-95, 296
Dundas, Henry, 165

East India Bill (1783), 20-21, 23, 122, 182, 255; Burke's comments on, 193-94, 201-4; constitutional crisis associated with, 144, 145; defeat of, 129-30, 142, 43; opposition to, 126, 127-29, 132, 133, 134, 135-37
East India Company, 2, 7, 40, 350; and anti-Company discourse, 276-81,

282; anxieties associated with, 45-46, 315-16; Burke's concerns about, 122-23, 165-66, 316; corruption associated with, 4, 47-50, 165; financial problems of, 23, 52, 120-21; as governmental agent, 3, 4, 43, 45-46; as hybrid of business, government, and military, 4, 122, 123-24, 199, 262; legislation affecting, 121, 122; military actions of, 260, 261, 269-70, 271, 274-75, 317, 322; theatrical allusions to, 16, 20-21, 24-27, 65-66, 127, 157, 271, 272. *See also* Hastings, Warren, impeachment trial of
Edgeworth, Maria, 117
effeminacy, 41, 154, 276, 339
Eidophusikon, 96-97
Elliot, Gilbert, 168-70
elocution. *See* oratory
empire, defined, 2. *See also* British Empire
"An Epistle from Mr. Banks, Voyager, Monster-hunter, and Amoroso, to Oberea, Queen of Otaheite," 77-79, 109
ethical spectatorship, 36
ethnography: and commedia dell'arte, 76; and pantomime as manifested in *Omai*, 74-75, 101, 113-14. *See also* autoethnography

Fabian, Johannes, 74
family as instrument of government, 15
Fatal Curiosity, 15
Favart, Charles Simon: *Soliman II*, 17
Ferguson, Frances, 189
Figueira, Dorothy M., 300
Foote, Samuel, 17. *See also The Bankrupt; The Nabob*
Fordyce, Alexander, 44; allusions to in Foote's *Nabob*, 55-56, 64, 68-69; bankruptcy precipitated by, 51-55;

and Falkland Island affair, 54, 369n32; as macaroni gambler, 68

Foreman, Amanda, 137

Foucault, Michel, 5, 8, 88, 268; concept of governmentality, 1-2, 15, 26; on the early modern state, 267; on race and power, 28, 29, 262-63; on regulation of the body, 121, 313, 315; on sexuality, 30, 88-89

Fox, Charles James, 9, 117; and Mrs. Armstead, 219-20; Burney's remarks on, 234-41; compared to Cromwell, 135-36; "death" of, 143, 144; and the defeat of the East India Bill, 140-42, 143; as depicted by Dent, 179-81, 192; as depicted by Sayers, 127-28, 130-31, 179, 216-17; East India Bill proposed by, 20-21, 23, 27, 122, 126, 127-28, 205; and Hastings's impeachment, 25, 26, 27, 119, 175-77, 179-81, 224-26, 239-41, 242-44; as sexual deviant, 129-30; as Shylock, 224-26; "Speech on the Benares Charge (1787)," 175-77, 234-36, 239-40; on wars against India, 260-62. *See also* East India Bill

France, military engagement with, 352, 399nn14-16

Francis, Philip, 166, 191, 278, 297, 380n3

French Revolution, 7, 119-20, 143, 298-99, 352, 379n45

Furneaux, Tobias, 79, 106

gambling, as emblematic of excess, 54, 67-70, 284, 292-93

Garrick, David, 18, 67, 110

gender. *See* masculinity; sexuality; women

Gentleman, Francis: *The Dramatic Censor*, 18

geographical morality, 214-15, 232-33, 238-39, 246, 251

George II, 328

George III, 2, 5, 23, 24, 78, 196; depicted as despot, 130-31, 137; and the East India Bill, 128-29; Fox's remarks on, 239-40; jurisprudence under, 156-57; and opera glass, 174, 224; as subordinate to Hastings, 171, 172, 199, 224

George, Dorothy, 172-74

Genest, John, 395n57

Gibbon, Edward, 44

Gillray, James, 22, 194; *A Bow to the Throne*, 172, 174; *Camera Obscura*, 195-99, 204; *The Coming on of the Monsoons*, 317-318; *Impeachment Ticket*, 181; *A Sale of English Beauties in the East Indies*, 291-92

Gilroy, Paul, 28

Glyn and Halifax, 51

Gould, Eliga, 118

governmentality: changes in, 23; of the East India Company, 4, 123; Foucault's concept of, 1-2, 15, 29; women's perspective on, 24, 117. *See also* sovereignty, imperial

Graham, Dr., 20

Great Chain of Being, 37

Green, Katherine, 378n30, 378n33

Grenville, George, 140-41, 367n4

Grosrichard, Alain, 132, 137, 142, 148, 155

Guha, Ranajit, 298

Habermas, Jürgen, 34

Haider Ali, 23, 270, 316, 322

Hall, Catherine, 361n14, 363n56

Hamlet (Shakespeare), 198-99, 341

Handel, George Frideric, 328

Hastings, Warren, impeachment trial of, 13, 31, 116-17, 118, 120, 122-23, 124, 165-70; as addressed in eighteenth-century theatre, 24-27, 127, 157, 272, 278-80, 294; and the Begams of Oudh, 200-221; Burke's role in, 25, 26, 118, 119-20, 144, 159, 165-66, 167,

surrogation, 261, 313

Sussman, Charlotte, 363-64n56

Sutherland, Dame Lucy, 368n12

suttee, 300, 303-4, 305, 306, 390n48.
See also *The Widow of Malabar*

The Sword of Peace (Starke), 30, 31,
266-67, 319; character and caricature in, 281-96; as critique of the
East India Company, 271-81; public
reception of, 296-97; reviews of,
277, 282, 287

Tacitus, 203

Tahiti. See *Omai; or, A Trip round the
World*

Tasch, Peter, 362n32

Taylor, John, 125-26

Teltscher, Kate, 120, 265, 281, 316, 318,
322, 329

The Tempest; or, The Enchanted Isle
(Davenant and Dryden), 129

Temple, Lord, 129, 138, 140, 153

theatre, British: audience-performer
interaction at, 11, 30, 31, 35-36; as
autoethnography, 11-21, 22, 28, 73,
350; as barometer of taste, 12-13;
character in, 11-12; gender transformations in, 41; legislation affecting,
178; military as represented in, 267,
270-71; precinematic technologies
as used in, 312; race as represented
in, 31-32, 76; regulation of, 13-14; social change as manifested in, 6-7, 11,
12-14. *See also* military spectacles;
names of specific plays

Thompson, E. P., 8, 298

Thurlow, Lord Chancellor, 171, 175-77,
196, 224, 225

Tipu Sultan, 23, 260, 269, 270, 275,
296, 340, 350; French involvement
with, 321; in Mysore Wars, 317, 318;
paintings of, 397n71; as portrayed
in British theatre, 314, 320-21, 323-

32, 341-42, 344-48, 355; as portrayed
in Cobb's *Ramah Droog*, 314, 333,
334; sons of taken as British
hostages, 329-30, 334, 341; as threat
to British, 316, 317, 322

The Ton (Wallace), 116, 305

Tone, Wolfe, 334, 340

Tuite, Clara, 34, 35

virtue: and Anglophone political theory, 5; Captain Cook as exemplar
of, 76; and corruption, 73; in Montesquieu's *Spirit of the Laws*, 145,
156; as portrayed in eighteenth-century theatre, 14, 156, 161, 163

Wahrman, Dror, 7, 118, 265, 307

Wallace, Lady Eglantine, 116, 304-5

Walpole, Horace, 50, 54, 61

warfare, 32; dramaturgy of, 320, 321; in
India, 260-62; race as aspect of, 262-
64. *See also* military, British; military action; military spectacles;
Mysore Wars

Wazir of Oudh (Awadh), Nawab, 200,
201, 208-9, 210, 214

Webber, John, 75, 82, 90-91, 95-96, 97

Wellesley, Lord, 260, 261

Westminster Hall, 171-73, 177; as camera
obscura, 198; as raree show, 172-75

Whale, John, 354

Wheeler, Roxann, 35, 283

Whig party, 3, 9, 22; concepts of liberty and property, 39-40, 360n8;
disintegration of, 143-44; and the
East India Bill, 138, 139, 142-43, 161-
62; George III as viewed by, 130,
140; and Hastings's impeachment,
166, 182

The Widow of Malabar (Starke), 30,
31, 267, 299; as private theatrical,
301; reviews of, 302; suttee in, 300,
303-4

Wilks, Mark, 322-23

Wilson, Kathleen, 12, 28, 36, 74-75, 86-87, 118

Wollstonecraft, Mary, 117

women: as barometers of historical progress, 12-13; at the Hastings trial, 24-25, 124, 169-70, 212; in Moslem society, 213-14; in *Ramah Droog,* 338-40; and social regulation, 117. *See also* Begams of Oudh (Awadh)

Wordsworth, William, 351

Wyndham (Windham), William, 235, 243, 249; on Burke's eloquence, 244-47; and Samuel Johnson, 236; role of in Burney's narrative, 228-29, 251-57